POPE FRANCIS,

Evangelii Gaudium,
and the Renewal
of the Church

edited by
DUNCAN DORMOR *&* **ALANA HARRIS**

Paulist Press
New York / Mahwah, NJ

Cover photo copyright © by L'Obsservatore Romano
Cover design by Lightly Salted Graphics
Book design by Lynn Else

Library of Congress Cataloging-in-Publication Data

 Names: Dormor, Duncan J., editor. | Harris, Alana, 1973– editor.
Title: Pope Francis, Evangelii gaudium, and the renewal of the church / edited by Duncan Dormor and Alana Harris.
Description: New York : Paulist Press, 2017. | Includes bibliographical references.
Identifiers: LCCN 2017010393 (print) | LCCN 2017040483 (ebook) | ISBN 9781587687372 (ebook) | ISBN 9780809153671 (pbk. : alk. paper)
Subjects: LCSH: Francis, Pope, 1936– | Catholic Church. Pope (2013– : Francis). Evangelii gaudium. | Church renewal—Catholic Church. | Evangelistic work—Catholic Church. | Catholic Church—Doctrines.
Classification: LCC BX1378.7 (ebook) | LCC BX1378.7 .P655 2017 (print) | DDC 266/.2—dc23
LC record available at https://lccn.loc.gov/2017010393

ISBN 978-0-8091-5367-1 (paperback)
ISBN 978-1-58768-737-2 (e-book)

Published by Paulist Press
997 Macarthur Boulevard
Mahwah, New Jersey 07430

www.paulistpress.com

Printed and bound in the
United States of America

Contents

Acknowledgments and Permissions vii

Common Abbreviations ix

List of Contributors xi

Introduction. *Evangelii Gaudium*: The Key to
Francis's Papacy 1
Duncan Dormor and Alana Harris

PART 1.
From the Heart of the Gospel: Theological Foundations 17

1. "The Ends of the Earth" Meets the *Caput Mundi*:
The Aparecida Document as Frame and Source for
Understanding Pope Francis's Thought in
Evangelii Gaudium 19
Eduardo Mangiarotti

2. Is Pope Francis a Liberation Theologian? 37
Paul Lakeland

3. From the Joy of the Gospel to the Joy of Christ:
Situating and Expanding the Christology of
Pope Francis 59
Philip McCosker

Contents

PART 2.
Renewing the People of God: Ecclesiology............................ 83

4. *Ecclesia et Pontifice*: Delivering on the Ecclesiological
   Implications of *Evangelii Gaudium* 85
   Paul D. Murray

5. "A Bride Bedecked with Her Jewels": Understanding
   Inculturation and Popular Piety as a *Locus Theologicus*
   in *Evangelii Gaudium* 112
   Jacob Phillips

6. Transforming Time: The Maternal Church and the
   Pilgrimage of Faith 135
   Tina Beattie

PART 3.
Together in Mission: *Evangelii Gaudium*
and Ecumenism 159

7. Ecumenism in Pope Francis: *Ad Intra* and *Ad Extra* 161
   Massimo Faggioli

8. "The Joy of the Gospel" and "Together towards Life":
   Comparing the Apostolic Exhortation of Pope Francis
   and the Statement of the World Council of Churches on
   Mission and Evangelism 190
   Kirsteen Kim

9. *Evangelii Gaudium*: Good News for Ecumenism 218
   Jeremy Worthen

PART 4.
Transforming the World: Catholic Social Teaching.......... 239

10. Is *Evangelii Gaudium* Disrupting or Enhancing Catholic
    Social Teaching? 241
    Augusto Zampini Davies

Contents

11. "Let Us Not Leave in Our Wake a Swath of Destruction and Death": *Evangelii Gaudium* and Socioecological Flourishing...274
    Christopher Hrynkow

12. *Evangelii Gaudium* and Amartya Sen's *Idea of Justice*: Informal Economy Workers in Argentina 308
    Séverine Deneulin

Transforming Words, Transforming Relationships:
    An Afterword...333
    Rowan Williams

Acknowledgments and Permissions

The editors wish to thank Brill Publishing for permission to reproduce the following three articles from *"Evangelii Gaudium and the Renewal of the Church,"* a special issue of *Ecclesiology* 12 (2016): 1–90, edited by Duncan Dormor and Alana Harris: Paul Murray, *"Ecclesia et Pontifice:* On Delivering on the Ecclesiological Implications of *Evangelii Gaudium,"* 13–33; Philip McCosker, "From the Joy of the Gospel to the Joy of Christ," 34–53; and Tina Beattie, "Transforming Time—the Maternal Church and the Pilgrimage of Faith," 54–72. Likewise, the editors express their gratitude for the inclusion of the chapter by Massimo Faggioli, which is a revised version of "Ecumenism in *Evangelii Gaudium* and in the Context of Francis' Pontificate," originally published in *Perspectiva Teologica* 48, no. 1 (2016): 17–35.

Common Abbreviations

AL   *Amoris Laetitia*: The Joy of Love, Post-synodal Apostolic Exhortation, April 8, 2016

EG   *Evangelii Gaudium*: The Joy of the Gospel, Apostolic Exhortation, November 24, 2013

GS   *Gaudium et Spes*: On the Church in the Modern World, Pastoral Constitution, December 7, 1965

LS   *Laudato Si'*: On Care for Our Common Home, Encyclical Letter, May 24, 2015

RN   *Rerum Novarum*: On Capital and Labor, Encyclical Letter, May 15, 1891

List of Contributors

Tina Beattie is professor of Catholic studies and director of the Digby Stuart Research Centre for Religion, Society and Human Flourishing and of Catherine of Siena College at the University of Roehampton. She has researched and written on sacramental theology, gender and psychoanalytic theory, on human dignity and women's rights, and on art, theology, and mysticism. As well as working with religious orders, NGOs, and other groups, she contributes widely to public debate on religion.

Séverine Deneulin is associate professor of international development in the Department of Social and Policy Sciences at the University of Bath. Her research in ethics and development policy focuses on the ethical framework of Amartya Sen's capability approach, and the role of religion in international development. She also teaches a module on the capability approach at the University of Bethlehem in Palestine, and is a visiting research associate at the Catholic University of Argentina.

Duncan Dormor is an Anglican priest and the dean, and former president, of St. John's College, Cambridge, where he teaches anthropology and sociology of religion within the university. A member of the Church of England's Mission Theological Advisory Group and of English ARC, he is the coeditor of *Anglicanism: The Answer to Modernity* (Continuum, 2003) and *An Acceptable Sacrifice? Homosexuality and the Church* (SPCK, 2007).

Massimo Faggioli is full professor in the Department of Theology and Religious Studies at Villanova University. His most recent publications in English include the books *Vatican II: The Battle for Meaning* (Paulist, 2012); *A Council for the Global Church: Receiving Vatican II in History* (Fortress, 2015); *The Legacy of Vatican II*, ed. Massimo Faggioli and Andrea Vicini (Paulist, 2015); and *The Rising Laity: Ecclesial Movements since Vatican II* (Paulist, 2016).

Alana Harris, a married lay Roman Catholic, is a lecturer in modern British history at King's College, London. Drawing upon her theological and ecumenical formation at the University of Divinity (Melbourne, Australia), she researches and publishes in areas related to the history of religion, ecumenical relations, and everyday "lived religion" (encompassing material cultures, pilgrimage, and popular devotion). These are issues explored in her most recent book, *Faith in the Family: A Lived Religious History of English Catholicism 1945–1982* (Manchester University Press, 2013).

Christopher Hrynkow is associate professor in the Department of Religion and Culture at St. Thomas More College, University of Saskatchewan, where he teaches courses in religion and culture, social justice and the common good, and Catholic studies. His principle research area for his appointment is Christianity and ecology. Hrynkow serves as the Graduate Chair for Religion and Culture at the University of Saskatchewan. Most importantly, he is the proud father of three energetic young boys.

Kirsteen Kim is professor of theology and world Christianity at Fuller Theological Seminary, USA, and was previously at Leeds Trinity University, UK. She edits *Mission Studies*, the journal of the International Association for Mission Studies, and a book series: Theology and Mission in World Christianity (Brill). She served as research coordinator of the Edinburgh 2010 project and as vice-moderator of the World Council of Churches' Commission for World Mission and Evangelism. She is the author of many publications and editor of *The New Evangelization* (Bloomsbury, 2014).

List of Contributors

Paul Lakeland is the Aloysius P. Kelley, SJ, Professor of Catholic Studies and founding director of the Center for Catholic Studies at Fairfield University, a Jesuit institution in Connecticut. He holds degrees from Heythrop Pontifical Athenaeum, Oxford University, the University of London and his PhD from Vanderbilt University. He is the author of ten books, the latest of which is *The Wounded Angel: Fiction and the Religious Imagination* (2017)

Eduardo Mangiarotti is a diocesan priest from San Isidro (Buenos Aires, Argentina). He has a master's degree in theology from the Catholic University of Argentina in Buenos Aires and is currently pursuing a PhD in dogmatic theology at the Gregorian University in Rome. His dissertation topic is "Rethinking the Institutional Church from the Mystery of the Church: Some Contributions from Postconciliar Theology and Perspectives for the Future."

Philip McCosker is director of the Von Hügel Institute for Critical Catholic Inquiry and Fellow of St. Edmund's College, Cambridge, and departmental lecturer in modern theology in the Faculty of Theology and Religion at the University of Oxford. He is the coeditor (with Denys Turner) of *The Cambridge Companion to the Summa Theologiae* (CUP, 2016) and author of *Christ the Paradox: Expanding Ressourcement Theology* (CUP, 2018). He is also the editor of the journal *Reviews in Religion and Theology*.

Paul D. Murray, a married lay Roman Catholic, is professor of systematic theology and director of the Centre for Catholic Studies at Durham University. He serves on the Anglican-Roman Catholic International Commission (ARCIC III). He is author of *Reason, Truth and Theology in Pragmatist Perspective* (Peeters, 2004); editor of *Receptive Ecumenism and the Call to Catholic Learning: Exploring a Way for Contemporary Ecumenism* (OUP, 2008); and coeditor of *Ressourcement: A Movement for Renewal in Twentieth Century Catholic Theology* (OUP, 2012).

Jacob Phillips is a lecturer in theology and program director of the theology MA at St. Mary's University, Twickenham, UK. He did his PhD on human subjectivity in the theology of Dietrich Bonhoeffer at King's College London, where he also completed his MA after undergraduate studies at Heythrop College. Jacob has taught at King's College London, the Universities of Winchester and Roehampton, and Allen Hall Seminary in London.

Rowan Williams is master of Magdalene College, Cambridge, and was Archbishop of Canterbury from 2002 to 2012. He has worked in university teaching as well as serving as a bishop in Wales, and has written a number of books in theology, spirituality, and the frontiers between faith, politics, and literature. He continues to be active in ecumenical discussion, and is also chair of the Trustees of Christian Aid.

Jeremy Worthen is the secretary for Ecumenical Relations and Theology at the Church of England's Council for Christian Unity. Prior to his current post, he worked for many years in theological education. An Anglican priest and honorary canon of Canterbury Cathedral, his publications include *The Internal Foe: Judaism and Anti-Judaism in the Shaping of Christian Theology* (Newcastle: Cambridge Scholars Press, 2009) and *Responding to God's Call: Christian Formation Today* (Norwich: Canterbury Press, 2012).

Augusto Zampini Davies is an Argentine lawyer, theologian, and Roman Catholic priest, currently working full time as the theological adviser to the UK aid-development agency CAFOD. He is also an honorary fellow at Durham University, Roehampton University, and Stellenbosch University on social ethics, development economics, and Catholic social teaching. He has also been a contributor to mainstream and Catholic media on matters pertaining to Pope Francis and social Catholicism in general.

Evangelii Gaudium

The Key to Francis's Papacy

DUNCAN DORMOR & ALANA HARRIS

Evangelii Gaudium or The Joy of the Gospel (*EG*), released on November 24, 2013, to widespread media coverage and praise from across the Christian churches, has been hailed by veteran Vatican analysts as a "Magna Carta for church reform"[1] or a latter-day "'I have a dream' speech."[2] While there have been subsequent Vatican pronouncements through which the nature and agenda of Francis's papacy have continued to take shape, chiefly his encyclical on ecology and climate change (*Laudato Si'*, May 24, 2015) and the controversial post-synodal Apostolic Exhortation *Amoris Laetitia* (The Joy of Love, March 19, 2016), *EG* remains a foundational manifesto or programmatic text for Jorge Mario Bergoglio's episcopacy as the Bishop of Rome. Inaugurating the pastoral register of all three documents with their emphasis on "joy," "praise," the "gospel message," and "mercy," the overarching focus of *EG* is primarily missiological and, therefore, inevitably ecclesiological. Full of bold and striking imagery and challenging, occasionally acerbic, words, *EG* must be understood (according to Cardinal Walter Kasper) against the background of Francis's theology of the people, *teología del pueblo*, of a "pilgrim and evangelizing people that transcends every (however necessary)

1

institutional expression," and of his deep commitment to the doctrine of the *sensus fidei*. As a consequence, for Kasper, Pope Francis is "thinking beyond the church's inner space": so his paradigm for the church is mission and it realizes its vocation when all its members are missionary disciples who go out—rather than merely reaching out—to the peripheries of God's world to encounter Christ. This necessitates dialogue and "a magisterium that listens."[3] Whether this is through the worldwide surveys that preceded the Synod on the Family (October 4–25, 2015),[4] the monumental gatherings at World Youth Day in Krakow (July 25–31, 2016) inspiring young people with the confidence to be "street preachers" (*callejeros de la fe*) (*EG* 106), or at the local level through a pastoral reappraisal of the sacrament of confession beyond its misuse as a "torture chamber" (*EG* 44), it is clear, as his multiple biographers have also recognized, that Francis's papacy marks a distinct break in style and substance from his predecessors.[5]

The material within this collected volume originated with a conference, "'Making All things New'? *Evangelii Gaudium* and Ecumenical Mission," held at St. John's College, University of Cambridge, from June 29 to July 1, 2015.[6] Unlike previous scholarly treatments of the Apostolic Exhortation,[7] it was conceived in quite a particular ecumenical setting, namely a meeting of English ARC, the Anglican–Roman Catholic Committee (of which the editors are both members) in March 2014, at which *EG* and its implications were discussed within a broader set of conversations about evangelization and mission in the UK and an ecumenical, pastoral guide to *EG* was commissioned (and has now been published).[8] In this regard, it is a companion piece to a recent special issue of the *International Review of Mission*, which provides a detailed summary of each chapter of *EG* and then systematically juxtaposes the Apostolic Exhortation with two other, recent ecumenical documents on mission.[9] This volume differs, however, in focusing exclusively on *EG* as interpreted from a variety of interdisciplinary and denominational perspectives, with a sharper focus on the ecclesiological as well as the ecumenical potentialities for the reform and renewal of the church contained within this reorientation and reappreciation of the church's primary mission to evangelization in the modern world.

From the Heart of the Gospel: Theological Foundations

Our opening section explores the theological foundations of *EG* through a consideration of context, theological method, and Christology. Eduardo Mangiarotti sets the scene with an invaluable introduction to the thinking of Pope Francis as it has been shaped by developments in Latin American theology over the last half-century. Paul Lakeland's chapter builds upon this with an exploration of the relationship between Pope Francis's thinking and liberation theology, the origins of which, of course, lie with the Latin American church. Finally, Philip McCosker explores how *EG* reveals the ways in which Francis's Christology lies at the heart of his theological thinking.

In the opening chapter of the volume, Eduardo Mangiarotti, a priest from the diocese of San Isidro, traces the provenance of *EG* within a distinctively Latin American theological context. While the journey begins in 1955 with the founding of the Latin American Episcopal Conference (CELAM), it is in the creative and organic appropriation of the teachings of Vatican II at the bishops' conference in Medellín, Colombia, in 1968 that a distinctively regional theological voice can first be discerned. In Mangiarotti's assessment, it is then to *Navega Mar Adentro* ("Launch out into the deep"), the Argentinean Bishops' Conference document of 2003, that the theologian's attention should be drawn. It is here that we find a pastoral and missiological articulation deeply responsive to the sense of political, cultural, and ecclesial crises that existed at that time in Argentina. *Navega Mar Adentro* in turn proves to be the catalyst for what is unmistakably the most immediate and formative textual influence on *EG*, namely the Aparecida document, which emerged from the Fifth Conference of the Latin American and Caribbean Bishops in 2007, drafted in large part by the then Cardinal Bergoglio. Mangiarotti concludes by drawing out some of the more important differences between this foundational text written for the church in Latin America and *Evangelii Gaudium* with its worldwide audience.

Is Pope Francis a liberation theologian or not? And what might the implications be? Liberation theology is a highly contested category, and in his chapter, Lakeland seeks to sift the

3

reality from the rhetoric. It is, of course, a particularly vexed question, as the pope's two immediate predecessors were the "principal collaborators in a sustained effort to destroy the influence of liberation theology in Latin America"—not, it should be stressed, primarily out of a concern that its economic analysis might be too indebted to Marxism (though that has drawn a good deal of criticism in other quarters), but on account of its ecclesiological implications that clashed with John Paul II's vision of a more centralized and hierarchical church.[10]

After a brief account of how the experience of the poor came to be understood as "the privileged locus of theology in Latin America," Lakeland takes the reader into a consideration of the principles and methods involved in being a liberation theologian. He then weighs the evidence by considering Jorge Bergoglio's actions as a Jesuit priest, archbishop, and indeed as pope, alongside his writings, most notably in the Aparecida document. In his assessment, it is clear that the natural concerns of liberation theology and Francis's program have a great deal in common: the learning from experience, the skepticism about global capitalism, the concern for the poor, an ecclesiology weighted toward the grassroots, and a focus on Scripture. In short, he concludes, if liberation theology is understood to involve a "shift toward a more grassroots church in which lay leadership plays a much greater role in the community of faith, in companionship with the poor, for the sake of the gospel," then the current pope is without doubt within that fold, as broadly conceived.

Despite being "textually restrained" and overlooked by many commentators whose interest is captured by other features of *EG*, for Philip McCosker it is Pope Francis's Christology that lies at the heart of this Apostolic Exhortation. With his emphasis on the simple principles that "realities are more important than ideas" (*EG* 231–33), and that at the heart of the Christian life lies the encounter with a person, it is difficult for the inexpert reader to discern the more particular theological contours and sources of Francis's Christology. Furthermore, as McCosker observes, for Francis, theology and Christology "are more verbs than nouns," with the latter characteristically rendered as "merciful, cordial, kerygmatic, active, adverbial." Yet, as he clearly establishes, Francis's reinvigorating christological emphasis is "rather deeply, if quietly and creatively resourced in the tradition." In McCosker's historically inflected survey of some of the *ressourcement* thinkers that inform Francis's emphasis on encounter and evangelization, underappreciated aspects of continuity, as well as the innovative dimensions for renewal (within and beyond the christological), are illuminated.

Renewing the People of God: Ecclesiology

Ecclesiological concerns lie at the heart of *EG* and indeed one of the central claims of the Apostolic Exhortation is that the church discovers its nature through reaching out, that is, through its engagement as a "community of missionary disciples." The opening chapter of the second section is therefore given over to a consideration of the wide-ranging ecclesiological implications of *EG*. Here, Paul D. Murray explores Francis's advocacy of reform against the inherited backdrop of an "entrenched climate of theological divorce and dysfunction within postconciliar Catholicism." Providing an assessment of the implications of *EG* for a number of "key sites of ecclesiological significance," Murray considers the challenges in three particular arenas: the relationship between the papacy and the college of bishops; the difficulties of empowering local churches against the backdrop of a long "history of reprisals" from the center; and the questions swirling around ordained ministry, not just the "hot button questions of access" (women, married men) but also, at a more basic level, the relationship between the clergy and the laity. In short, much of this boils down to the question, Who can have a voice within the Roman Catholic Church, and what can they legitimately say? In Murray's assessment, Francis's vision of a more decentralized church, which is shaped more profoundly by the needs of the poor and marginalized, is underwritten by a "whole-church ecclesial theology" that eschews theological binaries and entrenched hierarchies. This is deeply refreshing, but inevitably, warns Murray, there are significant challenges in turning vision into reality.

In his chapter, Jacob Phillips turns our attention to the intimate relationship between evangelization and inculturation in *EG*, and the central role played by practices of popular piety that, he argues in Francis's thinking, constitute "a *nota veritatis* of genuinely authentic evangelization." Given Pope Benedict's well-known criticism of inculturation, the subject matter also provides an excellent opportunity for Phillips to explore the widespread claim that there is significant divergence between Francis and his predecessor. Phillips traces the origins of inculturation, as idea and practice, back to the Spanish Jesuit Pedro Arrupe (1907–91) and demonstrates its deep roots in Jesuit theology, practice, and spirituality. Through a detailed consideration of Francis's advocacy of inculturation and Benedict's alternative construal of "interculturality," alongside their respective intellectual and ecclesial contexts, Phillips firmly rejects a "hermeneutic of rupture" in this regard between the two pontiffs. Rather, he points to their shared skepticism of many aspects of Western culture. Phillips concludes with a clear exposition of Francis's view that popular piety is "the result of authentic inculturation at its best" and that inculturated manifestations of faith, like those so prominently on display at the national shrine of Aparecida, are the jewels that bedeck the church as bride. This is a bride that for Francis is always, of her nature, poor—a confrontational assertion for a church whose central institutions are so deeply embedded within affluent Western culture.

In the final ecclesiological reflection in this section, Tina Beattie takes as her subject the two theological metaphors that dominate Francis's understanding of the church: pilgrimage (journeying) and motherhood (fruitfulness or gestation). Clearly within the Roman Catholic Church, these metaphors have different histories, resonances, and implications. The historical and theological legacies of these analogies, and how these ways of talking about the church might be resolved, form the focus of Beattie's contribution, pursued through an exposition of two of Francis's primary principles, that "time is greater than space" (*EG* 222–25) and that "the whole is greater than the parts" (*EG* 234–37).

In Beattie's assessment, Pope Francis is a communitarian mystic and a narrative theologian but also "surely one of [the church's] first great postmodern theologians." He is clearly "with the reformers," and this is most apparent in his reflections on inculturation and his unequivocal statement that popular piety is a *locus theologicus*. However, like other contributors, Beattie fully recognizes that Francis's commitment to the whole precludes him from taking sides within the deeply conflicted postconciliar church. Yet, in some of the strongest criticisms of *EG* within this volume, Beattie argues that this commitment comes at the cost of a striking inconsistency between his assertion that "realities are greater than ideas" (*EG* 233) and his construal of the maternal metaphor for the church that remains abstract and unrealistic, detached from the reality of the lives of women.[11] In short, Beattie argues that when it comes to the female body and the place of women within the church, there is a distinct possibility that Francis will remain trapped within the "nostalgic romanticisms" of his predecessors. In Beattie's assessment, there are signals here of the clear potential for renewal, and indeed the "reform" of the church within this programmatic document, but this can only happen if the church takes a leap of faith to acknowledge the sacramental significance of the female (as well as male) body. Perhaps, in the recently announced commission to study the issue of women deacons and their early mission in the church (August 2016), comprised of six men and women under the presidency of Archbishop Luis Ladaria Ferrer, there is a portent of an open-minded reappraisal on the horizon.

Together in Mission: *Evangelii Gaudium* and Ecumenism

It has been widely observed that *EG* has very little to say about ecumenism, as Bevn and Keum also acknowledge.[12] While it is true that relationships with other churches do not receive much explicit treatment, in different ways the authors of the next three chapters all argue that the ecumenical implications of *EG* are significant and far-reaching.

Massimo Faggioli's contribution takes us into ecumenical ecclesiology, which he argues is an area where the differences between Francis and his predecessor are brought into particularly sharp relief. For Faggioli, it is "immediately clear" that Pope Francis is breathing life back into the ecclesiological trajectory initiated by Vatican II and "reenacting Pope John XXIII's reorientation of the church's message." Hence, it is as much his commitment to a dynamic idea of Catholic Church structures, as his more directly ecumenical initiatives, that are important here. But as Faggioli points out, these connections between the intraecclesial landscape and the wider ecumenical scene have to be situated within Francis's wider commitment to a missionary church and to a theology that is deeply contextual and inductive in character. So, for example, his image of the church as a "field hospital"—engaged in an urgent task and responsive to all who are wounded—has profound ecumenical implications. For Francis, ecumenism is a fact, a reality rather than an idea, and his approach is essentially practical (or "existential," as the Orthodox bishop and theologian John Zizioulas has described it) rather than doctrinal in character. Allied to this, we should not forget that Francis's ecumenism is, as Faggioli frames it, "postconfessional"—that is, its field of vision and priorities are not limited to the boundaries, physical and intellectual, of Europe. He has, for example, witnessed firsthand the growth of Pentecostalism in South America over the course of his lifetime and for many years undertaken his pastoral duties in the *villas miseria* of Buenos Aires in close contact with evangelical pastors.

In a very useful, wide-ranging work of comparison, Kirsteen Kim considers the "striking convergences" between *EG* and the World Council of Churches' (WCC) position statement on mission and evangelism, "Together towards Life" (TTL).[13] Despite the obvious and radical differences in ecclesiology, namely the established unity of the Catholic Church in contrast with the inherent plurality and diversity of the WCC, Kim identifies some key thematic similarities. Most of these flow from the shift in the "center of gravity" from a Eurocentric to a world Christianities perspective that profoundly shape both TTL and *EG.* As a consequence, there is greater attentiveness in both documents to cultural diversity, to the poor and to those on the margins, and therefore to the perspectives of liberation and postcolonial theology than in their respective predecessors. Here, perhaps, one of the most obvious and interesting distinctions is regional: the WCC document being shaped predominantly by an Asian perspective, and *EG* by the Latin American context and theological tradition.

However, the clearest distinction lies in the fact that TTL presents its theology of mission within a pneumatological framework that is, of course, explicitly and consciously ecumenical, whereas *EG* firmly ties evangelization to ecclesial renewal. In addition to extensive convergence as a result of the mutual emphasis on decentralization, internationalization, and the preference for the poor, Kim also argues cogently that there are further possibilities for mutual enrichment. For example, a reading of TTL suggests that the ongoing Catholic discussions might benefit from a more critical reflection on the ambiguities of culture, and give greater and more explicit consideration to the issues raised by migration and religious conversion in multifaith societies. Equally, Kim suggests that the WCC could benefit from a deeper consideration of the concept of evangelization vis-à-vis mission.

Like our other contributors in this section, Jeremy Worthen acknowledges that there is little overt discussion of ecumenism in *EG*; nevertheless, he argues *EG* is good news for ecumenism. That claim is rooted in Pope Francis's deep commitment to an evangelical ecclesiology and to an ecclesial characterization of the gospel. As Worthen points out, the pope's insistence on the inseparability of gospel and church, and his belief that the deepest source for the church's renewal lies with the activity of evangelization, means that any partnership in mission *itself* will inevitably generate unity. Drawing on his Anglican background, and in conversation with recent ecumenical explorations of evangelization, Worthen takes the view that the vision outlined by Francis of the church as a "community of missionary disciples" has wide ecumenical appeal and application.

Transforming the World: Catholic Social Teaching

Our final section considers the implications of *EG* for Catholic social teaching (CST). Notwithstanding the fact that *EG* "is not a social document," much of the immediate critical response to its publication took issue with its social teaching. A good deal of this was fairly uninformed, simply the clattering hooves of "hobby horses"—although it should be admitted that Pope Francis's condemnation of the "darker" side of capitalism has been more pronounced than that of his predecessors, doubtless informed by his pastoral and political experience in Argentina. In the opening chapter of this section however, Augusto Zampini Davies considers (and rejects) more detailed claims that in *EG* Pope Francis has disrupted or distorted the tradition and "threatened the continuity of the social magisterium." Two chapters that bear witness to the fruitfulness of Francis's approach follow this: in the first, Christopher Hrynkow considers the implications of *EG* for thinking about the environment, and in the last chapter, Séverine Deneulin considers some of the promising implications for a more humane approach to economic development.

Zampini Davies opens with a clear and positive rebuttal of the methodological criticisms leveled at *EG* by the Argentinian moral theologian Gustavo Irrazábal, who argues that Francis has put at risk a whole tradition of thinking.[14] To the contrary, Zampini Davies argues, in *EG* Pope Francis is faithful to the inductive and ecumenical methodology of CST, yet through a "much stronger dialogical and ecumenical tone," he has renewed it rather than retreated to the "the safe fortress of deductive theology." For Zampini Davies, Pope Francis builds up an entirely legitimate critique of the prevailing economic model of progress, drawing attention to those practices that ferment "exclusion and inequality," in which "the "subject" of the economy is misconceived as a mere "object" of consumption. It is against this backdrop that Francis provides a refined elaboration of the CST notion of "integral human development." And indeed, as Deneulin also makes clear, far from putting at risk interdisciplinary work between theologians and economists, a deep affinity can be detected between the thinking of Pope Francis and that of the "capability approach" developed by the Nobel prizewinning economist Amartya Sen. Finally, Zampini Davies argues that critics have seriously underestimated the dialogical approach of Pope Francis. For example, his argument that there is a place for biblical narrative as a classic religious text in facilitating public dialogue, and indeed challenging root metaphors and the "exclusive utilitarian-ridden intention for decision-making," is, Zampini Davies argues, offered in a spirit that respects healthy and respectful pluralism. This is a contribution to the processes of inclusive public dialogue that is crucial to social transformation rather than an attempt to foreclose on an argument.

For Pope Francis, the cause of the poor is closely tied to concern for creation, and here too there is a clear commitment to openness and dialogue with other voices as well as an insistence on the role that spirituality has to play. Indeed, it is through our embodiment that Pope Francis suggests that "we can feel the desertification of the soil almost as a physical ailment" (*EG* 215). This theme of our responsibility to our common home is picked up in the next chapter by Christopher Hrynkow, who assesses the importance of *EG* as a contribution to Christian thinking about socioecological flourishing. Prefaced by a wide-ranging consideration of theological perspectives on the environment, Hrynkow considers how Pope Francis's thinking can be mapped onto the six green principles enunciated in the *Global Greens Charter* (2001):[15] ecological wisdom, social justice, participatory democracy, nonviolence, sustainability, and respect for diversity. Hrynkow then considers how *EG* trails some of the issues that are more fully developed in *Laudato Si'* before concluding that, in his view, *EG* offers "sound sources for constructing an integrated ethic of socioecological flourishing."

The section is completed by a fascinating account of informal economy work in Argentina from the perspective of development studies. Here Séverine Deneulin provides a clear illustration of the broad affinity between the capability approach of Amartya Sen's and the message of *EG*, as well as a good exemplar of the former's account of public reasoning. Taking as her case study the *cartoneros*, the waste pickers of Buenos Aires, Deneulin shows how theological resources (social teaching, ecclesiology, and liturgy) were deployed to give voice, generate empathy, and promote public dialogue that led to the empowerment of these marginalized workers. A key player in the transformation of this formerly illegal activity into employment work with a stable income within a cooperative was the city's cardinal, namely, one Jorge Bergoglio.

The volume concludes with a brief reflection from Rowan Williams that focuses on the nature of authentic evangelization in the light of what Pope Francis's describes as the "crisis of commitment" (*EG* 106). For Williams it is evident that evangelization is simply a "nonnegotiable" aspect of living faithfully, and involves being "transparent to Christ." Finally, he offers the suggestion that the vision of *EG* might be developed through an extended reflection on the practices of commitment entailed in the liturgical and sacramental life to ensure that worship and service are not falsely divided.

Select Bibliography

Bevans, Stephen. "The Apostolic Exhortation *Evangelii Gaudium* on the Proclamation of the Gospel in Today's World: Implications and Prospects." *International Review of Mission* 103, no. 2 (2014): 297–308.

Bevans, Stephen, and Jooseop Keum. "*Evangelii Gaudium* and Ecumenism." *International Review of Mission* 104, no. 2 (2015): 149–415.

Burns, Jimmy. *Francis, Pope of Good Promise.* London: St. Martin's Press, 2015.

Dormor, Duncan, and Alana Harris. "*Evangelii Gaudium* and the Renewal of the Church." *Ecclesiology* 12 (2016): 3–11 (and entire special issue, 1–90).

Gooder, Paula. *The Joy of the Gospel: A Six-Session Study Course in Sharing Faith.* London: Church House Publishing, 2015.

Iverleigh, Austin. *The Great Reformer: Francis and the Making of a Radical Pope.* London: Allen & Unwin, 2014.

Kasper, Walter. *Pope Francis's Revolution of Tenderness and Love.* New York: Paulist Press, 2015.

Gerard Mannion, *Pope Francis and the Future of Catholicism:* Evangelii Gaudium *and the Papal Agenda* (Cambridge: Cambridge University Press, 2017).

Vallely, Paul. *Pope Francis: Untying the Knots.* London: Bloomsbury, 2013.

Notes

1. Naomi O'Leary, "Pope Attacks 'Tyranny' of Markets in Manifesto for Papacy," *Reuters,* November 26, 2013, http://www

.reuters.com/article/us-pope-document-idUSBRE9AP0EQ201
31126.

2. John L. Allen Jr., "'Evangelii Gaudium' Amounts to Francis' 'I Have a Dream' Speech," *Reuters,* November 26, 2013, https://www.ncronline.org/news/theology/evangelii-gaudium-amounts-francis-i-have-dream-speech.

3. Walter Kasper, "How Pope Francis Sees the Church," *Commonweal,* March 13, 2015; see https://www.commonwealmagazine.org/open-house. See also Walter Kasper, *Pope Francis's Revolution of Tenderness and Love* (New York: Paulist Press, 2015).

4. See Alana Harris, "Councils and Synods: Reforming the Catholic Church in the Digital Age," *History and Policy,* November 11, 2015, http://www.historyandpolicy.org/opinion-articles/articles/councils-and-synods-reforming-the-catholic-church-in-the-digital-age.

5. See Jimmy Burns, *Francis, Pope of Good Promise* (London: St. Martin's Press, 2015); Austen Iverleigh, *The Great Reformer: Francis and the Making of a Radical Pope* (London: Allen & Unwin, 2014); Paul Vallely, *Pope Francis: Untying the Knots* (London: Bloomsbury, 2013); Andrea Tornielli, *Francis: Pope of a New World* (San Francisco: Ignatius Press, 2013); and Antonio Spadara, *My Door Is Always Open: A Conversation on Faith, Hope and the Church in a Time of Change* (New York: HarperOne, 2013). See also Rowan Williams, "Pope of the Masses: Is Francis Really the People's champion?" *New Statesman,* September 10, 2015, http://www.newstatesman.com/politics/religion/2015/09/pope-masses-francis-really-people-s-champion.

6. We would like to thank St. John's College, Cambridge, and the trustees of *The Tablet* for financial support in the organization of this conference.

7. The most substantial and creative theological reflections on *EG* that have emerged are those that seek to address the central challenges it poses for evangelization in a culturally diverse world. Here two collections stand out: the first is in the *Australian eJournal of Theology* (vol. 22, no. 1, April 2015), with contributions by Stephen Bevans, Gerard Whelan, Joseph Ogbonnaya, and Catherine Clifford—see http://aejt.com.au/2015/volume_22/vol_22_no_1_2015. Bevans has also written on *EG* within the World Council of Churches' journal—see "The Apostolic Exhortation

Evangelii Gaudium on the Proclamation of the Gospel in Today's World: Implications and Prospects," *International Review of Mission* 103, no. 2 (2014): 297–308. Unsurprisingly, a good proportion of the commentary on *EG* comes from the Spanish-speaking world, such as a collection of articles in *Scripta Theologica* 46, no. 2 (2014), which contextualizes *EG* with the papal encyclical *Lumen Fidei,* issued on June 29, 2013—see http://www.unav.edu/documents/29050/afdfff18-777b-4a30-a831-8c98f9a95882. Further contributions from the Spanish-speaking Catholic world can be found in the journal *Teología y vida* 55, no. 3 (2014). Two contributions provide interesting examples of moves to apply and contextualize Pope Francis's reflections on evangelization: Branko Muri in the context of a largely Catholic Croatia, see "The People of God as the Agent of Evangelization of the Church: *Evangelii Gaudium* and the Church's Missionary Transformation," *Ephemerides Theologicae Diacovenses* 22, no. 4 (2015): 469–95; and in a stimulating juxtaposition, Hannes Knoetze seeks to draw out "some specific African contextual considerations for a child theology" from *EG* in conjunction with the WCC document "Together towards Life"; see "Together towards Life and *Evangelii Gaudium*—Implications for African Child Theology Today," *Missionalia: Southern African Journal of Mission Studies* 43, no. 2 (2015): 218–31. Other articles of note include those by Gerard Mannion, "Time, Space and Magisterium: The Need for a Long-Range Perspective," *Australian eJournal of Theology* 21, no. 3 (2014); Robert Svatoň, "Unity and Mission: Impulses for Reflection on the Relationship," *Studia Theologica* (Czech Republic) 16, no. 3 (2014): 72–86, and the extensive references to *EG* in a special issue titled "Bioethics after Pope Francis," *Christian Bioethics* 21, no. 1 (2015).

8. Paula Gooder, *The Joy of the Gospel: A Six-Session Study Course in Sharing Faith* (London: Church House Publishing, 2015).

9. Stephen Bevans and Jooseop Keum, "*Evangelii Gaudium* and Ecumenism," *International Review of Mission* 104, no. 2 (2015): 149–415. Also recently published, see Gerard Mannion, ed., *Pope Francis and the Future of Catholicism:* Evangelii Gaudium *and the Papal Agenda* (Cambridge: Cambridge University Press, 2017).

10. The most authoritative critique of liberation theology was that issued by the Congregation for the Doctrine of the Faith in 1984, "Instruction on Certain Aspects of the Theology

of Liberation," which can be found at http://www.vatican.va/
roman_curia/congregations/cfaith/documents/rc_con_cfaith
_doc_19840806_theology-liberation_en.html.

11. See, for example, Catholic Women Speak Network, ed.,
Catholic Women Speak: Bringing Our Gifts to the Table (Mahwah, NJ:
Paulist Press, 2015).

12. Bevans and Keum, "*Evangelii Gaudium* and Ecumenism,"
149–51.

13. "Together towards Life: Mission and Evangelism in
Changing Landscapes," the new WCC affirmation on mission
and evangelism was released in September 2013, just two months
before the publication of *EG.*

14. The theological differences between Gustavo Irrazábal
and Jorge Bergoglio have a long history; see Vallely, *Untying the
Knots,* 96.

15. The *Global Greens Charter,* which draws upon the charters
and constitutions of green parties around the world, is the foundational document of the Global Greens. It has been updated
since 2001; the current, 2012 version, accessed August, 16, 2016,
can be found at https://www.globalgreens.org/globalcharter.

Part 1

FROM THE HEART OF THE GOSPEL

THEOLOGICAL FOUNDATIONS

1

"The Ends of the Earth" Meets the *Caput Mundi*

The Aparecida Document as Frame and Source for Understanding Pope Francis's Thought in *Evangelii Gaudium*

EDUARDO MANGIAROTTI

Introduction: From the Ends of the Earth

The memory of Pope Francis's election is still fresh in the life of the church, his first words as Bishop of Rome echoing even now in our hearts: the cardinals had gone "to the ends of the earth" to find the new pope. This was and is more than a romantic figure of speech: it provides the biographical, pastoral, and theological frame that allows us to delve with greater clarity and insight into Jorge Mario Bergoglio's pastoral project for the church, so clearly expressed in his Apostolic Exhortation *Evangelii Gaudium*. Even if his first encyclical was *Lumen Fidei* (2013), it is *EG* that has the privilege of being the pope's programmatic text, as is clearly expressed within the exhortation itself (see *EG* 25). This chapter will argue that a deeper comprehension of the Latin American context helps us to achieve a better understanding of *EG*, its style, its pastoral priorities, and its theological matrix.

There are a number of approaches that could be pursued. Perhaps the richest lies in considering the Fifth General Conference of the Latin American and Caribbean Bishops that took place at the Aparecida Shrine in Brazil in the year 2007, under the motto "Disciples and Missionaries of Jesus Christ, so That Our Peoples May Have Life in Him," and its concluding document, published in the same year.[1]

The grounds for such inquiry lie not only in the influence the conference had in the church in Latin America as a whole, but more specifically in the fact that Cardinal Bergoglio was both an important protagonist at the conference (where he served as president of the redaction commission) and author of its subsequent document, as well as an outspoken advocate of the ideas espoused. Therefore, a better knowledge of Aparecida can bring about a more profound and nuanced reading of *EG* and a richer understanding of Pope Francis's project for the church at this particular juncture of her ongoing pilgrimage.

The Road to Aparecida: A Young but Strong Tradition

When in 1955 the CELAM (Consejo Episcopal Latinoamericano, Latin American Episcopal Conference) was created at the request of the Latin American bishops, the first stone was laid to the paving of a road that would eventually lead to Aparecida. The conference helped to generate a growing self-awareness among the bishops of the specific concerns and urgencies of their region that led to them making a distinctive contribution to the Second Vatican Council.[2] More importantly still, this initiated a process of reception at the CELAM's Second General Conference held in Medellín, Colombia. This reception was not merely an uncritical application of the Council's documents and spirit, but instead a profoundly "creative" one.[3]

The bishops' desire was to pursue a contextualized application of the Council, one that would address the social, cultural, and pastoral situation in which the task of aggiornamento was to be undertaken. The development of this inculturated approach was quite different from that which took place in the European setting where the Council was held. It would come to define the reception of Vatican II within Latin America.[4]

Guided by the "see-judge-act" methodology, Medellín would soon become a reference point for the church in Latin America and thus set the groundwork for an original style of reflection that would have at its core, as Ernesto Valiente points out,

> (1) attention to the signs of the times as the point of departure for pastoral directives and pastoral reflection; (2) the adoption of the preferential option for the poor as the stance that ought to inform all aspects of the church; and (3) an ecclesiological vision rooted in the idea of communion and expressed in the formation of Christian base communities.[5]

The Medellín Conference would later be followed by Puebla (1979) and Santo Domingo (1992). Both would deepen the path set by Medellín and add their own contributions to what was already becoming a young but strong regional tradition. Nevertheless the meeting at Santo Domingo was also marked by significant tensions between those who wished to follow the method and priorities set by the former conferences and others who attempted to steer the conference in a different direction. Fifteen years later, the Aparecida Conference would be the context for both a clear reclamation of the theological-pastoral style developed by the bishops at Medellín (1968) and a bold new step forward. By the time of Aparecida in 2007, Jorge Mario Bergoglio had been archbishop of Buenos Aires for a few years. A brief reference to the cultural and ecclesial context in Argentina during that period can therefore help us understand the *sitz im leben* he found himself in when he participated in the conference. This also informs the worldview he brought with him to Rome as the first Latin American pope.

The Argentinean Church Ecclesial Context before Aparecida

The Aparecida document set out to return to the original path on which the church in Latin America had been walking from Medellín until Santo Domingo. The spirit of the document and indeed the context in which Bergoglio lives, thinks, and works can be very fittingly described by another Argentinean Bishops' Conference document, *Navega Mar Adentro* (Launch out into the deep),[6] written in 2003 to update the conference's Pastoral Lines for a New Evangelization from 1992. Argentina's political, cultural, and ecclesial context was described in the years previous to the Aparecida document as having reached a moment of crisis, in line with a much broader "crisis of our civilization" due to the epochal change the world was and is going through, with distinctive characteristics of its own.

Less than two years before *Navega Mar Adentro*'s publication, the country underwent one of its darkest hours, when, on December 2001, then president of the republic Fernando De La Rúa resigned during a financial crisis. This led to a time of turmoil that was specially felt in Buenos Aires and other Argentinean cities, where riots broke out during what would later be called by some the *Argentinazo* or the *Cacerolazo* ("beating on the pan," because of the use of pans to make noise during the protests). The crisis revealed and deepened wounds in the nation's already fragile social tissue. The lack of a vice president, who had already resigned early on during De La Rúa's presidency, resulted in a string of extremely short-lived presidencies (four in the course of two weeks), until Eduardo Duhalde assumed the role of president, providing some stability through what remained of the term of office. A political crisis of representation had been installed, along with the economic and social ones. The aftermath of the crisis was felt throughout 2002 and continued through to when *Navega Mar Adentro* was published.[7]

However bleak in some of its assessments, given the described situation, *Navega Mar Adentro* strives for a hopeful tone: this crisis (both global and national) is, above all, an opportunity, a "providential occasion"[8] for the nation to grow following Jesus's call. It is in this context that Bergoglio ministered as archbishop in the largest diocese in the country (he'd only been titular archbishop for five years before that) and that we can fully appreciate *Navega Mar Adentro*'s diagnosis of the Argentinean reality on a cultural, political, social, and religious level.

As previously stated, there is in the Argentinean Bishops' Conference an acute awareness of a shift in the social and cultural paradigm: "We are not merely going through a time of changes, but through an epochal change that seriously compromises our Nation's identity."[9] The extent of the transformation within different areas of society and culture reveals an underlying paradigm shift. As the culture changes, Argentinean society's shortcomings come to be seen in a new light, with political corruption and power struggles undermining the possibility for true progress;[10] a growth in crime and violence; and, especially, an ever-growing breach between the privileged ones and the huge masses who are already beyond poverty (*miseria*).[11] Family life is a victim of this fragmentation on two accounts: as a consequence of the cultural crisis, which relativized its value and importance, and as a result of the rampant economic crisis that ate away at the core of family life by disaggregating its members.[12] On a religious level, the bishops notice a "diffuse search for God," intertwined with contemporary individualism and religious indifference. Many Catholics have left the church for other communities, Christian or otherwise.[13] Yet a strong sense of belonging still remains in popular Catholicism, expressed mainly through the different manifestations of popular piety.[14]

It is worth pausing to evaluate the church's situation at this particular juncture. The exodus of many Catholics is partially acknowledged as a failure of the church, which has not always been able to provide the relief and the answers her people were looking for, and which has failed to work properly on her members' formation.[15] This is partly because the church has struggled to work in unity, and this has dented her efforts to be an effective presence in society. Lack of imagination and interest has also paralyzed many of her endeavours.[16]

It is worth noting that this last part of the "seeing" section of the document (following the traditional "see-judge-act" method) seems rather lukewarm in its attempt to identify the elements of the crisis *ad intra ecclesiae.* Other voices during the same year *Navega Mar Adentro* came out were more precise in their considerations, like that of the Argentinean theologian Marcelo González, who wrote a three-part article on the "uneasiness and emergencies in the pastoral life of the church in Argentina."[17] In that article, he argued that such uneasiness pervades all areas of the church's life, from the laity to the bishops, and crystalizes itself in inadequacy toward the different pastoral challenges that the communities face, estrangement from everyday reality and common language, and a lack of pastoral reaction[18] in an ever faster changing culture.

The Argentinean church's inadequacy shows itself, according to González, mainly in the widening gap between the growing pastoral needs and the lack of people (both consecrated and lay) to address them. This resulted in considerable burdens being placed on those already committed to different ministries and initiatives and a large number of clergy leaving the priesthood during the late 1990s and early 2000s.

At the same time, these two decades also saw the outbreak of internal conflict within the church and the undermining of traditional episcopal authority and diocesan structures. Particular tensions were created by the formation of new, but traditionally minded communities and the development of relationships between certain church personalities with members of the government creating a network of power and influence independent of the bishops' conference. Such developments eroded the church's strength and credibility.

However, González recognized that there were burgeoning pastoral initiatives as well that sought for new ways to address a new reality. As he poignantly wrote, "Today the Catholic Church in Argentina's pastoral life requires something unprecedented, a creative and audacious response. The pastoral crisis isn't conjectural but historic, and it is the fruit of a long deterioration process."[19]

In this regard, *Navega Mar Adentro* also calls for such a renewal by admitting that "we need to transparently and sincerely evaluate our way of being Church."[20] As stark as the document's perspective might be when it comes to the numerous difficulties the church in Argentina needs to address, it is also important to note that its tone is hopeful and positive: such difficulty is not seen as a problem but as a challenge, right from the very first paragraph, and in every reality there are signs of hope[21] or moral reserves[22] still to be found.

This contrast between a complex and challenging crisis and an energetic call for evaluation and renewal is the context in which the church in Argentina found herself in during Jorge Bergoglio's years as an archbishop. Already we can see some of the topics present both at Aparecida and in *EG* emerging with marked clarity, such as concern for church renewal, a positive appraisal of popular piety, and the need to be near the poor and marginalized.

Aparecida: The Joy of Encounter with Jesus and the Call to Mission

In 2003 Pope John Paul II agreed to convene a new conference, a decision sanctioned two years later by Benedict XVI. Aparecida's basilica in Brazil was to be the meeting point, which is one of the world's largest and most vital Marian shrines. This setting wasn't something merely incidental, as the bishops not only worked amid the countless pilgrims that visit the basilica every day but also prayed and celebrated the Eucharist with them. The resulting document from the conference was a hefty text composed of 555 paragraphs, divided in ten chapters and covering a wide range of topics. Despite its length and the immense number of people involved in one way or another in its composition, the document reveals an all-embracing tone, even if it remains the fruit of accords and consensus.[23] The cohesive, overarching message, the concluding document's spirit, is marked both by an underscoring of the elements seen as core to the church's path in Latin America and the need to apply them in a new social, cultural, economic, political, and ecclesial context. The awareness of the "many changes" the continent and the church underwent in the years following Santo Domingo leads to a call for a renewed impetus for evangelization.[24]

This desire for renewal is in continuity with the call to the "new evangelization" that John Paul II made in his opening discourse at Santo Domingo in 1992; but here, it is grounded both in a growing awareness of a rather visible "weakening" of Christian life (as it was described by Benedict XVI, who would later be quoted in the document on this regard)[25] and a desire to rekindle the fire of the Spirit. Hence the continued use of the *re* prefix (in the original Spanish version of the document), which seems to describe much of the new drive the church is called to have in this particular hour of her history in Latin America: "We must all start again from Christ."[26]

This mission doesn't unfold in a vacuum: the life of the Trinity that the church is called to share with the world reaches out to concrete peoples in a determined time and place. Human history unfolds under God's loving gaze;[27] guided by the Holy Spirit, the church always seeks to discern the signs of the times,[28] even if reality has now become more opaque and difficult to read.[29] Such a spiritual exercise is never a cause for discouragement or disillusion; in fact, the "seeing" chapter of the document is followed by a hopeful declaration on the joy of being missionary disciples. Latin America and the Caribbean is not a land of sorrow, but the continent of hope and love.[30]

"Starting again" is founded in the personal and communal encounter with Jesus Christ.[31] This is not just a moment in a Christian disciple's itinerary "but the leitmotiv of a process."[32] This is why the motto of the conference was "Disciples and Missionaries so That Our Peoples May Have Life in Him." The church is called to rediscover this fundamental personal dimension of her faith, but it is not to fall into a self-secluded intimism. The "and" in the "disciples and missionaries" binomial is fundamental: it reminds everyone of how every Christian is both things, as they are mutually intertwined, and there cannot be one without the other. There is no discipleship without mission, there is no mission without personal and collective intimacy with the Lord: "When awareness of belonging to Christ grows by reason of the gratitude and joy that it produces, the eagerness to communicate the gift of this encounter to all also grows."[33] The mission is a fruit born out of grace.[34]

This profoundly interpersonal vision of the church's apostolic work impregnates every aspect of her life and work. The encounter with Jesus transforms and fulfills all dimensions of human existence.[35] It is therefore impossible to think of faith as a menace to man.[36] On the contrary: it renews the human being. Jesus comes so that the peoples of Latin America may have life in him, a full, dignified life. Therefore, mission is seen in the Aparecida document as a sharing of the life we have received in our encounter with Christ.[37] This communication is nothing less than personal, organic, and humanizing. This is also one of the reasons why the document goes out of its way to stress that the church's missionary style is absolutely opposed to any kind of religious propaganda: "The church grows not by proselytizing but 'by attraction': as Christ 'attracts all to himself' with the power of his love."[38] This is especially important not only because of the way this conception of the mission sheds light on the church's apostolic work, but also for its ecumenical consequences. As the document makes clear,

> At this new stage of evangelization, we want dialogue and ecumenical cooperation to lead to promoting new forms of discipleship and mission in communion. We note that where dialogue is established, proselytism diminishes, mutual knowledge and respect increase, and possibilities for witnessing together expand.[39]

Ecumenical dialogue is therefore also strongly encouraged, with an emphasis on concrete gestures and activities.[40]

Mission and Pastoral Conversion

The Aparecida document highlights, as we have seen, the need for renewal in the Latin American and Caribbean church. However, the word *reform* is rarely used (only twice when it comes to the church),[41] and instead, the preferred term seems to be *conversion*, and in some very noteworthy paragraphs, *pastoral conversion*, which suggests at the same time the theological and missionary elements of the church's renewal. In what is probably one of its most relevant passages, the document affirms, "The pastoral conversion of our communities requires moving from a pastoral ministry of mere conservation to a decidedly missionary pastoral ministry."[42] Whenever the church goes forth on her mission, it is then that she finds the source for her renewal and that of her members. Mission nourishes discipleship, in a collective echo of what was said before on a more personal level. This dynamism reveals a very interesting and holistic perspective on church reform, even if some have criticized this view as excessively ecclesiocentric and therefore still insufficiently "ex-centrically" oriented.[43] This seems, however, too harsh a criticism. The document stresses again and again the importance of the church of being shaken and woken up, since "the Church needs to be jolted to prevent it from becoming well established in comfort, stagnation, and luke-warmness, aloof from the suffering of the continent's poor."[44]

As the Belgian-born but Brazilian-by-choice theologian José Comblin said, this is an ambitious project that, in his view, would require all of the twenty-first century.[45] In the meantime, the event and document of Aparecida seems to have been transported across continents and onto the larger canvas of the global church through the person of Pope Francis and his programmatic Apostolic Exhortation *EG*.

Aparecida and *Evangelii Gaudium*: A Church That Goes Forth Worldwide

Cardinal Jorge Mario Bergoglio was clearly a pivotal figure at the Fifth Conference of Aparecida,[46] and also a fervent supporter of its application,[47] whether in the archdiocese of Buenos Aires or the national context. After his election as pope, the conference seems to have also exerted an important influence in his writing of *EG*. Not only is it referenced twenty times, but these references seem to condense the essence of the document, and most emphatically the need for the church to grow in her missionary outreach. As one of Pope Francis's more authorized interpreters, the Argentinean theologian and Buenos Aires priest Carlos Galli says that Francis's proposal of a missionary church as the paradigm for the people of God (see *EG* 15) and his dream of an all-transforming missionary option (see *EG* 27) shows the impulse the Aparecida proposal has given to what is now a worldwide call to conversion and renewal for the Catholic Church.[48]

It is, of course, easy to identify differences in the scope and the contents of both documents. The mere nature of Aparecida as a work of discussion and consensus allows for what can be perceived as tensions in its propositions. *EG* is, instead, an extremely personal document, one that shows in every paragraph what we now have come to know as Pope Francis's predominant themes: a missionary church and the need for her reform; the importance of the poor not only as recipients but protagonists of the church's life and mission, especially through popular piety; the insistence on what we could call the basic aspects of Christian faith, with an emphasis on mercy, social justice, and discernment to find God's will for the church here and now. The common, concurrent agendas of both documents are palpable and it is these communalities that are illuminated within this analysis. The task the church has set herself in Latin America has now gained a global reach. More so, it is once again the church's mission that defines and molds the shape she is called to adopt in order to better fulfill her apostolic calling (see *EG* 25). By attraction and sharing of the life received from the Trinity, the church finds conversion and renewal in her missionary work (see *EG* 15).

Perhaps these two last elements are the most representative of the missionary spirit that Aparecida radiates and *EG* continues and refines. Reform is not achieved by looking inward, but by setting out into the world as missionary disciples of Christ. It is from this going forth that the dynamics of conversion within the church spring, a missionary conversion that now becomes the official agenda for the people of God (see *EG* 25). Nevertheless it is true that the "reform" facet seems to be more explicit, emphatic, and underscored in *EG*, a reform that every particular national church must undertake as part of a "resolute process" (*EG* 30). An interesting dimension of this reform is the importance of implementing it in a decentralized fashion. This is more than clear from the very beginning of *EG*, for "it is not advisable for the Pope to take the place of local bishops in the discernment of every issue which arises in their territory" (*EG*

16). While this may be somewhat of a new development when comparing *EG* to the bishops' propositions at Aparecida, it is certainly understandable when we take into account that Pope Francis comes from the one region in the world where the Second Vatican Council's reception was implemented on an organic continental level,[49] thus creating a keen awareness of the importance of discernment and action from a strongly local, parochial perspective. The fact that documents from bishops' conferences from all around the world are quoted in a consistent fashion is far from incidental.[50]

Consequently, the church is put in a constant state of outreach, a healthy tension that not only drives her forth toward the peripheries of the world (both geographical and existential) but also renders her more aware of her pilgrim condition (see *EG* 26). This also avoids the danger of a merely formal or cosmetic reform, which would be useless without a life that fills whatever ecclesial structure may be created. Awareness of her own precariousness makes ecumenical dialogue more fluent and fruitful: the church grows in unity by gazing outside, searching for God's face (see *EG* 244).

This is not a mere "internal affair" for the church. It is "a contribution to the unity of the human family." Francis's approach to ecumenism, as we can see not only in *EG* but in his numerous gestures toward members of the other Christian communities, is strongly based on friendship, prayer, and charity: "It is not just about being better informed about others, but rather about reaping what the Spirit has sown in them, which is also meant to be a gift for us" (*EG* 246). In this regard, a certain shift seems to happen between Aparecida and *EG*: Pope Francis seems to stress a more pastoral, interpersonal approach, more based on signs and vicinity and less on theological agreements, which are much more in evidence in Aparecida (even if a quote from Benedict XVI reminds readers at the end of the document's ecumenical section that concrete gestures are needed in order to grow toward a deeper unity).[51]

Aparecida: A Pilgrim, Missionary Church for the Twenty-First Century

Gustavo Gutiérrez said that the Aparecida Conference was, like the preceding ones, bound to impact the life of the church both in the continent and beyond it.[52] Little did he know the prophetic strength of his words. The event and the document that inspired a renewed vigor and a confirmation of the young but fruitful path of the Latin American church has stretched itself beyond its original borders. Pope Francis's dream of a missionary option (see *EG* 27) undoubtedly drinks from the well of Aparecida. As José Comblin said, this is neither an ordinary project nor a short-term one. It involves a true conversion in its most literal sense, a "renewal of the mind" (*metanoia*). But it is indeed this combination of inspiration and audacity that can hold one of the keys to church renewal in this current juncture. Both in the interior of the Catholic Church and in all its ecumenical initiatives, a missionary, pastoral conversion can only lead to a greater deepening of the bonds of communion. Neither the document of Aparecida nor *EG* answers every question. They do not provide a complete diagnosis of what the church is to do nor a concrete program of action. But the practical consequences of following the spirit that imbues both of them can only lead to a healthier, more open and vital church. We can only hope that from this missionary option, the seeds of a new Pentecost may be sown, that they in their time show a little more of what God dreams for all men and women, for "the pilgrim Church lives in anticipation the beauty of love, which will be achieved at the end of time in perfect communion with God and human beings."[53]

A More Personal Conclusion

Less than a year ago, I was fortunate enough to participate in a meeting of the pope with the priests living at the Argentinean

College in Rome.[54] During our conversation, I had the chance to ask him what he thought were the main challenges for theology today. He said he had already outlined them in *EG*, where the program for his pontificate had been set. He then described the Exhortation as a combination of the Aparecida Document with Paul VI's *Evangelii Nuntiandi* (the similarity between both titles, as we know, is far from coincidental).[55] This double influence converges organically in the document, since Paul VI's papacy had a huge influence on the church in Argentina and its pastoral and theological thought, and most particularly on Jorge Bergoglio,[56] whose active participation both in the composition and reception of the Aparecida document have been instrumental to its fruitfulness.

As Pope Francis's pontificate continues, we are beginning to see many of the intuitions contained in *EG* slowly start to develop. However universal such development may be, the elements of Francis's Latin American *forma mentis* can be continually seen, heard, and felt. Though his episcopacy, his pastoral style, and his persona are as particular as they can be, the ground from whence all this sprouted nevertheless remains easily recognizable. It remains to be seen how the church, both in Rome and worldwide, will receive and put in practice the novelty of this pope's teachings and proposals.

Select Bibliography

Codina, Víctor. "Eclesiología de aparecida." *Revista Iberoamericana de Teología* 6 (2008): 69–86.

Fernández, Victor Manuel. *Aparecida. Guía para leer el documento y crónica diaria.* Buenos Aires: San Pablo, 2007, 103–61.

Fifth General Conference of the Latin American and Caribbean Bishops. *Aparecida Document.*

González, Marcelo. "Repercusiones del cambio epocal en la vida pastoral de la Iglesia católica argentina: Malestares y emergencias." In *Crisis y reconstrucción. Aportes desde el pensamiento social de la Iglesia. Dimensión social y ético–cultural,* ed. Grupo Gerardo Farrell, 159–82. Buenos Aires: San Pablo, 2003.

Kasper, Walter. *Pope Francis' Revolution of Tenderness and Love: Theological and Pastoral Perspectives.* Mahwah, NJ: Paulist Press, 2015.

Piqué, Elisabetta. *Pope Francis: Life and Revolution: A Biography of Jorge Bergoglio.* Chicago: Loyola Press, 2015.

Rubin, Sergio, and Francesca Ambrogetti. *Pope Francis: Conversations with Jorge Bergoglio; His Life in His Own Words.* New York: G. P. Putnam's Sons, 2013.

Valiente, O. Ernesto. "The Reception of Vatican II in Latin America." *Theological Studies* 73 (2012): 795–823.

Yáñez, Humberto Miguel, ed. *Evangelii Gaudium: il testo ci interroga. Chiavi di lettura, testimonianza e prospettive.* Roma: Gregorian & Biblical Press, 2014.

Notes

1. Fifth General Conference of the Latin American and Caribbean Bishops, Aparecida Document, (Hereafter, DA).

2. A very good and updated survey on the recent bibliography on this subject can be found in Carlos Schickendantz, "Las investigaciones históricas sobre el Vaticano II. Estado de la cuestión y perspectivas de trabajo," *Teología y Vida* 55, no. 1 (2014): 105–41.

3. Cf. Agenor Brighenti, "Medellín-Aparecida. Pre-textos, con-textos y textos," *Pasos* 137 (2008): 14–20.

4. Cf. O. Ernesto Valiente, "The Reception of Vatican II in Latin America," *Theological Studies* 73 (2012): 805.

5. Ibid., 795–96.

6. Comisión Episcopal para la actualización de las Líneas Pastorales para la Nueva Evangelización, *Navega Mar Adentro*, accessed September 8, 2016, http://www.arquidiocesisbb.com.ar/download/cea/CEA%20-%20Navega%20Mar%20Adentro.pdf. (Hereafter, *NMA*). It bears mentioning that Pope Francis underscored both this document and Aparecida as the guiding lines for the church in Argentina when he wrote to the Bishops' Conference shortly after his election (see http://www.episcopado.org/portal/actualidad-cea/oficina-de-prensa/item/763-carta-del

-papa-francisco-a-los-obispos-argentinos-con-ocasi%C3%B3n-de
-la-105-asamblea-plenaria-de-la-cea.html).

7. The process and causes that lead to the crisis, its consequences, and possible solutions are far too complex to properly summarize. A brief but clear and insightful attempt can be found in Daniel García Delgado, "La ruptura de un contrato. Crisis de representación y gobernabilidad," in *Crisis y Reconstrucción. Aportes desde el pensamiento social de la Iglesia. Dimensión político-económica*, ed. Grupo Gerardo Farrell (Buenos Aires: San Pablo, 2003), 57–84. A more detailed account is told in Ceferino Reato, "Doce Noches. 2001: La caída de la Alianza, el golpe peronista y el origen del kirchnerismo" (Buenos Aires: Sudamericana, 2015).

8. *NMA* 28.

9. Ibid., 24: "No estamos sólo en una época de cambios sino ante un cambio de época que compromete seriamente la identidad de nuestra Nación."

10. Cf. ibid., 36–37.

11. Ibid., 36.

12. Cf. ibid., 40–41.

13. Cf. ibid., 30–31.

14. Cf. ibid., 33.

15. Cf. ibid., 30–31.

16. Cf. ibid., 46.

17. Marcelo González, "Repercusiones del cambio epocal en la vida pastoral de la Iglesia católica argentina: Malestares y emergencias," in Grupo Gerardo Farrell, *Crisis y reconstrucción*, 159–82.

18. Ibid., 161–74.

19. Ibid., 172: "Hoy la vida pastoral de la Iglesia católica argentina requiere algo inédito, una respuesta creativa y audaz. La crisis pastoral no es coyuntural sino histórica, y es fruto de un largo proceso de deterioro."

20. *NMA* 46: "Necesitamos evaluar con sinceridad y transparencia nuestro modo de ser Iglesia."

21. Ibid., 7, 28, 39, 48.

22. Ibid., 28.

23. Agenor Brighenti, "Criterios para la lectura del documento de Aparecida (II)."

24. DA 16.

25. Ibid., 100.

26. Ibid., 12.

27. Ibid., 30.

28. Ibid., 31.

29. Ibid., 36.

30. Ibid., 126–27.

31. Ibid., 11, 297.

32. Ibid., 278.

33. Ibid., 145.

34. Ibid., 347.

35. Ibid., 356.

36. Ibid., 29.

37. Víctor Manuel Fernández, "Estructuras internas de la vitalidad cristiana. La vida digna y plena como clave de interpretación de Aparecida," *Teología* 94 (2007): 419–43.

38. DA 159.

39. Ibid., 233.

40. Ibid., 234.

41. Ibid., 252, 367.

42. Ibid., 370.

43. Víctor Codina, "Eclesiología de aparecida," *Revista Iberoamericana de Teología* 6 (2008): 69–86.

44. DA 362.

45. José Comblin, "El proyecto de Aparecida," accessed May 29, 2015, http://www.alterinfos.org/spip.php?article1571.

46. For an Argentinean perspective on the conference and the redaction of the document, with a special attention on the role of Cardinal Bergoglio, see the journal of the conference written by Mons. Victor Manuel Fernandez in Víctor Manuel Fernández, *Aparecida. Guía para leer el documento y crónica diaria* (Buenos Aires: San Pablo, 2007), 103–61.

47. See, for example, Cardenal Jorge Mario Bergoglio, "El mensaje de Aparecida a los presbíteros," accessed May 29, 2015, http://aica.org/aica/documentos_files/Obispos_Argentinos/Bergoglio/2008/2008_09_11.html; "Dios vive en la ciudad," accessed May 29, 2015, http://pastoralurbana.com.ar/web/eventos/p2.php; also, some references in Francis, *Only Love Can Save Us: Letters, Homilies and Talks of Cardinal Jorge Bergoglio* (Huntington: Our Sunday Visitor, 2013).

48. Carlos M. Galli, "La teología pastoral de 'Evangelii Gaudium' en el proyecto misionero de Francisco," *Teología* 114 (2014): 32.

49. Carlos Schickendantz, "Único ejemplo de una recepción continental del Concilio Vaticano II. Convocatoria, desarrollo y estatuto eclesial-jurídico de la Conferencia de Medellín (1968)," *Teología* 108 (2012): 25–53.

50. For example, Oceania (*EG* 118); the Philippines (*EG* 215); the USA (*EG* 64); France (*EG* 66); and Congo (*EG* 230).

51. DA 234.

52. Gustavo Gutiérrez, "La V Conferencia en Aparecida y la Opción por los Pobres," in *El desafío de hablar de Dios en la América Latina del Siglo XXI*, ed. Gustavo Gutiérrez, Horacio Simián Yofre, and Cecilia Avenatti (Buenos Aires: San Benito, 2008), 13.

53. DA 160.

54. See http://www.aica.org/21517-francisco-al-colegio-sacerdotal-argentino-cuidar-la-oracion-predicar-palabra.html (accessed September 15, 2016).

55. For a more detailed compared analysis of *Evangelii Gaudium* and *Evangelii Nuntiandi*, see Daniel Juncos and Luis O. Liberti, "Evangelii nuntiandi y Evangelii gaudium: ¿El mismo paradigm misionero? Continuidades, novedades y desafíos," *Teología* 116 (2015): 49–71.

56. Galli, "La teología," 30. See also Rocco D'Ambrosio, "Comunicare con semplicità e profondità," in *Evangelii Gaudium: il testo ci interroga. Chiavi di lettura, testimonianza e prospettive*, ed. Humberto Miguel Yáñez, SJ (Rome: Gregorian & Biblical Press, 2014), 145–57.

2

Is Pope Francis a Liberation Theologian?

PAUL LAKELAND

The poor person, when loved, "is esteemed as of great value," and this is what makes the authentic option for the poor differ from any other ideology, from any attempt to exploit the poor for one's own personal or political interest. Only on the basis of this real and sincere closeness can we properly accompany the poor on their path of liberation.

—*Evangelii Gaudium* 199

Our preferential option for the poor must mainly translate into a privileged and preferential religious care.

—*Evangelii Gaudium* 200

The question of whether Pope Francis is or is not a liberation theologian cannot be solved by examining his concern for the poor or his commitment to the principles of Catholic social teaching (CST). It cannot even be a matter of recognizing his astonishing level of compassion and his driving commitment to the virtue of mercy, which Thomas Aquinas held was the fundamental virtue of Christian life. Both John Paul II and Benedict XVI in their different ways spoke courageously on behalf of the poor and were men of great compassion, but no one would describe them as liberation theologians. Indeed, they were the two principal collaborators in a sustained effort to destroy the influence of liberation theology in Latin America. All Christians know well the picture of the last judgment presented in chapter 25 of the Gospel of Matthew, and so all are aware that salvation is intricately connected to the performance of what are usually called the corporate works of mercy. When we feed the hungry, we are feeding Christ, says the Lord, and so we are saved and gain entry into the presence of God. But there is a difference, as not a few Latin American religious leaders have pointed out, between feeding the hungry and asking about the social, economic, and political realities that make them hungry and keep them hungry. The direct action gets you the label of saint, while the question arouses suspicion that you are a communist.[1]

Raising and attempting to answer the question "Is Pope Francis a liberation theologian?" requires a more complex approach than simply recognizing his powerful advocacy of the poor. In the first place, we need to look at what it is that makes social action a work of liberation theology, and so the first section of this chapter provides a summary outline of the basic principles and methods of this particular way of approaching Christian life.[2] Second, we shall need to look at what clues there might be to Jorge Bergoglio's ideas in his earlier years as a Jesuit priest in Argentina, given this was a time and place in which liberation theology was both passionately proclaimed and deeply vilified. Also relevant is his time as archbishop of Buenos Aires, the fifteen years immediately before he became pope, when he was one of the leading churchmen of Latin America. Here we shall need to ask if there are any clues to his attitude to liberation theology in the final document of the CELAM meeting in Aparecida in 2007,[3] a meeting in which he was a prime mover and editor of the lengthy final document that the bishops produced. However, it is obvious enough that the most important facts to consider are those that have appeared in Bergoglio's time as pope. What can we learn from Pope Francis's way of acting, and what can we discover from his writings? At the end of these considerations, we will be in a position to offer an answer to our question of whether or not Pope Francis is a "liberation theologian," and what the concrete consequences of that particular identity might be. Bearing in mind, of course, that many a philosopher and at least one US president has said in response to this kind of question, "Well, it all depends what you mean by 'is,'"[4] and that in Catholic circles at least, the label of "liberation theologian" is praise to many, condemnation to others, and confusion to more than a few.

Although liberation theology is a worldwide phenomenon, its origins surely lie in Latin America. If we think of it as an academic theological phenomenon, we can trace its roots in some ways to the series of books published by Juan Luis Segundo under the series title Theology for Artisans of a New Humanity,[5] but its emergence is more properly associated with the work of the Peruvian priest Gustavo Gutierrez, whose seminal *A Theology of Liberation* appeared in Spanish in 1971, to be followed two years later by an English translation.[6] However, as Gutierrez has warned more than most, the academic work of theology follows upon a prior pastoral experience. For Gutierrez, "Theology is reflection, a critical attitude. Theology *follows*; it is the second step."[7] So it builds upon the actual practice of the church, it is "critical reflection on praxis," and in Latin America, that means above all the praxis of the poor.[8]

Whatever else it was, liberation theology and the prior pastoral reality of the church of the poor was a surprising development in Latin America, since for centuries there had been a strongly sedimented alliance between the church and largely traditional political forces. Why this alliance broke down is a fascinating mixture of sociopolitical and religious factors. The sociopolitical factors are two. First was the phenomenon of economic stagnation for the majority of the continent's citizens, even and perhaps especially in the so-called development decade of the sixties.[9] The second was the emergence of the national security state, that is, the rise of authoritarian or totalitarian governments in many countries, marked by the abrogation of civil and human rights. The church was at that time, and to some degree still is, the only institution in Latin American culture able to challenge the political interests of the oligarchy. In some ways close to the people, the church could see the effects of continuing impoverishment and the extent of oppression and degradation, so the church therefore found itself becoming the voice of the voiceless and consequently suspect by the prevailing political forces. In many places, the church came to be seen as subversive of national security. At the same time, there were changes taking place in the shape of Catholicism, occasioned in large part by the Second Vatican Council from 1962 to 1965, in which all the bishops of the church gathered to read "the signs of the times." Particularly relevant to liberation theology was the rediscovery of the need for solidarity with the world and the consequent attention to social and political challenges.[10] Put the sociopolitical and religious factors together and the stage was set for a confrontation between the oligarchy and the church, one in which successive US administrations took the side of the former.[11]

As liberation theology developed, with sustained theological reflection on the pastoral practice of the grassroots church, certain key elements became clear. First, the experience of the poor was understood to be the privileged locus of theology in Latin America. Second, reflection on Scripture unlocked options for the poor to be found in the Hebrew prophets and the Gospel of Luke in particular, there for all to see but occluded in large part because the voice of the poor had not previously been heard in theological reflection. Third, these realizations led the Latin American church to a commitment to poverty for the sake of the gospel, a decision that changed the pastoral face of the church in most if not all sectors. And fourth, this meant a new form of church grassroots life, responding in part to the historic shortage of clergy, and in part to the concern that those on the margins of church and society should become subjects of their historical process and not merely victims.

The radical implications of liberation theology and the potential for ecclesial opposition are apparent from the very first pages of *A Theology of Liberation.* Theology as critical reflection on praxis will "necessarily be a criticism of society and the Church insofar as they are called and addressed by the Word of God."[12] It presupposes theology as wisdom and rational knowledge but "it necessarily leads to redefinition of these other two tasks."[13] And so "we have here a political hermeneutics of the Gospel."[14] In a few short pages, Gutierrez takes up the properly pastoral function of theology but applies it in a context in which more traditional theologians and church leaders will be made to feel uneasy, if not hostile. What is the relationship between this historical praxis, they will ask, and the properly religious understanding of salvation? Is salvation being reduced to historical liberation, particularly since Gutierrez invokes "the influence of *Marxist thought*, focusing on praxis and geared to the transformation of the world"? And although Gutierrez and countless others will explain at length that salvation is not to be equated with political liberation but does require historical praxis, and that the use of a Marxist critique of society does not mean acceptance of its dialectical materialism, many were not convinced.[15] And so, as we turn to Bergoglio, we need to be aware that his earlier life is lived in an ecclesial context of suspicion of liberation theology, if not condemnation, while recognizing that his pastoral orientation to the poor is quite consistent with its prioritization of the poor.

When Jorge Bergoglio was elected pope, it did not take the media long to trawl through his past life and come up with what they took to be evidence of conservatism, if not of something much worse, in his dealing as a very young provincial superior with two of his fellow Jesuits. During Argentina's 1970s "Dirty War," Orlando Yorio and Francisco Jalics were detained for several months in a torture center. Was Bergoglio complicit in their ill treatment, did he (as he claimed) move immediately but unsuccessfully to get them freed, or was he along with the rest of the Argentinian bishops, somewhere in between, effectively supporting the regime by his silence? This story has faded away over the past few years, but perhaps not the suspicion that Bergoglio (and maybe Francis) was no great friend of liberation theology. Back in the '70s and '80s, Bergoglio did appear to believe that the Jesuits should stick to their traditional roles as parish leaders and chaplains and steer clear of community activism. He seemed, in particular, to be suspicious of the use of Marxist categories in the social and economic analysis favored by the early liberation theologians, though by the time of the Argentinian economic crisis of 2001 and 2002, he was outspoken in denouncing the country's corrupt politicians for the major role they played fomenting the economic meltdown.

There is considerable consensus today that Bergoglio's conduct during the Dirty War was anything but collaborative. If Austin Ivereigh's latest book is to be believed, Francis is and always was a man of the center, and was elected pope because he is centrist and continues to be centrist, albeit centrist with a pronounced populist sensibility.[16] However, though he is like John Paul II and Benedict in some respects, he seems to be more open to progressive elements in the church than either of his two predecessors. His critique of capitalism is stronger than that of either John Paul or Benedict, and his clear suspicion of conservatism, especially liturgical conservatism, is quite marked. According to the *New York Times* columnist Ross Douthat in an article in *The Atlantic*, Francis's suspicion of traditionalism can be ascribed to what he learned during the Dirty War about the silent complicity of the Argentinian church with fascism.[17]

My own feeling is that we find a way to reconcile Francis's past and present if we focus on his evident distaste for ideology. Whether it be the warmed-over Marxism of some well-intentioned progressive elements among the Argentinian Jesuits in the 1970s; the violent fascism of the national security state of Jorge Rafael Videla, who was dictator from 1976 to 1981; or the closeted gossip of Vatican traditionalists up to the present day, Francis views them all through the lens of the gospel imperative to care for the poor. His perspective is, in fact, very like that suggested in the early years of liberation theology, a "pre-reflective" or even "pre-ideological" commitment to the oppressed. Ideologies distort our perception when, as they most often do, they reflect the interests of an elite social class.[18] One of the more interesting, if not unquestioned, views of Latin American liberation theology in its early years was that the poor and oppressed, because they have no vested interests to protect, are immune from ideological distortions of reality and can, in consequence, see the world as it really is. Hence, the call to the church issued by CELAM at Medellín in 1968, in effect to come down from the mountain and live on the dunghill, was a way of identifying the church with those who, because they have nothing to lose, have much to teach.

There are certainly those who believe that Francis's use of the term *ideology* sometimes gets a little out of control,[19] though when one sees his distaste for ideology as a consequence of the adoption of a consistently inductive method himself, it becomes more understandable. So, to take the most obvious and challenging example, his dismissal of discussions of gender on the grounds that it is ideological might seem to be embarrassingly naive. But is he actually dismissing gender *theory*, that is, dismissing it for its inevitably distorting deductivity rather than for the revelation of the complexity of human life that it intends? The remarks about gender theory that have occasioned the most comment appear in an interview conducted by *La Stampa*.[20] There he speaks critically of a number of failures to recognize "the order of creation," and includes gender theory. While there is no getting around the uncongenial and ill-informed attack on gender theory, in the context, Pope Francis is challenging a number of what he sees as efforts by the developed West to impose its own way of thinking upon cultures that would find them inimical. This is the man, let us recall, who very recently spoke out in favor of gender equity in the workplace, calling the failure to pay women and men at the same rates "pure scandal."[21] Francis's point seems not to be that women and men do not deserve equal treatment, but that theories that somehow bend our understanding of what it is to be a man and woman are dangerous. A note of criticism here: If Francis is right to point to the dangers of ideology, is he also in danger of making certain (essentialized) understandings of sex and gender into ideologies too, perhaps mistaking the perception of the gospel, which he calls the only worthwhile ideology, for those theories of human sexuality that claim gospel provenance but do not actually possess it?

His more general point is clearer if we look at his attack on the reduction of faith to ideology. In October 2013, he suggested that faith becomes ideology when it passes through "a distiller," becoming something rigid:

> And when a Christian becomes a disciple of the ideology, he has lost the faith: he is no longer a disciple of Jesus, he is a disciple of this attitude of thought....The knowledge of Jesus is transformed into an ideological and also moralistic knowledge, because these close the door with many requirements.[22]

So the enemy is deductive thinking, approaching the gospel with a preconceived commitment to an idea through which the gospel is then understood and, inevitably, distorted. You cannot use the gospel to condemn gays and lesbians, or to assert an unthinking fealty to the state, or to justify the depredation of the environment, or to justify slavery. But many have, and the failure arises with a false starting point, Francis thinks. Do not start with ideas. As he has said so many times, "Realities are greater than ideas" (*EG* 231). So start with the gospel and you will avoid all such distortions.[23]

The principal lessons that Francis seems to have learned from his life in difficult and sometimes turbulent times in Argentina coincide to a high degree with the perspectives of liberation theology, and have remained remarkably consistent over the years. Learning from experience, suspicion of global capitalism and concern for the poor, listening to the word of God in Scripture, an evangelical orientation to building the reign of God and the promotion of lay leadership in the church are all elements of liberation theology, as they are of Francis's program, then and now. Liberation theology method operates within what is often called "the hermeneutical circle," a context-based process of reflection upon the implications of Scripture for overcoming structural oppression in order to foster human dignity and initiate social change.[24] Much of this, though perhaps not all, is close to Francis's heart.

The Latin American Bishops' Conference (CELAM) meets every ten years. The best known of their meetings was the one that took place in Medellín, Colombia, in 1968, just three years after the end of the Second Vatican Council. At Medellín, CELAM set out to translate the universal message of Vatican II into the language and cultural context of Latin America, at a time in its history when country after country was falling to one form or another of the government of national security, described by the American journalist Penny Lernoux as "creole fascism," enabled for the most part by interference from successive US administrations.[25] Medellín critiqued the church's own romanticization of poverty, calling it simply "evil," but also called on the church itself to embrace poverty for the sake of the gospel. The bishops challenged the middle classes to become aware of the sinful structures of society in which they were complicit by their silence, encouraged the poor, and excoriated the wealthy for using social unrest as an excuse for increasing violations of human rights. They supported the growth of "mediating structures," including especially the emerging phenomenon of base Christian communities, and spoke sternly against revolutionary quick fixes, since they simply substitute a new form of oppression for the old. At the same time, they named unjust social structures as a form of violence and sympathized with, though they did not support, the "counterviolence" that was sometimes the only form of response.[26]

Since the historic meeting in Medellín, CELAM has met three times. In Puebla, Mexico, in 1979, despite the very conservative conference leadership of Cardinal Alfonso Lopez Trujillo, the bishops managed to maintain the church's commitment to the principles of Medellín. In Santo Domingo in 1992, they were less successful, since the 1980s had revealed consistent suspicion of liberation theology on the part of Pope John Paul II and his prefect at the Congregation for the Doctrine of the Faith (CDF), Cardinal Joseph Ratzinger, and episcopal appointments during John Paul's tenure had dramatically changed the face of the Latin American hierarchy. And so the stage was set for the latest meeting of CELAM, to take place in 2007 in Aparecida, Brazil.[27]

The final document from Aparecida runs to 276 pages in the Spanish original and is available to English speakers in a PDF of about 195 pages. It is wordy, redolent of the rhetorical style of the Spanish language, but direct and forceful. Cardinal Bergoglio was elected by his brother bishops to chair the committee that drafted the final document. Also on that committee was Honduran Cardinal Oscar Rodríguez Maradiaga, whom Pope Francis named to lead the team of cardinals he appointed to oversee the reform of the Roman curia. So it is surely not surprising to find that a reading of the Aparecida document sounds like a program for the papacy of Pope Francis as we now know him, or that to listen to Pope Francis is to find oneself in the world of Aparecida. Thanks to Aparecida, it is probably correct to say that as much as the church is in the hands of Pope Francis, it is in the hands of Latin America.[28] As the previous chapter also argues, the program laid out at Aparecida for the Latin American church has become the program of renewal for the universal church.

From the Heart of the Gospel

There are at least three important themes in the Aparecida document that seem to reflect the perspective of liberation theology and that will reappear in the papal letter *EG*.[29] First, there is the identification with the "see, judge, act" method that lies behind the hermeneutical circle of liberation theology, that was originally introduced into Latin America through the Young Christian Workers movement in the 1940s, and that is also close to the pedagogical method of the Society of Jesus. In essence, it calls for the application of inductive reasoning to the solution of problems, in contradiction of deductive methods that have historically been employed in Catholic theology that understood itself as proclaiming context-free "universal truth," and that harbor ideologies. Second, there are the words that simply repeat the call of Medellín for "a poor church for the poor." The third is the central and repeated emphasis on the need for Christians to understand themselves as "missionary disciples," an idea that comes directly from Vatican II's rediscovery of baptism as entry into a mission-oriented priesthood of all believers and that is central to the ecclesiology of the base Christian communities (*EG* passim, esp. 119–21).

The connections between Aparecida and Pope Francis are made even clearer in his address to the coordinating committee of CELAM, delivered in Rio de Janeiro in July 2013. In this brief statement, he makes explicit reference to the temptation to make the gospel message "an ideology," a temptation that "has been present in the Church from the beginning: the attempt to interpret the Gospel apart from the Gospel itself and apart from the Church." The only acceptable way of seeing is that of "discipleship," and, moreover, "the position of missionary disciples is not in the center but at the periphery: they live poised towards the peripheries...including the peripheries of eternity, in the encounter with Jesus Christ....The disciple is sent to the existential peripheries."[30]

And so we come to *EG*, where Francis is speaking to and about the global church, not simply that of Latin America. The message, however, is the same:

> The poor person, when loved, "is esteemed as of great value" and this is what makes the authentic option

for the poor differ from any other ideology, from any attempt to exploit the poor for one's own personal or political interest. Only on the basis of this real and sincere closeness can we properly accompany the poor on their path of liberation. Only this will ensure that "in every Christian community the poor feel at home. Would not this approach be the greatest and most effective presentation of the good news of the kingdom?" Without the preferential option for the poor, "the proclamation of the Gospel, which is itself the prime form of charity, risks being misunderstood or submerged by the ocean of words which daily engulfs us in today's society of mass communications." (*EG* 199)

In a series of reflections on Aparecida, Gustavo Gutierrez echoes these remarks. "To be a Christian," he writes, "is to walk, moved by the Spirit, in the footsteps of Jesus," and "this kind of discipleship is the root and the ultimate meaning of the preferential option for the poor."[31]

Evangelii Gaudium is a 2013 document written by Francis as, in theory, a summary of the deliberations of the Rome Synod of Bishops held the previous year, the last of the pontificate of Benedict XVI. The rules for these allocutions are treated with varying degrees of freedom by one pope or another, and in this case Francis seems to have decided to set out a kind of program for his papacy and to pay scant attention to the work done at the synod. One reason for this is perhaps that, as archbishop of Buenos Aires, Francis shared the general dissatisfaction of the bishops with the whole mechanism of the synods, and indeed in planning the two-part synod on the Family that took place in 2014 and 2015, he insisted that the bishops were to speak their minds, something not previously recommended to the synodal bishops. The consequence of that event was of course that a number of serious differences among the bishops became public, and the papal letter *Amoris Laetitia* attempted to address them.[32]

For our purposes it will be sufficient to take a look at *EG*'s section on "the inclusion of the poor in society" (*EG* 186–216), and especially sections 197–201, on "the special place of the poor in God's people." Section 198 begins with reference to the central tenet of liberation theology, "the option for the poor," but this is immediately glossed as "a theological category rather than a cultural, sociological, political or philosophical one." "The Church has made an option for the poor," writes Francis, and "this is why I want a Church which is poor and for the poor." The option for the poor or, as Gutierrez explains it, the *decision* for the poor, is not in the first instance about improving their social context. It has far more to do with recognizing and affirming the essential human dignity of the poor and, maybe surprisingly to some, of learning from them. "They have much to teach us and we need to let ourselves be evangelized by them." We are surely "called to find Christ in them, to lend our voice to their causes," but not this alone. We also have "to be their friends, to listen to them, to speak for them and to embrace the mysterious wisdom which God wishes to share with us through them" (*EG* 198).

As Francis goes on to develop these thoughts, he is insistent that the central need is to develop an attitude of "loving attentiveness." "The poor person," he thinks, "when loved, is esteemed as of great value." It is this that makes the authentic option for the poor differ from any other ideology, says Francis, because it is free "from any attempt to exploit the poor for one's own personal or political interest" (*EG* 199). He then turns to the language of accompaniment as the primary activity demanded of solidarity, echoing key ideas in Gutierrez and many others.[33] "Only on the basis of this real and sincere closeness can we properly accompany the poor on their path of liberation," he remarks, and brings these thoughts to a rousing conclusion with the claim that "our preferential option for the poor must mainly translate into a privileged and preferential religious care" (*EG* 200). Those who would wish to distance Francis from liberation theology will eagerly seize upon this last sentence. What it amounts to in the end, and how similar to or different from "true" liberation theology depends on what one understands by "liberation theology," and to that question we now turn.

It is standard practice in Roman documents that the condemnation of what are invariably referred to as "certain tendencies" is never accompanied by naming any names. Scrutinize Pius X's *Pascendi* with a microscope, and the names of the offending Modernists, proponents of "the heresy of all heresies," will not be found. Pore over Pius XII's frontal assault upon *la nouvelle théologie* in his 1950 encyclical, *Humani Generis*, and the theologians who were silenced as a result of his letter—Congar, Daniélou, Courtney Murray among others—are not listed. So it should come as no surprise to find that the Congregation for the Doctrine of the Faith, headed by Joseph Ratzinger, should produce a radical critique of liberation theology whose pages were bereft of the names of any miscreants. The "Instruction on Certain Aspects of the Theology of Liberation" (1984) paints the "dangerous tendencies" with very broad brush strokes.[34]

In the charged atmosphere of the times, the document was probably received less generously than was entirely fair. It opens with a couple of paragraphs that could have been written today by Pope Francis. "Liberation," the document proclaims, "is first and foremost liberation from the radical slavery of sin." Liberation seeks "the freedom of the children of God, which is the gift of grace," and so in consequence "it calls for freedom from many different kinds of slavery in the cultural, economic, social, and political spheres, all of which derive ultimately from sin, and so often prevent people from living in a manner befitting their dignity" (intro., para. 2). The text goes on, in a much less irenic tone:

> Faced with the urgency of certain problems, some are tempted to emphasize, unilaterally, the liberation from servitude of an earthly and temporal kind. They do so in such a way that they seem to put liberation from sin in second place, and so fail to give it the primary importance it is due. Thus, their very presentation of the problems is confused and ambiguous. Others, in an effort to learn more precisely what are the causes of the slavery which they want to end, make use of different concepts without sufficient critical caution. It is difficult, and perhaps impossible, to purify these borrowed concepts of an ideological inspiration which uses, in an insufficiently critical manner, concepts borrowed from various currents of Marxist thought. (intro., para. 2)

Because the text mentioned no names, the response to it was fairly predictable. Liberation theologians failed to see themselves in

49

the critique, pointing out that the use of Marxist terminology was opportunistic and purely analytical, and vehemently denying that liberation theology collapses the understanding of salvation into a purely historical liberation, the "tendency" referred to in the document as "historicist immanentism."[35] On the other hand, any more traditional theologian and any church member committed to the defense of hierarchicalism, conservative political and geopolitical worldviews, or simply the status quo in the very difficult political and economic context of Latin America in the later part of the twentieth century felt free to dismiss liberation theology entirely and to condemn anyone remotely associated with it.[36]

The most unfortunate consequence of the CDF documents, for all the fine words about the commitment to the preferential option for the poor, was that the papacy of John Paul II maintained a protracted attack upon liberation theology. Curiously, however, his motivation seems to have been less to weed out Marxist terminology, terminology that he used quite freely in his 1981 encyclical, *Laborem Exercens*, or to favor capitalism, which he challenged in very strong language in a number of further encyclical letters, but rather to contend with an ecclesiological vision with which he profoundly disagreed.[37] Before liberation theology is a theology, it is the praxis of a poor church suffering from a dire shortage of clergy and living in challenging and often oppressive social situations. In response to these conditions, the new ecclesial structure of the "base Christian community" emerged, in which noneucharistic worship led by lay Christians became the order of the day in many places. John Paul never looked kindly upon initiatives that did not grow out of commitment to the strongly hierarchical and centralized church he favored, and he did not trust the ordinary faithful to explore the gospel for themselves. The most telling image for this would be the public finger wagging to which he subjected Ernesto Cardenal, one of Latin America's most distinguished poets and a leader of the lay community of Solentiname, during his disastrous visit to Nicaragua in March 1983. And the best example of the vision of the church that John Paul thought he had to combat can surely be seen in the title of Leonardo Boff's 1986 slim book, *Ecclesiogenesis: The Base Communities Reinvent the Church*.[38] In his address at an open-air Mass in

Managua, John Paul said it was "absurd and dangerous to imagine that outside—if not to say against—the church built around the bishop there should be another church, conceived only as 'charismatic' and not institutional, 'new' and not traditional, alternative and as it has been called recently, a People's Church."[39] The Nicaraguan bishops were by and large a very unhappy bunch during the Sandinista government of the 1980s. An American religious sister who worked there at the time once told me that they were upset because "they were like children whose toys had been taken away." At the same time, five Catholic priests served as ministers in the revolutionary Sandinista government, at considerable cost to themselves and under constant Vatican pressure to abandon their roles.[40]

It is now possible to attempt an answer to our question about Pope Francis, because we can now see clearly that there are at least two possible understandings of liberation theology. Is it a movement for political and economic reform in which the gospel is harnessed to leftist social movements for the sake of the "crucified people"? Of course, but is it done in a way that diminishes the understanding of liberation and becomes the willing or unwilling servant of Marxist ideology? Or is it a shift toward a more grassroots church in which lay leadership plays a much greater role in the community of faith, in companionship with the poor, for the sake of the gospel? If it is the former, then Pope Francis is no liberation theologian. If it is the latter, then he surely is. But if it is the latter, then the ghost of John Paul II can be no happier with Pope Francis than he would be had he flown the hammer and sickle over the Vatican. Hyperbole, perhaps, but you get the point. And John Paul was no fool. He paid far less attention to combatting warmed-over Marxism than he did to reasserting a strongly hierarchical church. With which Bergoglio, in his turn, could not have been happy.

What, then, might be the consequence of papal identification, or not, with liberation theology? Internal political pressures make it extraordinarily difficult for a sitting pope to do or say the opposite of at least his most recent predecessors. So we could not expect Francis to repudiate the severe criticisms expressed by John Paul II and Benedict XVI, any more than he could just come out and say that Paul VI was misguided in his condemnation

From the Heart of the Gospel

of contraception in his 1968 encyclical, *Humanae Vitae*. A more acceptable approach to incremental change might be either to simply ignore previous popes' utterances, or perhaps to have the challenges to their positions uttered by a surrogate rather than by the pope himself. But the likeliest tack in the case of Francis himself is to sidestep the papal ukase and invoke the synodality of the bishops, if not of the whole church. And yet, if we examine either *Laudato Si'*, his encyclical on the environment and globalization, or scrutinize *Amoris Laetitia*, the document he wrote to "summarize" the views of the Rome Synod on the Family, a very clear and quite idiosyncratic papal voice can be heard.

If liberation theology was primarily concerned with the voice of the poor in the life of the church, Francis is painting on a bigger canvas, drawing attention to poverty as a worldwide issue, in large measure a product of globalization. But one important consequence of this is that his appeal is to the rich and powerful countries, and to a change of heart of those who live comfortably within them, to reorient their priorities. Moreover, the conversion that he calls for is necessary for the sake of the future of the planet and so in the interests of all human beings, rich and poor alike. So there is less emphasis on what the poor can and should do for themselves, much less attention to liberation theology's call for the poor to become subjects of their own history, and not its victims. There is more realism and less romanticism, perhaps, or maybe it is just that fifty years on the urgency for planetary change is more pressing. The liberation of the earth from the greedy despoiling of global capitalism is now the issue. But at the same time a preferential option for the earth is truly a preferential option for the poor, since they remain the principal victims of globalization, as Christopher Hrynkow explores in chapter 11.

I want to conclude by returning to the figure of Gustavo Gutierrez, the father of liberation theology. Those who have read his work know that he has always said that "theology comes after," that it is "the second act." The first is the religious reflection of the poor in their own context, responding to the message of Holy Scripture. At a meeting at Fordham University in 2015, Gutierrez said, among other things, that "liberation theology is anti-Marxist" and that if he ever found that liberation theology interfered with the preferential option for the poor, he would abandon it. "Liberation theology," he said, is just a tool. The preferential option for the poor must be at the center. In fact, he seemed to play down his designation as a theologian. "My first academic appointment," he said with a smile, "was at the age of seventy-five." And added, "I have always been first and foremost a parish priest." Though Gutierrez is not a bishop, Francis warms to him, among other reasons, because he smells strongly of the sheep. And if we needed further evidence of Francis's warmth toward liberation theology as an ecclesial reform movement, as a struggle for "a poor church for the poor," we need only look to the fact that one of the pope's first private conversations was with Gutierrez, and one of his most recent acts has been to name the diminutive Dominican to the leaders of the "Year of Mercy" to begin this fall. If Francis gets his way, we will all be liberation theologians before long.

Select Bibliography

Gutierrez, Gustavo. *A Theology of Liberation: History, Politics and Salvation.* Maryknoll, NY: Orbis, 1973.

Hennelly, Alfred T. *Liberation Theology: A Documentary History.* Maryknoll, NY: Orbis, 1990.

Kyongsuk Min, Anselm. *Dialectic of Salvation: Issues in the Theology of Liberation.* New York: SUNY, 1989.

Lernoux, Penny. *Cry of the People: The Struggle for Human Rights in Latin America—The Catholic Church in Conflict with U.S. Policy.* London and New York: Penguin, 1982.

McGovern, Arthur F. *Liberation Theology and Its Critics: Towards an Assessment.* Eugene, OR: Wipf and Stock, 2009.

Rourke, Thomas R. *The Roots of Pope Francis's Social and Political Thought: From Argentina to the Vatican.* New York: Rowman & Littlefield, 2016.

Scannone, Juan Carlos. "Pope Francis and the Theology of the People." *Theological Studies* 77, no. 1 (2016): 118–35.

Smith, Christian. *The Emergence of Liberation Theology: Radical Religion and Social Movement Theory.* Chicago: Chicago, 1991.

Notes

1. The words of Dom Helder Camara, archbishop of Recife in Brazil for many years, are well known: "When I fed the poor they called me a saint, when I asked why the poor are poor, they called me a Communist," quoted in John Dear, *Peace behind Bars: A Peacemaking Priest's Journal from Jail* (New York: Sheed and Ward, 1995), 65.

2. Those who are comfortable with the ideas of liberation theology can safely pass this section over, though not if they are too easily persuaded by the official suspicion surrounding them.

3. CELAM is the acronym for the Latin American Bishops' Conference, a meeting that occurs approximately every ten years and brings together representatives of each national hierarchy in the region. The most significant of these meetings was the 1968 gathering in Medellín, Colombia, where the assembled bishops gave their episcopal blessing to many of the ideas of liberation theology. The Aparecida document can be seen as a deeper theological reflection on much of that conference's conclusions.

4. For President Bill Clinton's use of this phrase, see his deposition in the office of the independent council on August 18, 1998, http://www.cnn.com/icreport/report/volume3/volume373 .html. For a more philosophical discussion of the same usage, see the consideration of C. E. M. Joad's catchphrase, "It all depends on what you mean by…," in Whately Carington, *Matter, Mind and Meaning* (London: Methuen, 1947), esp. 44.

5. Published initially in Spanish in Uruguay in the 1960s, the five volumes appeared in English under the Orbis imprint in 1973 and have been recently reissued by Wipf and Stock in 2011. They are *The Community Called Church; Grace and the Human Condition; Our Idea of God; The Sacraments Today;* and *Evolution and Guilt.*

6. *A Theology of Liberation: History, Politics and Salvation* (Maryknoll, NY: Orbis, 1973).

7. Ibid., 11.

8. The bibliography of liberation theology is vast. In addition to Gutierrez, the writings of Leonardo Boff and Jon Sobrino were among the most influential in the early decades, but there

have been many others, and once liberation theology began to be an influence beyond Latin America, the list of books simply exploded. Among the most useful general introductions are Alfred T. Hennelly's *Liberation Theology: A Documentary History* (Maryknoll, NY: Orbis, 1990); and the sociological study by Christian Smith, *The Emergence of Liberation Theology: Radical Religion and Social Movement Theory* (Chicago: University of Chicago Press, 1991). A shorter and simpler introduction can be found in Lakeland, "Theological Trends: Political and Liberation Theology II," *The Way* 26, no. 2 (April 1986): 145–54.

9. UNICEF's "development decade" (see http://www.unicef .org/sowc96/1960s.htm) was roundly criticized in the prevailing neo-Marxist theory of economic dependency at the time. For dependency theory, see André Gunder Frank, *Capitalism and Underdevelopment in Latin America: Historical Studies of Chile and Brazil*, rev. ed. (New York: Monthly Review Press Classics, 1967).

10. The principal document of the Council to address issues of church and world was the lengthy *Gaudium et Spes*, the Pastoral Constitution on the Church in the Modern World. In section 44, the Council fathers recognize that the church has learned from the world, and in the entire second half of the work, sections 46–93, they examine issues of culture, politics, economics, and world peace.

11. This sad story is told enormously well in Lernoux's now classic book *Cry of the People: The Struggle for Human Rights in Latin America—The Catholic Church in Conflict with U. S. Policy* (New York: Penguin, 1982).

12. Gutierrez, *Theology of Liberation*, 11.

13. Ibid., 14.

14. Ibid., 13.

15. The official disapproval of liberation theology is contained in Cardinal Ratzinger's 1984 document, "Instruction on Certain Aspects of the Theology of Liberation" (http://www .vatican.va/roman_curia/congregations/cfaith/documents/ rc_con_cfaith_doc_19840806_theology-liberation_en.html). See also Arthur F. McGovern, *Liberation Theology and Its Critics: Towards an Assessment* (Eugene, OR: Wipf and Stock, 2009).

16. Austin Ivereigh, *The Great Reformer: Francis and the Making of a Radical Pope* (New York: Henry Holt, 2015). For somewhat

different readings, see also Paul Vallely, *Pope Francis: The Struggle for the Soul of Catholicism* (New York: Bloomsbury, 2015); and Elisabetta Piqué, *Pope Francis, Life and Revolution: A Biography of Jorge Bergoglio* (Chicago: Loyola, 2014).

17. "Will Pope Francis Break the Church?" *The Atlantic*, May 2015, 4.

18. On this complex notion, see Anselm Kyongsuk Min, *Dialectic of Salvation: Issues in the Theology of Liberation* (New York: SUNY, 1989), esp.41 and 70.

19. See R. R. Reno in *First Things*, "Criticizing Pope Francis" (http://www.firstthings.com/blogs/firstthoughts/2015/01/criticizing-pope-francis).

20. *La Stampa*, April 15, 2015: http://www.lastampa.it/2015/04/15/vaticaninsider/eng/the-vatican/pope-with-the-gender-theory-there-is-a-risk-of-backtracking-1k5g1j38bvqJJxu9HYDeKI/pagina.html.

21. Nolan Feeney, "Pope Francis Calls for Equal Pay for Women and Men," *Time*, April 29, 2015, http://time.com/3840049/pope-francis-equal-pay/.

22. See the discussion of this issue by Hrafnkell Haraldsson, who makes the point that Francis's critique is primarily directed at the rigidity of right-wing, traditionalist Catholicism: "Pope Francis Condemns Christian Ideology Posing as Religion," *Politicsusa*, October 22, 2013, http://www.politicususa.com/2013/10/22/pope-francis-condemns-christian-ideology-posing-religion.html.

23. This pragmatic and inductive approach is often explained as Francis being influenced by the Argentinian "theology of the people," which is little other than liberation theology without the Marxism. Theologian Juan Carlos Scannone has an important article on this topic, "Pope Francis and the Theology of the People," *Theological Studies* 77, no. 1 (2016): 118–35. For an even more detailed and somewhat more popular discussion of the theology of the people that does not come to quite the same conclusions about the interchangeability of the two approaches, see Thomas R. Rourke, *The Roots of Pope Francis's Social and Political Thought: From Argentina to the Vatican* (New York: Rowman & Littlefield, 2016), 71–100.

24. Peter C. Phan, "Method in Liberation Theologies," *Theological Studies* 61 (2000):40–61.

25. See n7 above.

26. The five major documents of the 1968 meeting are most easily available online at https://educationforjustice.org/events/medellin-conference-documents-1968.

27. Aparecida is addressed in much greater detail by Eduardo Mangiarotti in the previous chapter.

28. See Ernesto Cevasso, SJ, "On the Trail of Aparecida," *America*, October 30, 2013. http://americamagazine.org/trail-aparecida.

29. See www.vatican.va/evangelii-gaudium/en/.

30. "Address to the Leadership of the Episcopal Conferences of Latin America during the General Coordination Meeting," section 5/1, https://w2.vatican.va/content/francesco/en/speeches/2013/july/documents/papa-francesco_20130728_gmg-celam-rio.html.

31. For the full text and commentary, see http://ncronline.org/blogs/ncr-today/gutierrez-vatican-church-must-be-samaritan-reaching-out-others.

32. The text is available on the Vatican website or at https://cruxnow.com/church/2016/04/08/read-the-popes-letter-amoris-laetitia-or-on-love-in-the-family/.

33. See Roberto S. Goizueta, *Caminemos Con Jesus: Toward a Hispanic/Latino Theology of Accompaniment* (Maryknoll, NY: Orbis, 1995) and *In the Company of the Poor: Conversations with Dr. Paul Farmer and Fr. Gustavo Gutierrez*, ed. Michael Griffin and Jennie Weiss Block (Maryknoll, NY: Orbis, 2013).

34. See http://www.vatican.va/roman_curia/congregations/cfaith/documents/rc_con_cfaith_doc_19840806_theology-liberation_en.html.

35. See here Juan Luis Segundo, *Theology and the Church: A Response to Cardinal Ratzinger and a Warning to the Whole Church* (London: Geoffrey Chapman, 1985).

36. Michael Novak, *Will It Liberate: Questions about Liberation Theology* (New York: Paulist Press, 1986).

37. See *Sollicitudo Rei Socialis* (1987) and *Centesimus Annus* (1991).

38. Maryknoll, NY: Orbis, 1986.

39. See Alan Riding's report in the *New York Times* for March 5, 1983: http://www.nytimes.com/1983/03/05/world/pope-says-taking-sides-in-nicaragua-is-peril-to-church.html.

40. See Teofilo Cabestrero, *Ministers of God, Ministers of the People: Testimonies of Faith from Nicaragua* (Maryknoll, NY: Orbis, 1983).

3

From the Joy of the Gospel to the Joy of Christ

Situating and Expanding the Christology of Pope Francis

PHILIP McCOSKER

Introduction

A quick reading might suggest that *Evangelii Gaudium* is only derivatively, or even tokenistically, christological. It is not a reflection on the metaphysics of Christ's person, but rather about what we do with his message, the good news of the gospel—how, in fact, we enact it, and the experience of joy that it brings. And it is true that the bulk of its text is concerned with mission, proclamation, and their social and political outworkings. Yet to focus exclusively on that extensive bulk would be to miss its significant generative theological heart; a closer look reveals that Pope Francis's comments on ecclesial mission, proclamation, and action in the world are driven by a rich, if somewhat etiolated, Christology.

The place given in *EG* to expounding this Christology may be small, but its dynamic role is clear. The central constellating importance of Christology for Pope Francis's thought is confirmed in his subsequent document, *Misericordiae Vultus* (*MV*), but also in his preaching and his much-followed tweets. There is a consistent christological heart in Pope Francis's witness that *EG* expresses, but that is missed in media commentary whose interests lie downstream.[1]

The Christological Heart of *EG* and Its Outworkings

What is the christological heart of *EG*? In this encyclical, Francis makes repeatedly clear that the gospel message that brings joy *is* Jesus Christ. The gospel is not in fact primarily a message, an idea, or even a program of action, but rather a person. Quoting his predecessor's *Deus Caritas Est*, he writes that "being a Christian is not the result of an ethical choice or a lofty idea, but the encounter with an event, a person" (*EG* 7).[2] Indeed, as he tweeted, "Christians are witnesses not to a theory, but to a Person: Christ risen and alive, the one Saviour of All."[3] Here Pope Francis situates himself on a particular strand among the many interpretations of the essence of Christianity, one particularly associated with the twentieth-century theologian Romano Guardini, to be explored further below. In fact, Guardini is as important to Jorge Maria Bergoglio/Francis as he is to Joseph Ratzinger/Benedict XVI.

For Francis, Jesus Christ reveals the infinite mercy and love of the Father. The "Spirit...leads us to believe in Jesus Christ who, by his death and resurrection, reveals and communicates to us the Father's infinite mercy" (*EG* 164).[4] In all his earthly life, his ministry and death, and now in his risen and ascended life, Christ manifests and *is* the love of the triune God. God is, as it were, mercy all the way down: Trinity, Christ, church, Christian, creature. Like isomorphic Russian dolls, all should bear the shape and dynamic of mercy and love that is revealed to humanity in the form of Christ.

This means that for Francis the separation between Christology and soteriology, between Christ's person and his work of salvation, makes no sense. For Francis, Christ manifests God's infinite love for each and every creature, for all: this is what is meant by God's salvation. Francis tells us that the primary proclamation of the Christian faith must be that "Jesus Christ loves you; he gave his life to save you; and now he is living at your side every day to enlighten, strengthen and free you" (*EG* 164). This is a thoroughly kerygmatic Christology, crafted for proclamation and mission.

The salvation that Christ is, is God's mercy, which is what Christians are called to proclaim and enact in their lives (*EG* 112). It follows that "being church...means proclaiming and bringing God's salvation into our world" (*EG* 114). The salvation experienced in encounter with Christ—being infinitely loved by God—is the motor of the impulse for evangelization: for Francis, Christ and what he does or achieves cannot be separated (*EG* 264).

Although Francis certainly does not ignore sin and its connection with salvation, there is a strong and persistent sense of the incarnation having of itself a divinizing role: "To believe that the Son of God assumed our human flesh means that each human person has been taken up into the very heart of God" (*EG* 178). Christ's incarnation is not just, or solely, a rescue mission for sin, but a manifestation of the power of God's love to transform our lives and actions from those of trapped sinners into merciful lives lived in the freedom of the risen Christ. Christ's incarnation as the world's peace unites in itself heaven and earth, God and humanity, time and eternity (*EG* 229). Christ's death on the cross bears the same "shape" as the rest of his life, the same "shape" as God: Christ's life and death are of a piece. "Jesus' sacrifice on the cross is nothing else than the culmination of the way he lived his entire life." (*EG* 269). Although the cross has a part in Francis's soteriology, it is not staurocentric.

For Francis's theology it is important that the trinitarian dynamic of mercy that the Son manifests as Christ spills over into our relations with each other.[5] Indeed he writes daringly that "our brothers and sisters are the prolongation of the incarnation for each of us" (*EG* 179). If our evangelization is authentic, it cannot be contained in some private realm, it overflows to others, hence the keynote of joy: "We Christians are called to go out of ourselves to bring the mercy and tenderness of God to all."[6] It is by focusing on Christ, and not on strictly secondary issues like moral doctrines or other subsidiary doctrines, that the church remains true to her missionary and evangelical, outward-focused, nature (*EG* 97).[7]

This overflow or extension of the incarnation in our fellow humans is the key link between Francis's Christology and the ethic of *EG*: each implicates the other. This is not simply a matter of implementing Jesus's message and following his commandments, but rather of continuing the trinitarian mission of love that Jesus Christ incarnated.[8] As Francis says, we are to think, "I am a mission" (*EG* 273). Our encounter with Jesus as the incarnation of mercy necessarily involves us in the same dynamic, if we truly encounter him. "Before all else, the Gospel invites us to respond to the God of love who saves us, to see God in others and to go forth from ourselves to seek the good of others" (*EG* 39).

Because God is ec-centric, or allo-centric,[9] we are called to enact that same dynamic. Francis sees secularization and the loss of a viable sense of the transcendent as leading to the privatization and personalization of religion, our closing in on ourselves, relationally but also economically and ethically. Our commodified age of economic and information exchange based on flat binary logics leads to squashed and narrowed moral compasses (*EG* 64). Our cities become places of isolation and neglect rather than fulfilling their rich potential for connection and relation (*EG* 76).

Jesus's incarnation of mercy enrolls us in its continuation. "True faith in the incarnate Son of God is inseparable from self-giving, from membership in the community, from service, from reconciliation with others. The Son of God, by becoming flesh, summoned us to the revolution of tenderness" (*EG* 88). This means finding "Jesus in the face of others, in their voices, in their pleas" (*EG* 91) and this without *any* exception (*EG* 48, 113). Not only are we, as humans, constituted in the image of the triune communion, and thus as persons in relation (*EG* 178), but God's incarnation in humanity confers infinite dignity on all humans.

Like Jesus, we are to enact mercy by finding him on the peripheries, among the poorest, the most rejected (*EG* 48). The scope of mercy, because it is divine, is universal. Like Christ, the church must constantly go outside herself and especially to the poorest (*EG* 97, 209); and not only because that is what Christ did and we imitate him, but also because it is Christ himself that we meet in the poor (*EG* 186). This is why Francis wants a "church which is poor and for the poor" (*EG* 198). Precisely as Christians we are called to "recognize the suffering Christ" in all forms of poverty and vulnerability and hunt out new and hidden forms of such alienation (*EG* 210). We see how for Francis Christology, soteriology, ecclesiology, anthropology, and ethics are intertwined and significantly of a piece.

Zooming In: Significant Features of Francis's Christological Vision

Several elements of Francis's christological vision call for brief comment before we attempt to situate it on a theological map. It is striking, first, how often Francis emphasizes the resurrection. He wants Christians who are not stuck in Lent, but who are Easter people. Our encounter is with the risen Christ, from whose heart springs life in the Spirit (*EG* 2, 3). He is our source of hope, the sign that our sinful state will change (*EG* 275). "Christ's resurrection is not an event of the past; it contains a vital power which has permeated this world. Where all seems to be dead, signs of the resurrection suddenly spring up. It is an irresistible force" (*EG* 276). In this respect, *EG* points to a recent upsurge in theological interest in the resurrection and, in particular, in its links with ethical action most recently and notably in the work of the Anglican theologian Sarah Bachelard,[10] helps to redress the relative dearth of work on the resurrection in twentieth-century theology and ethics.[11]

It is noticeable how often Francis underscores the primacy of God and God's action. God is the first evangelizer (*EG* 12); God has loved us first (*EG* 24); it is God's grace that draws creation to himself: that is the work of God's mercy (*EG* 112). Our activities as Christians are always a response to God's prior action. Francis seems to want to fend off any whiff of a Pelagianizing overemphasis on the role of the human in the church's work of proclamation and mercy.

Consonant with *EG*'s focus on proclamation and mission is a strong emphasis on affect and the heart. This is clear most obviously in the theme of joy: our affective, infectious response to the good news of God's love and mercy. But it is also striking how often Francis uses the imagery of the heart. The Spirit flows from the heart of the risen Christ (*EG* 2). Our joy responds to the joy brimming over from Christ's heart (*EG* 5, quoting John 15:11). The incarnation of the Son means that all humans are taken up into the "heart of God" (*EG* 178). Our hope flows from the "loving heart of Jesus Christ" (*EG* 183). Our intercessory prayer is "leaven" in the heart of the Trinity, and is a way of "penetrating the Father's heart" (*EG* 283). This is cordial theology in the etymological sense of that word. It is a popular theology that doesn't disdain popular piety. Indeed Francis specifically commends popular piety as incarnational and relational (*EG* 90, 122–24).[12]

Francis's focus on encounter—face-to-face and person-to-person—chimes well with mission and proclamation too. His vision is profoundly relational in its theology, anthropology, ethics, economics, and ecology. He seeks to redress a profoundly unrelational, individualized, postmodern context (*EG* 67). Our encounter with Jesus affects, effects, and orders our encounters with all others (*EG* 1, 8). We need to renew a "'mystique' of living together, of mingling and encounter, of embracing and supporting one another" and oppose the "bitter poison of immanence" (*EG* 87). Precisely by becoming incarnate does God privilege encounter, and we learn "to find Jesus in the face of others, in their voices, in their pleas" (*EG* 91) at any time in any place (*EG* 127). Interestingly, this chimes in with recent work in social neuroscience and on cooperation.[13] Encounter is a key theme of this pontificate.

Allied with this emphasis on the affective, the relational, and the personal is a downplaying of ideas, texts, and theories. As I have emphasized, this theology is animated by, and seeks to promote, transformative encounter with the person of Jesus Christ, not some version of his message, or a metaphysics of his person (though of course it cannot avoid implying both of these).[14] So Francis promotes intellectual diversity flowing out of the inexhaustible gospel, held together by the Spirit, rather than a "monolithic body of doctrine guarded by all" (*EG* 40), in which specific forms trump substance (*EG* 41). Indeed Francis warns that excessive attachment to doctrinal particularities or moral regulations are in fact deficiencies in christological or incarnational thinking, tending to either "gnosticism" or "promethean neopelagianism":

"in neither case is one really concerned about Jesus Christ or others" (*EG* 94). Once again Christology is key.

Because Christ is *encountered*, the gospel is never captured once and for all, but rather incarnated in diverse cultures and peoples, so we must avoid thinking that it must be "communicated by fixed formulations...or by specific words which express an absolutely invariable content" (*EG* 129). Preaching should be inculturated, "proclaiming a synthesis, not ideas or detached values" (*EG* 143). Our concern should not be about "doctrinal error, but...being faithful to this light-filled path of life and wisdom" (*EG* 194). Practice in the real world is prioritized over theory: Francis wants "practical real effects" not more "commentary or discussion" (*EG* 201).

Francis's prioritization of reality over ideas is one of the four cardinal principles that are a little tucked away toward the end of the document. The other three are "time is greater than space" (*EG* 222–25); "unity prevails over conflict" (*EG* 226–30); and "the whole is greater than the part" (*EG* 234–37). The four principles are ways of thinking through different aspects of differentiated unities, and I think this is a key theme of much of this text, as well as of other of his writings: holding together *both* difference *and* unity. Critically, he links the interpretation of these four guiding principles to Christ and Christology, where, he argues, they receive paradigmatic expression. In other words, his four guiding principles are christologically grounded.

It is hard to see how "time" could be greater than "space," as they are two different categories with insufficient commonality to make comparative judgments possible.[15] We never experience one without the other. But from his comments, I think Francis sees humans as poised or tensed between their limited spatialized finite realities and the plenitude of time, tensed between their past and present, and the beckoning future (*EG* 222). We always experience life in a finite way, but in the very finitude of that experience apprehend infinity. You could say our being and outlooks are stereoscopic.

The paradoxical, tensed nature of humanity seen in this light offers two counterpoised possible reductions: an exclusive focus on the finite and the here and now, or, contrariwise, a utopic disregard for the present in favor of some future plenitude. Francis argues that one should accept the tension, give room to both sides, but privilege what he calls "time": temporally stretched out processes, long-term programs rather than "space"; the lasting over the ephemeral (*EG* 223). It is here that Francis, in a very rare quotation of a contemporary or recent theologian, points to Romano Guardini's *The End of the Modern Age* (*EG* 224), on whom more will be discussed shortly.

Francis is a realist about conflict: "It has to be faced" (*EG* 226). But again it is a question of keeping the balance, keeping both poles of the tension in play, maintaining what we might call a "both/and" approach. This means not being solely focused on conflict and opposition but remembering the overall underlying unity of reality. Again, we have a portrayal of differentiated unity. In the face of conflict, Christians are called to be peacemakers, practicing solidarity so that "conflicts, tensions, oppositions can achieve a diversified and life-giving unity" (*EG* 228). As I have already noted, this unity is found and manifested in Christ, for it is he who "has made all things one in himself: heaven and earth, God and man, time and eternity, flesh and spirit, person and society. The sign of this unity and reconciliation of all things in him is peace. Christ 'is our peace' (Eph 2:14)" (*EG* 229). The diversified unity of peace is (also?) brought about by the Spirit, who "overcomes every conflict by creating a new and promising synthesis" (*EG* 230).

The final principle is mereological, looking as it does at the issue of differentiated unity from the perspective of parts and wholes. Francis first expresses this kind of tension as that between "globalization and localization" (*EG* 234). Again it is a case of paying attention to both sides of the tension, not letting one trump the other. We can get lost in an "abstract globalized universe" at the expense of living in the here and now, or contrariwise we can get trapped into the very particulars of our here and now without relation to the rest of the world or any sense of movement or novelty. We need to keep our eyes on the whole that is bigger than our part, and note that the whole is always greater than the sum of its parts (*EG* 235). Our outlook needs to be "glocal."

It is here that Francis produces his much commented on comparison between the sphere and the polyhedron (*EG* 236). I'm not sure that all the details of this comparison actually work, but the sense is clear. All the elements on the surface of the sphere, every pixel as it were, composes the whole, so that the sphere is the sum of its surface pixels and each is equidistant from the center. Each element of diversity has a flat, nonvariegated, relation to the center and to each other. With the polyhedron, by contrast, each element has a three-dimensional, differential relation with each other element and with the center. The latter model admits of different differences, the former does not.

Francis uses the image to contrast an evangelization of uniformity, indicated by the sphere, with an evangelization of ever-expansive unity and totality that respects the integrities of its ingredient elements. These are in fact differing views of the unity of catholicism, different views of the differentiated unity that is universal Christianity. In Francis's favored, polyhedral view, the gospel is incarnated in everyone who hears and responds to it, each in their own language, culture, context, and situation (*EG* 237). These "incarnations" do not displace each other, nor are they called to be identical, but they relate to each other in differentiated ways according to their varying relations with Christ. It is Christ who creates this "reconciled diversity" (*EG* 230).

This discussion is not without its difficulties. Francis seems to be comparing a curiously two-dimensional view of a sphere with a three-dimensional view of the polyhedron. The polyhedron only seems to promote a unity by juxtaposition—a rather static view of union for a theologian of encounter, dialogue, and mercy. And sometimes Francis's language—and this might be a difficulty of translation—seems to militate against the preservation of the integrity of the localized particular that he wants to guarantee. Talk of "synthesis" summons up Hegel: a thesis and antithesis that have been reconciled in a "synthesis" or "reconciled diversity" that is some *tertium quid* or an amalgam. But there are places where he tries to strike a more careful balance: "This is not to opt for a kind of syncretism, or for the absorption of one into the other, but rather for a resolution which takes place on a higher plane and preserves what is valid and useful on both sides" (*EG* 228). And indeed Nick Adams's recent rereading of Hegel suggests that he himself operated with a careful, Chalcedonian, logic of "oppositional pairs," guided by Christology, and not a logic of subsumption.[16] Francis himself echoes the famous alpha-privative adverbs

used in the symbol of Chalcedon to apophatically circumscribe
Christ's unique and ineffable union of divine and human in a
lecture on political anthropology from 1989; in it he talks about
Guardini's polar opposites of similarity/difference and unity/
multiplicity as being conjunctions that are *"indivise et inconfuse"*:
not divided and not merged.[17] This lecture echoes much in *EG*, as
well as demonstrating his early deep love of Guardini.

Leaving these quibbles aside for the moment, it is clear from
these four principles, which Francis enunciates in *EG* and has also
used much earlier elsewhere,[18] and which are clearly therefore
significant for him, that tension, difference, and opposition are
important, even fundamental. In many ways, this document is
about thinking through and ameliorating differentiated unities—
redeeming difference—and, as I have been trying to show, Francis
does this in a christological way.

The shape of love and mercy, manifested in Christ, and
taken on and grown into, falteringly, by the community of his
followers, is one in which differences are mutually related in an
inclusive way: the "evangelizing community...bridges differences,
it is willing to abase itself if necessary, and it embraces human
life, touching the suffering flesh of Christ in others" (*EG* 24).
This is a paradoxical faith that renders "our lives...wonderfully
complicated" (*EG* 270). The conjunction of opposites is a lens to
consider the Christian faith in which "we are challenged to discern how wine can come from water and how wheat can grow in
the midst of weeds" (*EG* 84). The "logic of the incarnation" would
be falsified if "we thought of Christianity as monocultural and
monotonous" (*EG* 117).

It is the work of the Spirit in particular to unite the different persons of the Trinity in love, just as it is the Spirit's role to
generate "a rich variety of gifts, while at the same time creating
a unity which is never uniformity but a multifaceted and inviting
harmony" (*EG* 117). The Christian community must be pneuma-
tologically ec-centric, seeking ever-greater diversity, and avoiding
"monolithic uniformity" at all costs.

Christ, as the Spirit-impelled and Spirit-imparting inexhaustible source of loving mercy, redemptive union of difference
and opposition, is also significantly thereby an endless source of
novelty. Francis quotes the famous phrase from Irenaeus's *Adversus*

Haereses: "By his coming, Christ brought with himself all novelty," which was so important to the christocentric theology of *ressourcement* theologian Henri de Lubac, SJ.[19] Christ's gospel with its eccentric posture, always encountering the other, must always engage and create the new, and this is how the Christian life and community is renewed. Jesus's novelty shows up our deficient comprehension of humanity: Christology dilates and expands anthropology. In our encounter with Jesus we "become fully human when we become more than human, when we let God bring us beyond ourselves in order to attain the fullest truth of our being" (*EG* 8). Authentic evangelization is always "new" (*EG* 11).

One final comment before trying to situate this captivating and promising Christology. It is a Christology always in act, resisting the deadening of definition and neat doctrinal packages. It is a Christology that is to be lived out, performed, improvised, continuing Jesus's story in the world. The focus on action is unmistakable: here *theology* and *Christology* are more verbs than nouns, more ways of life than topics for research. And more than that, there is a focus on future action, how Christology and theology are to be completed by us: theology in the gerundive. How does joy fit into this? I think joy is the relation that characterizes that christological action, so that one can call this an adverbial Christology as well as a cordial theology.

Ressourcement Influences on Francis's Christology: Romano Guardini and Josef Jungmann, SJ

Now, having given a christological account of *EG*, and highlighted what I think are its most striking features, it remains to attempt to situate that Christology within the sweep of recent theologies. Whom is Francis drawing on in developing this line of thinking and action?

The themes of Christology, difference, and union that we have been tracing in *EG* resonate greatly with many *ressourcement* theologians of the early twentieth century,[20] but particularly in the works of Romano Guardini.[21] This polymathic Italian theologian from Verona who spent most of his life in Germany is largely forgotten in the English-speaking theological world today, but his significance for twentieth-century theology has actually been considerable. Both Walter Kasper and Austen Ivereigh report on Jorge Maria Bergoglio's time spent in Germany in 1986 to start the doctorate he never completed: the topic was to have been Romano Guardini.[22] Clear evidence of this is seen in the impact of Guardini's thought—especially his writings on opposition and his apocalyptic announcement of the end of modernity—on Bergoglio's inaugural lecture in 1989.[23]

Like other theologians retrospectively grouped as *ressourcement* theologians, Guardini was not attracted by the regnant, syllogistic neo-Scholasticism when he was undertaking his ordination studies at the diocesan seminary in Mainz. This gave him a lifelong impulse to fertilize theological thinking with sources outside the usual neo-Scholastic theological canon: literature, liturgy, contemporary philosophy, and psychology. Most immediately, for his doctorate and then *Habilitationsschrift*, he studied not Aquinas, but Bonaventure, the Franciscan christocentric mystical theologian and champion of evangelical poverty. Joseph Ratzinger had also turned to Bonaventure for his doctorate.

Guardini's early theses link together opposition and Christology, as we have found in *EG*. Guardini notices in the first thesis, on Bonaventure's soteriology, how Christ for Bonaventure is the mediator or *medium*. Because of sin, the distance between Creator and creature has become an opposition, *Gegensatz*. God is merciful and so wills reconciliation with creation that a mediator is needed. Guardini highlights how for Bonaventure the *medium* "must be between two extremes, is differentiated from both, but is in relation with both and participates in the nature of both and is 'confected' out of both."[24] Christ, as mediator and *medium* between God and humanity, is one person of both natures. Guardini highlights how for Bonaventure Christ is the *medium* between God and the world as well as being the *medium* within the Trinity, and the *medium* between angels and humans. We have seen the same interlocking or cascading theology in *EG*: the "shape" of mercy manifested in Christ, revealing the loving relations of the triune God, which calls forth our ongoing incarnation of that merciful, joy-creating love.

But even more significant for our purposes are Guardini's next writings, explicitly on opposition.[25] Both in 1914, and then again in 1925, Guardini wrote works on opposition. In these he is seeking to tease out our perception of concrete reality and life as a unity always formed of opposites. Like other *ressourcement* theologians, Guardini was trying to reconnect our theorizing and theology with real concrete life, redressing the diremption between theology and life in neo-Scholastic theologies. The subtitle of his second work on opposition is key: "A Theory of the Living Concrete." Like Maurice Blondel before him, who influenced many of the *ressourcement* thinkers, truth could no longer be understood as the *adaequatio speculativa rei et intellectus* (the speculative correspondence between something and the intellect) but had rather to be understood as the *adaequatio realis mentis et vitae* (the real correspondence between life and mind).[26] You could say the history of twentieth-century theology is in significant part the story of patchy progress toward Blondel's insight. Francis is vigorously picking up that relay now.

At any rate for Guardini opposites, or *Gegensätze*, mutually define and implicate each other. We perceive life in and through these opposites. Our mind perceives these different facets of a united experience as opposed. The opposites must be thought with or in each other; we must see in the round, perceive the whole. We get more of an idea of what Guardini is after when we consider what he thinks of as opposites.[27] He divides up his system into two groups, categorial and transcendental opposites.[28] The former group is divided into a further two: intra-empirical and transempirical opposites. Intra-empirical opposites are things like dynamic and static; form and formlessness; integrity and differentiation. Transempirical opposites are things like production and disposal; originality and rule; immanence and transcendence. Guardini's transcendental opposites are affinity and particularity; unity and multiplicity. Whatever one makes of his particular taxonomy, the point is clear: we perceive aspects of reality as partial, but in perceiving them as partial, know their opposites at the same time. For Guardini, we perceive reality in a polar vision, focusing on one aspect but being at the same time aware of its polar opposite that completes it. It is as if we cannot focus on the whole at one time, but must focus on some part while being aware, on the periphery of our vision, of a greater whole. Not only are opposites key to perception of reality, but also to movement, which is necessarily oppositional: rhythm is a key theme of Guardini's dynamic enantiology. Guardini opposes his view of the relation of opposites and their various kinds with what he sees as the errors of the Hegelian and Romantic systems of thought on the one hand, and the Kierkegaardian on the other.[29] In his view, the former systems do not ultimately preserve the integrity of both poles, but sublate them into the final synthesis, eliminating difference.[30] By contrast, the Kierkegaardian view holds the poles too far apart in complete, contradictory otherness.[31] Both trajectories fail to maintain differentiated unity. Guardini's polar vision of reality resonates deeply with Francis's vision in *EG*.

Guardini relates his polar vision to Christology and catholicity in his later works too. In his inaugural lecture as professor of the philosophy of religion and the Catholic worldview at Berlin, Guardini argues that catholicity or universality is not a type among others, but the perception of the whole.[32] And that whole is the person of Christ. In his book *Das Wesen des Christentums*, undoing the eponymous works of Feuerbach and von Harnack, Guardini insists that the essence of Christianity is the person Jesus Christ, and not some moral or doctrinal package. Indeed he says in his major christological work, *The Lord*, that we are not to think "about Christ but think from him"; Christ is at the center of reality redefining it.[33] Other themes in his christological writings that chime with the priorities of Francis and *EG* are the newness and complete originality of Christ, as well as the central importance of encounter with the person of Christ, and others.[34] Because Christ is completely original and new, our response to him creates newness in us: his beginning and novelty calls forth our own novelty. For Guardini, this is the work of grace and redemption.[35] Key to this dynamic is our encounter with Christ.

Another frequently ignored *ressourcement* theologian whose influence can be seen in *EG* and Francis's theology more generally is Josef Jungmann, SJ. Josef Jungmann was an exponent of the *Verkündigungstheologie* (proclamation theology) of Innsbruck whose other prominent member was Hugo Rahner, SJ, Karl's brother. In its desire to reconnect the church's theology with the lived lives of those to whom it ministered, these theologians recalled theology to its kerygmatic, or proclamatory, heart, just as Pope Francis is doing. Jungmann is best known for his works on the Mass and liturgy, but an important but overlooked pedal-note in his writings is the theme of Christology. Jungmann had a heightened christological sensibility that can be seen most obviously in his first major work, *The Place of Christ in Liturgical Prayer*, and then again in his long article on the impact of Arianism on liturgical formulations.[36]

Elsewhere, in a significant but now overlooked article, "Christ as the Centre of Religious Education," Jungmann is looking for "the middle point, from which the whole Christian teaching can be unfolded, and to which every part can be led back."[37] He argues that theology has failed in its kerygmatic function by misplacing the middle, the heart, of the faith. His is a critique of contemporary catechetics: bad theology yields bad catechetics. In his view, the failed "centres" are such organizing principles as "serving God" (faith, prayer, sacraments), or the Trinity, or even the Mass and eucharistic piety. He argues that for the Christian on the street, Christ must be the ordering center or "middle-point" of religious life. Jungmann's polar form of differentiated unity is the idea of a middle that structures all around a constellating center, recalling Francis's images of the sphere and polyhedron.

Jungmann writes that "the given middle point of the faith is Christ."[38] Christ is the source and structuring principle of the other "centers" that Jungmann dismissed earlier: to the extent that they are not ordered to Christ, they are misleading. "Christ stands in the middle of this cosmos, not as an impersonal essence, but as a warm blooded person, this Person, who seeks and loves us humans with a strong love, so that we might be able to meet him in trust, love, and friendship."[39] Christ as middle point enables the Christian to engage the "whole of reality." Walter Kasper tells us that the work of Jungmann is important for Francis.[40] Indeed Francis has been a champion of the movement Communione e liberazione, founded by Luigi Giussani, which had a deep impact on Francis.[41] Jungmann's essay on the centrality of Christ was in turn key to Giussani's conception of education as an introduction to the whole of reality.[42]

Jungmann, like Francis, was a Jesuit, and this must be another point in situating the christological vision of *EG*. Pope Francis's long training and leadership in Ignatius's society has thoroughly

shaped his thought and action. One can point here to the centrality of mercy in the first week of Ignatius's *Spiritual Exercises,* and
its incarnational, christological shape in the second week.[43] More
generally the direct encounter with Jesus throughout the *Exercises,*
together with Ignatius's theology of election—personal decision for
Jesus and his kingdom that doing the *Exercises* is designed to lead
up to—resonate deeply with the shape and dynamism of Francis's
theology as seen in *EG,* as well as his close contacts with evangelical forms of Christianity. Moreover, Joseph Veale has argued that
the tensed conjunction of opposites thoroughly characterizes the
Constitutions of the Society of Jesus, its earliest institutional charter
for the charismatic communal life of the followers of Ignatius, as a
dynamic differentiated unity. *EG* also shares its circular dynamic of
mercy—from the Trinity, through Christ, and back to the Trinity in
the believer—with the *Constitutions.*[44]

Finally, and ecclesiologically, Francis's vision of a poor church
for the poor, resourced from the peripheries over the center, undertaking a program of "discernment, purification, and reform" (*EG*
30), shows significant resonances with the thought of the French
Dominican Yves Congar, so influential on Vatican II. One thinks
especially of his work on the poverty of the church and on the
nature on true reform.[45] Of particular interest for this chapter, and
its concerns with christological and pneumatological construals of
differentiated unities, is Congar's retrieval of Johann Möhler's contrast between positive opposition (*Gegensatz*) and destructive contradiction (*Widerspruch*): yet another possible source for Francis's
fascination with, and welcoming of, difference.[46] While Francis
seems to see both Christ and the Spirit as the principles of reconciled difference, Möhler moved from pneumatocentrism to chris-
tocentrism. Although resonances between Francis and Congar are
frequently noted, I have yet to find any textual evidence of Bergoglio's
dependence on these works.[47]

Deepening Francis's Christology

Having attempted to situate Francis's christological vision as
resonating variously with several elements of *ressourcement* theology,

what areas can be identified for expansion, deepening, or correction? Chief among these I think is the issue of different differences and oppositions, which I have argued are key. The *ressourcement* thinkers show how one needs to be alert to different kinds of difference even while uniting them in a greater unity, and so more investigation of these authors on this issue in connection with Francis's thought would be beneficial. For most of those thinkers, any unity is only possible because of the nonexclusive nature of the underlying ultimate difference: the differentiated unity of opposites in Christ is only possible because of the radical transcendence of the Creator God who creates out of nothing at all. This is most clear perhaps in Erich Przywara's understanding of analogy, but is clear too in the other *ressourcement* thinkers. If Pope Francis wants to take forward his view of "reconciled synthesis" and the union of opposites he picked up from Dorotheus, Ignatius, Möhler, Congar, and Guardini, he will need to think more clearly about different kinds of difference. One way to do this would be through consideration of creation and the Creator God, a process arguably begun in Francis's encyclical *LS*. As we stand now somewhere between late modern emphases on unity and postmodern emphases on diversity, a theology that wants to promote differentiated unity theologically, ecclesiologically, and ethically needs to consider the multiple kinds of diversity with urgency and greater analytical clarity.[48] This will be key to the ecumenical development of *EG* too: What is legitimate and illegitimate diversity, or, to put it in Möhlerian terms, when does opposition become contradiction? Also key to that ecumenical work will be noticing and enacting Francis's return to christological and soteriological basics: working from the center outward.

A greater sense of the radical transcendence of God, and therefore a greater sense of the apophatic, might make the very rapid transitions in *EG* from Trinitarian-differentiated unity to human-differentiated unity more circumspect and undercut possible criticisms of a noxious social trinitarianism in Francis's thought.[49] God's difference from creation is utterly unlike, though generative of, all intracreaturely differences. To ignore this carries the potential danger of anthropomorphizing God. Widening the "gap" between the divine and the human would not in any way limit the inclusive nature of Francis's gospel of mercy and the action and ethic that flow from it, but only serve to enhance its universal and utterly nonexclusive nature.

More attention needs to be paid to the relation between Francis's Christology and pneumatology. In *EG* he argues, in different places, that both Christ and the Spirit are the principle and source of diversity and differentiated unity, and both are at the root of the novelty of the gospel of mercy. And of course the Trinity is undivided, but an ambiguity remains in *EG* that could be fruitfully explored, especially in connection with recent work on Spirit christologies: Where does the priority lie?[50] This is especially important in the light of the global rise of Pentecostalism, especially in the southern migration of Christianity, and the emphases on mission, dialogue, and dynamism in the theologies that it is generating.[51] There is a link here with recent work arguing for a "spirit-led" approach to the Trinity, and on the ecumenical difficulties of the *filioque*.[52]

The universality of Francis's gospel of mercy means that the continuation of *EG* needs to engage with all disciplines beyond theology and ethics. Francis's focus on the embodied and social nature of the encounter with Christ and its outworkings in the Christian community will find rich resonance with several current areas of interest, for instance, in social cognition and neuroscience—what is known as the second person perspective—as well as cultural analysis more broadly.[53] Francis's paradoxical vision of the conjunctive, amplexive nature of mercy resonates here with the hugely suggestive cultural analysis of Iain McGilchrist.[54]

In looking at the Christology of *EG*, and identifying some of its tributaries in *ressourcement* theologies, we have seen that Francis's Christology is not radically innovative in its content, but rather deeply, if quietly and creatively, resourced in the tradition. It shares much with the Christology of his predecessor, while adding a dynamic, dialogical frame and a pneumatological supplement to Benedict's focus on Logos. But both pontiffs are united by drawing deep inspiration from Romano Guardini: not for nothing did Benedict choose to quote Guardini in his last official act as pope, and Guardini is the theologian most quoted in all of Francis's texts thus far.[55] But Francis's Christology is, however, different in its packaging, communication, and outworking.[56] This merciful, cordial, kerygmatic, active, adverbial Christology, centered on the ongoing reconciliation (but not elimination) of oppositions and differentiated unities being effected in us through Christ's Spirit, should prove key in dislodging recent deadening squabbles over the interpretation of Vatican II, as well as galvanizing ecumenical fatigue. Central to both will be a move from messages and programs, to renewed encounter with the person of Christ; not so much *evangelii gaudium* as *Christi gaudium*.

Select Bibliography

de Lubac, Henri. *Catholicism: Christ and the Common Destiny of Man*. San Francisco: Ignatius, (1938) 1988.

———. *More Paradoxes*. San Francisco: Ignatius, 2002.

———. *Paradoxes of Faith*. San Francisco: Ignatius, 1987.

Guardini, Romano. *The Church of the Lord*. Chicago: Regnery, (1965) 1966.

———. *The Lord*. London: Longmans, (1937) 1956.

Jungmann, Josef. *The Good News Yesterday and Today*. New York: William Sadlier, (1936) 1962.

McCosker, Philip. *Christ the Paradox: Expanding Ressourcement Theology*. Cambridge: Cambridge University Press, 2018.

Przywara, Erich. *Analogia Entis: Metaphysics; Original Structure and Universal Rhythm*. Grand Rapids: Eerdmans, (1962) 2014.

Notes

1. A recent set of interdisciplinary essays on *EG* only very occasionally mentions the place of Christ in the exhortation but does not explore its role or provenance: Humberto Yánez, ed., *Evangelii Gaudium: il testo ci interroga. Chiavi di lettura, testimonianze e prospettive* (Rome: Gregorian & Biblical Press, 2014).

2. Quoting Benedict XVI, *Deus Caritas Est* 1.

3. Pope Francis, Twitter post, May 28, 2015, https://twitter.com/pontifex.

4. Cf. *MV* 1: "Jesus Christ is the face of the Father's mercy. These words might well sum up the mystery of the Christian

faith....Jesus of Nazareth, by his words, his actions, and his entire person reveals the mercy of God."

5. Cf. *MV* 25.

6. Pope Francis, Twitter post, April 25, 2015, https://twitter.com/pontifex.

7. Note how frequently Francis employs the "hierarchy of truths" in order to refocus on Christ (e.g., *EG* 36, 37, 246).

8. Cf *MV* 9: "Jesus affirms that mercy is not only an action of the Father, it becomes a criterion for ascertaining who his true children are. In short, we are called to show mercy because mercy has first been shown to us."

9. I gratefully borrow this term from my student Peter Farrugia.

10. Sarah Bachelard, *Resurrection and Moral Imagination* (Farnham: Ashgate, 2013). This important work builds on key works by Oliver O'Donovan, Rowan Williams, James Alison, and Brian Robinette.

11. Cf. Brian Johnstone, "Transformation Ethics: The Moral Implications of the Resurrection," in *The Resurrection: An Interdisciplinary Symposium on the Resurrection of Jesus Christ*, ed. S. T. Davis, G. O'Collins, and D. Kendall (Oxford: Oxford University Press, 1997), 339–60.

12. This emphasis echoes the concluding document from CELAM V at Aparecida (see 37, 43, 93, 99, 99b, 258, 300, 549).

13. For straightforward accounts, see Susan Pinker, *The Village Effect: Why Face-to-Face Contact Matters* (London: Atlantic, 2014); and Richard Sennett, *Together: The Rituals, Pleasures and Politics of Cooperation* (London: Penguin, 2012).

14. There are many resonances between Francis's theology and the recent work of Oliver Davies. See his *Theology of Transformation: Faith, Freedom, and the Christian Act* (Oxford: Oxford University Press, 2013), chap. 1, for instance.

15. For a more charitable interpretation, see Giulio Maspero, "Il tempo superiore allo spazio (*EG* 222): Un principio teologico fondamentale per l'agire cristiano," *PATH* 13 (2014): 403–12.

16. See Nicholas Adams, *Eclipse of Grace: Divine and Human Agency in Hegel* (Oxford: Wiley-Blackwell, 2013), 8–10, 20–25.

17. Jorge M. Bergoglio, "Necessidad de un antropologia politica: un problema pastoral," *Stromata* 45, nos. 1–2 (1989): 173–

89, here 177n5. Bergoglio also uses this phrase in his texts on the monastic spirituality of Dorotheus of Gaza: *The Way of Humility: Corruption and Sin; On Self-Accusation* (San Francisco: Ignatius, 2014), 66.

18. He first gave three of the principles in an address to the Argentine Province of the Jesuits, when he was its provincial, on February 18, 1974, and then more fully as archbishop of Buenos Aires in 2010. See Juan Carlos Scanonne, "Papa Francesco e la teologia del popolo," *La Civiltà Cattolica* 3930 (March 15, 2014): 571–90.

19. See, for instance, Henri de Lubac, *Catholicism: Christ and the Common Destiny of Man* (San Francisco: Ignatius, 1988), 269; *The Mystery of the Supernatural* (New York: Herder, 1998), 83, among many others. For commentary, see Étienne Guibert, *Le Mystère du Christ d'après Henri de Lubac* (Paris: Cerf, 2006), part 1, esp. 166–69.

20. See Philip McCosker, *Christ the Paradox: Expanding Ressourcement Theology* (Cambridge: Cambridge University Press, 2018).

21. For a synchronic analysis of Guardini, see Hans Urs von Balthasar, *Romano Guardini: Reform from the Source* (San Francisco: Ignatius, 2010); and for a fuller, diachronic, somewhat downbeat account, see Robert A. Krieg, *Romano Guardini: A Precursor of Vatican II* (Notre Dame: University of Notre Dame Press, 1997).

22. See Walter Kasper, *Pope Francis' Revolution of Tenderness and Love* (New York: Paulist Press, 2015), 20; and Austen Ivereigh, *The Great Reformer: Francis and the Making of a Radical Pope* (London: Allen & Unwin, 2014), 197–98.

23. Bergoglio, "Necessidad," esp. 177, but *passim*. For an analysis of this text, see Diego Flores, "L'antropologia politica di papa Francesco," *La Civiltà Cattolica* 3928 (February 15, 2014): 345–60.

24. Romano Guardini, *Die Lehre des heil. Bonaventura von der Erlösung: Ein Beitrag zur Geschichte und zum System der Erlösungslehre* (Düsseldorf: L. Schwann, 1921), 48.

25. Romano Guardini, *Gegensatz und Gegesätze: Entwurf eines Systems der Typenlehre* (Freiburg: Caritas, 1914); *Der Gegensatz: Versuche zu einer Philosophie des Lebendig-Konkreten* (Mainz: Matthias Grünewald, 1925). For a full analysis of Guardini from the perspective of opposition, see Albino Babolin, *Romano Guardini: Filosofo dell'alterità*, 2 vols. (Bologna: Zanichelli, 1968–69).

26. Maurice Blondel, "Le point de départ de la recherche philosophique," *Annales de philosophie chrétienne* 151 (1906): 337–60; 152 (1906): 225–49, here 235.

27. Note the summary in Bergoglio, "Necessidad," 177.

28. Guardini, *Der Gegensatz*, chap. 2.

29. See Peter Šajda's highly informative essay, "Romano Guardini: Between Actualistic Personalism, Qualitative Dialectic and Kinetic Logic," in *Kierkegaard's Influence on Theology. Tome III: Catholic and Jewish Theology*, ed. Jon Stewart (Farnham: Ashgate, 2012), 45–74, esp. 54–56.

30. Guardini, *Der Gegensatz*, 42.

31. Ibid., 48.

32. Romano Guardini, "Vom Wesen katholischer Weltanschauung," in *Unterscheidung des Christlichen: Gesammelte Studien 1923–63* (Mainz: Matthias Grünewald, 1963), 13–33.

33. Romano Guardini, *The Lord* (London: Longmans, Green & Co, 1956), 436 and *passim*.

34. Guardini drew deeply on the dialogical thought of Martin Buber's conception of the I-Thou reciprocal encounter and the self's need of the other in knowing itself. For Guardini that dialogical reciprocity is based on the same relation between selves and God. See his *Welt und Person* (Wurzburg: Werkbund, 1939), chap. 2. For an account of his anthropology, see Robert Krieg, "Romano Guardini's Theology of the Human Person," *Theological Studies* 59 (1998): 457–74.

35. See Romano Guardini, *The Humanity of Christ: Contributions to a Psychology of Jesus* (London: Burns & Oates, 1958), 124.

36. Josef Jungmann, *The Place of Christ in Liturgical Prayer* (London: Geoffrey Chapman, [1925] 1965); "The Defeat of Teutonic Arianism and the Revolution in Religious Culture in the Middle Ages," in *Pastoral Liturgy* (New York: Herder, [1947] 1962), 1–101.

37. Josef Jungmann, "Christus, als Mittelpunkt religiöser Erziehung," *Stimmen der Zeit* 134 (1938): 218–33, here 218.

38. Ibid., 223.

39. Ibid., 227.

40. See Kasper, *Pope Francis' Revolution*, 97n2, where he mentions Jungmann's *Die Frohbotschaft und Unsere Glaubensverkündigung* (Regensburg: Pustet, 1936). See the abridged translation: *The Good News Yesterday and Today* (New York: Sadlier, 1962).

41. See Jorge Mario Bergoglio, "For Man," in *A Generative Thought: An Introduction to the Works of Luigi Giussani*, ed. Elisa Buzzi (Quebec: McGill-Queen's University Press, 2003), 79–83.

42. See Luigi Giussani, *The Risk of Education: Discovering Our Ultimate Destiny* (New York: Crossroad, 2001).

43. See Michael Ivens, *Understanding the Spiritual Exercises* (Leominster: Gracewing, 1998), 43–44, 75–77.

44. Joseph Veale, "How the *Constitutions* Work," *The Way Supplement* 61 (1988): 3–20, esp. 17–19.

45. Yves Congar, *Power and Poverty in the Church* (Baltimore: Helicon, 1964), and *True and False Reform in the Church* (Collegeville, MN: Liturgical, 2010), esp. 205–13.

46. Johann Adam Möhler, *Unity in the Church, or, The Principle of Catholicism Presented in the Spirit of the Church Fathers of the First Three Centuries* (Washington, DC: Catholic University of America Press, 1996), esp. 194–98. For good commentary on the role of opposition in Möhler's ecclesiology, see Rupert Geiselmann, *Johann Adam Möhler, Die Einheit der Kirche und die Wiedervereinigung der Konfessionen* (Vienna: Friedrich Beck, 1940), esp. 47–48, 167–68.

47. Cf. Ivereigh, *Reformer*, xv, 93–94, 120, 142, among others.

48. For a useful conspectus and discussion of some possibilities, see F. LeRon Shults, "The Philosophical Turn to Alterity in Christology and Ethics," in *Christology and Ethics*, ed. F. LeRon Shults and Brent Waters (Grand Rapids: Eerdmans, 2010), 179–211.

49. On the perils of social trinitarianism, see Karen Kilby, "Perichoresis and Projection: Problems with Social Doctrines of the Trinity," *New Blackfriars* 81, no. 957 (2000): 432–45, among many others.

50. See, for instance, Ralph del Colle, *Christ and the Spirit: Spirit-Christology in Trinitarian Perspective* (New York: Oxford University Press, 1994).

51. The recent works of Amos Yong come to mind here. See, for instance, his *Renewing Christian Theology: Systematics for a Global Christianity* (Waco, TX: Baylor University Press, 2014); *The Missiological Spirit: Christian Mission Theology for the Third Millennium Global Context* (Eugene, OR: Cascade, 2014); and *The Dialogical Spirit: Christian Reason and Theological Method in the Third Millennium* (Eugene, OR: Cascade, 2014).

52. See Sarah Coakley, *God, Sexuality, and the Self: An Essay "On the Trinity"* (Cambridge: Cambridge University Press, 2013), chap. 3 and pp. 327–34; Thomas Weinandy, "The *Filioque*: Beyond Athanasius and Thomas Aquinas; An Ecumenical Proposal," in *Ecumenical Perspectives on the Filioque for the 21st Century*, ed. Myk Habets (London: Bloomsbury T&T Clark, 2014), 185–97.

53. See the references in Warren S. Brown and Brad D. Strawn, *The Physical Nature of Christian Life: Neuroscience, Psychology, and the Church* (Cambridge: Cambridge University Press, 2012).

54. Iain McGilchrist, *The Master and His Emissary: The Divided Brain and the Making of the Western World* (New Haven, CT: Yale University Press, 2009).

55. See Benedict XVI, "Farewell Address," http://w2.vatican.va/content/benedict-xvi/en/speeches/2013/february/documents/hf_ben-xvi_spe_20130228_congedo-cardinali.html. The text is from Guardini's *The Church of the Lord* (Chicago: Regnery, 1966), 37. For Ratzinger's understanding of Guardini, see his "From Liturgy to Christology: Romano Guardini's Basic Theological Approach and Its Significance," in *Fundamental Speeches from Five Decades* (San Francisco: Ignatius, 2012), 231–58.

56. A recent study, "Twiplomacy," by PR company Burson Marsteller has found that Pope Francis is the most retweeted world leader, which apparently pushes his influence beyond Barack Obama, who has more followers than Francis, but fewer retweets, see http://twiplomacy.com/.

Part 2

RENEWING THE PEOPLE OF GOD

ECCLESIOLOGY

4

Ecclesia et Pontifice

Delivering on the Ecclesiological Implications of *Evangelii Gaudium*

PAUL D. MURRAY

Introduction

While Pope Francis's 2013 Apostolic Exhortation *Evangelii Gaudium* (*EG*)[1] may not have either the status or the sustained focus and political volatility of his 2015 encyclical *Laudato Si'*,[2] this somewhat odd exhortation—in terms of length and range of subject matter—will likely endure as the definitive articulation of the watershed nature of this papacy. Its game-changing nature was recognized immediately upon publication, engaging Catholic conversation on multiple fronts starved of oxygen throughout the two previous papacies, speaking into them with remarkable directness borne from pastoral concern to attend closely to lived realities (see *EG* 82, 96, 231–33).

Too long for a manifesto, at times somewhat rambling, we are nevertheless presented here with the distillation of a lifetime's reflections and convictions on the properly evangelical orientation of all aspects of Catholic life and structure. At multiple points, the continuities of voice, perspective, and position with the writings of the former cardinal archbishop of Buenos Aires are tangible,[3] as also with the "Concluding Document" of the Fifth General Conference of the Latin American and Caribbean Bishops (CELAM) at Aparecida in 2007, on which he had significant influence.[4] But here we have far more than a compendium of Pope Francis's personal theological synthesis and spirituality. He is outlining a wide-ranging proposal for cultural change within Catholicism, one undoubtedly borne from his long experience in the local church in Argentina but that now needs to extend well beyond his own papacy if it is to come to fruition.[5]

Nor is this any detached bureaucratic presentation of a fully detailed program and "complete diagnosis" (*EG* 108) but an urgent plea to a renewal of mind, action, and priority throughout Catholicism, the implications of which are yet to be worked out in specific detail. He urges each individual and each community to discern how most appropriately to take the issues forward in their own circumstances (see *EG* 108; also 17 and 33).

Approaching this exhortation from the perspective of a systematic theologian with interests in ecclesiology and ecumenical theology,[6] my concern in this chapter is first to identify and then to analyze the specifically ecclesiological implications of the process of change that *EG* seeks to promote.[7]

From the outset it is worth noting that given that Pope Francis writes not as an academic theologian but as a wise pastor intent on promoting cultural change within Catholicism, we would look in vain in *EG* for anything approaching systematic ecclesiological analysis. Theology is here put in its proper ecclesial context of emerging out of and addressing issues arising in the life of the church—what Richard Gaillardetz, borrowing from Christoph Theobald, refers to as "the pastorality of doctrine."[8] What *EG* does is to identify various sites urgently requiring sustained formal attention in Catholic ecclesiology, many of which have already received significant informal attention since Vatican II. But the actual work of formally and systematically attending to them is left outside the scope of *EG*. It follows that the work of seeking to deliver on the implications of these sites and the issues they raise is properly and necessarily an analytical and constructive exercise and not simply a descriptive one. Consequently the force of this chapter is about identifying what the Catholic community—Catholic ecclesiologists in particular—now need to do if we are to live into the ways of Catholic renewal that Francis advocates.

It pursues its diagnosis in three steps. The first, expository, section identifies the key sites of ecclesiological significance in *EG*. Here the concern is simply to let the force of the document speak as clearly as possible. Given that some key aspects of *EG* are yet to be received into the common sense of formal Catholic theology, this is a worthwhile exercise in its own right and not simply as set-up for the analysis that follows. The second section then offers some initial reflections on the broad implications of *EG* for the contemporary task of Catholic ecclesiology—and Catholic theology more generally—concerning the manner in which these tasks should appropriately be pursued. The third then identifies something of the range of specific issues and potential ways ahead pertaining to the various sites of ecclesiological significance in *EG* and representing the work now needing to be done.

The Key Sites of Ecclesiological Significance in *Evangelii Gaudium*

Pope Francis's extended reflection on what it means for the whole life of the church to be rooted in and called to "attractive witness" (*EG* 99; also 15) to the "joy of the Gospel" has implications for every member of the church and every facet of church life, placing mission as primary for both individual and institution alike. Echoing Aparecida, the leitmotiv is, "Throughout the world, let us be 'permanently in a state of mission'" (*EG* 25).[9]

At the institutional level, the church exists not for itself (*EG* 95), with only exceptional overflow into mission; but for the sake of and only as a result of such mission, so all the institutional dimensions of the church, even when recognized as divinely willed, need to be properly oriented to and placed in effective service of this mission.[10] This is expressed most clearly in *EG* 27, where we find, "I dream of a 'missionary option,' that is, a missionary impulse capable of transforming everything, so that the church's customs, ways of doing things, times and schedules, language and structures can be suitably channelled for the evangelization of today's world rather than for her self-preservation."

Correlatively, mission is not the calling of the exceptional few but the ordinary calling of every individual. "No one," he tells us, "should think that this invitation is not meant for him or her" (*EG* 3). On the contrary, "grounded in their baptism and confirmation" (*EG* 102, 120) and the gifting of the Spirit therein, the call to "missionary discipleship" (*EG* 24, 50, 119–21) and a sharing in the *sensus fidei*[11] is normative for all. As such not only do laypeople represent the "majority of the people of God," their formation and the correlative "evangelization of professional and intellectual life" represents the most pressing "pastoral challenge" (*EG* 102). In this context he regards the parish as still the normal place of formation and training for most Catholics (*EG* 28), which is a little surprising given his Global South perspective wherein parishes can be significantly larger geographical entities than many dioceses in the global North.

Rather than defining the church relative to the hierarchical ordering of the clergy, with the "rest of the faithful" simply as "passive recipients" (*EG* 120), the clergy should be defined in relation to the laity whom they exist to serve (*EG* 102, 104). He makes clear acknowledgment of the potential pathology of an "excessive clericalism" that can neglect to allow room for the laity "to speak and to act" and that "keeps them away from decision-making" (*EG* 102). Here particular emphasis, albeit in somewhat essentialist terms,[12] is placed on the "need to create still broader opportunities for a more inclusive female presence in the Church," acknowledging that "many women share pastoral responsibilities with priests, helping to guide people, families and groups and offering new contributions to theological reflection" (*EG* 103).

Similarly, if the diocese, as a "particular...portion of the Church under the leadership of its bishop," is to fulfill its "missionary impulse," it needs "to undertake a resolute process of discernment, purification and reform" (*EG* 30). Episcopal leadership in "vision and hope needs also to allow the flock to strike out on new paths," to include an ability "simply [to] be in their midst," and "to encourage and develop the means of participation proposed in the Code of Canon Law, and other forms of pastoral dialogue, out of a desire to listen to everyone and not simply to those who would tell him what he would like to hear" (*EG* 31).

In turn, and with reference to Pope St. John Paul II's remarkable 1995 request of church leaders and theologians from other traditions to help with reimagining the ministry of the Bishop of Rome (see *Ut Unum Sint* 95–96),[13] Pope Francis frankly acknowledges the disappointing progress since *Ut Unum Sint* and reiterates that "the papacy and the central structures of the universal Church also need to hear the call to pastoral conversion" (*EG* 32).[14] He continues, "Excessive centralization, rather than proving helpful, complicates the Church's life and her missionary outreach" (*EG* 32).[15] With reference to section 23 of Vatican II's Dogmatic Constitution on the Church, *Lumen Gentium*, particular mention is made both of the potential role of episcopal conferences in offsetting this excessive centralism and of the way in which this potential has been hampered by the lack of any clear juridical support for their ordinary teaching authority(*EG* 32).[16] Surprisingly notable by omission, however, is any mention of the synod of bishops, particularly so given the significant steps that Pope Francis has already taken to reshape the culture and procedures of synodal processes.[17]

Related also to the need to overcome this Catholic default to excessive centralism are a number of ways in which Pope Francis advocates for a full and proper catholicity. First are his reflections on there being a legitimate internal diversity of local expressions of Catholic life and structure around the world, each bringing diverse "facets of the inexhaustible riches of the Gospel" to expression (*EG* 40; also 44, 115–18, esp. 116). From this diversity the Spirit creates a unity "which is never uniformity but a multifaceted and inviting harmony" (*EG* 117).[18] There needs, consequently, to be appropriate freedom to explore, without fear, what it means to discern and respond to the mystery of Christ in a given context and to ask what rethinking this may require.[19]

The correlate follows that authentic catholicity is served neither by the eradication of legitimate "multiplicity" in favor of a "monolithic uniformity" nor by the absolutizing of diversity into a fragmented and fragmenting difference. Such situations require docility to the Holy Spirit, who "alone can raise up diversity, plurality and multiplicity while at the same time bringing about unity" (*EG* 131; also see 226–30). He continues, "This is not to opt for a kind of syncretism, or for the absorption of one into the other, but rather for a resolution which takes place on a higher plane and preserves what is valid and useful on both sides" (*EG* 228). It is just such a "reconciled diversity," borrowing a term from ecumenical discourse, that should be sought after within intra-Catholic situations of disagreement and dispute.[20]

As this might suggest and as doubtless influenced by his reading of John Paul II's aforementioned *Ut Unum Sint*, Pope Francis's approach to inter-Christian ecumenical engagement is in sympathy with the key principles of what in recent years has come to be developed as receptive ecumenism, which itself draws key inspiration from *Ut Unum Sint*.[21] As we find in *EG* 246, "If we really believe in the abundantly free working of the Holy Spirit, we can learn so much from one another! It is not just about being better informed about others, but rather about reaping what the Spirit has sown in them, which is also meant to be a gift for us."[22] He continues, "To give but one example, in the dialogue with our Orthodox brothers and sisters, we Catholics have the opportunity to learn more about the meaning of episcopal collegiality and their experience of synodality" (*EG* 246).[23]

It is important, however, to be aware that appearances to the contrary based on *EG*'s irenic tone notwithstanding, none of these conversations in service of a full and diverse catholicity are envisaged as being conducted without either the checks of responsible discernment or the possibility of formal limits. In the latter regard, it is notable if predictable, and no less a cause of disappointment to many on that account, that in *EG* the only such formal limit to Catholic conversation explicitly touched upon is that pertaining to discussion of women's ordination. In the context of appreciating women's contributions to pastoral ministry, we nevertheless find the bald statement that "the reservation of the priesthood to males, as a sign of Christ the Spouse who gives himself in the Eucharist, is not a question open to discussion" (*EG* 104). The baldness of which is not reduced by his attempt to parse sacramental power from sociopolitical power.

As with each of the other key sites of ecclesiological significance here identified, this requires full analysis, development, and testing. Before turning, however, in the third part of the chapter to identify something of the range of relevant issues and constructive proposals needing to be considered here, it is fruitful to note some more fundamental implications for the nature of the Catholic ecclesiological task and how it should be conducted.

Some Fundamental Implications of *EG* for the Catholic Ecclesiological Task

It is a commonplace that the twin papacies of John Paul II and Benedict XVI were marked by increased polarization within Catholic life, most evident in North America, and frequently but unhelpfully referred to with the binary categories of "conservatives" and "progressivists." Mapping how these categories play out in lived ecclesial reality is a complex matter, with many anomalies and crossovers.[24] The most influential and most self-consciously theological construal of this basic polarity, at least insofar as it relates to mainstream Catholicism, employs a contrasting pair of ideal types, with each pole representing the prioritization of one of the twin streams of theological renewal that flowed, frequently intermingled and mutually supporting, into Vatican II.

On the one hand, the aggiornamento concern for renewal of the tradition in the light of contemporary questions came to be associated with the theological corpus of Karl Rahner, the journal *Concilium*, and a retrieved Thomistic view of graced nature. Here the world is regarded as *both* oriented toward the consummation of truth in Christ as known in the church *and* as being already engaged with aspects of this truth in ways from which the church can itself potentially learn, not least in relation to the church's own need for reform.[25] On the other hand, the *ressourcement* concern for the transformative retrieval of the full riches of the tradition came to be associated with Hans Urs von Balthasar, Henri de Lubac, SJ, and the journal *Communio*, of which Joseph Ratzinger was a founding editor in a breakaway move from the *Concilium* board. This perspective is frequently characterized by an Augustinian judgement on the world as in error and in need of the saving truth to be found within the church, together with a consequent dual emphasis on the need for mission and resistance to ecclesial criticism.[26]

A properly Catholic theology arguably needs to hold both these voices in dialectical tension, and it is notable that the respective greatness of Rahner and de Lubac enabled each of them to do so.[27] But given that official approval very definitely resided with the second—John Paul II had referred to Balthasar as his favorite theologian and Joseph Ratzinger, as noted, was a founding member of the *Communio* board of editors—together with a mindset given to perceiving all criticism as a dangerous act of disloyal dissent, an unhealthy balance of power and corresponding binary reduction of theological options frequently resulted. While many supporters of the second set of sensibilities have tended toward being content to expound the perceived beauty and wisdom within formal Catholic theology, those committed to the first set of concerns sank into a slump of seemingly permanent opposition, manifesting the range of responses this might suggest.

Where some variously proceeded in modes of frustrated grumbling,[28] others mounted the barricades with prophetic counterblast, serving to keep alternative voices heard but also inevitably reinforcing the apparent binary divorce in the process.[29] Other minority options included attempts, on the one hand, to undermine and collapse the binary by patiently seeking to show quite what room for movement is available within the existing system[30] and, on the other hand, to outflank the limits of court theology by articulating alternative theological visions unconstrained by any felt need even to engage the prevailing polarities.[31]

This entrenched climate of theological divorce and dysfunction within postconciliar Catholicism, long prevailing by the time of Pope Francis's election, sets the watershed nature of his papacy and the staggering freshness of *EG* in clearer perspective. A number of factors combine to show that this is all considerably more than just a change of mood music: his consistent encouragement of honest exploration and voicing of concerns—repeated also to the bishops of the world in preparation for the 2014 and 2015 dual synod process; his clear advocacy of ecclesial reform; and his emphasis upon the need to learn both from experienced pastoral reality and the wisdom of other traditions and perspectives. At minimum it marks the end of the privileging of a chosen school of court theology and the welcoming back to formal Catholic conversation of those shaped by different theological instincts— literally so in the case of Leonardo Boff in relation to *Laudato Si'*.

It would be wrongheaded, however, to see in this any straight- forward reversal of the basic binary—the same game continued only with a different distribution of power and patronage. While Bergoglio/Francis is primarily a wise pastor rather than a theo- logical ideologue, he is nevertheless a man of profound theologi- cal instincts, and these instincts defy easy categorization within the prevailing Catholic binary.[32]

It is not that he comes down in favor of *ad-intra* ecclesial reform rather than *ad-extra* mission, but that he refuses and transcends the supposed tension, viewing them as necessary cor- relates. It is the demands of mission that themselves require eccle- sial reform: for the sake of missional effectiveness; for the sake of ecclesial vitality; and for the sake of the quality and integrity of Catholic witness—that we might be what we preach (see *EG* 27).[33] In this perspective, the life of the church *ad intra, including* the church's structures and internal organization, is not properly understood simply as the background against which the church engages the world. Rather, the life, practices, and structures of the church *are* the primary statement the church makes to the world, prior to any specific initiatives or actions *ad extra*. This is the core principle in Boff's groundbreaking 1981 work, *Igreja: Carisma e poder* (*Church: Charism and Power*).[34] Consequently, mat- ters of ecclesial reform do not simply reduce to matters concern- ing the church's internal organization and structures of authority. They relate directly to the sacramentality and sign value of what the church is *before* God and *for* the world, and directly, therefore, to the church's witness and mission.[35]

Similarly, it is not that he comes down in favor of theological challenge and criticism rather than doctrinal fidelity and eccle- sial loyalty, but that he again refuses and transcends the disjunc- tion. It is precisely fidelity to what the church most deeply *is* that frees him to engage ecclesial difficulties with honesty and confi- dence, clear in his mind that none of the fundamental commit- ments of the faith can or need be compromised.[36] Indeed, not only does he seek to avoid being caught between specific substantive

expressions of the prevailing binary, he actively promotes, as earlier noted, the overcoming of this destructive binary in principle,
which serves only to diminish the quality of the church's catholicity.[37] If the younger son has been brought in from the cold, then it
is not a victory feast to which he has been called but to the communion table.

So prior to identifying the various substantive issues and
proposals pertaining to the sites of ecclesiological significance in
EG and beginning to reflect on how each might be approached, it
is important to ask more fundamentally after *EG's* broader implications for how the basic task of Catholic ecclesiology is to be
pursued. What does it mean for us to be called to lay down, or at
least to recalibrate, our theological arms when a formal cease-fire
is encouraged in the Catholic culture wars?

Where for one, the "conservative," it might mean learning
that constructive articulation of the riches of the tradition is not
incompatible with critical analysis of points of difficulty, for the
other, the "progressivist," it might mean learning to forego the
voice of protest and to hear again the invitation to constructive
contribution. For both it means the need to resist the common
tendency to speak, effectively, only to our own in-group, those
with whom we are already in agreement, simply reaffirming each
other with already familiar tropes, commitments, and shared
vision. By contrast, each needs instead to learn to pursue a whole-
church orientation in Catholic theology: to learn to speak—and
prior even to that, to learn—in a cross-bench fashion.

For those of us concerned to contribute to the process of
ecclesial reform, seeking to serve the process of conceiving change
within Catholicism by ministering therapeutically to its wounds,
this means being prepared to take the time patiently to test and
to demonstrate how the options we have before us—even those
that are novel and apparently discontinuous—can be appropriately integrated with received formal Catholic understanding.[38] It
means being prepared to take the time to show how any proposed
changes to the sedimented deposits of the tradition are benign,
even vital, rather than destructively invasive. This is a task requiring fine-detailed needlework and keyhole surgery rather than set-
tling either for broad-brush painting of desirable directions of
travel or sweeping polemic and posture.

In some respects it is a work of self-abnegation, of dusting off the prior work of others, the sheet music languishing in the ecclesial piano stool, and exploring how it might now be put to work in a discriminating way. Most of all this is to view the work of theology as a properly collective, ecclesial task and responsibility and not simply a personal endeavor. It is properly more about serving and building consensus and communion than it is about a virtuoso solo performance concerned to distinguish itself over against others. It is in this spirit of whole-church ecclesial theology, concerned to scrutinize and test how the web of Catholic belief and practice might be virtuously and appropriately rewoven, that we turn now in the third section to identify briefly the set of substantive issues pertaining to the sites of ecclesiological significance touched on in *EG*.

Specific Issues and Proposals Pertaining to the Key Sites of Ecclesiological Significance in *EG*

The single largest site of ecclesiological significance within *EG*—largest in terms of its density and the number of issues pertaining to it—is that concerning the need to overcome excessive centralism and to deepen the relationship between the papacy and the college of bishops. Here Pope Francis has already taken certain steps, including: (1) restructuring the current synod process into a two-stage affair that allows for greater deliberation and local consultation;[39] (2) strongly encouraging the bishops to bring the concerns and perspectives of their particular and local churches to clear voice within the synod process without fear of recrimination;[40] (3) identifying the need for the juridical status of national and regional bishops' conferences and their ordinary teaching authority to be strengthened (see *EG* 32);[41] (4) appointing eight senior cardinals from different regions of the world church, together with the secretary of state, to advise on the governance of the church (the "C9"); and (5) initiating a comprehensive review of the workings of the Roman curia and seeking to eliminate career curialism.[42] In each case, however, there is still further work to be done.

As regards the synod of bishops, quite apart from such practicalities as to how often the synod should meet, in what format, and with what modes of prior consultation, the key issue that has yet to be addressed is whether it should move from being a purely consultative body to being a genuinely deliberative body.[43] A number of related issues come into play here: Does a deliberative function for the synod already properly belong to it as an expression of the college of bishops? Or must deliberative power be delegated to it by the papacy? If the latter, does this imply that such delegation could later be revoked? And behind this lies the crunch question of all: Were the synod to be accorded a fully deliberative function, how would this cohere with the primacy of the Bishop of Rome as head of the college?

Would it imply the possibility both of limits being placed on the initiating function of the Bishop of Rome and of there being an appropriate mechanism for resistive pressure from the college of bishops acting against the papacy's own limiting function?[44] Can formal Catholic theology and canon law, as currently configured, be shown to allow for such possibilities? Or would one or both have to be reconfigured and, if so, on what basis? Again, following Pope Francis's lead and the developed strategy of receptive ecumenism, what fruitful learning in transposition might Catholicism here pursue in relation to other traditions? Similar questions as have been provoked here by focusing on the synod of bishops could be asked throughout in relation to the C9 group of key cardinal advisors; and for its own part, it should be noted that the receptive ecumenical question is pertinent to practically every other question posed throughout this entire subsection of the chapter.

In turn, these questions about the relationship between papacy and collegiality arising out of a focus on the synod could be pressed further in two directions. On the one hand is the question as to what models and mechanisms there might be for preserving a properly executive function for the papacy in a context in which genuine forms of deliberative power were to be operative within the college of bishops. Could, for example, Catholic theology and canon law develop in such a direction as would allow the college (or the synod, or any formally representative group of bishops on behalf of the college) to bring a proposal for consideration to a given pope as head of the college on up to three occasions before that pope could rule it out of court for the duration of his papacy (or a shorter time if deemed appropriate)?[45] Similarly, might it develop in such a direction as would correlatively require the pope to bring any significant proposed innovation with bearing on the universal church for consideration by the college or its representatives?[46]

On the other hand, there is the question as to what voting system would be employed if a deliberative function were indeed to be associated with the synod. Presumably in this day and age this would be an electronic system? If so, this could be extended to the entire episcopate, at least in relation to crucial matters. This would provide both a means for efficiently consulting the entire episcopate in relation to the mind of the ordinary magisterium— for which no mechanism currently exists—and an alternative to gathering the bishops in full council, which is now almost certainly impractical with over five thousand bishops in the world.

As regards the desire to enable the voices and concerns of the local churches to be heard more clearly at the level of the universal church, encouraging the bishops to speak with boldness and confidence is all well and good, as too is the prospect of strengthening the juridical status and teaching authority of bishops' conferences. But we need not be naive about the differential power distribution between Rome and the local churches, nor blind to the further structural changes required before diocesan bishops and local bishops' conferences will feel confident in voicing criticism to Rome. This is particularly so in light of the history of reprisals that has been taken since the Council in situations in which Rome judged that the voice and initiative of the local church needed to be reined in. This all comes to focus in the current system of centralized episcopal appointments, which acts as a highly effective mechanism for exerting centralized control over the local churches. What is required here is exploration and testing of appropriate means of returning episcopal appointments to the local churches while preserving appropriate Roman involvement and potential veto *in extremis*.[47]

Let us move now beyond asking where the initiatives already set in train by Pope Francis might need to develop further, and turn to consider some pertaining to the vitality of Catholic life at the level of diocese and parish alike, which, while their desirability is highlighted in *EG*, are not yet on his implementation list. One nodal issue here—in some respects analogous to those pertaining to the papacy-college issue—relates to the decision-making structures that exist at parish and diocesan levels: their nature and status. Is it conceivable for laity to be accorded a genuinely deliberative role while preserving the appropriate executive functions of parish priest and bishop, respectively? By what criteria and by whom should decisions be made as to whether a given member of the faithful is a reliable witness to the *sensus fidelium*? By what criteria and through what processes should the local church and parochial community seek to discern and make good judgements?

Also significant here, although in a more formal manner, is the question of appropriate structures and procedures for genuinely representative and whole-church theological consultation at the levels of dioceses (particular church), bishops' conferences (local church), and universal church.[48]

In turn, another nodal point relates to ordained ministry and the range of issues involved here, such as the hot-button questions of access to ordained ministry relative both to the ordinary requirement of celibacy within Western Rite Catholicism and to the restriction of ordination to men throughout the Catholic Church (as similarly throughout the Orthodox churches). As regards the former issue—essentially a disciplinary matter, supported by the theology, spirituality, and pastoral practice of ordained ministry that have grown up around it—Pope Francis is reported as having already indicated his willingness, in conversation with a Brazilian bishop, to engage requests from bishops' conferences to reconsider the current discipline, indeed as encouraging such requests to be made.[49] By contrast, as earlier indicated, as regards the restriction of ordination to men, he follows in line with the two previous papacies in regarding this as closed to discussion (*EG* 104). Given, however, its relationship to some of the other issues already touched on here, this last point is worthy of brief comment.

The formal Catholic position currently rests with John Paul II's 1994 letter *Ordinatio Sacerdotalis*, where his argument essentially comes down to the church not judging herself authorized to introduce such innovation into the tradition.[50] This was underlined the following year with a letter from the Congregation for the Doctrine of Faith (CDF). Here it was maintained that while the issuing of *Ordinatio Sacerdotalis* was not itself intended as an act of papal infallibility, the teaching it articulates is nevertheless to be understood as coming under the infallibility pertaining to the ordinary magisterium of the universal teaching of the Catholic bishops and, as such, is to be held as absolutely binding and utterly closed.[51] It is not clear, however, that things are as straightforward here as this would suggest.

First, while it is certainly conceivable that this is indeed the universal teaching of the Catholic bishops in such a fashion as brings it under the infallibility of the ordinary magisterium, the earlier noted problem is that currently there is no way of knowing this with certainty, given that there is no efficient and canonically authenticated means of ascertaining what the universal teaching of the bishops is on a given subject.[52] Moreover, while it is clear that neither of the previous two papacies—nor, it would seem, the current papacy—has been prepared to countenance the ordination of women, the combination of the highly divisive nature of the issue, the depth of feeling it arouses, and the fact that thus far it has not been allowed full airing within Catholic conversation suggest that even were it possible to devise an appropriate means of ascertaining the universal teaching of the bishops, it would at this point be pastorally and theologically imprudent—even illegitimate—to push the matter through to infallible status. If from the perspective of the formal magisterium the point is to make clear that for the foreseeable future the church has no intention of doing other than reject the possibility of ordaining women, then there are ways of doing this that stop short of binding the church to absolute closure in such a fashion as would make heretics of those who are of a different conviction and who are still exploring how this might in fact be done with Catholic integrity.

More generally, Catholicism would do well to seek to regain, strengthen, and further develop a broader set of strategies for classifying and handling disputed questions beyond a tendency to an overly bald polarity between the seemingly open and innocuous, on the one hand, and the absolutely closed, on the other hand. Inadequate in this regard is the overly broad and underdefined, yet now common, appeal to the notion of "definitive teaching." While this is generally used by the CDF to refer to teaching that is judged as needing to be taken very seriously even though it is recognized that no infallible judgment has been pronounced in its regard, the CDF does not thereby intend to suggest that there is any legitimacy to continuing debate in such regards. On the contrary, the intention is to support and enforce the prevailing judgement of the CDF on given issues by moving them, even while full consideration is de facto still in train, into apparent company with those matters already settled, seeking thereby to close down consideration prematurely.[53]

Alongside these hot button questions concerning access to ordained ministry, other questions also exist, albeit at somewhat cooler temperatures, concerning existing patterns of ordained ministry within Catholicism and whether these might evolve to allow for the kinds of part-time nonstipendiary and local ordained ministry that we find in other traditions, such as Anglicanism. In such traditions, a mixed economy prevails, with part-time non-stipendiary and local ordained ministers working alongside full-time salaried ordained ministers. Given the frequently parlous state of parochial and diocesan Catholic finances even in affluent countries such as the United Kingdom, this is an issue with direct practical bearing on the aforementioned possibility of an unexceptional married priesthood within Western Rite Catholicism.

Similarly there are questions as to whether there are also other ministerial models in other traditions, such as the formal office of reader within Anglicanism and of lay preacher within Methodism, which could fruitfully be considered within Catholicism, thus allowing, for example, lay theologians and suitably qualified catechists and teachers of religious education to be commissioned and licensed to preach.

In turn, lying behind all such issues in Catholic culture and its default habits, structures, and practice of ministry, authority, and accountability, is the question of the lay-clerical relationship and the lack of an integrated theology of ministry in postconciliar Catholicism. Here the question is whether Catholic understanding of the lay-clerical relationship can be reconfigured in a way that does justice to the proper dignity of both while overcoming any suggestion of the destructive two-tier view of Christian existence that has so bedeviled Catholicism. The earlier noted binary tendencies in postconciliar Catholicism have been characterized by diametrically opposed approaches in this regard: one maintaining the necessity of an ontological distinctiveness that appears to elevate the ordained to the detriment of the laity; the other tending to flatten ecclesial ministry and so failing to account for the sacramental distinctiveness of the ordained.

Given how fundamental it is to so much else within Catholic life and how fulcrum the response given, of all the sites of required ecclesiological investigation prompted by *EG*, this presents as the logical first and most pressing. The conviction here is that the route to an understanding capable of integrating relevant Catholic conviction around it lies in the overcoming of the artificial distinction between the ordained as *representatio Christi* and as *representatio ecclesiae* and the articulation of ordained ministry as the authenticated, public, and sacramentally representative performance of Christ's one pluriform ministry in the Spirit-filled, charism-endowed body of the church. But that is to bring us to the limits of one contribution and the anticipation of another.[54]

Select Bibliography

Faggioli, Massimo. *Pope Francis: Tradition in Transition.* New York: Paulist Press, 2015.

Gaillardetz, Richard P. *An Unfinished Council: Vatican II, Pope Francis, and the Renewal of Catholicism.* Collegeville, MN: Liturgical Press, 2015.

Kasper, Walter. *Pope Francis' Revolution of Tenderness and Love: Theological and Pastoral Perspectives.* New York: Paulist Press, 2015.

Politi, Marco. *Pope Francis among the Wolves: The Inside Story of a Revolution.* New York: Columbia University Press, 2015.

Rausch, Thomas R., and Richard R. Gaillardetz, eds. *Go into the Streets! The Welcoming Church of Pope Francis.* New York: Paulist Press, 2016.

Wills, Gary. *The Future of the Catholic Church with Pope Francis.* New York: Viking, 2015.

Notes

1. Pope Francis, "*Evangelii Gaudium*: Apostolic Exhortation to the Bishops, Clergy, Consecrated Person, and the Lay Faithful on the Proclamation of the Gospel in Today's World," November 24, 2013 (henceforth *EG*), available at http://w2.vatican.va/content/francesco/en/apost_exhortations/documents/papa-francesco_esortazione-ap_20131124_evangelii-gaudium.html.

2. Pope Francis, "*Laudato Si*': Encyclical Letter on Care for Our Common Home," May 24, 2015, available at http://w2.vatican.va/content/francesco/en/encyclicals/documents/papa-francesco_20150524_enciclica-laudato-si.html.

3. See, e.g., Jorge Mario Bergoglio and Abraham Skorka, *On Heaven and Earth: Pope Francis on Faith, Family, and the Church in the Twenty-First Century*, ed. Diego Rosemberg, trans. Alejandro Bermudez and Howard Goodman (New York: Image, 2013 [2010]). Variously useful in this regard are Paul Vallely, *Pope Francis: Untying the Knots* (London: Bloomsbury, 2013); and Austen Ivereigh, *The Great Reformer: Francis and the Making of a Radical Pope* (New York: Henry Holt, 2014), pursuing different lines on the extent to which Bergoglio, following his controversial years as Jesuit Provincial in Argentina, underwent a significant conversion and strategic and theological reorientation.

4. CELAM, "Concluding Document," Aparecida, June 29, 2007.

5. In *EG* 25, he writes, "I want to emphasize that what I am trying to express here has a programmatic significance and important consequences. I hope that all communities will devote the necessary effort to advancing along the path of a pastoral and missionary conversion which cannot leave things as they presently are." For a selection of other papal addresses outlining his vision, see Pope Francis, *The Church of Mercy: A Vision for the Church*, ed. Giuliano Vigini (Chicago: Loyola, 2014).

6. See Paul D. Murray, "Searching the Living Truth of the Church in Practice: On the Transformative Task of Systematic Ecclesiology," *Modern Theology* 30 (2014): 251–81.

7. Significant here is Richard R. Gaillardetz, "The Francis Moment: A New Kairos for Catholic Ecclesiology; Presidential

Address to the Catholic Theological Society of America," *Proceedings of the CTSA* 69 (2014): 63–80, which focuses on Pope Francis's ecclesial vision across five key themes. For a first book-length systematic analysis of the pastoral concerns of this papacy and its ecclesial context, see Walter Kasper, *Pope Francis' Revolution of Tenderness and Love,* trans. William Madges (Mahwah, NJ: Paulist Press, 2015). In addition, readers may wish to consult Thomas R. Rausch and Richard R. Gaillardetz, eds., *Go into the Streets! The Welcoming Church of Pope Francis* (New York: Paulist Press, 2016); Richard P. Gaillardetz, *An Unfinished Council: Vatican II, Pope Francis, and the Renewal of Catholicism* (Collegeville, MN: Liturgical Press, 2015); Gary Wills, *The Future of the Catholic Church with Pope Francis* (New York: Viking, 2015); and Catherine Clifford, "Pope Francis' Call for the Conversion of the Church in Our Time," *Australian eJournal of Theology* 21, no. 1 (April, 2015): 33–55, esp. 46–54. Complementing each of these works, this chapter focuses less on the wider ecclesial vision and context of *EG*—although something of this is done in the second main section—and more on its specifically ecclesiological implications, in the formal, institutional, and doctrinal sense.

8. See Gaillardetz, *op. cit.*; compare Christoph Theobald, "The Theological Options of Vatican II: Seeking an 'Internal Principle of Interpretation,'" in *Vatican II: A Forgotten Future. Concilium* (2005/4), ed. Alberto Melloni and Christoph Theobald (London: SCM, 2005), 87–107.

9. Citing CELAM, "Concluding Document," 551.

10. In *EG* 17, we hear of the need for the "reform of the Church in her missionary outreach" and in *EG* 26, citing both Paul VI and Vatican II's Decree on Ecumenism, *Unitatis Redintegratio,* of the need "to make clear that renewal does not only concern individuals but the entire Church."

11. See "As part of his mysterious love for humanity, God furnishes the totality of the faithful with an instinct of faith—*sensus fidei*—which helps them to discern what is truly of God. The presence of the Spirit gives Christians a certain connaturality with divine realities, and a wisdom which enables them to grasp those realities intuitively, even when they lack the wherewithal to give them precise expression." *EG* 119; also 31, 139, 154, 198.

12. For further information, see the chapter by Tina Beattie in this volume.

13. See Pope St. John Paul II, "*Ut Unum Sint.* Encyclical Letter on Commitment to Ecumenism," May 25, 1995, available at http://www.vatican.va/holy_father/john_paul_ii/encyclicals/documents/hf_jp-ii_enc_25051995_ut-unum-sint_en.htm.

14. Among the welter of material stimulated in this regard by *Ut Unum Sint,* particularly useful is the series published by Herder & Herder: Michael J. Buckley, *Papal Primacy and the Episcopate: Towards a Relational Understanding* (New York: Crossroad, 1998); Hermann J. Pottmeyer, *Towards a Papacy in Communion: Perspectives from Vatican Councils I & II,* trans. Matthew J. O'Connell (New York: Crossroad, 1998); Phyllis Zagano and Terrence W. Tilley, eds., *The Exercise of the Primacy: Continuing the Dialogue* (New York: Crossroad, 1998); John R. Quinn, *The Reform of the Papacy: The Costly Call to Christian Unity* (New York: Crossroad, 1999).

15. Also "Nor do I believe that the papal magisterium should be expected to offer a definitive or complete word on every question which affects the Church and the world. It is not advisable for the Pope to take the place of local Bishops in the discernment of every issue which arises in their territory" (*EG* 16).

16. With reference to John Paul II's Motu Proprio, *Apostolos Suos* (May 21, 1998), available at http://w2.vatican.va/content/john-paul-ii/en/motu_proprio/documents/hf_jp-ii_motu-proprio_22071998_apostolos-suos.html. It is significant that in *EG*, Pope Francis frequently cites from the teaching documents of regional bishops' conferences, thereby de facto according them the status of authoritative teaching documents of the local church, see *EG* 51.

17. See Paul Vallely, "Tectonic Plates Are Shifting," *The Tablet* (November 21, 2015): 14–16; and Vallely, "The 2015 Synod and Beyond," *The Tablet* (November 28, 2015): 14–16.

18. The resonance here with Johann Adam Möhler's 1825 classic, *Die Einheit in der Kirche,* is notable. See *Unity in the Church or the Principle of Catholicism: Presented in the Spirit of the Church Fathers of the First Three Centuries,* ed. and trans. Peter C. Erb (Washington, DC: Catholic University of America Press, 1996), e.g., no. 32 (pp. 157–60), no. 5 (pp. 167–68), no. 46 (pp. 194–98), no. 48 (pp. 201–5), also no. 70 (p. 262). In his own contribution to this

special edition, Philip McCosker traces this to Bergoglio's time in Germany in 1986 pursuing potential research into the work of Romano Guardini.

19. E.g., in the context of inviting people "to be bold and creative in this task of rethinking the goals, structures, style and methods of evangelization in their respective communities," he emphasizes, "I encourage everyone to apply the guidelines found in this document generously and courageously, without inhibitions or fear" (*EG* 33; also 49).

20. See "The message of peace is not about a negotiated settlement but rather the conviction that the unity brought by the Spirit can harmonize every diversity. It overcomes every conflict by creating a new and promising synthesis. Diversity is a beautiful thing when it can constantly enter into a process of reconciliation and seal a sort of cultural covenant resulting in a 'reconciled diversity'" (*EG* 230). For "reconciled diversity" in ecumenical discourse, see Yves Congar, *Diversity and Communion*, trans. John Bowden (London: SCM, 1984 [1982]), 149.

21. The essential principle at work in receptive ecumenism is that in the context of mature dialogues, the current moment requires primary emphasis to be placed not on what the ecumenical other needs to learn from one's own tradition but on what one's own tradition can and needs to learn with dynamic integrity from the other. See Paul D. Murray, ed., *Receptive Ecumenism and the Call to Catholic Learning: Exploring a Way for Contemporary Ecumenism* (Oxford: Oxford University Press, 2008), particularly Murray, "Receptive Ecumenism and Catholic Learning: Establishing the Agenda," 5–25; also "Receptive Ecumenism and Ecclesial Learning: Receiving Gifts for Our Needs," *Louvain Studies* 33 (2008): 30–45; and "Introducing Receptive Ecumenism," *The Ecumenist: A Journal of Theology, Culture, and Society* 51 (2014): 1–8.

22. Also "Let us ask for the grace to rejoice in the gifts of each, which belong to all" (*EG* 99); and "We must never forget that we are pilgrims journeying alongside one another" (*EG* 244).

23. The clearest resonance of all with receptive ecumenism is to be found in Pope Francis's January 22 General Audience Address during the 2014 Octave of Prayer for Christian Unity: "It is good...to find in other Christians something of which we are in need, something that we can receive as a gift from our brothers

and our sisters. The Canadian group that prepared the prayers for this Week of Prayer has not invited the communities to think about what they can give their Christian neighbours, but has exhorted them to meet to understand what all can receive from time to time from the others." Available at http://www.vatican .va/holy_father/francesco/audiences/2014/documents/papa -francesco_20140122_udienza-generale_en.html.

24. E.g., someone with a preference for a highly traditional Catholic aesthetic and liturgy may nevertheless be in profound sympathy with the communion ecclesiology of Vatican II and its resituating of order within the body of the baptized, the pilgrim people of God; others who trenchantly maintain a hieratic understanding of the church and its teaching authority may be highly selective in their obedience to specific teachings around one or more of sexual ethics, the death penalty, or social justice, calmly considering the magisterium to be wrong and irrelevant on such matters.

25. Note that while all the statements made here are descriptively accurate of Rahner's theology, they do not by themselves represent a sufficient or comprehensive description, which would show him as transcending the very binary of which his opponents claimed him to be an exemplar. To take just one example, he was as influenced by his close reading of St. Bonaventure as he was by his reading of St. Thomas. Again, his work on penance was precisely in the mode of *ressourcement.*

26. For an earlier discussion of some of the tensions and options within Catholic theology since the Council, see Paul D. Murray, "Roman Catholic Theology after Vatican II," in *The Modern Theologians: An Introduction to Christian Theology since 1918*, ed. David F. Ford and Rachel Muers (Oxford: Blackwell, 2005), 265–86, esp. 265–70.

27. On Rahner, see n. 25 here. In the case of de Lubac, it is in turn notable that his work was shaped in key part through close engagement with and retrieval of St. Thomas's theology of grace. Indeed, given how deeply Augustinian St. Thomas himself was—with St. Augustine's writings acting as a constant source of authoritative reference—the binary categories that have infected too much of Catholic ecclesial and theological sensibility since

the 1970s represent a reductionist distortion of the authentic capacious richness of Catholic tradition.

28. By the 1990s, something of this mindset was frequently in evidence in the pages of *Concilium* and is reflected also in the title given to the volume of late interviews with Karl Rahner, *Faith in a Wintry Season: Conversations and Interviews with Karl Rahner in the Last Years of His Life*, ed. Paul Imhof and Hubert Biallowons, trans. Harvey D. Egan (New York: Crossroad, 1990).

29. A particularly clear and entertaining example of this provocative genre is Tina Beattie, *New Catholic Feminism: Theology and Theory* (London: Routledge, 2006).

30. Perhaps the best example of this is Francis A. Sullivan, *Creative Fidelity: Weighing and Interpreting the Documents of the Magisterium* (Mahwah, NJ: Paulist Press, 1996). In fact this represents a strategy far closer to that which characterized the work of Rahner in the 1940s and 1950s than does the stance of oppositional counterblast that later frequently appealed to—or became pejoratively associated with—his legacy. Among the younger generations of Catholic theologians who have pursued versions of this strategy, Richard Gaillardetz stands out.

31. One interesting example is James Alison, *Faith beyond Resentment: Fragments Catholic and Gay* (London: DLT, 2001). The work of Elizabeth A. Johnson, CSJ, has also been exemplary. As with all such classifications of theological types, this fourfold sketch of diverse modes of theological resistance to the hegemony of court *Communio* theology under John Paul II and Benedict XVI is not a description of pure forms. In reality, there is overlap and interrelationship between them, with a given theologian—as Rahner exemplifies—capable of adopting different modes on different occasions, in a context-specific way. Indeed, a proficient singer with range can switch keys even within the same song. Nevertheless, this fourfold sketch does articulate something of the range of fundamental stances and strategies characterizing the work of diverse theologians of resistance, at least at various points in their work.

32. See Kasper, *Pope Francis*, 9–13, in particular: "He doesn't fit into our scheme of progressive or conservative, which in the meantime has become somewhat worn-out and outdated," 9; and "He is a conservative, but a conservative who, just like John XXIII

and the subsequent popes down to Benedict XVI, knows that one can only preserve the heritage of tradition if one does not regard it like a dead coin that is passed on from hand to hand until, in the end, it is totally worn, or does not treat it like a beautiful museum piece stored in a glass case," 13. For a superb relevant discussion, see Eamon Duffy, "Who Is the Pope?" *The New York Review of Books,* February 19, 2015, 11–13.

33. Also Francis, "Address to the Leadership of the Episcopal Conferences of Latin America during the General Coordinating Committee," July 28, 2013, available at http://w2.vatican.va/content/francesco/en/speeches/2013/july/documents/papa-francesco_20130728_gmg-celam-rio.html.

34. See Leonardo Boff, *Church: Charism and Power. Liberation Theology and the Institutional Church,* trans. John W. Diercksmeier (London: SCM, 1985 [1981]).

35. See Paul Murray, "Redeeming Catholicity for a Globalising Age: The Sacramentality of the Church," in *Exchanges of Grace: Essays in Honour of Ann Loades,* ed. Natalie K. Watson and Stephen Burns (London: SCM, 2008), 78–91.

36. See Pope Francis, "Introductory Remarks by the Holy Father at the First General Congregation of the 14th Ordinary General Assembly of the Synod of Bishops," October 5, 2015, available at http://w2.vatican.va/content/francesco/en/speeches/2015/october/documents/papa-francesco_20151005_padri-sinodali.html.

37. For the most sustained articulation of this, see Pope Francis, "Address for the Conclusion of the Third Extraordinary General Assembly of the Synod of Bishops," October 18, 2014, available at https://w2.vatican.va/content/francesco/en/speeches/2014/october/documents/papa-francesco_20141018_conclusione-sinodo-dei-vescovi.html.

38. In his masterly, if demanding, work on the discernment of doctrinal development, John Thiel seeks to demonstrate *both* that the tradition provides good precedent for the discerning of the novel and the immediately, even persistently, discontinuous *and* that in such instances the instinct is ultimately to seek to integrate this with a reconfigured appreciation of the plain sense of the tradition; see John E. Thiel, *Senses of Tradition: Continuity*

and Development in the Catholic Faith (New York: Oxford University Press, 2002), particularly 100–128 and 3–30.

39. For Pope Francis's most developed comments at the time of writing on the place of the synod in the life of the church, see "Ceremony Commemorating the 50th Anniversary of the Institution of the Synod of Bishops," October 17, 2015, available at http://w2.vatican.va/content/francesco/en/speeches/2015/october/documents/papa-francesco_20151017_50-anniversario-sinodo.html.

40. See "Greeting of Pope Francis to the Synod Fathers during the First General Congregation of the Third Extraordinary General Assembly of the Synod of Bishops," October 6, 2014, available at http://w2.vatican.va/content/francesco/en/speeches/2014/october/documents/papa-francesco_20141006_padri-sinodali.html.

41. For initial discussion of some of the pertinent issues, literature, and historical precedent, see Michael J. Buckley, SJ, "What Can We Learn from the Church in the First Millennium?" in *The Catholic Church in the 21st Century: Finding Hope for Its Future in the Wisdom of Its Past,* ed. Michael J. Himes (Liguori, MO: Liguori, 2004), 11–28 (22–25); also Francis A. Sullivan, "The Teaching Authority of Episcopal Conferences," *Theological Studies* 63 (2002): 472–93.

52. See Pope Francis, "Presentation of the Christmas Greetings to the Roman Curia," December 22, 2014, available at https://w2.vatican.va/content/francesco/en/speeches/2014/december/documents/papa-francesco_20141222_curia-romana.html. For a sobering assessment of the difficulties facing any attempts at effective curial reform, see Franz-Xaver Kaufmann, "The Miseries of Roman Centralism," *ET Studies* 4 (2013): 253–62 (esp. 254–75), which concludes, "It would require almost superhuman powers, very loyal collaborators, highly successful teamwork, and support from the universal church for a Pope to bring about real reform of the Curia, according to the principles of 'good governance.'"

43. See James Coriden, "The Synod of Bishops: Episcopal Collegiality Still Seeks Adequate Expression," *The Jurist* 64 (2004): 116–36. As regards such practicalities as to how often the synod should meet and in what format, Gaillardetz proposes, "The

creation of a permanent synod of bishops with deliberative and not merely consultative authority, crafted according to the model of the synods of the eastern churches....One possibility would be to have a permanent synod comprised of all the metropolitan archbishops in the universal Church that would meet twice a year to deliberate with their head, the bishop of Rome, over matters of concern for the universal Church." Gaillardetz, "What Can We Learn from Vatican II?" in Himes, *Catholic Church*, 80–95 (93). A related issue provoked by the 2015 Ordinary Synod on the Family is as to who should be allowed to vote in synodal processes. Hitherto the determining factor had been assumed to be ordination. At the 2015 Synod, however, a consecrated religious brother was allowed to vote; thus appearing to open the way to nonordained lay participants more generally also being able to vote. Unfortunately, while the religious brother was invited to share in the vote, none of the participating religious sisters were so invited, thus raising the worrying prospect that while ordination may no longer be the deciding criterion, maleness nevertheless is.

44. See Patrick Granfield, *The Limits of the Papacy: Authority and Autonomy in the Church* (New York: Crossroad & DLT, 1987).

45. The inspiration for this proposal—requiring rigorous testing—lies in Church of England Anglican synodical practice wherein the house of laity and the house of clergy can bring a proposal to the house of bishops up to three times within a given period even if it is rejected by the house of bishops on the first two occasions. This allows for accountability and testing in each direction while preserving the executive function of the house of bishops.

46. This has some relevance for the 2015 Ordinary Synod on the Family, where the indications are that, had a deliberative vote been taken, then it would not have been in support of the innovation that Pope Francis appears to favor in relation to permitting divorced and remarried Catholics, in certain circumstances, to receive the Eucharist. Deliberative mechanisms can themselves be viewed as moments within broader processes of ecclesial discernment.

47. For initial discussion again see Buckley, "What Can We Learn from the Church in the First Millennium?" 12–19, which concludes, "If the present system for the selection of bishops is

not redressed, all other attempts at serious reform will founder";
and Catherine M. Mooney, "What Can We Learn from the Medieval Church?" in Himes, *Catholic Church,* 29–55 (29–38); also useful is Quinn, "The Appointment of Bishops and Christian Unity,"
in *The Reform of the Papacy,* 117–39; and Gaillardetz and John Huels,
"The Selection of Bishops: Recovering the Enduring Values of
Our Tradition," *The Jurist* 59 (1999): 348–76.

48. Compare "These structures, like the present International Theological Commission, must represent a genuine diversity of theological perspectives, and allow for legitimate and
respectful dissent from authoritative, non-infallible teaching."
Gaillardetz, "What Can We Learn from Vatican II?" 94.

49. See David Gibson, "Are Married Priests Next?" *America,*
April 25, 2014; see http://www.americamagazine.org/issue/are
-married-priests-next?lite.

50. See Pope St. John Paul II, "*Ordinatio Sacerdotalis:* Apostolic
Letter on Reserving Priestly Ordination to Men Alone," May 22,
1994, available at http://w2.vatican.va/content/john-paul-ii/en/
apost_letters/1994/documents/hf_jp-ii_apl_19940522_ordinatio
-sacerdotalis.html.

51. CDF, "Concerning the Reply of the Congregation for the
Doctrine of the Faith on the Teaching Contained in the Apostolic Letter *Ordinatio Sacerdotalis,*" October 28, 1995, available
at http://www.vatican.va/roman_curia/congregations/cfaith/
documents/rc_con_cfaith_doc_19951028_commento-dubium
-ordinatio-sac_en.html.

52. See Sullivan, "Guideposts from Catholic Tradition,"
America, December 9, 1995, 5–6.

53. See Paul D. Murray, "On Valuing Truth in Practice:
Rome's Postmodern Challenge," *International Journal of Systematic
Theology* 8 (2006): 163–83.

54. For an initial foray in this direction, now in process of
full articulation, see Paul D. Murray, "The Need for an Integrated
Theology of Ministry within Contemporary Catholicism: A Global
North Perspective," in *Ministries in the Church. Concilium* (2010/1),
ed. Susan Ross, Maria Clara Bingemer, and Paul D. Murray (London: SCM, 2010), 43–54.

5

"A Bride Bedecked with Her Jewels"

Understanding Inculturation and Popular Piety as a *Locus Theologicus* in *Evangelii Gaudium*

JACOB PHILLIPS

Introduction

The first two years of Francis's papacy featured a remarkable amount of attention from the Western media. This coverage proved striking not only through its sheer quantity, but also its quality. After a period in which the Catholic hierarchy was generally represented negatively by large segments of the media, to see a pope being positively praised was as surprising as it was—at times—bizarre and perplexing. In this chapter, I want to work from two popular conceptions about Francis in the discussions surrounding the early stages of his papacy—both with important ecclesiological subtexts—and cast some light on the issues at stake by examining *EG*. The first is an apparent "hermeneutic of rupture" between Pope Francis and Benedict XVI, where Francis is sometimes heralded as an antithesis to his predecessor. Of course anyone versed in the Catholic scene knows this to be an oversimplification, but establishing the precise nature of a "hermeneutic of continuity" between the two remains something of a challenge. Of course, my application of the language of "hermeneutics of continuity/discontinuity" draws directly on Pope Benedict XVI's analysis of the conciliar legacy given in his Christmas address to the curia in 2005, and in 2007's *Sacramentum Caritas*. Here, Benedict put forward the idea that *both* archtraditionalist and archprogressivist interpretations of the Council were guilty of the same hermeneutic: namely rupturing the Council from the centuries that preceded it, claiming it to be either a woeful and ultimately invalid break from authentic tradition in the first place, or a wonderful liberation from an inauthentic and misconstrued tradition in the second. To speak of a hermeneutic of continuity is to highlight reform over discontinuity, or "reform within tradition."[1] My contention is that we saw this shared hermeneutic underlying interpretations of the first months of Francis's papacy, with many commentators taking either an archtraditionalist or archprogressivist interpretation of Bergoglio as personifying a dramatic rupture with his predecessor.

The second conception I want to discuss involves Francis's oft-repeated condemnations of "proselytism,"[2] which have been praised ad infinitum by some secularly oriented voices. This is perhaps because seeking to convert people is often seen today as a particularly misguided expression of religious fervor. But Francis's condemnation of proselytism is sharply counterbalanced by his far more exuberant commendation of evangelization, which is nowhere more apparent than in *EG*. This leaves us with a question regarding where the boundary between proselytism and evangelization lies, or rather, how we might ensure that evangelization, or mission, does not slip into proselytism.

These two questions are related to two aspects of *EG*, and highlighting these aspects will show how both issues are interlinked. First, *EG* emphatically links evangelization with inculturation. Inculturation is clearly close to the heart of the "new chapter of evangelisation" Francis wants to instigate in this Apostolic Exhortation, for he claims it is "through inculturation" that the church "introduces peoples" into "her own community" (*EG* 1).[3] Looking closely at the notion of inculturation promises to shed some light on the apparent hermeneutic of rupture between Benedict and Francis. The former, Joseph Ratzinger, gained notoriety for criticizing this approach to evangelization, claiming "we should no longer speak of inculturation" during a speech in 1993 in which he articulates an alternative approach termed "inter-culturality."[4] Prima facie, this might appear to be a rupture between Francis and Benedict, but looking closely at the substance of *EG* will show that Francis has a complex standpoint on culture, which can accommodate some of Ratzinger's criticisms of certain cultural settings as inimical to Christian teaching, namely, the dominant culture of the West.[5] Second, it is clear from *EG* that, for Francis, the expression of faith in practices of popular piety constitutes a *nota veritatis* of genuinely authentic evangelization; he describes it as "a true expression of the spontaneous missionary activity of the people of God" (*EG* 123). Bearing in mind the difficulty of distinguishing between evangelization and proselytism, Francis's comments promise to show how to demarcate between the two. That is, popular piety is for him an exemplary instantiation of evangelization proper, and thus presumably free from what he associates with proselytism. Analyzing this issue through *EG*, it becomes clear that for Francis, popular piety is the fruit of healthy inculturation, precisely because it functions in evangelization in a way that challenges the inherent dangers of contemporary Westernized thinking. This will be seen below to be demonstrated particularly through popular piety's situatedness at the heart of concrete lived experience *in* faith, over against an abstract and conceptual understanding *of* faith, a feature that is exemplified in its prevalence among the poor. For the victims of the "economy of exclusion" (*EG* 53–54), abstract and idealized conceptions are less likely to usurp the urgency of lived reality.

In this sense, we can begin to understand how the two questions I seek to investigate connect: for, although Francis's appraisal of inculturation seems at first sight starkly to contradict Ratzinger's criticism of it, Francis's reasons for emphasizing inculturation are based on an unease about *Western* culture, specifically, and his unease about contemporary Western culture is actually shared by Benedict XVI/Joseph Ratzinger.[6] We shall see therefore that, when Francis strikingly describes the inculturated church as "a bride bedecked with her jewels"—quoting the Vulgate translation of Isaiah 61:10 (*sponsa ornata monilibus suis*)[7]—this should be understood by thinking of the church as a "*poor* bride," uncorrupted by the destructive effects of dominant Western thinking. That is, Francis contends the culture of the West threatens to deaden a "thirst for God" (*EG* 123)[8] through its aspirational promises of material contentment and prosperity, and he holds that this thirst can only be fulfilled by the joy of the gospel.

Inculturation and Interculturality

To commence with investigating the first issue of an apparent "hermeneutic of rupture" between Benedict and Francis on the issue of inculturation, I will first provide the necessary historical background for understanding this concept. This will disclose how inculturation has historically presupposed a generally optimistic view of human culture, considering culture itself as *by definition* able to host Christian teaching. From this, Benedict's critique of inculturation will be examined, showing his concern that certain cultures can be hostile to Christian teaching, and thus deficient in their potential to inculturate the faith. Benedict's alternative notion of "inter-culturality" can then be outlined, enabling us to ask if Francis's commendation of inculturation in *EG* constitutes a rupture from the teaching of his predecessor. This discussion will show that Francis's understanding of inculturation is actually highly nuanced, and his understanding of culture is closer to Benedict's than it seems due to a shared skepticism on the matter of Western culture. This suspicion of the West will then be shown to underlie Francis's affection for popular piety, explored in the second part of this chapter.

Before examining the concept of inculturation directly, it is necessary to bring into view some of the background to the discussions around this concept, which stem from the Vatican II's Pastoral Constitution on the Church in the Modern World, *Gaudium et Spes* (*GS*). To this end, I want to highlight a certain ambiguity in the way the word *culture* is understood in that document, for we shall see this ambiguity resurfaces in the discussions surrounding inculturation, and indeed arguably perdures in *EG* itself.[9] Article 53 of *GS* states, "The word 'culture' in its general sense indicates everything whereby man develops and perfects his many bodily and spiritual qualities." It also defines some of those qualities as including "the goods (*bona*) and values (*valoresque*) of [human] nature" (*GS* 53). In this explicit definition of *culture*, the word is being interpreted in its classical sense. It originates in the Latin *cultura*, which is an agricultural term referring to the cultivating of plants and crops, and in *GS*, *culture* means "cultivation": fostering the goods and values of human nature into fruition, culture as that which edifies.

However, there are good grounds to suggest that—implicitly at least—there is another understanding of culture at work in *GS*, which, rather than seeing culture as intrinsically edifying, acknowledges that certain cultures can be misguided or even destructive. This issue comes to the fore when the document lists various positive aspects of the so-called culture of modernity and then sounds a note of caution for each, with a corresponding corrective impulse from the conciliar fathers. For example, the fact that "historical studies tend to make us view things under the aspects of changeability and evolution" is praised, but shortly afterward, the question is asked, "How is the dynamism and expansion of the new culture to be fostered without losing the living fidelity to the heritage of tradition?" (*EG* 54, 56). The definition of *culture* at work here seems more ambivalent than the explicit definition that considers culture to be inherently edifying, for the "culture of modernity" seems to involve both positive and negative facets. The implicit definition of *culture* at work in *GS* therefore seems closer at times to a definition like T. S. Eliot's, who defines the word straightforwardly as referring to "all the characteristic activities and interests of a people."[10] A mere collection of "characteristic activities and interests" can of course work for good or ill, unlike that which intrinsically edifies the "goods and values" of human nature.

We shall see shortly that this ambiguity bears directly on discussions surrounding inculturation, which depends in part on an optimistic approach like *GS* 53. Before looking at this, it needs to be borne in mind that the ambiguity of *GS* has been highlighted by some who present the thinking of Benedict XVI to provide a stark alternative. One example is Tracey Rowland, who considers the document to exhibit an "explosive problematic." She also urges the church to question its optimism about the culture of modernity and adopt a countercultural position to the dominant thinking of the secularized West.[11] Rowland orients her position firmly with the *Communio* school, quoting Benedict XVI at length,[12] mentioning his comment that cultures "cannot be saved" except through Christ, who is "the repudiation of evil."[13] Moreover, Rowland is not only critical of the culture of modernity, but draws in other non-Christian cultures, mentioning the "pantheistic or polytheistic 'traditional wisdom' of pre-Christian cultures" as those viewed too positively by *GS*.[14] She therefore asserts that *GS*'s optimistic view of culture as that which edifies human nature should be questioned, insofar as cultures can be deeply antithetical to the business of evangelization. For Rowland, it seems that Ratzinger's early criticism of the language surrounding free will in *GS* 17 (as "downright Pelagian") is connected to issues surrounding culture through a broad interpretation of his condemnation of the document's "optimistic atmosphere."[15]

The ambiguity highlighted above impacts on the concept of inculturation, because inculturation presupposes an essentially positive or optimistic view of culture, seeing different cultural settings as all able to bring Christ to birth in their own terms, or in terms of their distinctive means of cultivating the goods and values of human nature. However, inculturation becomes problematic if we define culture more ambivalently and acknowledge that some cultures might be hostile to Christ, a position Rowland associates with Benedict XVI. If Benedict's thinking is antithetical to inculturation, and Francis approaches evangelization as inculturation in *EG*, maybe we have a specific point of rupture between the two after all, challenging my attempt to establish a hermeneutic of continuity between them. To see if this is indeed the case, we need to examine the concept of inculturation more closely to discern exactly what it means.

The term *inculturation* is generally thought to have developed from two concepts in cultural anthropology: acculturation and enculturation. *Enculturation* usually refers to the process by which children learn the rudiments of acceptable social behavior and the collective expectations that enable them to function in the culture where they are growing up, or the process by which someone coming into contact with a new culture undergoes "the process of socialisation into that new culture."[16] The prefix *en-* indicates that this refers to the process of becoming "cultured" *in* terms of a specific community. The second related word, *acculturation*, refers to a contact between two cultures, and specifically the changes that result from this contact, where one culture is altered or adjusted *to* another, in becoming a-cculturated to it.[17] *Inculturation* arose originally in a theological context, for as acculturation presupposes two cultures, it would not suffice for describing contact with a new culture through evangelization, because the gospel is not merely a culture. Moreover, as enculturation presupposes an individual approaching a new or alien culture as a *tabula rasa*, it would not suffice for evangelization, because with the latter a specific message is being brought to life in a new cultural context. This bringing to life resonates with the doctrine of the incarnation, and so the *in-* of inculturation directly points to the incarnation, and we shall see shortly that this is intrinsic to its meaning.

The first formal definition of *inculturation* is commonly held to be found in the writings of the former Superior General of the Society of Jesus, Pedro Arrupe. Arrupe was Superior General of the Order between 1965 and 1983, and after Jorge Bergoglio was ordained a Jesuit priest in 1969, he worked under Arrupe as the provincial of Argentina from 1973. Although the dynamics of their professional relationship are complex,[18] the appraisal of inculturation in *EG* evinces the general tenor of the Order under Arrupe's leadership, insofar as Francis mentions the "legitimate autonomy" of culture (referencing *GS*) and calls the content of the gospel "transcultural" (*EG* 115, 117). To understand how these sentiments connect with the genesis of the term *inculturation* in Arrupe's writings, let us consider first that, when Arrupe took the helm of the Order, he had the task of leading the Jesuits through the upheavals following Vatican II. An indication of how far reaching these upheavals were is provided by his description of the General Congregations of the Society of Jesus that took place on either side of the Council, in 1965 (while the Council was still in session) and then subsequently in 1974–75. Arrupe describes how, in 1974, the church was rather different from 1965, and he maintains that this was when *inculturation* was "born."[19] He relates that the common language had been Latin at the 1965 meeting, but by 1974, the Jesuits were speaking in their respective vernaculars, so there was suddenly a plethora of tongues in use. Now the Jesuits were operating in deep plurality, and this is perhaps why Arrupe began at this juncture to present inculturation as an approach for evangelizing that is sensitive to the polyphonic and multivalent diversity of global humanity.

Arrupe offers a definition of *inculturation* that has since become classic. He writes,

> The fundamental and valid principle is that inculturation is the incarnation of Christian life and of the Christian message in a particular cultural context, in such a way that this experience not only finds expression through elements proper to the culture in question (this alone would be no more than a superficial adaptation), but becomes a principle that animates, directs and unifies the culture, transforming and remaking it so as to bring about a "new creation."

He goes on, "The Christian experience is that the People of God...lives in a definite cultural space and has assimilated the traditional values of its own culture."[20]

Arrupe is concerned that evangelization should not superimpose alien elements of culture on its host setting. Rather, the gospel should be incarnated in the terms of the host culture and expressed in a manner proper and authentic to it. He envisages that this should ultimately lead to a point whereby the gospel serves as the central pivot of the host culture itself, being disclosed as its intrinsic essence, the point to which this culture is implicitly directed through its distinctive cultivating of the goods and values of human nature. We can therefore see how this resonates directly with the explicit definition of culture in *GS*, as that which edifies. Arrupe envisages different cultures as each seeking to bring human nature to bear fruit, and the best fruit of being human to be exhibited in the person of Christ. Therefore, all cultures are—for Arrupe—in some way gesturing toward Christ himself.

Arrupe asserts that inculturation is deeply linked with the Jesuit charism, linking it with St. Ignatius of Loyola's maxim: *Non cohiberi a maximo, contineri tamen a minimo, divinum est.* We could translate this as, "Not to renounce the greatest, but be concerned with the least, is holiness." Arrupe claims this "challenges us to

119

hold on to the concrete and particular, even to the last cultural detail, but without renouncing the breadth and universality of those human values which no culture, nor the totality of them all, can assimilate and incarnate in [a] perfect and exhaustive way."[21] By this, Arrupe means that the task of an evangelizer is to focus his or her attention on the specific circumstances of the cultural context in question—however lowly and unpromising—being fully attentive to the work of human beings being edified through that context. That is, to locate what *GS* calls the "goods and values" of human nature that are being cultivated by that people. Yet, in doing so, an evangelizer is commended not to surrender to the particular, and certainly not to surrender to anything like relativism. Rather, he or she should trust that in this specific context, genuinely universal human values can be disclosed, values that perhaps might not be disclosed in the same way in any other context.

Arrupe also refers to a link between inculturation and the *Spiritual Exercises*, citing the 106th exercise, from the meditations on the birth of Christ and the mysteries of the incarnation. Here, a retreatant is encouraged to enter into the mystery of Jesus's birth by imagining the three divine persons of the Blessed Trinity looking down "upon the face and circuit of the world, filled with people" and how they, "on seeing that all were going down to Hell," then "decreed in their eternity that the Second Person would become human to save the human race."[22] Arrupe is drawing a parallel here between the breadth of the range of evangelization as inculturation, and the breadth of range of the incarnation of Jesus Christ: being for all people in all times and places. The implication is that—just as no one is excluded from the outpouring of God's love in the incarnation—no *culture* is excluded from bringing Christ to birth in its own terms, from incarnating the gospel as the heart of its own cultivation of the goods and values of human nature. So there is here a clear difference between Pedro Arrupe's understanding of culture, resting on the explicit definition of *GS*, and the Ratzinger presented by Rowland, who highlights the hostility to Christ of some cultures. Moreover, Arrupe's classically Jesuit approach to evangelization as inculturation resonates strongly with *EG*, which claims for example that "each portion of the people of God" translates "the gift of God into its own life and in accordance with its own genius" (*EG* 122). To see if this genuinely constitutes a "rupture" from his predecessor, we need now to discern why Ratzinger is critical of inculturation, and to delineate his alternative approach that he terms "inter-culturality."

In order to define *interculturality*, it is necessary to point out that Benedict XVI is of course indelibly marked by the German intellectual tradition, which has its own trajectory of interpreting culture through the distinctively German concepts of *Kultur* and *Bildung*, particularly.[23] On the basis of this inheritance, it was perhaps inevitable that Benedict would critique inculturation, for it involves a far less sophisticated awareness of the radical differences between cultures, and their being inextricably intertwined with diverse temporal and geographical factors. For this reason, Benedict challenges a notion of inculturation that assumes the gospel is somehow *extra*-cultural, or what Francis terms "trans-cultural" (*EG* 117), and thus capable of being "inserted" into any other setting. He holds that we cannot suppose the gospel is "faith stripped of culture," and claims there is no such thing as "naked faith."[24] Moreover, he claims that the cultures that missionaries or evangelizers come into contact with are unavoidably interrelated with religious commitments and faith orientations. He writes, "In all known historical cultures, religion is the essential element of culture, indeed it is its determining core."[25] He therefore maintains there are problems with the concept of inculturation, because by inculturating the gospel into another cultural context, what he calls two "organisms" (each with their own respective intertwining of religious and cultural elements) come into contact, and so "it is difficult to see how a culture, living and breathing the religion with which it is interwoven, can be translated into another religion without both of them going to ruin."[26] That is, he claims, if "you implant" a "new" and "Christian heart" into a host culture, it is unavoidable "that the new organism…will reject the foreign body."[27]

It is for precisely this reason that Benedict makes the comments that seem very different to the position articulated in *EG*. He asserts that "we should no longer speak of inculturation but of the meeting of cultures or 'inter-culturality,' to coin a new phrase."[28] He goes on to criticize inculturation as "artificial and unrealistic" for presuming "a faith stripped of culture is transplanted into a religiously indifferent culture whereby two subjects, formerly unknown to each other, meet and fuse."[29] So the task for this chapter is now to assess whether or not Benedict's interculturality genuinely contradicts or challenges the inculturation Pope Francis speaks of as an "imperative" bearing on the readers of his Apostolic Exhortation. The *inter-* of interculturality refers to a thoroughgoing interchange or intercourse between two organisms, one of which has grown around the gospel, so that a "profound evolution" occurs by way of mutual interpenetration, which he terms a "successful transformation."[30] What is necessary for this, Benedict claims, is that the host culture, with which the gospel-rooted culture interrelates, is directed to the "truth." Benedict presents the directedness to truth of human cultures as demonstrative of an innate thirst driving human endeavor, a thirst that is a universal endowment of human nature. He writes that the human being is "touched in the depth of his [or her] existence by truth," and this points to a "fundamental openness of each person toward the other" that "can only be explained by the hidden fact that our souls have been touched by truth." He claims that "this explains the essential agreement which exists even between cultures most removed from each other."[31] Indeed, there are good grounds to consider truth as the cohesive theme of Benedict XVI's oeuvre, from his discussion of the Scholastic *verum est ens* (Being is truth) in *Introduction to Christianity*, right up to the discussion of his episcopal motto "co-worker in truth" in his final autobiographical work, *Last Testament*.[32]

In this, we can see Benedict presenting a sort of collective cultural version of the Augustinian *inquietum,* where the resting place of the human soul is the place of *truth,* toward which human cultures are directed to varying degrees. With this he is drawing on the work of Theodor Haeckel, who presented the great cultures of antiquity as pointing to Christ in their pursuit of the truth, a characteristic he called *adventistischen Heidentum* (adventistic paganism).[33] Ratzinger claims that Christ is the epitome of truth, saying that "Christian faith is certain that in its core it is the self-disclosure of truth itself."[34] Insofar as Ratzinger's interculturality is presented by him as a stark alternative to inculturation (which he dismisses as "artificial and unrealistic"), there still seems to be a rupture between his thinking and that of Pope Francis.

Bearing in mind Ratzinger's view that certain cultures are directed to the truth, however, Rowland's interpretation of his thinking appears somewhat injudicious. Ratzinger is not as antithetical to all non-Christian cultures as she claims, and so there does not seem to be an outright contradiction between Ratzinger and Francis, but rather a relatively subtle difference of nuance based on their differing intellectual and ecclesial contexts. The fundamental issue here is whether or not Francis approaches inculturation as necessitating an entirely optimistic view of culture, and whether he can accommodate a certain ambiguity toward culture, as *GS* does implicitly, and Benedict does explicitly under the aegis of truth. On this front, for all Francis's commendations of inculturation, he does differ from Arrupe—and sits closer to Ratzinger—in his marked pessimism about certain aspects of contemporary *Western* culture. In *EG*, there are criticisms of "the prevailing culture" (*EG* 62), regarding which Francis's criticisms can be linked to both sides of the *Non cohiberi* maxim. First, the *maximo* that Arrupe translates as pointing to "the breadth and universality" of "human values," is undermined by what Francis describes as a situation where "each person wants to be a bearer of his or her own subjective truth," meaning "it becomes difficult for citizens to devise a common plan which transcends individual gain and personal ambitions" (*EG* 61). Second, the *minimo*, which Arrupe describes as "the concrete and particular, even to the last cultural detail,"[35] is undermined by Francis's comments about Western-led globalization, for he claims that "in many countries globalisation has meant a hastened deterioration of their own cultural roots and the invasion of ways of thinking and acting proper to other cultures which are economically advanced but ethically debilitated" (*EG* 62). It is clear that Francis considers the prevailing Western model as bearing negative, unedifying facets. This same stance is also prevalent throughout *LS* (nos. 27, 51), and in his comments on Western "cultural tendencies" affecting family life in *AL* (no. 41).

Francis criticizes the prevalence of Western technology in connection with this, quoting Paul VI's comment that "technological society has succeeded in multiplying occasions of pleasure, yet has found it very difficult to engender joy" (*EG* 7), and Francis's unease about the "globalisation of the technological paradigm" is also expounded at length in *LS* (nos. 106–14). Perhaps surprisingly, this directly resonates with the speech in which Benedict XVI is most critical of inculturation. Benedict criticizes the over-simplification involved in dismissing all evangelization of other cultures in history as mere imperialism and colonialism (though elsewhere he acknowledges the mistakes involved as well).[36] He gives two examples of attempts to untangle the apparent imposition of European culture on other nations, including the *teología India* of Latin America, which sought to rediscover and perpetuate the indigenous religiosity of the American continent prior to European imperialism.[37] But the important point is not that the ancient culture this movement seeks to rediscover is primitive or inferior, but that seeking what he terms "a simple return to the past"[38] is problematic because the geographical settings of these movements are already unavoidably infiltrated by Western technology. He claims that, for the peoples of Latin America, "the diffusion of technological civilisation is irrevocable," and that "modern civilisation is not mere multiplicity of knowledge and know-how" but "deeply encroaches upon the basic understanding of man, the world and God." His concern, then, is the selectivity of seeking to disentangle European impositions and return to ancient expressions of culture, while "at the same time, technology, though nonetheless Western, is passionately adopted and exploited."[39] It is this intrinsic dislocation that constitutes the problem for Ratzinger, in that Western heritage is divided "into the useful, which one accepts, and the foreign, which one rejects," and moreover insofar as Western technology promises mastery over the world, its endurance in the context of an indigenous culture fosters the world-mastering tendencies inherent in that original culture.[40] Ratzinger includes both means of world mastery as forms of "magic in the broadest sense of the word."[41]

We thus see a certain harmoniousness between Francis and Benedict here, in that both want to preserve what is *true* in evangelized cultures, and see contemporary Western, technological globalization as a potentially dubious element effecting cultures elsewhere. Now that we have grasped how Francis understands inculturation, and how his approach is closer to Ratzinger's than it seems at first glance, we can begin to see why he speaks of the church made up of evangelized cultures as "a bride bedecked with her jewels." That is, he claims that, in taking up "the values of different cultures," these become the jewels of the *sponsa ornata*. This harmoniousness is based on Ratzinger's and Francis's respective suspicions of the contemporary West, and turning to the second issue I outlined in the introduction, we shall see how this suspicion is related to the latter's condemnation of proselytizing.

Popular Piety

Francis considers popular piety to be the result of authentic inculturation at its best, particularly in *EG*'s subsection "The Evangelising Power of Popular Piety" (nos. 122–26).[42] He argues that "once the Gospel has been inculturated in a people, in their process of transmitting their culture, they also transmit the faith in ever new forms," and claims that "herein lies the importance of popular piety, a true expression of the spontaneous missionary activity of the people of God" (*EG* 122). It is in the practices of popular piety, for Francis, that we can "see how the faith, once received, becomes embodied in a culture" (*EG* 123), so we can discern that the establishment of pious practices is, for him, a *nota veritatis* of effective inculturation. That is, to quote Arrupe, when the Christian message relates to a positive "host" setting, it becomes "a principle that animates, directs and unifies the culture, transforming and remaking it so as to bring about a 'new creation,'"[43] and for Francis this issues in distinctive forms of popular catholic devotionalism. The question arises here as to what practices Francis has in mind. He mentions "mothers tending their sick children" who "cling to a rosary" and "the hope poured into a candle lighted" with "a prayer for help from Mary" and "the gaze of tender love directed to Christ crucified" as three examples (*EG* 125). So Francis considers popular piety to include Marian devotions, which are often localized (as with Our Lady of Guadalupe or England's Walsingham, for example), and things like novenas or pilgrimages in honor of national or local saints. I would suggest that the Divine Mercy Devotion of the Polish nun St. Faustina

Kowalski seems particularly apposite here, considering Francis's affection for Divine Mercy Sunday and his calling of a Jubilee Year of Mercy commencing in Advent 2015.[44]

My question is how passing on the faith through practices like those just mentioned might give us some insight into distinguishing between evangelization and proselytism. Francis recently raised eyebrows by saying in an interview that "proselytism is solemn nonsense, it makes no sense" (*Il proselitismo è una solenne sciocchezza, non ha senso*).[45] Despite various attempts to discern what this means, and how it might be squared with his evangelizing zeal,[46] a conclusive answer has not yet been forthcoming. But we can shed some light on this issue by examining some of Francis's comments about popular piety, such as his assertion that it "discovers and expresses [the content of the faith] more by way of symbols than by discursive reasoning, and in the act of faith greater accent is placed on *credere in Deum* than on *credere Deum*" (*EG* 124). This *credere* distinction comes from Aquinas, who distinguishes believing *in* God (a living, relational, and dynamic faith), and believing *that* God exists (a proposition about God).[47] Given Francis's affection for "the evangelising power of popular piety," and his association of this piety with Thomas's *credere in Deum*, there are good grounds to explore the possibility that *credere Deum* is related to what he terms proselytism: to proselytize is to try and gain an assent from others to propositional, conceptual knowing "that"—rather than believing "in." The distinction between a living and relational knowledge and a propositional conceptual knowledge is reminiscent of John Henry Newman's distinction between "notional" and "real" apprehension" in *An Essay in Aid of a Grammar of Assent*.[48] Although Francis is not himself drawing on Newman in *EG*, he would surely applaud Newman's assertion that "simple assent" (or believing "in" lived realities) is more important than "complex assent" (or believing "that" interrelated conceptual propositions are true). For Newman, the priority of simple assent is related to the fact that belief "in" lived realities can become a motive for "faithful obedience,"[49] whereas holding "that" conceptual propositions are true does not. This is closely related to Newman's concern for the industrial poor in the context of Victorian Britain, who would be largely uneducated or "unlearned," and for whom complex assents are simply not at stake. He considers that the "learned" have lost sight of simple assent through a preoccupation with establishing the theoretical validity and verifiability of things like the doctrine of the Trinity, and seeks to redress the balance by asserting that simple assent is "*imperative* on learned as well as unlearned."[50] For Newman, complex, inferential theological deliberations are seen as *having* to follow from simple assent to religious truth. Indeed it is worth mentioning here that Newman himself bore a long-standing affection for the popular piety of his day, as evinced by argument that "the theologian should respect the Neapolitan crone chattering away to a crucifix, for beneath her seeming idolatry lies a kernel of true devotion."[51]

We can glean from bringing Newman into this discussion why Francis considers proselytism to make no sense. This is because to posit conceptual, propositional truths apart from their rootedness in lived relationality is to argue for second-order truths without the first order of simple and fundamental grounding from which they follow. This is exemplified further in Francis's discussion of "reality and ideas," which Zampini Davies has discussed in chapter 10 in relation to Catholic social teaching. Francis argues that "[r]ealities simply are, whereas ideas are worked out," and that "realities are greater than ideas." He claims that "conceptual elaborations—are at the service of communication, understanding and praxis," but "ideas disconnected from realities" are "capable at most of classifying and defining, but certainly not calling to action," mirroring almost exactly Newman's comment about simple assent being able to lead to faithful obedience. Francis goes on to claim that "religious leaders" may lack followers "because they are stuck in the realm of pure ideas."[52] If popular piety is a locus of evangelizing power and a sign of effective inculturation through being emblematic of *credere in Deum* over against *credere Deum*, fleshing this out with Newman's *Grammar* allows us to see that proselytism is, for Francis, about being "stuck in ideas" over against realities, and allowing realities to fall out of view through a preoccupation with "conceptual elaborations." In short, he is calling the church back to something like Newman's simple assent, for he claims that in the preoccupation with ideas, some have "left simplicity behind" (*EG* 232). Evangelization over proselytism, then, is about the simplicity of lived faith that we see at its fullest in popular piety.

Conclusion

EG envisages an outwardly directed, evangelizing church that can inculturate the faith in manifold cultural contexts, and flourish in forms proper to different peoples so the values of the diverse collective members of the human family become like the jewels bedecking the church as bride. But we would be doing Francis an injustice if we left the discussion here, for he implies that the church is not merely to be understood as a bride, but as a *poor* bride, bringing in one of the most pervasive themes of his writings and speeches: the love of the poor. The *sponsa* image comes from Isaiah 61:10, but it should be recalled that this verse of Isaiah provides a mariological type for Luke's Magnificat, where the former's statement "my soul rejoices in my God" is applied to the "lowly handmaid" Mary.

By mentioning the Marian element to Francis's exhortation here, it becomes necessary briefly to situate my argument in relation to Beattie's subsequent chapter, which highlights an incongruity between Francis's occupation with "the 'fleshy' devotions of popular religiosity (*EG* 90)" when "female fleshiness bars women from speaking…in the context of the Mass, which is at the very heart of Catholic devotional life."[53] Francis's description of "mothers tending their sick children" who "cling to a rosary," and so on, might well be considered a bit "soft focus" or even trite, but Beattie's observation is more serious insofar as it might lead to an interpretation of Francis's love of popular piety as an avoidance of calls for reexamining the role of women in the church. Such a contentious and complex set of issues cannot be dealt with fully here, although it is worth mentioning that Francis's call for a more "incisive" role for women in the church, for example, would seem to lead naturally toward involvement in homiletics.[54] But, it is important to bear in mind that, for Francis, the domestic, social, worldly, or "fleshly" realm and the sphere of popular devotionalism are by no means secondary to liturgy and the sacraments proper. Francis's theology is predicated on the center of gravity of Christian life being self-sacrificial service of others ("the most important thing is the person in front of you"[55]), and the formative, nourishing, and vivifying practices of piety that feed into that service. In fact, a notable differentiation between Francis and his predecessors is the degree to which he is far less eucharistically centered than John Paul II and Benedict XVI.[56] This is important because if the Eucharist is not so much the center of Christian life compared to ethical immediacy of the "person in front of you," and this immediacy is brought into pious practices far more readily than the celebration of the Mass (hence the mothers tending their sick children who cling to a rosary), then the issues surrounding a sacerdotal role are arguably placed on a different footing. That is, for Francis, service of others is the "source and summit" of Christian life, and ministering to the needs of others is something from which no one is precluded. Indeed, Francis's frequent and sharp condemnations of clerical-ism should also be read from this viewpoint: those in priestly min-istry should wield no sense of sacramental power or privilege.

To return to my focus in this section—examining Francis's love of the poor—we soon see this reveals further links between inculturation and popular piety, which allows us to discern why the poor are so central to Francis's wider vision, because it is through the example of the piety of the poor that we can redis-cover something like what Newman calls "simple assent."

Pope Francis claims that the "missionary impulse" he wants to instigate should "above all" be directed at "the poor," meaning "those who are usually despised and overlooked, 'those who can-not repay you' (Luke 14:14)" (EG 48). He quotes Benedict XVI in describing the poor as "the privileged recipients of the Gospel," and claims "there is an inseparable bond between our faith and the poor" (EG 48n52). Moreover, later in the document, he con-nects this centrality of the poor explicitly with popular piety—the supreme exemplar of authentic inculturation—quoting Paul VI's comment that popular piety "manifests a thirst for God which only the poor and simple can know" (EG 123n100). He makes some bold claims in this connection, maintaining that "expressions of popular piety have much to teach us; for those who are capable of reading them, they are a *locus theologicus* which demands our attention" (*EG* 126). So in what way is popular piety a *locus theologicus* in *EG*?

The point here seems to be twofold. First, insofar as the poor are inhibited by their earthly circumstances from participation in the privileged business of intellectual inquiry (Newman's "notional assent," Francis's "conceptual elaboration," or Thomas's *credere Deum*), looking to devotional practices among the poor will enable us to avoid getting ensnared in trying to proselytize people into assenting to ideas and propositions. This can be seen in Francis's comment that popular piety works "more by way of symbols than discursive reasoning," and his highlighting of the need to approach the practices of popular piety with an "affective connaturality born of love" (*EG* 126). Second, however, and perhaps more challengingly, *EG* presents the poor as those closest to God, on account of "a thirst for God which only [they] can know" (*EG* 123n100). This is a thirst for joy, which can be discerned in popular piety particularly, because the poor are not caught up in what Francis calls the contentment of "prosperity" that "deadens" us (*EG* 54). That is, dominant Western culture, with its aspirational promises of material comfort, personal fulfillment, and self-realization, deadens the thirst for God that can meet its fulfilment only in the joy of the gospel. For this reason, Francis commends us to look to the "poor and simple" to free us from the "prevailing culture." In doing so, we are provided with an image of the church as a *poor* bride bedecked with her jewels, with the values of diverse peoples flourishing through the gospel, and issuing forth in popular devotionalism. This is a church with the poor and simple at the center: proclaiming words of joy over against the empty happiness of the economy of exclusion.

Select Bibliography

Arrupe, Pedro. *Jesuit Apostolates Today: An Anthology of Letters and Addresses III*. Edited by Jerome Aixala, SJ. Anand, India: Sahitya Prakash, 1981.

Lemna, Keith, and David H. Delaney. "Three Pathways into the Theological Mind of Pope Francis." *Nova et Vetera* 12, no. 1 (2014).

Newman, John Henry. *An Essay in Aid of a Grammar of Assent.* South Bend, IN: Notre-Dame Press, 1979.

Phillips, Jacob. *Mary, Star of Evangelization: Tilling the Soil and Sowing the Seed.* Mahwah, NJ: Paulist Press, forthcoming.

Ratzinger, Joseph. *Christianity and the Crisis of Cultures.* San Francisco: Ignatius Press, 2006.

Rowland, Tracey. *Culture and the Thomist Tradition after Vatican II.* London: Routledge, 2003.

Vallely, Paul. *Untying the Knots.* London: Bloomsbury, 2013.

Notes

1. See chap. 6 by Tina Beattie in this volume, which highlights how "reform" was substituted for "continuity" in Benedict's writing between 2005 and 2007.

2. Pope Francis's comments about proselytism occurred in an interview with Eugenio Scalfari in the Italian newspaper *Repubblica,* http://www.repubblica.it/cultura/2013/10/01/news/papa_francesco_a_scalfari_cos_cambier_la_chiesa-67630792/.

3. For more examples of Pope Francis's ongoing concern with culture, cf. the integration of culture into ecology as "integral ecology" in *Laudato Si'* 143–46 and *Amoris Laetitia* 3.

4. Joseph Ratzinger, "Christ, Faith and the Challenge of Cultures," Speech to the Presidents of the Asian Bishop's Conference, March 1993, http://www.ewtn.com/library/CURIA/RATZHONG.HTM.

5. On this point about Western culture, specifically, Francis's attitude to culture in *EG* seems closer to the definition used in the World Council of Churches document *Teaching towards Life* than Kim concludes in chap. 8 of this volume.

6. Joseph Ratzinger will be referred to as Benedict XVI throughout this chapter, although the key texts being used predate Ratzinger's enthronement in 2005.

7. Image taken from the Vulgate trans. of Isa 61:10, quotation from John Paul II, n92 *EG* 116.

8. Quoting Paul VI, n100, *EG* 123.

9. This analysis of *GS* is discussed in more detail in my book, *Mary Star of Evangelization: Tilling the Soil and Sowing the Seed,* forthcoming from Paulist Press.

10. T.S. Eliot, *Notes toward a Definition of Culture* (London: Faber & Faber, [1948] 1962), 31.

11. Tracey Rowland, *Culture and the Thomist Tradition after Vatican II* (London: Routledge, 2003), 11.

12. Ibid., 37.

13. Ibid.

14. Ibid., 23.

15. Ratzinger in *Das Zweite Vatikanische Konzil: Dokumente und Kommentare,* ed. Herbert Vorgrimler, vol. 3 (Freiburg: Herder, 1968) 313–54; translated as *Commentary on the Documents of Vatican II,* vol. 5 (New York: Herder and Herder, 1969), 115–63.

16. Peter Schineller, *A Handbook on Inculturation* (New York: Paulist Press, 1990), 22.

17. Ibid.

18. Cf. Paul Vallely, *Untying the Knots* (London: Bloomsbury, 2013), 52–56.

19. Pedro Arrupe, *Jesuit Apostolates Today: An Anthology of Letters and Addresses III,* ed. Jerome Aixala, SJ (Anand, India: Sahitya Prakash, 1981), 171.

20. Ibid., 173.

21. Ibid., 176.

22. Ignatius of Loyola, *The Spiritual Exercises of Ignatius of Loyola,* trans. Michael Ivens, SJ (London: Gracewing, 2004), 33.

23. For a basic but accessible discussion of these concepts, cf. Peter Watson, *The German Genius* (London: Simon & Schuster, 2010).

24. Ratzinger, "Christ, Faith and the Challenge of Cultures."

25. Ibid.

26. Ibid.

27. Ibid.

28. Ibid.

29. Ibid., wording altered slightly as original erroneously has "formally" in place of "formerly."

30. Ibid.

31. Ibid.

32. Joseph Ratzinger, *Introduction to Christianity* (London: Burns & Oates, 1969), 34; Benedict XVI and Peter Seewald, *Last Testament*, trans. Jacob Phillips (London: Bloomsbury, 2016), 241.

33. Theodor Haeckel, *Vater des Abendlandes* (Leipzig: 1931); analogous standpoints toward Greco-Roman culture are of course found as far back as the church fathers, and in the twentieth-century in C. S. Lewis, but the focus on *truth* as the "adventistic" element of ancient pagan cultures is taken from Haeckel.

34. Ibid.

35. Arrupe, *Jesuit Apostolates Today*, 176.

36. He states that "in the history of evangelisation, there were certainly mistakes, about this no one would disagree," in Joseph Ratzinger, "Some Reflections on the Encyclical Letter Fides et Ratio," a speech given at St. Patrick's Seminary, New York, 1999, http://www.ratzinger.us/modules.php?name=News&file=article&sid=105.

37. Joseph Ratzinger, "Christ, Faith and the Challenge of Cultures."

38. Ibid.

39. Ratzinger, "Some Reflections."

40. For the background to this discussion, see Ratzinger's discussion of *techne* in his genealogy of knowledge in the opening chapter of *Introduction to Christianity*, 30.

41. Ibid.

42. This is of course rooted in the Argentinian movement of *teología del pueblo* (theology of the people), associated particularly with Juan Carlos Scannone, SJ. See Scannone's article, "Pope Francis and the Theology of the People," *Theological Studies* 77, no. 1 (2016): 118–35, and Keith Lemna and David H. Delaney's "Three Pathways into the Theological Mind of Pope Francis," *Nova et Vetera* 12, no. 1 (2014): 25–56.

43. Arrupe, *Jesuit Apostolates Today*, 173.

44. For an excellent discussion of the Divine Mercy devotion, see Alana Harris and Jane Garnett, "Canvassing the Faithful: Image, Agency and the Lived Religiosity of Devotion to the Divine Mercy," in Giuseppe Giordan and Linda Woodhead, eds., *Prayer in Religion and Spirituality* (Leiden-Boston: Brill, 2013), 77–102.

45. Scafari interview, see note 2 above.

46. Cf. John L. Allen Jr., "When Pope Francis Rips 'Proselytism,' Who's He Talking About?" *Crux*, January 27, 2015, *passim*, http://www.cruxnow.com/church/2015/01/27/when-francis -rips-proselytism-whos-he-talking-about/.

47. *S.Th.*, II–II, q.2, a.2.

48. John Henry Newman, *An Essay in Aid of a Grammar of Assent* (South Bend, IN: Notre-Dame University Press, 1979), 15ff.

49. Ibid., 108, 115, and 122.

50. Ibid., 131, my emphasis.

51. Discussed by Sheridan Gilly in "Life and Writings," in *The Cambridge Companion to John Henry Newman*, ed. Terrence Merrigan and Ian Ker (Cambridge: Cambridge University Press, 2009), 1–28, at 24.

52. Ibid., 231–33, 111–12; this same standpoint is seen in *Amoris Laetitia* 2, where Francis criticizes "an attitude that would solve everything by applying general rules or deriving undue conclusions from particular theological considerations."

53. See chap. 6 by Tina Beattie in this volume.

54. John L. Allen Jr., "Pope Wants 'Capillary and Incisive' Role for Women in Church," *National Catholic Reporter*, January 25, 2014, https://www.ncronline.org/blogs/francis-chronicles/ pope-wants-capillary-and-incisive-role-women-church.

55. Vallely, *Untying the Knots*, 112.

56. John Paul II's Encyclical *Ecclesia de Eucharistia* (2003) and Joseph Ratzinger, *The Spirit of the Liturgy* (San Francisco: Ignatius Press, 2003).

6

Transforming Time

The Maternal Church and the Pilgrimage of Faith

TINA BEATTIE

In section 3 of *Evangelii Gaudium,* Pope Francis lists "four principles related to constant tensions in every social reality" that must be addressed in the quest to build just and peaceful communities. These principles are the following: time is greater than space; unity prevails over conflict; realities are more important than ideas; and the whole is greater than the part (*EG* 221). I focus primarily, though not exclusively, on the first of these principles—"time is greater than space." I see this as crucial to understanding Francis's ecclesiology, his spirituality, and his style of leadership, and it provides the interpretive context for the other three principles.

The restoration of a sense of temporality to the church's doctrine and mission is a subtle but radical way of reanimating the historical, contextual ecclesiology of the Second Vatican Council, which gave way to more static and absolutist doctrinal principles under the papacies of John Paul II and Benedict XVI. However, Francis emphasizes the importance of a mystical dimension to his contextualized vision of the church in time. This suffuses what might otherwise be simply another political/liberationist ecclesiology with a profound awareness of the timeless otherness and mystery of God glistening darkly through and beyond all our time-bound endeavors, doctrines, and theologies, most sublimely encountered in the theophany of the Mass. This is why we need to weave together the two metaphors of pilgrimage and motherhood, journeying and gestating, that shape his vision of the church.

Psychoanalysts identify the adult's imagined infant relationship with the maternal body as the source of repressed fears and desires, but also as that aspect of imagination and creativity that eludes the control of the conscious, rational mind. The maternal, Marian aspect of the church has always been expressive of the mystical dimension of Catholic consciousness and of the paradoxical intimacy in otherness of Catholic liturgy and devotion. It has also inspired the most sublime (and some of the most ridiculous!) examples of Catholicism's cultural and artistic forms of expression. When this dimension is emphasized at the expense of historical and contextual realities, then we risk a form of infantilized escapism. However, if we overemphasize the historical and contextual without the mystical and sacramental, then we reduce the Christian life to one of political activism.

With this in mind, I begin by commenting briefly on the conflicted ecclesiology of the postconciliar church, before going on to explore the relationship between time and space in *EG* and in some of Francis's other published interviews and homilies. Finally, I ask how far his preferred metaphor of the maternal, Marian church coheres with this sense of history as salvation and as the self-revelation of God in the time of human becoming. I am aware that the significance of Mary for ecclesiology and redemption remains one of the most vexed issues dividing churches within the broad Orthodox/Catholic spectrum from those within the equally broad Protestant/evangelical spectrum. It is beyond the scope of this essay to explore these issues, but I acknowledge the bemusement that some evangelicals might feel on reading what follows.

Conflicted Ecclesiologies in the Postconciliar Church

Two opposing factions have emerged among Catholics since the Council, operating with divergent interpretations of tradition.

This is reflected in the debate sparked by Pope Benedict XVI when, in a lecture on hermeneutics to the Roman curia in December 2005, he contrasted "a hermeneutic of discontinuity and rupture" with "the hermeneutic of reform."[1] Citing these terms a couple of years later in his 2007 Apostolic Exhortation *Sacramentum Caritatis*, he substituted "continuity" for "reform," so that the emphasis on a hermeneutic of continuity eclipsed the language of reform.[2] Francis is clearly with the reformers, but he offers the church a potentially deeper and richer theology than either the progressivist and liberationist movements of the 1970s and 1980s, or the doctrinally rigid and romanticized nuptial ecclesiology that was the dominant theological trend under Pope John Paul II in particular.

The gendered relationship between the maternal church and the fatherhood of God has been a near-constant feature of Catholic ecclesiology arguably since the Letter to the Ephesians,[3] but it is difficult to find any such gendered language in the writings of Catholic theologians from the late 1960s to the 1980s.[4] It returned with a vengeance in John Paul II's nuptial ecclesiology and theology of the body, and with the promotion of Hans Urs von Balthasar rather than Karl Rahner as the magisterium's theologian of choice—a shift that was at least in part a reaction against feminism, homosexuality, and women's ordination.[5] Yet even if this reactionary trend is open to criticism, it also invites reflection on how the Council continues to be interpreted in response to the rapidly changing global context in which we find ourselves. Did Vatican II throw both mother and baby out with the bath water?

The Council's abandonment of the idealized ecclesiology of Vatican I in favor of an image of the church as the pilgrim people of God has fueled a progressive ecclesiology, often driven by Western liberal ideas of progress and democracy informed by a rationalized and politicized understanding of faith. While many liberals and liberationists have embraced this modernizing change, some feminists as well as conservatives have expressed dismay at the loss of the maternal ecclesiology of the preconciliar church. For example, Catholic feminist Charlene Spretnak, in her book *Missing Mary*, appeals for a rediscovery of the Catholic Church as "a container and guardian of mysteries far greater than itself." She observes, "We who once partook of a vast spiritual banquet with boundaries beyond our ken are now allotted spare rations, culled by the blades of a 'rationalized' agenda more acceptable to the modern mindset."[6] Von Balthasar, an archrival of feminism, writes of the church since the Council as having "put off its mystical characteristics" and becoming preoccupied with meetings, structures, and organizations dominated by political theology. This is, he says, "more than ever a male Church, if perhaps one should not say a sexless entity, in which woman may gain for herself a place to the extent that she is ready herself to become such an entity." He goes on to ask, "May the reason for the domination of such typically male and abstract notions be because of the abandonment of the deep femininity of the Marian character of the Church?"[7]

I ask how far Francis is able to bring about some reconciliation between a politically engaged, historically contextualized church in solidarity with the poor, and a more traditional ecclesiology of the maternal church as an organic body of gestation, nurture, and spiritual growth, redolent with a sense of sacramental mystery. In order to address these questions, we have to appreciate that it is impossible to separate the style from the substance of Francis's theology, so let me say a little about Francis's theological style in the context of the themes I am addressing.

Francis's Ecclesiology: A Mother on the Move

If Benedict XVI could be described as one of the church's last great modern theologians, Francis is surely one of her first great postmodern theologians. He is a communitarian mystic, a narrative theologian who seeks truth in the carnivalesque exuberance of popular devotions and the faithful inconsistency of ordinary Catholics doing their best and often getting it wrong. In the press conference at the launch of *EG*, Archbishop Claudio Maria Celli, president of the Pontifical Council for Social Communication, drew attention to "the simple, familiar and direct language which has been the hallmark of the style that has emerged in the months of [Francis's] pontificate."[8] Francis's narrative style is earthed in the lives of the poor, in such a way that it is impossible to separate his personal experience of Latin America from his theological concerns. If Benedict's church was the church of Christ enthroned in glory far above the squalor and struggle of earthly existence, Francis's is the church of Jesus the Galilean, the barefoot storyteller trudging through the heat of the day in the midst of the people.

Everywhere we look, Francis's God is on the move. In one of his daily Mass reflections, he speaks of encountering God "walking, walking along the path," and he describes the mystery of the incarnation as "a history of walking...the Lord is still saving us in history and walking with his people."[9] His encyclical *LS* extends this to encompass the whole of creation moving toward its fulfilment. We are, says Francis, "journeying towards the sabbath of eternity....In union with all creatures, we journey through this land seeking God" (*LS* 243).

Without directly criticizing his predecessors, Francis is unleashing doctrine from its moorings in absolutist and closed spaces of interpretation, setting it free to journey and develop through time with and for the people of God, constantly open to new interpretations and revelations in the context of different cultures and changing circumstances. This explains his insistence that "realities are greater than ideas" (*EG* 231; see also *LS* 110). Ideas must be connected to realities. They must, says Francis, be "at the service of communication, understanding, and praxis" (*EG* 232). Evangelization requires an incarnational reality, the reality "of a word already made flesh and constantly striving to take flesh anew" (*EG* 233). He refers to this as "the unruly freedom of the word" (*EG* 22).

Alongside this metaphorical dynamism is the language of fecundity—the fruitfulness of the maternal church. The word *fruitful* appears repeatedly in *EG*. "An evangelizing community is," writes Francis, "always concerned with fruit, because the Lord wants her to be fruitful" (*EG* 24). We are called to be "mysteriously fruitful" (*EG* 280) by surrendering our desire to plan and control our lives and trusting the guidance of the Holy Spirit. He quotes Isaac of Stella, who writes that every Christian is in a way "believed to be a bride of God's word, a mother of Christ, his daughter and sister, at once virginal and fruitful" (*EG* 285).[10]

This is the metaphorical terrain within which my chapter is situated—journeying and fruitfulness. Francis paints a prismatic image of the story of salvation that is at one and the same time a journey through time, a process of gestation and growth like the child in the womb, and a fecundity of living like the maternal body. In all these images, the human individual in his or her cultural context and the body of the church are involved in a continuous process of movement, development, and change. So let me turn now to consider how this plays out in the context of his claim that "time is greater than space."

Time Is Greater Than Space

As Philip McCosker rightly cautions in chapter 3,[11] we cannot push Francis's contrast between time and space too far or take it literally, because we never experience time without space. However, we need to remember that Francis is not concerned with presenting theology as a series of systematic arguments or rational propositions. His language is poetic and evocative, a colorful assemblage of metaphors intended to evoke a response and inspire action among ordinary people, rather than an exercise in intellectual persuasion for theological elites. In *EG*, he affirms the importance of doing theology "in dialogue with other sciences and human experiences," but goes on to caution against "a deskbound theology" that forgets the church's raison d'être of evangelization (*EG* 133).

In privileging time over space, Francis seeks to balance the "constant tension...between fullness and limitation. Fullness evokes the desire for complete possession, while limitation is a wall set before us" (*EG* 222). To experience ourselves in time is to accept the limitation of each passing moment, without ever losing sight of the connectedness of time that draws us forward in hope. It is to be patient in order to cope with failure and finitude, to remain conscious of the promise of the future while dealing with the inevitable difficulties and obstacles of the present. It enables us to live, says Francis, "poised between each individual moment and the greater, brighter horizon of the utopian future as the final cause which draws us to itself" (*EG* 222). To give priority to time is to be "concerned about initiating processes rather than possessing spaces. Time governs spaces, illumines them and makes them links in a constantly expanding chain, with no possibility of return" (*EG* 223).

By contrast, the sociopolitical activity of our present world order is, Francis argues, sometimes dominated by the privileging of space over time—by short-term goals that result in "madly attempting to keep everything together in the present, trying to possess all the spaces of power and of self assertion." This is, he says, "to crystallize processes and presume to hold them back" (*EG* 223). Francis's concern throughout *EG* is with the temporal processes by way of which human endeavors bear fruit and seeds of transformation are given time to develop and grow in the incarnational contexts of people's lives. Space precludes any in-depth exploration of the intellectual hinterland to Francis's understanding of the question of time and space—a question that was a major preoccupation of early twentieth-century thinkers such as Henri Bergson, Sigmund Freud, and Marcel Proust, and of course Martin Heidegger. However, it is worth noting that, in the interview he gave in September 2013 to Antonio Spardaro, SJ, editor in chief of the Italian Jesuit journal *La Civiltà Cattolica*,[12] Francis refers to the little-known French novelist Joseph Malègue (1876–1940). Malègue was deeply influenced by Bergson,[13] so at least implicitly we might detect early-twentieth-century phenomenological concerns with the nature of time in relation to space, even if these influences should not be exaggerated.

A more important factor in Francis's emphasis on time and process is the significance of discernment for the formation of Ignatian spirituality—a theme to which he repeatedly returns. In the Spadaro interview, he says that "the wisdom of discernment redeems the necessary ambiguity of life." Also in that interview, he touches on the theme of time and space, of process, in the context of revelation in history and of history as revelation. He observes that "we must initiate processes rather than occupy spaces. God manifests himself in time and is present in the processes of history. This gives priority to actions that give birth to new historical dynamics. And it requires patience, waiting." Themes of patience and mercy go hand in hand with those of process and discernment. In the Spadaro interview, Francis speaks of patience in terms of "the common sanctity" of the people of God. In *EG*, he argues that "evangelization consists mostly of patience and disregard for constraints of time" (*EG* 24). Those who accompany others in faith "need to accompany with mercy and patience the eventual stages of personal growth as these progressively occur" (*EG* 44). Mercy, then, is intrinsic to the related themes of process, patience, and discernment. If we want to see how all this finds practical expression in Francis's style of leadership, we might consider his declaration of 2016 as a Holy Year of Mercy, in the context of the second of his four principles—"unity prevails over conflict" (*EG* 226–30).

The Holy Year of Mercy followed upon the two Synods on the Family, in October 2014 and October 2015. By calling these a year apart, Francis initiated a process in 2014 that brought to the surface all the tensions, conflicts, and challenges that have been fermenting among the church's leaders in recent years. This is a quest for healing and harmonization not through the avoidance of conflict, but through facing it head on and going through a tense and painful process of seeking resolution. By declaring 2016 a Year of Mercy, Francis seeks to shift the church from a journey of intense but necessary struggle, to a journey of forgiveness and reconciliation.

This is a model of church leadership that makes manifest his fundamental theological beliefs about time and space, discernment and process, patience and mercy. Respect for process leads him to seek a middle road—neither an artificially imposed unity nor an irreconcilable conflict, but a process of struggling toward reconciliation, toward a solidarity that, "in its deepest and most challenging sense,…becomes a way of making history in a life setting where conflicts, tensions and oppositions can achieve a diversified and life-giving unity" (*EG* 228). Whether or not this is a Hegelian view of history depends on how we read Hegel.[14] Francis's vision of history is not in any sense directed toward the overcoming of diversity. It is rooted in "the conviction that the unity brought by the Spirit can harmonize every diversity" (*EG* 230). This is not only a movement between peoples but also within ourselves. Citing Gospel passages that refer to the unity, peace, and reconciliation offered by Christ, Francis observes that "the locus of this reconciliation of differences is within ourselves, in our own lives, ever threatened as they are by fragmentation and breakdown. If hearts are shattered in thousands of pieces, it is not easy to create authentic peace in society" (*EG* 230).

Mystery and Eternity

This emphasis on history, context, and process could be described as the horizontal dimension of Francis's theology, exploring as it does the immanent aspect of God from the perspective of the temporality and materiality of human existence. However, Francis is a mystical theologian and a Thomist, and this means that all his reflections on the human in creation are immersed in the mystery of the Creator. His emphasis on the importance of time and process entails at every turn a radical openness to the God who comes to meet us, who interrupts us on the way, who renders mysterious the mundane realities of time and space by penetrating them with an unfathomable and eternal otherness.

In his proclamation of the Holy Year of Mercy, Francis takes the refrain from Psalm 136—"For his mercy endures forever" (*MV* 7).[15] The repetition of this refrain, he says, "seems to break through the dimensions of space and time, inserting everything into the eternal mystery of love" (*MV* 7). This is not a dissolution of God's eternal being into the process of human becoming. It is rather a codependent duality of time—a call to discern the timeless presence of God within the temporal affairs of history. In the Spadaro interview, Francis acknowledges that his insistence on the need to encounter God in the present, "walking, along the path," might be interpreted as a form of relativism. It would be relativism if it amounted to "a kind of indistinct pantheism," but not if we understand it in the biblical sense, "that God is always a surprise, so you never know where and how you will find him....You must, therefore, discern the encounter. Discernment is essential."

The Christian life, as Francis portrays it, is a journey to the far horizons, lived out on the edge of the receding horizon of eternity. He tells Spadaro, "You cannot bring home the frontier, but you have to live on the border and be audacious." This call to be audacious means being creative and imaginative, and it also means embracing the risk and the doubt of faith. Like St. Augustine, we must "seek God to find him, and find God to keep searching for God forever." Our journeying is often a journey where we feel blind, but it is also a journey in which God comes to meet us in our quest—"God is always first and makes the first move."

History unfolds as salvation and participates in the mystery of God without that mystery ever collapsing into the mundane. Yet all we can know of God we discover through contemplation on the self-revelation of God as history. This comes together in a vivid and intense way in the theophany of the Mass, where we encounter God as really present. In a daily Mass reflection, Francis speaks of "putting ourselves…in God's time, in God's space, without looking at our watches. The liturgy is precisely entering into the mystery of God."[16] This acute sensitivity to the mystery and otherness of God gives Francis a deeper theological perspective than that of many postconciliar liberal theologians. In the Spadaro interview, he expresses his closeness to Jesuit mystics such as Louis Lallement, Jean-Joseph Surin, and Peter Faber. He links this to "the mystical dimension of discernment [that] never defines its edges and does not complete the thought."

In all this, however, we might ask how Francis accounts for the inescapably spatial dimension of incarnation—material bodies occupy spaces even as they are caught up in the slipstream of time as it flows toward the mystery of God. Here, we have to turn not only to Francis's passionate concern for social justice engaged with the messy realities of material life in its poorest and most abject situations, but also to his insistence upon the incarnational significance of cultures and local communities.

Culture and Incarnation

Francis speaks of "a *mystical* fraternity, a contemplative fraternity," constituting "a fraternal love capable of seeing the sacred grandeur of our neighbour, of finding God in every human being" (*EG* 92). This refers to the vocation to neighborly love and social justice, but it can also be read in the context of Francis's emphasis on culture as the privileged locus of incarnation. Inculturation flourished in the aftermath of Vatican II, with the widespread adaptation of liturgies to accommodate local forms of cultural expression. However, this trend enjoyed little support and was at times actively obstructed during the papacies of John Paul II and Benedict.[17]

According to Francis, "The People of God is incarnate in the peoples of the earth, each of which has its own culture" (*EG* 115). As individuals, we derive our identities and our experience of God within our different cultures, for "grace supposes culture, and God's gift becomes flesh in the culture of those who receive it" (*EG* 115). It is interesting to note how Francis substitutes culture for nature here, in the more familiar Thomist axiom that grace supposes nature.

The Holy Spirit works to bring communion and harmony within and among our diverse cultures, but evangelization requires inculturation—the adaptation of the Christian message so that it reflects and transforms the cultures within which it is incarnate. Once again, we see the importance of history and temporality for this vision: "Culture is a dynamic reality which a people constantly recreates; each generation passes on a whole series of ways of approaching different existential situations to the next generation, which must in turn reformulate it as it confronts its own challenges" (*EG* 122).

For Francis, communities and cultures constitute the incarnate living out of the history of salvation. In the Spadaro interview, he says that "no one is saved alone, as an isolated individual, for God draws us to himself through the complex web of interpersonal relationships which constitute the human community. God enters into this dynamic of the people." This is the context in which we need to understand his references to popular piety as "the people's mysticism…a spirituality incarnated in the culture of the lowly" (*EG* 124)—terms that he takes from the Aparecida document of which, as Cardinal Bergoglio, he was one of the main authors.[18] Popular piety is, he says, a "*locus theologicus* that demands our attention" (*EG* 126).

We can explore Francis's emphasis on the significance of culture in the context of the fourth of his principles—"the whole is greater than the part"—where he addresses the "innate tension… between globalization and localization" (*EG* 234). To reconcile the particular and the global requires us to affirm different cultures and contexts without getting caught up in the glitter of "an abstract, globalized universe" or turning our culture "into a museum of local folklore…incapable of being challenged by novelty or appreciating the beauty which God bestows beyond their borders" (*EG* 234). This means we need "to sink our roots deeper into the fertile soil and history of our native place, which is a gift of God. We can work on a small scale, in our own neighbourhood, but with a larger perspective" (*EG* 235).

This theological vision of a temporal, communal, incarnational unfolding of the story of salvation is woven upon the loom of the doctrine of the Trinity. Human beings are essentially relational with regard to one another and to God, working through the Holy Spirit: "the very mystery of the Trinity reminds us that we have been created in the image of that divine communion, and so we cannot achieve salvation or fulfilment purely by our own efforts" (*EG* 178). Cultural diversity is not a threat but, when open to the Holy Spirit, participates in the "perfect communion of the blessed Trinity, where all things find their unity" (*EG* 117). This is true not just for humans, but for the whole of creation. In *LS*, Francis writes that

> the human person grows more, matures more and is sanctified more to the extent that he or she enters into relationships, going out from themselves to live in communion with God, with others and with all creatures. In this way, they make their own that Trinitarian dynamism which God imprinted in them when they were created. Everything is interconnected, and this invites us to develop a spirituality of that global solidarity which flows from the mystery of the Trinity. (*LS* 240)

Francis's account of historical becoming is not a dialectical struggle between the one and the many, but a reconciling movement through time toward the communion of all created beings in the mystery of the Trinity.

This brings me to the last part of my argument, where I am more critical of Francis's thought. How far does his preference for maternal ecclesiology cohere with his understanding of revelation as history, and what does this say with regard to the place of women in Francis's church?

The Church as Mother

In a general audience, Francis declared himself "extremely fond of [the] image of the Church as mother."[19] Developing this theme, he speaks of the mother who shows her children "the right path to take through life...with tenderness, affection, and love" (*GA* 1). When the children grow up, the mother continues to accompany them with patience, following them with discretion, always ready to defend them, always giving of herself, always praying for her children and entrusting them to God.

Themes of journeying along a path with patience, mercy, and discernment are implicit here too, but the mother, in this model, is not the wayfarer but the guide. That is a potentially rich image of the church. However, for real mothers attempting the complex and challenging task of mothering and often getting it wrong, this may not be a helpful image if there is no creative gap between mundane reality and imaginative sacramentality. The maternal church as represented by Francis is neither inculturated nor contextualized within the incarnate experiences and relationships of maternal life. Rather, mothers are assumed to behave in ways that conform to a model of the ideal church. Women have yet to find a meaningful place in Francis's church, whether or not they are mothers.

In a doctoral thesis on the motherhood of the church, Cristina Lledo Gomez has shown how, in the early church, maternal ecclesial metaphors drew their potency from their capacity to break open existing, culturally constructed expressions of motherhood to new meanings. In the documents of Vatican II and in the contemporary church, on the other hand, she argues that there is no such connection to culturally recognizable models. The motherhood of the church has become a "dead" metaphor, as this term is understood in Janet Soskice's work on metaphor.[20]

Alongside his unrealistic representation of motherhood, there is a more fundamental problem to do with Francis's appropriation of maternal language to describe roles from which women are excluded on account of their female bodies. For example, in *EG*, he writes about homiletics under the title "*A Mother's Conversation.*" The church "preaches in the same way that a mother speaks to her child" (*EG* 139). The Christian faith must be communicated in "our 'mother culture,' our native language," (*EG* 139) in a setting that is "both maternal and ecclesial" (*EG* 140).

This inculturated preaching requires a synthesis that comes from the passionate heart of the preacher, rather than "ideas or detached values" (*EG* 143). Yet the idea of a priest speaking as a mother, in a role that female bodies are prohibited from occupying, is detached from any incarnate maternal context. What does it mean to insist upon the affective dimension of preaching as a maternal activity, if women's bodies are denied sacramental significance? Francis's richly incarnational vision unravels in the face of such abstractions.

Francis has reiterated the teaching that the question of women's ordination is closed (*EG* 104). According to canon law, only priests and deacons are permitted to preach the homily during the Mass,[21] so women cannot initiate the mother's conversation that is the homily. Francis speaks of the "fleshy" devotions of popular religiosity (*EG* 90), but female fleshiness bars women from speaking when the maternal voice is heard in the context of the Mass, which is at the very heart of Catholic devotional life.

The idea of a maternal ecclesiology finds its focus in Mary— "the Mother of the Church which evangelizes" (*EG* 284). Mary walks with us on our journey to God—she "shares the history of each people which has received the Gospel and she becomes a part of their historic identity" (*EG* 286). These familiar themes of history and journeying shape Francis's understanding of Mary, who "let herself be guided by the Holy Spirit on a journey of faith towards a destiny of service and fruitfulness" (*EG* 287). Mary is Jesus's gift to the church from the cross, "because he did not want us to journey without a mother....The Lord did not want to leave the Church without this icon of womanhood" (*EG* 285).

This language of the icon is particularly problematic, given that similar language is used to justify the exclusion of women from the sacramental priesthood on the basis that the priest is an icon of Christ.[22] In the latter sense, the icon is exclusive—it is claimed that only men can be icons of Christ. However, in the former sense it is inclusive—men as well as women are called to be mothers or indeed women, since the mother is in this case "an icon of womanhood" identified with the motherhood of the church, which of course incorporates male and female bodies alike. This asymmetrical gendering of the iconic potential of the human body, pushed to its limit, shows the female body to be superfluous in the economy of salvation, apart from the procreative function needed to sustain the species. The icon is a work of art, a transformation of natural materials into a medium that mediates something of the presence of the divine beyond mere representation.[23] Where language really matters—where language becomes fleshy and bodies become sacraments—only male bodies count. In the maternal church, men are the true "icons of womanhood"—the priests who occupy the sacramental role of the mother—just as they are the icons of Christ. Women's bodies, lacking iconic significance, are confined to the biological function of the womb, a mammalian function that fails to transform the animality of the human creature into the sacramentality of the person as icon of Christ.

The elision of any significant distinction between womanhood and motherhood means that women remain trapped in the function of the womb—the role of providing space for others, while never occupying their own time and space in the human story. In other words, defined within this symbolic of the maternal, women do not change and develop through time; we do not incarnate the revelation of God in our particular cultures and contexts, but remain always available as the repository of men's fantasies of maternal nurture and feminine genius.[24] Addressing women at an event organized by the Pontifical Council for Culture, Francis said, "You, women, know how to show the tender face of God, his mercy, which translates in the availability to give time more than to occupy spaces, to welcome rather than to exclude. In this sense, I like to describe the feminine dimension of the Church as a welcoming womb that regenerates life."[25]

This reiterates the themes of time and space I have been exploring in this chapter. Yet what does it mean to say that women are available "to give time more than to occupy spaces"? And how can we square this with being likened to "a welcoming womb that regenerates life"? Surely, in the latter image, the womb is a space within which time unfolds. I am not suggesting that these informal observations and conversations should in themselves be given too much weight, but taken together they are revealing of Francis's underlying mentality when it comes to reflecting on the place of women in the church.

As Luce Irigaray suggests in her disruptive interventions into the Western philosophical and theological traditions, "The feminine is experienced as space,...while the masculine is experienced as time."[26] Irigaray refers to Kant's identification of temporality with the interiority of the subject and space with exteriority. Francis's subject is a more dynamic model than Kant's, but his ambulatory historical subject still looks to the womb/woman/mother/church to provide the space of his redemption, the space of his coming to be in God. For Irigaray, masculinity signifies the enclosure and sealing of spaces, whether these are the bodily boundaries of the modern subject, or the sealed boundaries that mark out property and territory in the modern capitalist state. She observes that "their fatherland, family, home, discourse, imprison us in enclosed spaces where we cannot keep on moving, living, as ourselves. Their properties are our exile."[27] This as an apt criticism to level at Francis, for while he seeks to render porous these masculine boundaries, the female body remains on the outside of the sealed borders of sacramental significance, unable to move because she is the space for his becoming, his dynamism.

Maternal Reconciling

I suggested in the first part of this chapter that Francis's vision of a mystical, maternal church has the potential to enrich the ecclesiology of the Second Vatican Council, restoring the sense of the church as "a container and guardian of mysteries far greater than itself," which was sacrificed to the more politicized agendas of the postconciliar era. At the same time, Francis not only preserves but deepens and develops the sense of the pilgrim people of God called to radical solidarity with the poor and the marginalized in their journey through time.

However, if this restoration of the maternal church is not simply to perpetuate the nostalgic romanticisms of his two predecessors—John Paul II, in particular—then women need to be liberated from bearing the burden of an archaic yearning associated with the maternal relationship, in order to play a full and equal role as persons in the church. Of course, the maternal body is female, but not every female is maternal, and a mother is a person before she is a mother.

Symbols of motherhood and fatherhood, of phallic power and maternal nurture, constitute the complex scaffolding of the human spirit with regard to some of our deepest desires and fears. These desires and fears are ineluctably entangled with the sexual bodies that we are, but gender is a fluid linguistic concept that allows the sexed body some finite freedom to give expression to a range of relationships and identities. Sacramentally, gendered identities are not tied to particular sexual bodies. They acquire a poetic potency that enables them to give expression to our most profound desires, our most unattainable yearnings, woven around the imagined ideal of the perfect lover, mother, or father. This is the language of contemplative prayer and mystical insight, when the self is lost in Christ in a way that finds partial expression through the appropriation of metaphors of nuptial and parental union, both paternal and maternal.

In the liturgy of the Mass, the fecundity of the fatherhood and motherhood of God become an expression of our hope, drawing on the most evocative and resonant symbols of birth, identity, desire, intimacy, and belonging to give an opaque sense of the hope that draws us forward through time toward the far horizon of eternity. This is the movement of which Marilyn Robinson speaks in her novel *Housekeeping*, when she writes,

> The force behind the movement of time is a mourning that will not be comforted. That is why the first event is known to have been an expulsion, and the last is hoped to be a reconciliation and return. So memory pulls us forward, so prophecy is only brilliant memory—there will be a garden where all of us as one child will sleep in our mother Eve, hooped in her ribs and staved by her spine.[28]

151

Francis describes the believer as "essentially one who remembers" (*EG* 13). Psychoanalysis tells us that remembering is more than a stringing together of events. It is our personal, unconscious history of desire, which is "remembered" in our drives and our instincts, in our dreams and our nightmares, suffusing our conscious memories with an uncanny bodily otherness and allowing intimations of a dark desire to ooze through the linguistic and social structures of our ordered worlds.

To bring such psychoanalytic insights to our understanding of sacramentality is in no way to deny that God, the transcendent Other, is the source of these elusive desires. It is rather to realize that holiness and madness, the mystic and the hysteric, dwell within each of us as the tabernacle wherein we encounter the God beyond all knowing and naming.

David Power describes sacramental ritual as a "language event" with a disruptive capacity to traverse boundaries and to interrupt the predictable rhythms of our daily routines. Rituals are, writes Power, "disclosures of human vulnerability and incompleteness. Bodily rites, in their very intensity of rhythm, bring to the surface the modes of being in time and space, together with the tensions inherent to the condition of being human."[29] He describes sacramental celebration as a linguistic excess that entails orality beyond the written word, so that speech is opened up to otherness and marginality.

There are deep resonances between Power's account of liturgy and Francis's understanding of popular piety as a *locus theologicus.* Yet such linguistic freedom and creativity is necessarily constrained when it must also police its boundaries in order to keep the female body at bay, excluding it from any participation in the church's performative maternal rituals of preaching and teaching, guiding and nurturing, worshiping and consecrating.

The alternative is to recognize that the priestly body makes sacramentally present that mystery of union discovered in trinitarian relationality that is the deepest desire of our human hearts. Neither father nor mother, male nor female, this body occupies God's time, God's space. It is a theophany in which the individual steps back from the mundane body in order to let the sacramental body manifest its mystery. The pilgrim seeks Sabbath rest from his or her journey through time, drawing nourishment and inspiration from the maternal body of Christ made flesh in Mary in the order of temporality and in the Eucharist in the order of sacramentality, in order to mother others along the pilgrim path of time.

In the postconciliar church, the pilgrim people of God travel through the time-space continuum of trinitarian otherness, manifesting to us in the sacramentality of all creation and in the theophany of the Mass wherein we become what we are not yet, before and beyond all that we know ourselves to be. This constitutes both immanence and transcendence, blindness and revelation, knowing and unknowing. It is the direction that Francis's vision could move in, if he acknowledged the iconic, sacramental potency of the female flesh. To discover the joy of the gospel in a way that is relevant for our times, we must also focus our gaze on the women who surround Jesus and ask anew what these models of female discipleship are telling us. In the scriptural and sacramental inheritance of the Christian faith, women's stories are yet to be given evangelical expression and sacramental embodiment.

Select Bibliography

Beattie, Tina. *New Catholic Feminism: Theology and Theory.* New York: Routledge, 2006.

Catholic Women Speak Network. *Catholic Women Speak: Bringing Our Gifts to the Table.* Mahwah, NJ: Paulist Press, 2015.

Irigaray, Luce. *An Ethics of Sexual Difference.* Translated by Carolyn Burke and Gillian C. Gill. New York: Continuum, 2004.

Kerr, Fergus. *Twentieth-Century Catholic Theologians: From Neoscholasticism to Nuptial Mysticism.* Malden, MA: Blackwell Publishing, 2007.

Power, David. "The Language of Sacramental Memorial: Rupture, Excess and Abundance." In *Sacramental Presence in a Postmodern Context,* edited by Lieven Boeve and Lambert Leussen. Sterling, VA: Leuven University Press, 2001.

Spretnak, Charlene. *Missing Mary: The Queen of Heaven and Her Re-emergence in the Modern Church.* New York: Palgrave Macmillan, 2004.

Notes

1. Pope Benedict XVI, "Address to the Roman Curia Offering Them His Christmas Greetings," December 22, 2005, http://w2.vatican.va/content/benedict-xvi/en/speeches/2005/december/documents/hf_ben_xvi_spe_20051222_roman-curia.html.

2. Pope Benedict XVI, Post-Synodal Apostolic Exhortation on the Eucharist as the Source and Summit of the Church's Life and Mission, *Sacramentum Caritatis*, February 22, 2007, http://w2.vatican.va/content/benedict-xvi/en/apost_exhortations/documents/hf_ben-xvi_exh_20070222_sacramentum-caritatis.html. See also Tracey Rowland, "Vatican II: A Hermeneutic of Continuity or Reform?" *Crisis Magazine*, November 15, 2012, http://www.crisismagazine.com/2012/vatican-ii-a-hermeneutic-of-continuity-or-reform.

3. Cf. Cristina Nava Lledo Gomez, "The Church as Mother: The Maternal Ecclesial Metaphor in the Vatican II Documents," PhD thesis, Charles Sturt University, Sydney, Australia, 2015; Joseph Conrad Plumpe, *Mater Ecclesia: An Inquiry into the Concept of the Church as Mother in Early Christianity.* The Catholic University of America Studies in Christian Antiquity (Washington, DC: The Catholic University of America Press, 1943).

4. Cf. Elizabeth Johnson, "Mary and Contemporary Christology: Rahner and Schillebeeckx," *Église et Théologie* 15 (1984): 155–82.

5. See Tina Beattie, *New Catholic Feminism: Theology and Theory* (New York: Routledge, 2006). See also Fergus Kerr, *Twentieth-Century Catholic Theologians: From Neoscholasticism to Nuptial Mysticism* (Malden, MA: Blackwell Publishing, 2007).

6. Charlene Spretnak, *Missing Mary: The Queen of Heaven and Her Re-emergence in the Modern Church* (New York: Palgrave Macmillan, 2004), 9. See also Beattie, *God's Mother, Eve's Advocate: A Marian Narrative of Women's Salvation* (New York: Continuum, 2002); Sarah Jane Boss, *Empress and Handmaid: Nature and Gender in the Cult of the Virgin Mary* (New York: Cassell, 2000).

7. Hans Urs von Balthasar, *Elucidations*, trans. John Riches (London: SPCK, 1975), 70.

8. Junno Arocho Esteves, "*Evangelii Gaudium*' (The Joy of the Gospel) Released Today," November 26, 2013, Zenit.org, http://www.zenit.org/en/articles/evangelii-gaudium-the-joy-of -the-gospel-released-today.

9. Pope Francis, "We Are History," Morning Meditation in the Chapel of the *Domus Sanctae Marthae*, Thursday, December 18, 2014, http://w2.vatican.va/content/francesco/en/cotidie/2014/ documents/papa-francesco-cotidie_20141218_we-are-history .html.

10. Isaac of Stella, *Sermo* 51: PL 194, 1863, 1865.

11. See Philip McCosker's chapter, "From the Joy of the Gospel to the Joy of Christ: Situating and Expanding the Christology of Pope Francis," chap. 3 in this volume.

12. See Antonio Spadaro, SJ, "A Big Heart Open to God," *America*, September 30, 2013, http://www.americamagazine.org/ pope-interview. All subsequent quotations are from this online translation of the interview.

13. See William Marceau, *Henri Bergson et Joseph Malègue: La Convergence de Deux Pensées*, Stanford French and Italian Studies (Stanford, CA: Stanford University Press, 1987).

14. See Philip McCosker's chapter in this volume, p. 67.

15. Pope Francis, Bull of Indiction of the Extraordinary Jubilee of Mercy, *Misericordiae Vultus*, April 11, 2015, http://w2.vatican .va/content/francesco/en/apost_letters/documents/papa -francesco_bolla_20150411_misericordiae-vultus.html.

16. Pope Francis, "At Mass without a Watch"—Morning Meditation in the Chapel of the *Domus Sanctae Marthae*, Tuesday, February 10, 2014, http://w2.vatican.va/content/francesco/en/ cotidie/2014/documents/papa-francesco-cotidie_20140210_mass -without-watch.html.

17. The best example of this would be the rejection by the Vatican Congregation for Divine Worship of an English translation of the Mass prepared by the International Commission on English in the Liturgy (ICEL). The translation sent to Rome in 1998 had been approved by all the bishops' conferences in the English-speaking church, but it was rejected by the Vatican. A more literal translation from the Latin prepared by a group of bishops appointed by Pope John Paul II was imposed from the first Sunday of Advent 2011, despite widespread and continuing

dismay about the awkwardness of the translation and the departure from Vatican II's emphasis on the importance of the vernacular for the liturgy. Cf. "Recover What Was Lost in the Translation," editorial, *The Tablet*, March 12, 2015, http://www.thetablet.co.uk/editors-desk/1/4936/recover-what-was-lost-in-the-translation.

18. Fifth General Conference of the Latin American and Caribbean Bishops, Aparecida Document, June 29, 2007.

19. Pope Francis, "General Audience," St. Peter's Square, September 18, 2013, https://w2.vatican.va/content/francesco/en/audiences/2013/documents/papa-francesco_20130918_udienza-generale.html.

20. Gomez, *The Church as Mother*. See Janet Martin Soskice, *Metaphor and Religious Language* (New York: Clarendon Press/Oxford University Press, 1985).

21. *Code of Canon Law*, book III, chap. 1, can. 767, no. 1, accessed August 1, 2015, http://www.vatican.va/archive/ENG1104/_P2J.HTM.

22. Cf. *Catechism of the Catholic Church*, part 2, sec. 1, chap. 2, art. 1, no. 1142, accessed August 1, 2015, http://www.vatican.va/archive/ENG0015/__P37.HTM. See also Sacred Congregation for the Doctrine of the Faith, "Declaration on the Question of Admission of Women to the Ministerial Priesthood," *Inter Insigniores*, October 15, 1976, http://www.vatican.va/roman_curia/congregations/cfaith/documents/rc_con_cfaith_doc_19761015_inter-insigniores_en.html.

23. See Thomas J. McGovern, *Priestly Identity: A Study in the Theology of Priesthood* (Eugene, OR: Wipf and Stock Publishers, 2010), 81–83.

24. For further development of these ideas, see Beattie, *God's Mother, Eve's Advocate.*

25. Elise Harris, "Society's Dire Need for the 'Female Soul'—Pope Francis Speaks to Women," *Catholic News Agency*, February 7, 2015, http://www.catholicnewsagency.com/news/societys-dire-need-for-the-female-soul-pope-francis-speaks-to-women-20605/.

26. Luce Irigaray, *An Ethics of Sexual Difference*, trans. Carolyn Burke and Gillian C. Gill (New York: Continuum, 2004), 9.

27. Luce Irigaray, *This Sex Which Is Not One*, trans. Catherine Porter (Ithaca, NY: Cornell University Press, 1985), 212.

28. Marilynne Robinson, *Housekeeping* (New York: Farrar, Strauss & Giroux, 1980), 192.

29. David N. Power, "The Language of Sacramental Memorial: Rupture, Excess and Abundance," in *Sacramental Presence in a Postmodern Context*, ed. Lieven Boeve and Lambert Leussen (Sterling, VA: Leuven University Press, 2001), 144.

Part 3

TOGETHER IN MISSION

EVANGELII GAUDIUM AND ECUMENISM

1

Ecumenism in Pope Francis

Ad Intra and *Ad Extra*

MASSIMO FAGGIOLI

Introduction

From the beginning of Pope Francis's pontificate, it was immediately clear that the new pope intended to revive the ecclesiological shift of Vatican II. The "communitarian" development (in an experiential more than a theoretical sense) of the latest generation of Catholic movements, for example, met Pope Benedict's idea of a church made of "creative minorities" within a "minority" church in the modern world, which posits a certain understanding of the relationship between Catholicism and the modern world, but also between Catholicism and the non-Catholic churches. The difference between Benedict XVI and Francis in the use of Vatican II, and in particular of the Pastoral Constitution on the Church in the Modern World, *Gaudium et Spes*, is a key element in order to understand the difference between the ecclesiology of Joseph Ratzinger and his successor.[1]

This constitutes one of the key discontinuities between Jorge Mario Bergoglio and his predecessor. Francis's focus on mercy and on the poor—two key terms that go back straight to Vatican

II and the pope who called for it, John XXIII[2]—does not aim at a doctrinal redefinition of new boundaries of church membership, assuming the church as a fixed, unmoving, and unmoved body. The focus on mercy, on the poor, and on the existential peripheries means a redefinition of the very idea of an ecclesiology defined in terms of in/out, that is, of visible boundaries.[3] What is particularly impressive about Pope Francis's ecumenism is the fact that he is accomplishing this work of Catholic ecumenism both *ad intra* and *ad extra*—within the Catholic ecclesial environment and in the ecumenical world at large. In this sense, the ecumenism of Francis is the embodiment of the postconciliar impression that the most difficult ecumenism is the one you try to build with the members of your own church with whom you disagree.[4]

Francis's pontificate has met with enthusiasm from many non-Catholics alongside the opposition of some Catholics.[5] This fact is not to be measured in terms of popularity, but in terms of the adequacy of his call for Christian unity in churches that are now internally more divided than fifty years ago. In other words, Francis's ecumenism is also indirectly an assessment of the ecclesial and ecumenical context that he found when he was elected. Pope Francis's "practical ecumenism" is capacious and comprehensive, extending not only to relations between Catholics and non-Catholic churches but also encompassing reconciliatory initiatives within Catholicism and across a very broad and fractious theological spectrum.

The Context: Ecumenical and Intra-ecclesial Reception of Vatican II

The theology of Pope Francis is deeply *contextual and existential*. For Francis, context is a key source for pastoral reflections on evangelization.[6] This has profound consequences for our understanding of his pontificate, and especially of his interpretation of Vatican II and its legacy—including its ecumenical legacy. Vatican II is not just a "text": for Francis, the Council is also an act and its ecumenical trajectories are already contextual, that is, part of the present theological and ecclesial landscape.

The *theological-ecumenical legacy* that Pope Francis found in 2013 is a complex one, but it is also clear that the pope does not see the signs of an "ecumenical winter": the ecumenical dialogue since Vatican II has produced many results (more than expected fifty years ago) on Scripture and Tradition, on justification, on ecclesiology, on baptism and the Eucharist.[7] Francis does not share the pessimism of those who see in the ecumenical scene at the beginning of the twenty-first century a stalemate or a fruitless series of dialogues. It is not an accident that the first direct quotation of Vatican II in his pontificate took place on March 20, 2013, at a meeting with representatives of non-Catholic churches and other religions. Part of his reception of the ecumenical path of Vatican II is the choice to describe himself as "Francis, Bishop of Rome" (with all the other titles moved to another page) in the edition of the *Annuario Pontificio 2013*, just a few weeks after his election.[8]

Nevertheless this is also an ecumenical landscape that has changed tragically as a consequence of the wars that target religious minorities—Christians included—in Africa, the Middle East, and Asia. What he called the "ecumenism of blood" is certainly part of the ecumenical outlook for Pope Francis, as he said many times and especially in his December 14, 2013, interview with Andrea Tornielli of the Italian newspaper *La Stampa*:

> For me, ecumenism is a priority. Today, there's the ecumenism of blood. In some countries they kill Christians because they wear a cross or have a Bible, and before killing them they don't ask if they're Anglicans, Lutherans, Catholic or Orthodox. The blood is mixed. For those who kill, we're Christians.…That's the ecumenism of blood. It exists today too, all you have to do is read the papers.[9]

Finally, there is also a perception by Pope Francis of an *intraecclesial landscape* that is divided, polarized, and fragmented. The firm and fervent messages of Pope Francis to bishops, to the clergy, and to Catholic movements about unity reveal the concern of the pope for the condition of the church today.[10] The emphasis on unity in his pontificate matches the same emphasis in John XXIII's teaching during the preparation of Vatican II. But Francis emphasizes unity in a very different historical-theological condition: in the church of today there are different interpretations of Vatican II that reflect the situation of tension and separateness between different versions of Catholicism in which some local Catholic communities (especially, but not only in the United States) live their faith.

Ecumenism is one of the trajectories of Vatican II that has suffered from a lack of energy during the years before the election of Francis—or, at least, ecumenism went through a redefinition of the coordinates of ecumenical dialogue and relations between churches (for example, with the decision to create a special ordinariate for former Anglicans, the apostolic constitution *Anglicanorum Coetibus*, November 4, 2009).[11] Pope Benedict's pontificate put the emphasis on the priority of the doctrinal consensus—in absence of which all the rest of the ecumenical relations suffered. The preeminence of the pastoral and existential dimension in Pope Francis is a departure from the previous ecumenical language used by his predecessors. Another departure, which is part of Francis's perception of the ecclesial landscape, consists in Benedict's attempt to re-Europeanize Catholicism (culturally and institutionally)—an attempt that had significant consequences for the importance of ecumenism in globalized Christianity. On the other hand, a shift in the institutional church on the relationship between the European identity of Catholicism, the catholicity of the church, and mission was visible already at the Bishops' Synod of October 2012 on evangelization, a synod that had been called by Benedict XVI. The synod of 2012 offered some interesting insights about the contribution of non-European bishops to the debate on evangelization in the global world.[12] This synod was the starting point of Francis's programmatic document, the exhortation *Evangelii Gaudium*.

Ecumenism in *Evangelii Gaudium*

The Apostolic Exhortation *Evangelii Gaudium* (*EG*) plays a special role in the corpus of the writings of Jorge Mario Bergoglio.

It is not an encyclical, but it has had the same effect as an encyclical in terms of an announcement of the priorities of the pontificate: in a sense, it was a document on the *environment in the church.* But if *EG* is a programmatic document, we must remember that Pope Francis does not present himself as a systematic thinker. The content of the exhortation is not a real plan but an organized collection of Francis's insights about evangelization in light of the present context. It is emblematic of his inductive method, and intended as a meaningful reception of teaching of the previous tradition—most importantly of the national and continental bishops' conferences. *EG* therefore reflects Francis's pastoral experience more than his theological preferences, or better, Francis's theology as the fruit of his pastoral experience—something that is typical of Francis much more than for his predecessors.[13]

One of the words seen most frequently in *EG* is *dialogue*—it appears altogether fifty-nine times, but only on a few occasions in the sense of "ecumenical dialogue":

> Evangelization also involves the path of dialogue. For the Church today, three areas of dialogue stand out where she needs to be present in order to promote full human development and to pursue the common good: dialogue with states, dialogue with society—including dialogue with cultures and the sciences—and dialogue with other believers who are not part of the Catholic Church. (*EG* 238)

The section properly devoted to ecumenism encompasses paragraphs 244–46. As it is often the case with Francis's language, there is not much need for commentary.

> Commitment to ecumenism responds to the prayer of the Lord Jesus that "they may all be one" (John 17:21). The credibility of the Christian message would be much greater if Christians could overcome their divisions and the Church could realize "the fullness of catholicity proper to her in those of her children who, though joined to her by baptism, are yet separated from full communion with her." We must never forget that we are

pilgrims journeying alongside one another. This means that we must have sincere trust in our fellow pilgrims, putting aside all suspicion or mistrust, and turn our gaze to what we are all seeking: the radiant peace of God's face. (*EG* 244)

In *EG* 245, Francis connects ecumenism with the universal role of the Catholic Church: "In this perspective, ecumenism can be seen as a contribution to the unity of the human family. At the Synod, the presence of the Patriarch of Constantinople, His Holiness Bartholomew I, and the Archbishop of Canterbury, His Grace Rowan Williams, was a true gift from God and a precious Christian witness."

This global claim of the Catholic Church at the service of the "unity of the human family" is presented in *EG* with a new urgency, given the threats to interreligious coexistence in the world of today, and Francis sees this as a sign of our times that directs the church's commitment to ecumenism:

Given the seriousness of the counter-witness of division among Christians, particularly in Asia and Africa, the search for paths to unity becomes all the more urgent.... Signs of division between Christians in countries ravaged by violence add further causes of conflict on the part of those who should instead be a leaven of peace. How many important things unite us! If we really believe in the abundantly free working of the Holy Spirit, we can learn so much from one another! It is not just about being better informed about others, but rather about reaping what the Spirit has sown in them, which is also meant to be a gift for us. To give but one example, in the dialogue with our Orthodox brothers and sisters, we Catholics have the opportunity to learn more about the meaning of episcopal collegiality and their experience of synodality.... Through an exchange of gifts, the Spirit can lead us ever more fully into truth and goodness. (*EG* 246)

Two elements stand out here in respect of a particular reception of Vatican II in an ecumenical trajectory. The first element is the reference to Asia and Africa and "countries ravaged by violence" (*EG* 246) as a test case for the importance of ecumenism. This is part of the "world-church turn" embodied by Pope Francis: ecumenism is no longer only part of the self-satisfied narrative on the peaceful nature of post–World War II Europe after the centuries of interreligious wars. Ecumenism is part of those areas of the world where religion is intertwined with violence (whether sectarian, ethnic, or nationalist). Pope Francis's ecumenism is an "existential ecumenism" (as Orthodox bishop John Zizioulas called it in the press conference for the presentation of the encyclical *Laudato Si'* [*LS*] in the Vatican on June 18, 2015). In a way, this is a return to the ecumenical urge of the theologians of Vatican II who developed a new thinking about the unity of the church between World War I and World War II.

The second element is the direct reference to the importance of ecumenism for the opportunity to learn about collegiality and synodality from the Orthodox churches in *EG* 246. Ecumenism here represents the gateway toward the advancement of Catholic conversations about inner reform from "collegiality" (concerning bishops and the pope) to "synodality" (concerning the whole church).[14]

There are then the passages where ecumenism is not the subject, but the decree of the Council on ecumenism, *Unitatis Redintegratio* (*UR*, November 21, 1964), is crucial for the text. As we have already seen, *EG* 244 quotes *Unitatis Redintegratio*. But there are two other passages where *UR* is quoted. The first is in *EG* 36, which quotes *UR* 11, and especially the notion of a "hierarchy of truths," one of the most important legacies of Vatican II for Pope Francis. For example, Francis uses *UR* 11 to recenter the life of the church around the gospel:

> All revealed truths derive from the same divine source and are to be believed with the same faith, yet some of them are more important for giving direct expression to the heart of the gospel. In this basic core, what shines forth is the beauty of the saving love of God made manifest in Jesus Christ who died and rose from the dead. In this sense, the Second Vatican Council explained, "in Catholic doctrine there exists an order or a 'hierarchy'

of truths, since they vary in their relation to the foundation of the Christian faith." This holds true as much for the dogmas of faith as for the whole corpus of the Church's teaching, including her moral teaching. (*EG* 36)

Institutional centralization is a major concern about the church for Francis in *EG*. But in a similar way, dogmatism is also a hindrance to a missionary church. The quotation of the Council's decree on ecumenism is a key principle in Francis's theology that is evident throughout his work.[15] For Francis, the missionary activity makes of the church "a missionary disciple":

The Church is herself a missionary disciple; she needs to grow in her interpretation of the revealed word and in her understanding of truth. It is the task of exegetes and theologians to help the judgment of the Church to mature. The other sciences also help to accomplish this, each in its own way. With reference to the social sciences, for example, John Paul II said that the Church values their research, which helps her "to derive concrete indications helpful for her magisterial mission." Within the Church countless issues are being studied and reflected upon with great freedom. Differing currents of thought in philosophy, theology and pastoral practice, if open to being reconciled by the Spirit in respect and love, can enable the Church to grow, since all of them help to express more clearly the immense riches of God's word. For those who long for a monolithic body of doctrine guarded by all and leaving no room for nuance, this might appear as undesirable and leading to confusion. But in fact such variety serves to bring out and develop different facets of the inexhaustible riches of the Gospel. (*EG* 40)

Francis is talking here of a theology that is much more ecumenical than could have been imagined fifty years ago. A second passage where the conciliar legacy is overt is the quotation of *UR* 6 in *EG* 26:

Paul VI invited us to deepen the call to renewal and to make it clear that renewal does not only concern individuals but the entire Church. Let us return to a memorable text that continues to challenge us. "The Church must look with penetrating eyes within herself, ponder the mystery of her own being....This vivid and lively self-awareness inevitably leads to a comparison between the ideal image of the Church as Christ envisaged her and loved her as his holy and spotless bride (cf. *Eph* 5:27), and the actual image which the Church presents to the world today....This is the source of the Church's heroic and impatient struggle for renewal: the struggle to correct those flaws introduced by her members which her own self-examination, mirroring her exemplar, Christ, points out to her and condemns." The Second Vatican Council presented ecclesial conversion as openness to a constant self-renewal born of fidelity to Jesus Christ: "Every renewal of the Church essentially consists in an increase of fidelity to her own calling.... Christ summons the Church as she goes her pilgrim way...to that continual reformation of which she always has need, in so far as she is a human institution here on earth." [*UR* 6]

There are ecclesial structures that can hamper efforts at evangelization, yet even good structures are only helpful when there is a life constantly driving, sustaining and assessing them. Without new life and an authentic evangelical spirit, without the Church's "fidelity to her own calling," any new structure will soon prove ineffective.

Ecumenism is also relevant for Francis's view of the church in its institutional aspect. In *EG* 25, there is a section devoted to the relations between pastoral activity and conversion that opens by underlining the shift from an administrative and institutional church to a missionary church:

I am aware that nowadays documents do not arouse the same interest as in the past and that they are quickly forgotten. Nevertheless, I want to emphasize that what I am trying to express here has a programmatic significance and important consequences. I hope that all communities will devote the necessary effort to advancing along the path of a pastoral and missionary conversion that cannot leave things as they presently are. "Mere administration" can no longer be enough. Throughout the world, let us be "permanently in a state of mission." (*EG* 25)

This shift from an administrative and institutional church to a missionary church has ecumenical consequences that are clearer to some in the church than to others. If in the post–Vatican II period popes have often talked about the irreversibility of ecumenism as a commitment (see John Paul II in the encyclical *Ut Unum Sint*, 1995), here with Pope Francis ecumenism is more a given fact than a commitment. Francis receives the post–Vatican II doctrinal policy about non-Catholic churches—especially the distinction between "churches" and "ecclesial communities" (*EG* 183; *LS* 7), but he transcends the distinction because his ecumenism is not based on considerations of ecclesiological proximity, but on a strong christological and pneumatological center on one side, and on the common challenges all Christians face on the other. This allows Francis to avoid so-called culture wars, where theology becomes subject to the ideological manipulations in the left-right cultural clashes and "identity politics."[16] Francis's ecumenism is an "ecumenism of blood," not an "ecumenism of the trenches" (to quote the expression coined by Charles Colson, president Richard Nixon's aide turned evangelist and prison minister).[17]

Francis's ecumenism is open to crossing old ecclesiological boundaries, but it is not unqualified: it is defined nondogmatically and rejects fundamentalism. In *EG*, Francis presents a problematic view of the "new religious movements":

The Catholic faith of many peoples is nowadays being challenged by the proliferation of new religious movements, some of which tend to fundamentalism while others seem to propose a spirituality without God. This is, on the one hand, a human reaction to a materialistic, consumerist and individualistic society, but it is also a means of exploiting the weaknesses of people living in poverty and on the fringes of society, people who make ends meet amid great human suffering and are looking for immediate solutions to their needs. (*EG* 63)

Pope Francis does not explicitly mention Christian groups among these new movements; instead his vision of ecumenism is connected to an understanding of religious faith as incarnate and not alienated from the existential circumstances.

Vatican II, Ecumenism, and Church Reform in *EG*

Ecumenism in *EG* must therefore be traced not only in those paragraphs where the word *ecumenism* is directly used, but also throughout in tone, tenor, and invocation. A mere three paragraphs devoted to ecumenism, out of 288 paragraphs in the entire exhortation, might lead us to conclude that ecumenism plays a secondary part in Francis's thinking. But if we take a look at the role of Vatican II in *EG*, the ecumenical tone of the exhortation is very visible. Of the quotations from conciliar documents, the most important quotation from Vatican II in *EG* is at no. 41 on the relationship between the deposit of faith and the way to express it. Here Pope Francis quotes from John XXIII's opening speech of the Council—not strictly a final conciliar document voted and approved by the Council fathers, but a key document for the hermeneutic of Vatican II:[18]

> At the same time, today's vast and rapid cultural changes demand that we constantly seek ways of expressing unchanging truths in a language that brings out their abiding newness. "The deposit of the faith is one thing...the way it is expressed is another" [John XXIII, *Gaudet Mater Ecclesia*, October 11, 1962]. There are times when the faithful, in listening to completely orthodox language, take away something alien to the authentic Gospel of Jesus Christ, because that language is alien

171

to their own way of speaking to and understanding one another. With the holy intent of communicating the truth about God and humanity, we sometimes give them a false god or a human ideal which is not really Christian. In this way, we hold fast to a formulation while failing to convey its substance. This is the greatest danger. Let us never forget that "the expression of truth can take different forms." The renewal of these forms of expression becomes necessary for the sake of transmitting to the people of today the Gospel message in its unchanging meaning. [John Paul II, encyclical *Ut Unum Sint* (1995) 19] (*EG* 41)

The other most important quotation of *Gaudet Mater Ecclesia*, though, concerns the challenges to evangelization and the lack of hope that is typical of our times:

The joy of the gospel is such that it cannot be taken away from us by anyone or anything (cf. John 16:22). The evils of our world—and those of the Church—must not be excuses for diminishing our commitment and our fervor. Let us look upon them as challenges which can help us to grow. With the eyes of faith, we can see the light which the Holy Spirit always radiates in the midst of darkness, never forgetting that "where sin increased, grace has abounded all the more" (Rom 5:20). Our faith is challenged to discern how wine can come from water and how wheat can grow in the midst of weeds. Fifty years after the Second Vatican Council, we are distressed by the troubles of our age and far from naïve optimism; yet the fact that we are more realistic must not mean that we are any less trusting in the Spirit or less generous. In this sense, we can once again listen to the words of Blessed John XXIII on the memorable day of 11 October 1962: "At times we have to listen, much to our regret, to the voices of people who, though burning with zeal, lack a sense of discretion and measure. In this modern age they can see nothing but prevarication and ruin....We feel that we must disagree with those prophets of doom who are always forecasting disaster, as though the end of the world were at hand. In our times, divine Providence is leading us to a new order of human relations which, by human effort and even beyond all expectations, are directed to the fulfillment of God's superior and inscrutable designs, in which everything, even human setbacks, leads to the greater good of the Church. (*EG* 84)

In this section of the Apostolic Exhortation, and especially with this quotation, Pope Francis is reenacting Pope John XXIII's reorientation of the church's message, thus showing many parallels between the church at the end of Pius XII's pontificate and at the beginning of Pope Francis's.[19] Like John XXIII, the election of Francis happened in difficult times for the church not only through a myriad of external factors and internal scandals, but also for the unstated and at the same time clear sense of exhaustion of a given theological-cultural paradigm in relation to the pastoral needs of the time, and the need to reframe and rephrase the message of the church in a new setting. It is no surprise then that the resistance and fear of change met by John XXIII at the time of the Council is similar to the reception of Pope Francis in some quarters of the Catholic Church today.[20]

The section on "worldliness" is significantly the one where the paragraph on the liturgy develops as a statement against those prone to nostalgia for pre–Vatican II liturgies: "In some people we see an ostentatious preoccupation for the liturgy, for doctrine and for the Church's prestige, but without any concern that the gospel have a real impact on God's faithful people and the concrete needs of the present time. In this way, the life of the Church turns into a museum piece or something which is the property of a select few" (*EG* 95). The ecumenical spirit of the liturgical legacy of Vatican II is part of this reflection of Pope Francis, reinforced further if we remember how he has celebrated the fiftieth anniversary of the reform recently.[21]

Ecumenism is also part of Francis's reception of Vatican II ecclesiology, and especially of *Lumen Gentium*. Pope Francis's claim about the church in the modern world is also visible in the quotation of *Lumen Gentium*:

In all the baptized, from first to last, the sanctifying power of the Spirit is at work, impelling us to evangelization. The people of God is holy thanks to this anointing, which makes it infallible *in credendo*. This means that it does not err in faith, even though it may not find words to explain that faith. The Spirit guides it in truth and leads it to salvation. (*LG* 12) As part of his mysterious love for humanity, God furnishes the totality of the faithful with an instinct of faith—*sensus fidei*—which helps them to discern what is truly of God. The presence of the Spirit gives Christians a certain connaturality with divine realities, and a wisdom which enables them to grasp those realities intuitively, even when they lack the wherewithal to give them precise expression. (*EG* 119)

This passage about the *sensus fidei* is even more remarkable because *EG* 119 is the only passage of the exhortation that talks about infallibility, and it does that in terms of infallibility *in credendo* of the people of God. The ecclesiological constitution of Vatican II, *Lumen Gentium*, is also quoted a few lines after: "The Holy Spirit also enriches the entire evangelizing Church with different charisms. These gifts are meant to renew and build up the Church [*LG* 12]" (*EG* 130).

Lumen Gentium 12 plays an important role in the exhortation: it is clearly the intent of the document to rephrase, once again, the infallibility of the magisterium as based on the infallibility of the people of God. This key element of Catholic ecclesiology builds a connection between infallibility and the charismatic structure of the church: charisms are not extraordinary and exceptional in the church, they are rather common, diverse, inclusive, and universal. The church is all-charismatic, and the value of every charism must be measured against the good of the people of God.

An ecumenical idea central to the exhortation is the idea of dialogue. The section on dialogue comes after the four principles (*EG* 222–33): "Time is greater than space," "Unity prevails over conflict," "Realities are more important than ideas," and "The whole is greater than the part." The first axiom—"Time is greater than space"—is particularly relevant for ecumenism. Francis privileges time over space: he is a pope of "process" (as he said in the groundbreaking interview with Antonio Spadaro, SJ, editor of *Civiltà Cattolica* in September 2013).[22] The second axiom is directly talking about diversity and the Spirit:

> The message of peace is not about a negotiated settlement but rather the conviction that the unity brought by the Spirit can harmonize every diversity. It overcomes every conflict by creating a new and promising synthesis. Diversity is a beautiful thing when it can constantly enter into a process of reconciliation and seal a sort of cultural covenant resulting in a "reconciled diversity." (*EG* 230)

The third axiom is also particularly relevant for ecumenism: "Ideas—conceptual elaborations—are at the service of communication, understanding, and praxis. Ideas disconnected from realities give rise to ineffectual forms of idealism and nominalism, capable at most of classifying and defining, but certainly not calling to action" (*EG* 232). The fourth axiom talks about a model of the church that is about preserving distinctiveness: "Here our model is not the sphere, which is no greater than its parts, where every point is equidistant from the centre, and there are no differences between them. Instead, it is the polyhedron, which reflects the convergence of all its parts, each of which preserves its distinctiveness." (*EG* 236). These four axioms—the importance of time, unity over diversity, praxis over abstract ideas, the church as a polyhedron—speak to and reflect the history of the ecumenical movement in this last century. We could rephrase these axioms through an ecumenical lens as ecumenism as a long-term project, the emphasis on invisible unity already existing between Christians, the ecumenism of "life and work" as evidence of a relationship nurtured by the Spirit, and an ecclesiology open to different relations between the center and the parts of the church.

However, in Francis's language, there is a renewed and very visible use of the word *dialogue* as part of papal teaching. Dialogue is the focus of chapter 4, titled "Social Dimension of Evangelization," which follows on sections on social and community repercussions of evangelization (chapter 1), on the poor (chapter 2), and on the common good (chapter 3). Dialogue concludes chapter 4 and it is part of a reflection on dialogue "as a contribution to peace" (*EG* 238–58), and in particular dialogue with reason and science, ecumenical dialogue, relations with Judaism, interreligious dialogue, and dialogue in the context of religious freedom. Dialogue is part of the inductive method, and spiritual discernment is part of ecumenism: ecumenism *ad intra* and *ad extra*. Francis keeps porous the boundaries of the Catholic Church and, in a different way, also the boundaries between the churches. Pope Francis is unquestionably a pro–Vatican II pope, and the issue of a reconciliation with a group like the SSPX, whose only reason for existence is the rejection of the Second Vatican Council and the denunciation of its teaching as heresy, is part of Francis's view of the ecumenical agenda of the Catholic Church today. It is also clear to Francis that full reconciliation with the SSPX cannot be at the expense of the theology of ecumenism of the Second Vatican Council.[23]

The ecclesiology of *EG* is committed to a dynamic idea of the structures of the church, and this has deep repercussions for the way the exhortation envisions ecumenism. The correlation between different poles of Catholic ecclesiology is visible in both the intra-Christian sphere and in the interreligious dialogue. The discussion about catholicity and ecumenism (*EG* 244) quotes *UR* 4, being aware of the historical centrality of the Catholic Church in the history of the Christian theological tradition—at least, a centrality in the mind of the fathers and theologians of Vatican II. In a similar way, Francis does not see a contradiction between dialogue and proclamation, thanks to a reference in the footnote from the decree on the missionary activity of the church, *Ad Gentes* (no. 9):

> In this dialogue, ever friendly and sincere, attention must always be paid to the essential bond between dialogue and proclamation, which leads the Church to maintain and intensify her relationship with non-Christians. A facile syncretism would ultimately be a totalitarian gesture on the part of those who would ignore greater values of which they are not the masters....Evangelization and

interreligious dialogue, far from being opposed, mutually support and nourish one another. (*EG* 251)

The Para-text: The Ecumenism of Francis's Gestures

The papacy in the world of today conveys its message not solely through official documents, but more dramatically through other kinds of texts (interviews, video messages) and, especially, gestures and a certain style. The papal mystique is being redefined—something that started with the election of John XXIII in 1958. Among the most dramatic gestures redefining this papacy are those concerning ecumenical dialogue and they occupy a special place in recent history.

For Francis, this begins with the liturgy for the beginning of the pontificate, in the presence of the Patriarch of Constantinople Bartholomew on March 19, 2013. In that first month, the decision to make official the preeminence of the title "Bishop of Rome" in the *Annuario Pontificio* is the manifesto of the self-understanding of the pope. Many more meetings with leaders of other churches followed: the meeting with Tawadros, head of the Coptic Orthodox Church of Egypt on May, 10, 2013;[24] the audience with Justin Welby, the archbishop of Canterbury and primate of the Anglican Communion on June 14, 2013;[25] the audience with Karekin II, Supreme Patriarch and Catholicos of all Armenians on May 8, 2014;[26] the visit with Patriarch Bartholomew in Jerusalem on May 26, 2014,[27] which took place fifty years after the first meeting between Paul VI and Athenagoras and was followed by another meeting in Turkey six months later (November 28–30, 2014);[28] the visit to the small community of Pentecostals near Naples on July 28, 2014 (a first for a pope);[29] the letter to Christians in the Middle East of December 23, 2014, which pointed out the relations between ecumenism and peace;[30] the audience with the female Lutheran archbishop of Uppsala in Sweden, Antje Jackelén, on May 4, 2015;[31] the wish, expressed at the beginning on June 12, 2015, for a common date for the celebration of Easter; the clearly ecumenical tone of the presentation in the Vatican and of the very text (from the introduction to the final ecumenical prayer) of the encyclical *LS*, On the Care of Our Common Home;[32] the visit to the temple of the Waldensians near Turin (the first for a pope) on June 22, 2015;[33] the visit to Rome's Christuskirche, a parish of the German Evangelical Lutheran Church in Rome on November 15, 2015;[34] the ecumenical meetings (especially with Anglicans and evangelical communities) during the journey to Kenya, Uganda, and the Central African Republic of November 25–30, 2015;[35] the visit to the refugees on the Greek island of Lesbos together with Ecumenical Patriarch Bartholomew of Constantinople and Archbishop Ieronymos of Athens and All Greece on April 16, 2016;[36] his trip to Armenia of June 24–26, 2016 and to Georgia and Azerbaijan September 30–October 2, 2016; and finally his trip to Sweden of October 31, 2016 for the commemoration of the five hundred years of the Lutheran Reformation.

There are, however, other elements of Francis's papacy that also represent his new approach to the need to give voice to the diverse cultures within the Catholic Church: for example, the creation of the council of cardinals (April 13, 2013) representing the Catholic church from different areas of the world as an acknowledgment of the need to rebalance the church structure in a fashion more respectful of the reality of the universal church of today, with cardinals coming from areas of the world where the state of ecumenism is quite different from the perception in Rome. His description of the church as a "field hospital" has ecumenical resonances because it responds to the "hierarchy of truths," as does the frequent invitations to Catholic bishops and priests not to deny baptism to anyone. To this could be added his repeated criticisms against all forms of clericalism in the church. Furthermore, the calling of the synod of 2014 and 2015 to discuss family and marriage, and the constant encouragement to the new Catholic movements to work for the unity of the church, and not for supremacy in the church, have both occurred at a time when there are visible tensions between different and sometimes seemingly incompatible interpretations (liturgically and politically) of Catholicism within the Roman Catholic Church. In this sense, Francis's idea of dialogue is relevant for ecumenical dialogue between the Catholic Church and other churches, as well as for an intra-Catholic ecumenism.

All these are genuinely intra-Catholic ecumenical moves because they acknowledge honestly a situation of division and they start a process of recreating a movement toward unity within the Catholic Church, as part of a new sense of unity among all Christians. In this sense, Pope Francis's encyclical On Care for Our Common Home, *Laudato Si'*, is not only a text on Catholic environmentalism, but also part of Francis's "ecclesial ecology," part of his "human ecology."[37] The ecumenical element in *LS* is evident in the important quotations of Patriarch Bartholomew of Constantinople (in California, 1997 and two other of his speeches of 2003 and 2012, *LS* 7–9) and in Francis's wish "to enter into dialogue with all people about our common home" (*LS* 3). The two prayers at the conclusion of the encyclical are full of Francis's keywords. In the interreligious prayer, there is reference to tenderness, the poor, and the phrase the "struggle for justice, love and peace." The ecumenical "Christian prayer in union with creation" has a prophetic tone for the conversion of the rich and powerful so that they can love the common good, protect the poor and the earth. Telling of Francis's view of ecumenism in *LS* is the preference for sources coming from the Eastern Orthodox tradition and the absence of references to the work on theology and environment done by other ecumenical bodies.

The ecumenical element in the post-synodal exhortation (March 19, 2016) on love in the family, *Amoris Laetitia* (*AL*), is in the attempt to create the conditions for a more welcoming church for all its members.[38] For the pressing issues (in some cultural contexts) of divorced and remarried couples, of homosexuals, and other people living in "irregular situations," the exhortation makes clear that they should be made to feel part of the church. Pastors must meet people where they are, in order to "avoid judgments which do not take into account the complexity of various situations" (*AL* 296). It is yet another example of Francis's ecumenism *ad intra*, which was initiated by a renewed use of the Bishops' Synod, after fifty years of marginalization of that institution. Francis's exhortation represents the first attempt by a pope to demonstrate how the episcopal collegiality of Vatican II is supposed to work. However, *AL* denotes also a step forward from the ecumenical ecclesiology of Vatican II. Paramount within Francis's ecumenical ecclesiology is the reconfiguration of the papal ministry in a way that is of

179

great interest from the point of view of ecumenism, and Francis makes this clear right at the beginning of the exhortation:

> Since "time is greater than space," I would make it clear that not all discussions of doctrinal, moral or pastoral issues need to be settled by interventions of the magisterium. Unity of teaching and practice is certainly necessary in the Church, but this does not preclude various ways of interpreting some aspects of that teaching or drawing certain consequences from it. This will always be the case as the Spirit guides us towards the entire truth (cf. John 16:13), until he leads us fully into the mystery of Christ and enables us to see all things as he does. Each country or region, moreover, can seek solutions better suited to its culture and sensitive to its traditions and local needs. For "cultures are in fact quite diverse and every general principle…needs to be inculturated, if it is to be respected and applied." (*AL* 3)

Francis's ecumenism cannot be separated from his practiced ecclesiology, with his stress on diversity, inclusion, and inculturation. This stems from a lived experience of Catholicism that, for Francis, is made of a new kind of relationship between the center (and its European-Western tradition) and the peripheries of the global church (and their many traditions that make Catholicism universal).

Conclusion

In Francis's pontificate there have been few dramatic breakthroughs concerning official, bilateral ecumenism. Rather, we have seen a constant ecumenical approach that reveals much not only of the ecumenical theology of Francis, but also of his view of the role of the papacy in the church and in Christianity today vis-à-vis theology.

In a video message on the occasion of the Day for Christian Unity, which took place in Phoenix, Arizona, in the United

States on May 23, 2015, Pope Francis articulated sentiments crucial to understanding not just his idea of ecumenism, but also of the relationship between the papal ministry and the ministry of theologians—precisely in light of the ecumenical future of the church:

> Together today, I here in Rome and you over there, we will ask our Father to send the Spirit of Jesus, the Holy Spirit, and to give us the grace to be one, "so that the world may believe." I feel like saying something that may sound controversial, or even heretical, perhaps. But there is someone who "knows" that, despite our differences, we are one. It is he who is persecuting us. It is he who is persecuting Christians today, he who is anointing us with [the blood of] martyrdom. He knows that Christians are disciples of Christ: that they are one, that they are brothers! He doesn't care if they are Evangelicals, or Orthodox, Lutherans, Catholics or Apostolic... he doesn't care! They are Christians. And that blood [of martyrdom] unites. Today, dear brothers and sisters, we are living an "ecumenism of blood." This must encourage us to do what we are doing today: to pray, to dialogue together, to shorten the distance between us, to strengthen our bonds of brotherhood. I am convinced it won't be theologians who bring about unity among us. Theologians help us, the science of the theologians will assist us, but if we hope that theologians will agree with one another, we will reach unity the day after Judgment Day. The Holy Spirit brings about unity. Theologians are helpful, but most helpful is the goodwill of us all who are on this journey with our hearts open to the Holy Spirit![39]

From what we have seen of the ecumenism of Francis in *EG* and in his whole pontificate, it is possible to draw some provisional conclusions.

First of all, ecumenism is one of the areas in which the transition from the "theologian" Benedict XVI to Francis has made a dramatic impact. Francis's teaching has addressed the role of theologians in the church only indirectly and occasionally. But Francis's detached relationship with academic theologians both as a Jesuit priest and as a pope must be part of our understanding of his ecumenism and of his theology in general. Ecumenism is one of those fields in which the task, method, and goals of academic theologians and of church leaders are—and must be—in constant dialogue but, simultaneously, are and must be different.

Second, Francis's ecumenism is not systematic. It is contextual and inductive. It is spiritual, not dogmatic. Again, this is an element that is key for the whole of Pope Francis, not just for his ecumenism; for the papacy as such, not just for Francis's pontificate. The relationship between papacy and ecumenism in Francis needs to be further explored. It is interesting to see that Vatican II and ecumenism are very present in the Aparecida document of 2007, but in that document (largely the fruit of Bergoglio's crucial role at that conference of CELAM, as Mangiarotti explores in this volume), John XXIII is not mentioned. Bergoglio's closeness to Roncalli and Francis's understanding of the papacy in relation to John XXIII seemed to have been activated by the conclave of 2013 and his election to the papacy.[40]

Third, Francis's ecumenism is "postconfessional" in the sense that it breaks the boundaries of post-Reformation European *Konfessionalisierung*. Francis is representative of the post-European papacy, and this helps in redefining European cultural-theological boundaries that, in the previous century, shaped the parameters of ecumenical dialogue. Global Christianity seen from a non-European perspective is helping the Catholic Church to exit an early modern European history of confessionalization, followed by secularization. *LS* has provided us with more elements to understand the relationship between Francis's teaching and the world of ecumenism—especially the difference between the Orthodox churches and the churches of the Reformation as sources for his theology and his documents. The visibility given to the Orthodox churches in *LS* is revealing of the silence in his documents about the churches of the Reformation and the WCC, though there are some clear parallels, as Kim's chapter explores.

Fourth, Francis's is an "existential ecumenism," that is, part of his efforts is to address systemic social challenges, to care for the poor and disenfranchised. It is not the ecumenism of the satisfied but of the hungry. For this, the ecumenical tone of *LS* is an integral part of this "existential ecumenism." It is not the same "ecumenism of the trenches" that neoconservative American Catholics and non-Catholics have talked about in this last decade: Pope Francis is not a cultural warrior. He is not only nonideological, he is anti-ideological, and this is key to understanding his ecumenism.

Fifth, Francis's ecumenical ecclesiology is a step forward from the mixed ecclesiology(ies) of Vatican II, where institutional ecclesiology had the last word over ecumenical ecclesiology—especially in the reception of the documents during the post–Vatican II period. Francis receives from the magisterium the distinction between "churches" and "ecclesial communities" (*EG* 183; *LS* 7), but he transcends it. Francis's ecumenical ecclesiology receives, but goes beyond, *Gaudium et Spes* and *Unitatis Redintegratio*. Francis's ecumenism is nonecclesiocentric, but it is in line with the ecumenism of Vatican II in the sense that there is a direct connection between ecumenism and ecclesial renewal/reform in the direction of a change not exclusively focused on the structure and institution.

The conclave in 2013 and the election of Francis have returned the Catholic Church to its global dimension—in a sense, trying to restore the promise made at Vatican II. The church has realigned itself to a more "world church" dimension, just as it was in that Council: from *urbs* to the *orbis terrarum*, the *oikumene*. In this sense, Pope Francis's encyclicals, exhortations, and actions mark a new chapter in the history of ecumenism.

Select Bibliography

Faggioli, Massimo. *Pope Francis: Tradition in Transition*. New York: Paulist Press, 2015.

Pope Francis. "Address during the Visit to the Community of Pentecostals near Naples," July 28, 2014. http://w2.vatican.va/content/francesco/en/speeches/2014/july/documents/papa-francesco_20140728_caserta-pastore-traettino.html.

————. "Joint Declaration with Ecumenical Patriarch Bartholomew of Constantinople and Archbishop Ieronymos of Athens and All Greece, Island of Lesbos," April 16, 2016. https://w2.vatican.va/content/francesco/en/speeches/2016/april/documents/papa-francesco_20160416_lesvos-dichiarazione-congiunta.html.

————. "Joint Declaration with Ecumenical Patriarch Bartholomew of Constantinople during Their Visit of Jerusalem," May 25, 2014. https://w2.vatican.va/content/francesco/en/speeches/2014/may/documents/papa-francesco_20140525_terra-santa-dichiarazione-congiunta.html.

————. "Joint Declaration with Ecumenical Patriarch Bartholomew of Constantinople in Istanbul," November 30, 2014. http://w2.vatican.va/content/francesco/en/speeches/2014/november/documents/papa-francesco_20141130_turchia-firma-dichiarazione.html.

————. "Letter to Christians in the Middle East," December 23, 2014. http://w2.vatican.va/content/francesco/en/letters/2014/documents/papa-francesco_20141221_lettera-cristiani-medio-oriente.html.

————. "Speech for the Fifty Years of the Creation of the Bishops' Synod." October 17, 2015. http://w2.vatican.va/content/francesco/en/speeches/2015/october/documents/papa-francesco_20151017_50-anniversario-sinodo.html.

Spadaro, Antonio. "Intervista a papa Francesco." *Civiltà Cattolica*, 3918 (September 19, 2013), 449–77 (in English as *A Big Heart Open to God: A Conversation with Pope Francis*. Interview by Antonio Spadaro, SJ. New York: HarperOne, 2013).

Notes

1. For Joseph Ratzinger's approach to *Gaudium et Spes*, see his introduction, in the series of his complete works, to the first of the two volumes dedicated to Vatican II: "Vorwort," in *Zur Lehre des Zweiten Vatikanischen Konzils. Formulierung—Vermittlung—Deutung*, Joseph Ratzinger Gesammelte Schriften, vol. 7/1 (Freiburg i.B.: Herder, 2012), 5–9, esp. 6–7. See also Carlos Schickendantz, "¿Una

transformación metodológica inadvertida? La novedad introducida por *Gaudium et Spes* en los escritos de Joseph Ratzinger," *Teología y Vida* 57, no. 1 (2016): 9–37; Theobald, *La réception du concile Vatican II. Vol. I. Accéder à la source* (Paris: Cerf, 2009) 641–54, esp. 652–53.

2. Massimo Faggioli, "The Parallel Lives of Two Surprising Popes: John XXIII and Francis," *Japan Mission Journal* 70, no. 2 (Summer, 2016): 75–85.

3. Christoph Theobald, "Mistica della fraternità. Lo stile nuovo della chiesa e della teologia nei documenti programmatici del pontificato," in *Il Regno—attualità* 9 (2015): 581–88 (from the lecture delivered at the University of Vienna on October 15, 2015).

4. About this particular feature of contemporary Christianity and Francis's ecumenism, see Walter Kasper, "L'unità attraverso la diversità," in *Il Regno—attualità* 9 (2015): 623–29 (lecture delivered at the Ecclesiological Investigations conference at Georgetown University in Washington, DC, May 21–24, 2015, originally published in *Origins* 45 (2015): 153–59.

5. See, for example, Marco Politi, *Francesco tra i lupi. Il segreto di una rivoluzione* (Roma-Bari: Laterza, 2014. English translation: New York, Columbia University Press, 2015).

6. See Gerald Whelan, "*Evangelii Gaudium* come 'teologia contestuale': aiutare la chiesa ad 'alzarsi al livello dei suoi tempi,'" in *Evangelii Gaudium: il testo ci interroga. Chiavi di lettura, testimonianze e prospettive*, ed. Humberto Miguel Yanez (Roma: Gregorian and Biblical Press, 2014), 23–38.

7. For more on this, see Walter Kasper, *Harvesting the Fruits: Basic Aspects of Christian Faith in Ecumenical Dialogue* (New York: Continuum, 2009).

8. See *Annuario Pontificio 2013*, 23.

9. See Pope Francis's interview with Andrea Tornielli of the Italian newspaper *La Stampa*, December 14, 2013, http://www.lastampa.it/2013/12/15/esteri/vatican-insider/it/mai-avere-paura-della-tenerezza-1vmuRIcbjQlD5BzTsnVuvK/pagina.html.

10. A significant example is the tone of Francis's messages to the new ecclesial movements in the first two years of pontificate: see Massimo Faggioli, *Sorting Out Catholicism: A Brief History of the New Ecclesial Movements* (Collegeville, MN: Liturgical, 2014); and

Massimo Faggioli, *The Rising Laity. Ecclesial Movements after Vatican II* (New York: Paulist Press, 2016).

11. For a critical assessment of *Anglicanorum Coetibus*, see *La costituzione Anglicanorum Coetibus e l'ecumenismo*, ed. Giuseppe Ruggieri (Bologna: EDB, 2012).

12. Stephen Bevans, "Beyond the New Evangelization: Toward a Missionary Ecclesiology for the Twenty-First Century," in *A Church with Open Doors: Catholic Ecclesiology for the Third Millennium*, ed. Richard R. Gaillardetz and Edward P. Hahnenberg (Collegeville, MN: Liturgical, 2015), 3–22.

13. See the most important biographies of Jorge Mario Bergoglio—Pope Francis: Elisabetta Piquè, *Pope Francis: Life and Revolution: A Biography of Jorge Bergoglio* (Chicago: Loyola Press, 2014, original Spanish 2013); Austen Ivereigh, *The Great Reformer: Francis and the Making of a Radical Pope* (New York: Holt, 2014); Paul Vallely, *Pope Francis: Untying the Knots; The Struggle for the Soul of Catholicism* (New York: Bloomsbury, 2015, first edition 2013).

14. About the relations between synodality and ecumenism in Francis, see the speech to the Bishops' Synod of October 17, 2015: "For this reason, speaking recently to a delegation from the Patriarchate of Constantinople, I reaffirmed my conviction that 'a careful examination of how, in the Church's life, the principle of synodality and the service of the one who presides are articulated, will make a significant contribution to the progress of relations between our Churches.'" http://w2.vatican.va/content/francesco/en/speeches/2015/october/documents/papa-francesco_20151017_50-anniversario-sinodo.html.

15. About the role of *Unitatis Redintegratio* 11 and the "hierarchy of truths" in Francis, see the book-interview conducted by Paolo Rodari with Archbishop Víctor Manuel Fernández, one of the closest advisors to Jorge Mario Bergoglio, *Il progetto di Francesco. Dove vuole portare la chiesa* (Bologna: EMI, 2014).

16. About the culture wars in the United States, see Andrew Hartman, *A War for the Soul of America: A History of the Culture Wars* (Chicago: University of Chicago Press, 2015). About Francis and the culture wars in the United States, see John Gehring, *The Francis Effect: A Radical Pope's Challenge to the American Catholic Church* (Lanham, MD: Rowman & Littlefield Publishers, 2016).

17. See Rod Dreher, "The New 'Ecumenism of Trenches,'"

The American Conservative, June 9, 2015, http://www.theamerican
conservative.com/dreher/christianity-islam-ecumenism
-trenches-colson-neuhaus/. The expression has been widely used
in neoconservative circles in the United States: see http://www
.firstthings.com/web-exclusives/2015/03/introduction-to-the
-first-ect-statement.

18. See Giuseppe Alberigo, "Critères herméneutiques pour
une histoire de Vatican II," in *À la Veille du Concile Vatican II. Vota
et Réactions en Europe et dans le Catholicisme oriental,* ed. Mathijs
Lamberigts and Claude Soetens (Louvain: Faculté de Théologie,
Centre Lumen Gentium, 1992), 12–23.

19. About the impact of John XXIII's *Gaudet Mater Ecclesia*
on Vatican II, see John W. O'Malley, *What Happened at Vatican
II* (Cambridge, MA: Belknap Press of Harvard University Press,
2008), 93–96; Andrea Riccardi, "The Tumultuous Opening Days
of the Council," in *History of Vatican II,* ed. Giuseppe Alberigo,
English edition by Joseph A. Komonchak, vol. 2 (Maryknoll, NY:
Orbis, 1997), 14–19.

20. See Massimo Faggioli, *Pope Francis: Tradition in Transition*
(New York: Paulist Press, 2015), 61–84.

21. For the relationship between liturgical reform and ecumenism, see Massimo Faggioli, *True Reform: Liturgy and Ecclesiology in
Sacrosanctum Concilium* (Collegeville, MN: Liturgical Press, 2012).

22. See Antonio Spadaro, *Intervista a papa Francesco,* in
"Civiltà Cattolica" 3918 (September 19, 2013), 449–77.

23. Pope Francis mentioned the importance of Vatican II for
the negotiations with the SSPX in his interview with La Croix of May
17, 2016 (English translation in http://www.globalpulsemagazine
.com/news/interview-with-pope-francis-by-la-croix/3184). During
the summer of 2016, there has been a pushback from the SSPX:
see the communiqué from the Superior General of the SSPX,
Bernard Fellay, on June 29, 2016, http://www.dici.org/en/news/
communique-from-the-superior-general/.

24. See http://w2.vatican.va/content/francesco/en/speeches
/2013/may/documents/papa-francesco_20130510_tawadros
.html.

25. See https://w2.vatican.va/content/francesco/en/speeches
/2013/june/documents/papa-francesco_20130614_welby
-canterbury.html.

26. See http://w2.vatican.va/content/francesco/en/speeches/2014/may/documents/papa-francesco_20140508_patriarca-armeni.html.

27. For the joint declaration of Francis and Bartholomew of May 25, 2014, see https://w2.vatican.va/content/francesco/it/speeches/2014/may/documents/papa-francesco_20140525_terra-santa-dichiarazione-congiunta.html.

28. For the joint declaration of November 30, 2014, see http://w2.vatican.va/content/francesco/en/speeches/2014/november/documents/papa-francesco_20141130_turchia-firma-dichiarazione.html.

29. See http://w2.vatican.va/content/francesco/en/speeches/2014/july/documents/papa-francesco_20140728_caserta-pastore-traettino.html. About this, see Raffaele Nogaro and Sergio Tanzarella, *Francesco e i pentecostali. L'ecumenismo del poliedro* (Trapani: Il Pozzo di Giacobbe, 2015).

30. See http://w2.vatican.va/content/francesco/en/letters/2014/documents/papa-francesco_20141221_lettera-cristiani-medio-oriente.html.

31. See http://w2.vatican.va/content/francesco/en/speeches/2015/may/documents/papa-francesco_20150504_chiesa-evangelico-luterana-svezia.html.

32. *Laudato Si'* is dated May 24, 2015, and was presented on June 18, 2015, in the Vatican also by Orthodox bishop John Zizioulas.

33. See http://w2.vatican.va/content/francesco/it/speeches/2015/june/documents/papa-francesco_20150622_torino-chiesa-valdese.html.

34. See http://w2.vatican.va/content/francesco/it/speeches/2015/november/documents/papa-francesco_20151115_chiesa-evangelica-luterana.html.

35. See https://w2.vatican.va/content/francesco/en/travels/2015/outside/documents/papa-francesco-africa-2015.html.

36. See https://w2.vatican.va/content/francesco/en/travels/2016/outside/documents/papa-francesco-lesvos-2016.html.

37. "Human ecology" is in Francis, encyclical *Laudato Si'* (May 24, 2015), no. 5, that quotes John Paul II, encyclical *Centesimus Annus* (May 1, 1991), no. 38.

38. See Francis, post-synodal Apostolic Exhortation *Amoris Laetitia* (March 19, 2016).

39. Pope Francis, video message on the occasion of the Day for Christian Unity, which took place in Phoenix, Arizona, in the United States on May 23, 2015, http://www.news.va/en/news/pope-sends-greetings-for-us-christian-unity-event.

40. About this, see Massimo Faggioli, "The Parallel Lives of Two Surprising Popes: John XXIII and Francis," *Japan Mission Journal* 70, no. 2 (Summer 2016): 75–85.

8

"The Joy of the Gospel" and "Together towards Life"

Comparing the Apostolic Exhortation of Pope Francis and the Statement of the World Council of Churches on Mission and Evangelism

KIRSTEEN KIM

Earlier in the same year that Pope Francis published the Apostolic Exhortation on evangelization, *Evangelii Gaudium* or "The Joy of the Gospel" (*EG*), the World Council of Churches (WCC) published a position statement on mission and evangelism, the first for thirty years, which was titled "Together towards Life: Mission and Evangelism in Changing Landscapes" (TTL). The appearance of these two documents on such similar themes together in 2013 gives an excellent opportunity for a comparative study of the contemporary mission thinking of two global bodies that claim respectively upward of one-half and one-third of all the world's Christians. This chapter will first consider the different origins and processes that produced each of these documents. Then, second, it will analyze their contents from the perspective of the theology and history of mission in order to identify convergences and differences. Finally, it will argue that the implications of the documents for ecumenical mission[1] include a renewed understanding of catholicity and ecumenism that is international and intercultural; the development of mission spirituality; and a rethinking of the terminology of mission/evangelization.

Origins and Processes of TTL and *EG*

TTL and *EG* originate from global bodies with different constitutions and ways of operating. Before any comparison is made, it is helpful to consider the provenance and nature of the two documents.[2] In this section, I will introduce TTL and, although the background to *EG* is also treated in other chapters in this volume, I shall draw attention to some aspects of the exhortation that are relevant to TTL.

TTL, subtitled "Mission and Evangelism in Changing Landscapes," was the work of the WCC Commission for World Mission and Evangelism (CWME). The origins of the commission are in the International Missionary Council, which was created to continue the work of the World Missionary Conference in Edinburgh in 1910 and joined the WCC in 1961. The Commission started working on a new affirmation on mission and evangelism following the assembly of the World Council of Churches at Porto Allegre in 2006. To date, the only WCC position statement on mission and evangelism was "Mission and Evangelism: An Ecumenical Affirmation" (EA) from 1982.[3] While recognizing the enduring validity of that document, considering the changes in the global landscape since then, the new commissioners made expressing an ecumenical theology of mission for today the main aim of their work. The commission had twenty-five members plus about five WCC staff, including a Catholic consultant seconded by the Vatican. Fifty percent of the commissioners represented WCC member churches (Protestant and Orthodox), 25 percent were from mission bodies associated with member churches, and 25 percent of the commissioners were representatives from nonmember churches. The latter category included evangelical, Pentecostal, and Catholic representatives.

The process adopted for composing the new document was a consensual one. After identifying together the four main sections of the document, the commissioners worked in groups on each, while the introduction and conclusion were drafted by Dr. Jooseop Keum, director of the Commission. The drafting group aimed to preserve the integrity of each contribution while combining these into one coherent document. The final draft of the complete document was scrutinized by the two hundred delegates at the CWME preassembly mission conference in Manila in 2012. As a result, it underwent some further revision before being presented to the WCC Central Committee, which unanimously approved it at its meeting at the Orthodox Academy in Crete in September 2012. "Together towards Life" was published in 2013 and formed the basis of one of the plenary sessions of the general assembly of the WCC in South Korea later that year.[4] As an official statement it informs WCC policy and is commended to all member churches for study and reflection.

The opening section of TTL has a series of faith statements that are amplified in the main body of the document and result in a series of affirmations and action points at the end. The four main sections deal with the mission of the Spirit, mission from the margins, church and mission, and evangelism. The distinctive feature of TTL as compared not only with EA but also with other previous WCC policy documents is its use of a pneumatological framework for theology of mission. This approach is justified and amplified in the first main section of the document, "Spirit of Mission: Breath of Life." Despite earlier controversy over pneumatology at the seventh WCC general assembly in Canberra (Australia) in 1991,[5] the CWME pursued this approach for multiple theological reasons. These included biblical reflection on the Spirit as "the guiding and driving force of mission";[6] Orthodox insistence on the need for proper attention to pneumatology in ecumenical theology; the liberating work of the Spirit as noted by liberation theologians who saw that "the Spirit of the Lord is upon me" meant "good news to the poor" (Luke 4:18); the desire to reach out to the rapidly growing Pentecostal churches and address their focus on the power and gifts of the Holy Spirit; the rich resources of creation pneumatology for the development of theologies of eco-justice; the use of pneumatology as the justification for dialogue; and the pneumatological approach developed by CWME to healing and reconciliation in preparation for the conference in Athens in 2005.[7] Other more immediate reasons were, first, that a pneumatological approach would complement the Christology of the 1982 document; second, it would allow for a direct contribution to the theme of the WCC's forthcoming thirteenth assembly, which was "God of life, lead us to justice and peace;" and third, the Commission's involvement in the Edinburgh 2010 (centenary) project suggested that a pneumatological approach would have an appeal beyond WCC member churches to reach all strands of Christianity.[8] The second theme of "mission from the margins" was partly a development of the concern for the poor expressed in EA to include all categories of marginalization. It drew especially on the work of the WCC's Just and Inclusive Communities program and Dalit experience in India, which stressed the agency of the marginalized.[9] The work on the third part, mission ecclesiology, reflected collaboration of CWME with the WCC Commission on Faith and Order between the twelfth and thirteenth assemblies.[10] Development of the final main section of TTL on evangelism was greatly helped by CWME involvement in the production of the document "Christian Witness in a Multi-Religious World: Recommendations for Conduct" jointly by the WCC, the Pontifical Council for Interreligious Dialogue (PCID), and the World Evangelical Alliance.[11]

"The Joy of the Gospel" reveals the concerns of Pope Francis himself and is his authentic voice.[12] However, the exhortation also needs to be understood in its context as the Apostolic Exhortation following the thirteenth Synod of Bishops (October 7–28, 2012). The theme for the synod had been set by Pope Benedict XVI, namely, "The new evangelization for the transmission of the Christian faith." He described the aim of the new evangelization as a re-presentation of the gospel in regions where the process of secularization had led to "abandonment of the faith," which were to be found especially in Europe and the West.[13] The *Lineamenta* prepared by a specially created dicastery, the Pontifical Council for Promoting the New Evangelization,[14] emphasized the duty to evangelize in obedience to the missionary mandate of Mark 16:15 and Matthew 28:20 (nos. 11, 18) and the primary model of the evangelist was the Apostle Paul, who preached the gospel with urgency, whether or not it was requested.[15] The new evangelization was said to depend on faithful proclamation of the word of

God (no. 13), renewed emphasis on catechesis and the catechu-menate (no. 14), the agency of local churches (no. 15), and the ability of all Christians to give an account of their faith (no. 16). However, the *Propositions* coming out of the Synod were consider-ably more wide-ranging than the preparatory documentation had suggested. They showed that the rest of the world did not share the preoccupation with Europe or agree with the narrowing of evangelization, especially as this might detract from attention to issues of justice and peace.[16]

Evangelii Gaudium is generally in line with these proposi-tions, to many of which it refers.[17] In marked contrast to views that focused evangelization on proclamation and catechesis, the pope describes it broadly as turning the church outward rather than toward its own survival (*EG* 27). Furthermore, *Evangelii Gaudium* synthesizes mission *ad gentes* with the new evangeliza-tion. This is indicated by Francis's use of two key sources for the meaning of evangelization: first, the usage of Pope Paul VI in his exhortation *Evangelii Nuntiandi* (*EN*, 1975) and, second, the origi-nal Latin American coinage of "new evangelization." In *EG*, Pope Francis refers to documents of Paul VI far more than any other pope, and significantly, he even uses Paul VI for the joy that is the theme of the exhortation (*EG* 3, 10). In particular, following *EN*, he takes Jesus—rather than Paul—as the model evangelizer (*EG* 12), sees the renewal of the church as integral to evangelization (*EG* 26), and promotes a broad understanding of evangelization encompassing proclamation, social justice, inculturation, and pastoral ministry (*EG* 26, 176, 181, 186, 190, 219).[18] Regarding the second source, the term *new evangelization* was coined in Latin America. When John Paul II referred, at the nineteenth general assembly of the Latin American Bishops' Conference in Haiti in 1983, to "a commitment...of a new evangelization—new in its fer-vor, in its methods, and in its expression,"[19] he was using a term he had already encountered in meetings with the Latin American Episcopate. There *new evangelization* signaled primarily a depar-ture from the methods of the first, brutal evangelization by the empires of Spain and Portugal to one that more fully embraced the particular concerns of Latin America. As such it had a new content of social change, a new method of participation with the various cultures present in the continent and new expressions in the cultural profiles of the people, and it would result in new life for the poor.[20] Unsurprisingly, Pope Francis's usage is closer to the Latin American meaning. *EG* is most directly indebted to the final document of the Latin American Bishops' Conference at Aparecida (CELAM VII), for which Francis himself chaired the drafting group.[21] In sum, *EG* puts forward a renewed and comprehensive understanding of evangelization informed by reflection on the world church in much the same way as TTL expresses a fresh and holistic view of mission resulting from global Christian conversation.

Significant Convergences and Differences between TTL and *EG*

In this section, I will discuss significant convergences between TTL and *EG* under six headings. I see these convergences as including, first, two tools of analysis of the context of mission/evangelization: world Christianity and cultures. Second, from my perspective, all four themes of TTL loom large in *EG* as well: margins, the church, evangelism, and pneumatology. During the discussion, I shall also note some themes that are particular to one document or the other.

First, both documents recognize the global or "world" nature of the Christian faith and, related to that, the need to evangelize in a way that is respectful of cultural diversity. TTL is shaped by the approach of "world Christianity," which originates in the work of Andrew F. Walls. Walls drew attention to the recent "shift in the centre of gravity" of Christianity from the Global North to the South and to the dominance of Asia and Africa in the early spread of Christianity.[22] The study of world Christianity utilizes demographic, theological, geographical, sociological, historical, and ecclesiological methods to study Christianity as globally widespread, locally rooted in different regions, and transnationally connected in multiple directions.[23] The Edinburgh 2010 project illustrated world Christianity in its polycentric study project, in its celebration of the way in which Christianity is no longer a predominantly European religion, and in the book series that emerged from it that is inclusive of all forms of Christianity and all regions. Similarly, TTL was drafted by a globally as well as ecclesially diverse commission. Some of the effects on TTL of the world Christianity approach are its use of liberation and post-colonial theological discourses; its stress on the agency of those perceived to be marginalized; its attention to migration and its role in spreading the gospel; its affirmation of popular evangelical and Pentecostal movements; and its acknowledgment of the influence of non-Western Christianity on recent developments in theology and mission.

Although the term *world Christianity* is not generally used in Catholic discourse, some of the same perspectives can be seen in the Apostolic Exhortation. The first pope from outside Europe for 1300 years rejects any European cultural imperialism and the "hallowing" of any particular culture (*EG* 117, 118). He stresses the global and local nature of the church and the polycentric and multidirectional nature of mission (nos. 20, 25, 30). This decentralization implies changes in the exercise of primacy. So the pope relativizes his own position, describing himself as Bishop of Rome (only) and refusing to pronounce on topics that are within the competence and jurisdiction of the local church (nos. 32, 184). Furthermore, it implies internationalization of the administration and magisterium, which Francis has been pursuing.[24] The pope states his intention to realize the potential of the episcopal conferences (no. 32) and demonstrates this by quoting and including references to the statements of bishops from different parts of the world in the exhortation itself (e.g., nos. 25, 110, 118, 191, 230). The pope's perspective from outside the West is evident not only in the recognition of the geopolitical and cultural diversity of the Catholic Church and the concern to restructure it to make it more representative. It is also apparent in the attention given to socioeconomic issues, which we shall deal with later, and also to the topic of inculturation.

The second tool of analysis in both documents is "culture." TTL always refers to culture as a plural concept. The world is seen as multicultural and, in a way that is closely linked to that, multireligious (no. 9). TTL envisages multiple "economic, social, cultural, and political systems" (no. 41) that include "societies, cultures, civilizations, nations, and even churches" (no. 42) that are mutually overlapping (no. 71). The document sees "cultural difference as a gift of the Spirit" (no. 75; cf. no. 27) and discusses multicultural and "intercultural engagement" positively (no. 70). Like *EG*, it envisages a "multicultural church" (TTL 75)—"a people of many faces" (*EG* 117). Altogether, it celebrates the riches of world Christianity.

In *EG*, culture is defined as that which "embraces the totality of a people's life," and multiple cultures are recognized (no. 115) but these are treated separately from religions. *EG* is positive about culture as the receptacle in which "God's gift [of grace] becomes flesh" (no. 115) and evangelization as "enriching" and "transforming" communities (no. 116). As befits a Jesuit pope, Francis stresses "evangelization as inculturation" (no. 122) through socialization and education (no. 129; cf. nos. 68–69) and theological "dialogue" with "sciences and human experiences" (no. 133).[25] Like TTL, the primary usage of culture is from cultural anthropology, which has dominated mission studies and tended to encourage the categorization of people by culture.[26] However, *EG* does point out that culture is not self-determining; rather, it is "a dynamic reality which a people constantly recreates" (no. 122).

Whereas *EG* is overwhelmingly positive in its reference to culture, TTL divides cultures into those that are "life-affirming" and those that are not. It seeks to work with the former (nos. 27, 110) but takes a countercultural, confrontational approach to the latter (nos. 37, 49, 108). These colonial or neocolonial cultures are accused of generating and sustaining "massive poverty, discrimination, and dehumanization" and of exploiting or destroying people and the earth (no. 37). So TTL overlays the multicultural model with an ideological distinction between the market, or mammon, on the one hand, which is culturally hegemonic (no. 98), and the Spirit of life on the other, which is liberating. In contrast, Francis emphasizes that "realities are greater than ideas" and puts ideology aside in favor of practice (*EG* 233). Although he refers similarly to a destructive "prevailing culture" brought about by globalization (no. 62; cf. also nos. 53, 54, 79), he affirms European cultures as among those that can be said to have been evangelized—a condition chiefly recognized by a "Christian substratum," especially in the realm of values (no. 68). Although the faith must be inculturated, Francis believes there are universal and "objective moral norms" (no. 64), and one of these is "the option for the poor" (no. 198). For Francis, these universal obligations that transcend local concerns are theological. However, TTL is dominated by a relativist approach in which everything is cultural and there are multiple theologies. The only transcendent reality is life, which is given by the Spirit.

Third, the poor and the margins constitute a key theme in both *EG* and TTL. The Apostolic Exhortation of the first ever pope from Latin America unsurprisingly shows the influence of liberation theology and may even be counted as the work of a liberation theologian.[27] In any case, at least since John Paul II's *Centesimus Annus* (*CA*, 1991), "the option for the poor" has been official Catholic teaching (nos. 11, 57), and one of the key challenges to the new evangelization was its near-absence from the initial agenda.[28] In *EG*, Francis makes evangelization into "good news to the poor" (no. 197). There is no "option": evangelization means "human advancement" (no. 178), the kingdom of God (no. 180) and "a better world" (no. 183). In passages echoing liberation theologians,[29] as well as the church's teaching on solidarity, he insists that the poor are part of human society and should be treated as neighbors (nos. 186, 204) with a special concern for the vulnerable (no. 209). Beyond organizing for the poor, the Pope commends "loving attentiveness" and accompaniment on the "path of liberation" (no. 199). Furthermore, he completes the action-reflection hermeneutical circle by asserting that the poor themselves are agents of evangelization (no. 198).[30]

TTL is more influenced by Asian than by Latin American liberation theologies and also by postcolonial studies. This is shown in its preference for "marginalization" rather than liberation. It is used to examine power relations more generally and to take account not only of economic status but also of race, caste, and community. As its title implies, the section on mission *from* the margins (nos. 36–54) emphasizes even more the evangelizing potential of the poor. In this perspective, the aim of mission is "not simply to move people from the margins to centers of power" but to include everyone (nos. 46–49) by transforming power structures (no. 40) and recognizing the personhood of all human beings (no. 42). In *EG* too, themes of inequality, exclusion, and violence recur[31] and "the marginalized" are also referred to (*EG* 53, 60). The liberationist emphasis in *EG* on sin being not only personal but also structural is found as well in the call for justice and peace with justice (nos. 217–21). Like TTL, the pope explicitly criticizes the ideology of the capitalist system and condemns its effects of indebtedness and consumerism (nos. 53–57, 60, 69, 202, 204), calling instead for an inclusive economy (nos. 53–54) and an ethical approach to economics (202–8).

Being addressed "to all Christians everywhere" (no. 3), *EG* challenges injustice by using chiefly biblical resources and adds an appeal to the "common good" as developed in Western ethics. However, this approach has limitations when seeking cooperation with other religions, or those of no religion, and especially where Christians are a minority, such as in most countries of Asia. Consequently, TTL prefers the wider category of "life." In TTL "life in all its fullness" (John 10:10), including not only human life but the whole created world, is the defining goal of mission. Life is the criterion for discernment in mission (TTL 102); mission is defined as finding out where the Spirit of life is at work and joining in (nos., 18, 25, 110) or engagement in whatever is life-affirming and resistance to whatever is life-denying (e.g. nos. 2, 102). Throughout most of the document, it is assumed that what constitutes life is recognizable to all human beings, although the document also points to Jesus Christ as "the life of the world" (no. 1; cf. no. 112).

Fourth, both *EG* and TTL stress the missionary nature of the church locally as well as globally. The missionary "impulse" is seen as integral to the Christian life because it is a response to the love of God (*EG* 262–63; TTL 55–56). Therefore all Christians and the "entire people of God" (*EG* 111) are evangelizers or missionaries, or "missionary disciples" in the phraseology of *EG*. All areas of church life are "missional" or "missionary" (TTL 10) and "missionary outreach" is "paradigmatic for all the Church's activity," including pastoral ministry (*EG* 15).[32]

Each of the statements devotes space to the structures of the church as the instrument of God's mission (*EG* 26–27; TTL 67–79) and to the qualities of those carrying out mission or evangelization. *EG* stresses the need for the renewal of the church to be "for the evangelization of today's world rather than for her self-preservation"

199

(no. 27). Francis envisages an open and engaged church (no. 46, 49). In TTL, the church is less prominent (and in lower case) because mission is defined primarily as God's mission and the focus is on "life," which is manifested especially in the church, but encompasses the whole creation (e.g., no. 58). Within this, the existence of the church is said to be "for the sake of mission" (no. 57). In TTL, the renewal of the church for mission is primarily in terms of rediscovering its unity in diversity as well as its communal nature and its inclusivity. As far as the evangelists are concerned, *EG* discusses the need for pastoral workers to overcome various temptations (nos. 76–109) and for evangelization to arise from a personal encounter with Christ (nos. 264–67). TTL calls for "authentic" witness and evangelism in the way of Christ (nos. 86–92). Both documents enjoin a missionary or mission spirituality (*EG* 78–80, 102–6; TTL 30–33). *EG* stresses the empowerment of the whole church, in virtue of baptism (no. 120), to become "Spirit-filled evangelizers" (no. 259). However in TTL, mindful of the triumphalism of colonial mission (nos. 27, 98), the emphasis is more on self-emptying than on empowerment, and on vulnerability and humility in evangelizing (e.g., nos. 8, 23, 33, 62, 71, 87, 89, 92, 106).

Fifth, both documents give attention to proclamation, preaching, and the call to conversion. TTL treats this under "evangelism," which it defines as "mission activity which makes explicit and unambiguous the centrality of the incarnation, suffering, and resurrection of Jesus Christ" (no. 80). Much like the "new evangelization" presented to the synod, "evangelism" is a particular expression of mission or witness that includes an "invitation to personal conversion to a new life in Christ" (no. 85). The TTL statement on evangelism affirms proclamation while, on the one hand, reigning in proselytizers, whose activities threaten community cohesion in various parts of the world, and on the other, combining the socially prophetic with the more religious dimensions of Christian witness. It does so in several ways: first, it focuses on the sacrificial way of Jesus in the Gospels (nos. 86–92); second, by advocating a dialogical approach to evangelism that affirms diversity (nos. 93–100); and third, by returning to a definition of the WCC from 1951: evangelism is "the communication of the whole gospel to the whole of humanity in the whole world" (no. 80).[33] The focus of TTL statements on evangelism are on the contentious issue of religious conversion.[34] However, *EG* avoids this topic because it uses *conversion* only with reference to the church. Perhaps because Pope Francis comes from a predominantly Christian context, he does not discuss the challenges to evangelization in multireligious contexts, which are treated instead in the short section on dialogue (*EG* 247–54).

In *EG*, chapter 3 is devoted to proclamation. Francis echoes the WCC definition (consciously or not) when he declares that "the entire people of God proclaims the gospel" (no. 111) "for everyone" (no. 112–14) in all cultures (nos. 115–18) and when he inserts "the social dimension" into the project of the new evangelization. Although he stresses that popular piety is a means of evangelization (nos. 122–26), in his consideration of proclamation, he also highlights the more professional activities of preaching and the homily (nos. 135–59) and catechesis (nos. 163–68), following the topics of the synod of bishops. The latter activities are hardly mentioned in TTL because matters of faith and order, life and work are the business of other parts of the WCC. Consequently, TTL is mainly concerned with the world beyond the church, with the danger that mission is seen as peripheral to church life.

Finally, among the significant convergences, in both statements the Trinity is the starting point and the end of mission, and both pay particular attention to the work of the Holy Spirit. In accord with its theme of mission, TTL stresses the *sending* of the Spirit, which redounds to the glory of the triune God who invites all to the "Feast of Life" (nos. 101–12).[35] TTL's attention to the distinct mission of the Spirit in the world results in a predominantly pneumatological understanding of mission as finding out where the Holy Spirit is at work and joining in (nos. 18, 25, 110).[36] The churches are urged to discern the Holy Spirit among many other spirits by the criterion of life and to respond to the Spirit's leading with participation in God's mission (especially nos. 1, 24–28, 102). The intention is to encourage not only ecumenical cooperation (no. 63) but also to work with life-affirming cultures and religions (nos. 27, 110) and to partner the poor and marginalized (nos, 98, 107).

The pneumatological underpinnings of *EG* are not quite as dominating as in TTL, but an emphasis on the Holy Spirit is apparent at the outset, and it is interwoven throughout. The Holy Spirit is the source of the joy that is the means by, and the medium in which, the gospel is proclaimed (nos. 5, 141). The Spirit animates ministry (no. 15), impels evangelization (nos. 119, 130), guides the evangelizer (nos. 14, 119, 139), and nourishes the missionary disciple (nos. 50, 84, 97, 145, 280). The Spirit raises up communities of evangelism (no. 29), is manifested in "works of love" (no. 37) and "loving attentiveness" (no. 199), and reconciles different parts of the church (no. 40, cf. nos. 131, 230, 246). The mission pneumatology comes to a climax in the last chapter in which the spirit of the new evangelization is likened to the Spirit of Pentecost and Mary is described as its supreme exemplar.

As its title implies, joy typifies the approach of *EG* much as life does in TTL. Moreover, the two themes are also closely linked in that joy is due to resurrection life (*EG* 2–3; cf. no. 93) and the aim of the document is that dignified and fulfilled life of the Spirit of Christ (no. 2). Furthermore, like the "joining in with the Spirit" model of TTL, the pope envisages the church as "inserting ourselves into the divine initiative" (*EG* 112) and being led by the Spirit in evangelization (*EG* nos. 12, 119; cf. no. 21). In *EG*, the Holy Spirit is the principal agent of evangelization (no. 122; cf. nos. 68, 116, 178, 197) and goes ahead of the church (no. 279; cf. nos. 29, 47, 105, 112, 254, 265). Moreover, as in TTL, the prerequisite for this is discernment of spirits—drawn in Pope Francis's case from Ignatius of Loyola (*EG* 45, 51). Therefore, *EG* too may be said to express a mission pneumatology.

However, there is a significant pneumatological difference between *EG* and TTL. The latter envisages the Holy Spirit working freely in the whole cosmos and generating life in a broad sense, whether or not this is explicitly related to the church or to Christ, whereas in *EG*, the discussion of pneumatology is limited to the Spirit's redemptive work in human beings.[37] This difference between Catholic and ecumenical pneumatologies was pointed out by the Protestant theologian Jürgen Moltmann in the context of the Canberra Assembly, the theme of which was "Come, Holy Spirit, renew the whole creation!" and the publication the previous year (1990) of the encyclical *Redemptoris Missio* by John Paul II.[38] WCC development of a creation or cosmic pneumatology was in dialogue with Orthodox theologians, who give greater prominence than Western theology to the themes of creation and cosmos and relate these to the economic Trinity and to the distinct mission of the Spirit. It was also linked with growing ecological concern in mission. In 1990, "the integrity of creation" was added to the justice and peace agenda of the WCC, forming the JPIC movement that was particularly influential at Canberra.[39]

The link of the Spirit with life in TTL means it is not only a statement on mission but also on ecology. Pope Francis has produced a second document on evangelization and ecology— *Laudato Si'* (*LS*)—but *EG* and *LS* do not appear to share a common theological theme.[40] There is a remarkable reference in *EG* to the Trinity from the perspective of the economy: "The fire of the Spirit is given in the form of tongues and leads us to believe in Jesus Christ who, by his death and resurrection, reveals and communicates to us the Father's infinite mercy." (no. 164). Conversely, in *LS*, there is a perspective attributed to the Brazilian bishops that exhibits a creation pneumatology: "nature as a whole not only manifests God but is also a locus of his presence. The Spirit of life dwells in every living creature and calls us to enter into relationship with him. Discovering this presence leads us to cultivate the 'ecological virtues'" (*LS* 88). There are also several calls to avoid opposing the spiritual and the material. Development of this view of the mission of the Spirit in the creation is not foreign to Catholic theology[41] and could provide common ground for further exploration of the ecological dimensions of evangelization.

Some Implications of *EG* and TTL for Ecumenical Mission

Since TTL was in process from 2007 and involved Vatican representatives and other Catholics, the drafters of *EG* may have been aware of it, but there is no evidence of any direct dependence of *EG* on TTL. The striking convergences could equally result from more general, global theological conversation. The extent of confluence of the two documents has at least three consequences for ecumenical mission: a renewed understanding of catholicity and ecumenism that is international and intercultural, the development of mission spirituality, and a rethinking of the terminology of mission/evangelization.

The Catholic Church is one church throughout the world—a "Church without frontiers" (*EG* 210)—but Pope Francis has embraced the option for the poor, and an agenda of decentralization and internationalization of the church, in a way that is redefining catholicity.[42] The WCC, conversely, represents multiple churches striving for unity. Nevertheless, both *EG* and TTL speak positively about diversity as something that comes from the Holy Spirit (*EG* 131; TTL 66) and both call for charisms, especially arising from cultural diversity, to be recognized and also integrated into the church for the sake of mission (*EG* 131; TTL 27). The WCC would agree with Francis that "cultural diversity is not a threat to Church unity" but rather, the Holy Spirit creates "a unity which is never uniformity but a multifaceted and inviting harmony" (*EG* 117). TTL, which also frequently refers to charisms (as "gifts"), joins the papal plea to receive from one another "through an exchange of gifts" so that "the Spirit can lead us ever more fully into truth and goodness" (*EG* 246; cf. TTL 63).

Where *EG* encourages diversity within an established unity, TTL works in the opposite direction. Stemming from its conception in the colonial period, the ecumenical movement has referred primarily to overcoming denominational barriers of polity and doctrine and bringing visible and structural unity to global churches or church families. In TTL, the ecclesial categories have grown to include "Catholic, Orthodox, Anglican, Protestant, Evangelical, Pentecostal, and Indigenous churches" (no. 65), which include strong Christian movements emerging from outside the West (no. 5). However, the unity and "common witness" (no. 63) called for is increasingly across regional rather than denominational boundaries. In other words, *ecumenical* is used more in its meaning as applied to the early church councils and in the sense in which it is used in *EG*: the churches from around the world. Together TTL and *EG* draw attention to catholicity as cultural diversity. Furthermore, TTL recognizes that any local church may be described as much by its "geo-political and socio-economic context" (no. 78) or "ethnic and cultural" composition (no. 70) as by its denominational identity (if it has one). Together with *EG*'s decentralization, this would seem to open the possibility for deeper local expressions of ecumenism involving Catholics—indeed Pope Francis himself exemplified this in Buenos Aires.[43]

Migration is an additional challenge to unity and a feature of TTL, but it is mentioned only briefly in *EG* (no. 210). From the perspective of the study of world Christianity, TTL sees contemporary migration as one of the key issues "reshaping the Christian landscape" (nos. 5, 70). Churches without borders, or across boundaries, and increasingly "on the move" (TTL 55 title) pose a challenge to the settled churches of European tradition organized within national borders and into parishes, which are the focus of *EG*. Considering that in the New Testament, evangelization is accomplished through the scattering of churches as well as by missionary movements, in the present context of global migration there is room for further common reflection on migration and mission.[44]

Second, the two documents agree that mission/evangelization is the way of Christ (*EG* 21; TTL 88), which makes it not only central to faith but also to spirituality. This connection of mission and spirituality is used to bring together parts of the church that have often been separated. Pope Francis applies Ignatian spirituality to the whole church for the work of evangelization and develops a contemporary mission spirituality as he advises preachers, catechists, and evangelizers to trust in the Holy Spirit and cultivate Spirit-filled lives (*EG* 259–88). In this way, Pope Francis brings the life of the missionary communities into the heart of the life of the church, which is missionary. Furthermore, the pope also uses mission spirituality to affirm popular piety (no. 124) and the exercise of various charisms (no. 130). Both the religiosity of the poor and the charismatic renewal among the middle classes are appealed to here. Rather than being causes of heresy or schism, these movements are drawn closer into the people of God and through the Holy Spirit are said to adorn and pour out treasures on the church in mission (nos. 116–17).

Mission spirituality is also a significant theme of TTL that is linked to its pneumatological framework. Its development of mission spirituality is against a background of the association of mission with activism, and even violence, and of spirituality with quietism.[45] A century ago at Edinburgh in 1910, Protestant mission thinkers were so focused on achieving the task of world evangelization and on discussing the most effective policies and strategies to bring this about, that the Holy Spirit was barely referred to except as the "super-human factor" that would bring about the victory of the missions.[46] A century later, their lack of critical reflection on their missionary methods and colonial power relations is glaring. The political theologies of the 1960s and '70s raised awareness of such structural violence in mission, but at the same time, they were tempted to support violent methods in service of mission goals of liberation.[47] Following the example of liberation theologians,[48] and in the context of the WCC's Decade to Overcome Violence, which culminated in the International Ecumenical Peace Convocation in Jamaica in 2011,[49] CWME explicitly rejected violence as a means of mission (cf. TTL 47, 77, 90, 92).

The rejection of violence is also a key theme in *EG*.[50] Like the Catholic Church, the WCC had been apprised in the previous two decades of the centrality of reconciliation to the theology of mission[51] and had connected this with the mission of the Spirit and mission in the Spirit.[52] In paying attention to the means and processes of mission rather than only to its end result (TTL 29), the development of mission spirituality was also a way of emphasizing the need for an ethical approach in mission.[53] The twelve principles already prepared by the WCC and the PCID on ethical witness in multireligious contexts could be jointly applied for any mission context. They enjoin love of neighbor, the exercise of virtue, service, respect, truthfulness, and building relationships.[54]

The third of the implications for ecumenical mission that I wish to consider is the terminological one of mission as evangelization. In *EG*, Pope Francis uses *evangelization* and *mission* interchangeably. TTL does not use *evangelization* except with reference to other bodies, but it does refer to "the call to evangelize" (nos. 81, 85) and to "evangelism" in the narrower sense of communicating the message. However, *evangelization* is not a term foreign to the ecumenical movement. *Evangelization* was the main term in late nineteenth-century Protestantism and the World Missionary Conference in 1910 considered evangelization as the goal of missions.[55] This included Christianization and social transformation.

Catholic adoption of *evangelization* in the early twentieth century to refer to the work of preaching to and teaching people outside Christendom and bringing them into the church[56] was partly due to Protestant usage.[57] This was the sense in which Pope Pius XII used it in his encyclical *Evangelii Praecones* (1951) on foreign missions. However, at the Second Vatican Council, in the context of decolonization, there was a rethinking of missions. In the documents of the Second Vatican Council, *evangelization* was used in three different senses: as missionary preaching, as the entire ministry of the word, and as the church's whole ministry.[58] But, significantly, in the decree of the Second Vatican Council on the missionary activity of the church, *Ad Gentes*, the words *mission* and *evangelization* were used synonymously to refer generally to "spreading the good news" (no. 35)[59] and the body responsible for the mission *ad gentes*—the Propaganda Fide—was renamed the Congregation for the Evangelization of Peoples. As we have seen, in *EN* in 1975, Pope Paul VI, drawing on the Vatican Council and also the third synod of bishops, refreshed the understanding of mission by using *evangelization*.[60]

EN regrounded mission in the work of Jesus Christ in proclaiming the gospel of the kingdom of God (nos. 6–13). This had several important corollaries: first, mission as evangelization was no longer limited to the mission *ad gentes*, but Europe and the West could now be included among the countries in need of an evangelization (nos. 18–20); second, evangelization became the work of the whole church—not only professional missionaries—in continuing Christ's mission (nos. 14–16); and third, mission was defined holistically to encompass good news to the poor and oppressed (nos. 31–39) as well as proclamation of the gospel message and church planting. Evangelization was related not only to *Ad Gentes* but also to *Gaudium et Spes* and even to the Dogmatic Constitution on the Church, *Lumen Gentium*.[61] Rather than "preaching the Gospel in ever wider geographic areas or to ever greater numbers of people" (*EG* 19), Paul VI laid emphasis on the depth of evangelization and its transforming effect not only on individuals but also on cultures (*EN* 20) and societies (nos. 23–24).[62]

The ecumenical movement went through a similar rethinking but adopted the term *mission* instead. Between the assemblies at New Delhi in 1961 and Canberra in 1991, although the proclamation and call of the gospel, confession and witness, and the meaning of conversion and salvation were discussed, the word *evangelism* was rarely used in WCC assemblies.[63] The reasons for this were partly to do with the influence of the Orthodox churches that joined the WCC from 1961. Because historically they had bad experience of Western missions and evangelism, as a condition of their joining the WCC, they condemned "proselytism" as a "corruption of Christian witness" in which "cajolery, bribery, undue pressure or intimidation is used—subtly or openly—to bring about seeming conversion."[64] There were other reasons for the reluctance of CWME to address the evangelism part of its mandate. One was that contemporary practice of evangelism looked too much like self-promotion by the church, a commodification of the gospel for sale in the marketplace, or an aggressive targeting of "non-Christians." Another was that postcolonial theologians saw evangelizing as damaging to the Christian cause, for example, in Latin America, where people had been baptized at the point of a sword, or in India, where anticonversion laws had been passed in several states. A third reason was the misuse of evangelism to promote conservative ideology and support right-wing regimes.[65] From the 1920s, Protestant missionaries became divided between a focus on eternal salvation or on the "social gospel." This exacerbated division during the Cold War era as the new era of "development" encouraged a secularization of mission by ecumenicals and an ideological use of evangelism by evangelicals.[66]

Instead of using *evangelization* or *evangelism*, in the postcolonial period, the ecumenical movement developed a theology of *missio Dei*.[67] *Missio Dei* recognized that mission was not primarily a sending overseas, as it had been understood in the colonial period, but the participation by all churches everywhere in the triune God's saving work in the world. This emphasized mission as the sending activity of God, rather than missions and missionaries, and local "witness" to that mission that was socially rather than mainly personally transformative.[68] Meanwhile, at the insistence of Latin American members influenced by liberation theology, evangelicals in the Lausanne Covenant of 1974 made an explicit commitment to "social responsibility," although evangelism was declared to be primary.[69] The 1982 statement (EA) arose as a response both to the *Lausanne Covenant* and to Paul VI's *Evangelii Nuntiandi*. It used the term *witness* rather than *evangelize* and drew on *missio Dei* theology and the insights of liberation theology to take a holistic approach to "mission in Christ's way" and the kingdom of God.[70]

In putting forward its pneumatological approach, TTL is careful to set this within the theology of *missio Dei* (nos. 2, 19). However, I hope that the dialogue around *EG* will revive the use of *evangelization* in ecumenical and Protestant circles as a synonym for *mission and evangelism*. There are two main reasons for this: first, because the combination of *mission and evangelism* tends to separate what are integral. Popes Paul VI and Francis have shown how these can be held together in their use of *evangelization*. The second reason is because of contemporary difficulties with the theology of mission. The *missio Dei* paradigm is increasingly open to criticism—among other reasons for its dependence on a social understanding of the Trinity—and a fresh approach is needed.[71] Biblically, evangelization—"effecting good news"— could be regarded as simply the Lukan version of the Johannine mission—or "sending."[72] However, in an era when *mission* is used by all sorts of organizations, businesses, and so on, and not necessarily accompanied by the love John attaches to it, *evangelization* helps to identify the Christian agenda since the term *gospel* is joined with it. I concede that the connection of *evangelization* with good news is lost on most English speakers, but nevertheless *evangelization* more obviously relates to the practice of Jesus Christ, and this is a sounder starting point than the theological model of mission. Since both Protestants and Catholics have used *evangelization*, there is the opportunity now to bring the churches together for a new consensus around this term.

In conclusion, our examination of the respective approaches and teachings of *EG* and TTL shows a considerable convergence in theology of mission and many issues of common concern. Both documents recognize the global diversity of the church as an expression of catholicity and take cultures seriously as a tool of analysis in mission/evangelization. They both share a special focus on the poor and marginalized, aim to mobilize the whole church for mission/evangelization and emphasize the importance of proclamation and communicating the gospel message, and they both privilege pneumatology of mission and develop mission spirituality. The divergences between the documents are mainly to do with the different ecclesiological perspectives of a church vis-à-vis a council of churches, different starting points for pneumatology, and the terminology of *mission* versus *evangelization*. While the differences are not insignificant, the striking convergence of these documents gives great potential for ecumenical mission. The renewed understanding of catholicity and ecumenism that is international and intercultural cuts across ecclesial divides. The development of common mission spirituality encourages shared action despite theological differences. Last, rethinking the terminology of *mission/evangelization* is mutually enriching and tends in the same direction toward an integrated "evangelizing mission" (*EG* 121).

Select Bibliography

Bevans, Stephen B., ed. *A Century of Catholic Mission*. Oxford: Regnum Books, 2013.

Edwards, Denis. *Breath of Life: A Theology of the Creator Spirit*. Maryknoll, NY: Orbis, 2004.

Grogan, Paul, and Kirsteen Kim, eds. *The New Evangelization: Faith, People, Context and Practice*. London: T&T Clark, 2015.

Kim, Kirsteen. *The Holy Spirit in the World: A Global Conversation*. Maryknoll, NY: Orbis Books, 2007.

Kim, Sebastian, and Kirsteen Kim. *Christianity as a World Religion*, 2nd ed. London: Bloomsbury, 2016.

Pontifical Council for Interreligious Dialogue (PCID), World Council of Churches, and the World Evangelical Alliance. "Christian Witness in a Multi-Religious World: Recommendations for Conduct." 2011. Available from each of the respective websites.

Rajkumar, Peniel, Joseph Dayam, and I. P. Asheervadham, eds. *Mission at and from the Margins: Patterns, Protagonists and Perspectives*. Regnum Edinburgh Centenary Series. Oxford: Regnum Books, 2014.

World Council of Churches. "Together towards Life: Mission and Evangelism in Changing Landscapes." Geneva: WCC Publications, 2013. Available from www.oikoumene.org.

Notes

1. This comparative study is done from the perspective of a lay Protestant woman who is a theologian of mission. In my role as vice moderator of the Commission for World Mission and Evangelism of the World Council of Churches from 2007 to 2013, I was the chair of the drafting group for TTL. In another capacity as professor of theology at Leeds Trinity University, which is a Catholic foundation, I co-organized a conference on "the new evangelization" in June 2012 and coedited the book of the conference. Paul Grogan and Kirsteen Kim, eds., *The New Evangelization: Faith, People, Context and Practice* (London: T&T Clark, 2015).

2. Whereas the authoritative version of *EG* is in Latin, that of TTL is in English. This paper uses the English versions of both, which are available from the Vatican and WCC websites.

3. WCC, "Mission and Evangelism: An Ecumenical Affirmation," in *"You Are the Light of the World": Statements on Mission by the World Council of Churches 1980–2005*, ed. Jacques Matthey (Geneva: WCC, 2005), 4–38.

4. A video recording of the mission plenary is available at www.wcc2013.info.

5. The conference was divided by the question of the relationship of the Holy Spirit with the spirits of this world and of pneumatology with Christology, as raised by the plenary presentation of the Korean theologian Chung Hyun Kyung. See Michael Kinnamon, ed., *Signs of the Spirit*, Official Report of the Seventh Assembly of the World Council of Churches, Canberra, 1991 (Geneva: World Council of Churches, 1991); Kirsteen Kim, *The Holy Spirit in the World: A Global Conversation* (Maryknoll, NY: Orbis Books, 2007).

6. David J. Bosch, *Transforming Mission: Paradigm Shifts in Theology of Mission* (Maryknoll, NY: Orbis Books, 1991), 113.

7. Conference website, www.mission2005.org. For documentation of the Athens conference, see Jacques Matthey, ed., *Come, Holy Spirit, Heal and Reconcile*, Report of the World Council of Churches Conference on Mission and Evangelism, Athens, May 2005 (Geneva: World Council of Churches, 2008). For background, see Kim, *The Holy Spirit in the World*.

8. Catholic, Orthodox, Protestant, Pentecostal, and indigenous churches were full members of this project. See the project website, www.edinburgh2010.org, from which the "Common Call" can be downloaded. See also the Regnum Edinburgh Centenary Series published by Regnum Books, Oxford.

9. See Peniel Rajkumar, Joseph Dayam, and I. P. Asheervadham, eds., *Mission at and from the Margins: Patterns, Protagonists and Perspectives*, Regnum Edinburgh Centenary Series (Oxford: Regnum Books, 2014).

10. This collaboration contributed to Commission on Faith and Order, *The Church: Toward a Common Vision*, available at www.oikoumene.org. See also Kirsteen Kim, "Mission Theology of the Church," *International Review of Mission* 99, no. 1 (April 2010): 39–55, and other articles in this issue, which record the joint consultation of CWME and Faith and Order in Hungary in 2009.

11. Available from each of the respective websites.

12. See, for example, Richard Lennan, "*Evangelii Gaudium*: The Good News from Pope Francis," *Compass* 48, no. 1 (Autumn 2014): 3–8, who notes differences from the synod's texts, terms characteristic of Ignation spirituality, and Francis's own particular concerns, especially mercy.

13. Benedict XVI, *Ubicumque et semper*, Apostolic Letter issued motu proprio "Establishing the Pontifical Council for Promoting the New Evangelization" (September 21, 2010).

14. Synod of Bishops, *Lineamenta*, "The New Evangelization for the Transmission of the Christian Faith" in preparation for the XIII Ordinary General Assembly of the Synod of Bishops from October 7 to 28, 2012 (February 2, 2011).

15. See the texts chosen to head each section of the *Lineamenta*.

16. Synod of Bishops, Final List of Propositions, October 27, 2012. For further comment, see Kirsteen Kim, "Introduction," in Grogan and Kim, *The New Evangelization*, 1–11.

17. Of the fifty-eight propositions, *EG* cites the following (twenty-seven in total): 1, 4, 6, 7, 8, 9, 11, 13, 14, 16, 17, 20, 25, 26 (twice), 27, 30, 38, 41, 42, 44, 45, 51, 52, 53, 54, 55, 56.

18. Altogether Francis makes seventeen references to Paul VI, mostly to *EN*. The others are in nos. 51, 123, 146, 150, and 156. For further discussion of the breadth of evangelization in magisterial

teaching, see Philip Knights and Andrea Murray, *Evangelisation in England and Wales: A Report to the Catholic Bishops* (London: Catholic Bishops' Conference, 2002), 11–54.

19. Quoted in Leonardo Boff, *Good News to the Poor: A New Evangelization* (Maryknoll, NY: Orbis Books, 1992), xii.

20. John F. Gorski, "From 'Mission' to 'Evangelization': The Latin American Origins of a Challenging Concept," in Grogan and Kim, *The New Evangelization*, 31–44 (38–42). Cf. Boff, *Good News to the Poor*, xii–xiv.

21. See the chapters by Eduardo Mangiarotti and Paul Lakeland in this volume.

22. Andrew F. Walls, *The Missionary Movement in Christian History* (Maryknoll, NY: Orbis Books, 1996); *The Cross-Cultural Process in Christian History* (Maryknoll, NY: Orbis Books, 2002).

23. See Sebastian Kim and Kirsteen Kim, *Christianity as a World Religion*, 2nd ed. (London: Bloomsbury, 2016).

24. See, for example, Austin Ivereigh, *The Great Reformer: Francis and the Making of a Radical Pope* (London: Allen & Unwin, 2015), 372–74.

25. For further discussion of Pope Francis's approach to culture, see the chapter by Jacob Phillips in this volume.

26. For discussion of the use of the culture concept in mission theology, see Stephen B. Bevans, *Models of Contextual Theology*, 2nd ed. (Maryknoll, NY: Orbis Books, 2002); Kirsteen Kim, "Doing Theology for the Church's Mission: The Appropriation of Culture," in *The End of Theology: Shaping Theology for the Sake of Mission*, ed. Jason Sexton and Paul Weston (Minneapolis: Fortress Press, 2016).

27. For discussion of whether or not Pope Francis can be called a liberation theologian, see the chapter in this volume by Paul Lakeland and Ivereigh, *The Great Reformer*. Both answer in the affirmative while qualifying what is meant by *liberation theology*.

28. See Susan K. Wood, "The Church: A People Sent in Mission," in Grogan and Kim, *The New Evangelization*, 65–78.

29. For example, the references in *EG* to the exodus (no. 187) and to Jesus as poor (no. 197).

30. In the same paragraph, it is clear that the inclusion is not yet complete. Although the poor are included, the pope can still refer to "them" and "us."

31. *EG* 52–61, 69, 74, 98, 113, 131, 202, 212, 218–19.

32. There is much in common here with the "missional church" movement in Protestant ecclesiology, which draws on the theology of Lesslie Newbigin. See, for example, Darrell L. Guder, *The Continuing Conversion of the Church* (Grand Rapids, MI: Eerdmans, 2000). The missional church movement emphasizes that each local church is missionary.

33. WCC, *Minutes and Reports of the Fourth Meeting of the Central Committee, Rolle, Switzerland, 1951* (Geneva: WCC, 1951), 66. This definition is used intentionally to reach out to evangelical Protestants who have also adopted a similar statement. See Lausanne Movement for World Evangelization, *The Lausanne Covenant* (1974), no. 6. Available at www.lausanne.org.

34. Tensions around religious conversion are especially strong in India. See, for example, Sebastian C. H. Kim, *In Search of Identity: Debates on Religious Conversion in India* (Delhi: Oxford University Press, 2002); Chad M. Bauman, *Pentecostals, Proselytization, and Anti-Christian Violence in Contemporary India* (Oxford: Oxford University Press, 2014).

35. In *EG*, we find the same eschatological sense, but couched mainly in the language of "kingdom" (esp. 180–81).

36. The development of mission pneumatology has been strongest in Pentecostal circles; see especially Amos Yong, *The Missiological Spirit: Christian Mission Theology in the Third Millennium Global Context* (Eugene, OR: Wipf and Stock, 2014) and other works by him. See also, Kirsteen Kim, *Joining In with the Spirit: Connecting World Church and Local Mission* (London: SCM, 2012). For some reservations about this model, see Kirsteen Kim, "Edinburgh 1910 to 2010: From Kingdom to Spirit," *Journal of the European Pentecostal Theological Association* 30, no. 2 (2010): 3–20.

37. Note, however, that *EG* does recognize the work of the Holy Spirit in individuals and peoples even before any conscious response to the gospel (e.g., no. 265).

38. See Jürgen Moltmann, *The Spirit of Life: A Universal Affirmation* (ET London: SCM Press, 1992), 1, 312nn4, 8.

39. See Kim, *The Holy Spirit in the World*, x–xiii. The recent statement "The Mission of the Orthodox Church in Today's World" produced the Synaxis of Orthodox Primates meeting at

Chambésy on January 21–28, 2016 bears out the Orthodox emphasis on ecological issues.

40. Christopher Hrynkow in this volume argues that *EG* nevertheless encourages ecological flourishing.

41. Catholic voices connecting these include Samuel Rayan, *The Holy Spirit: Heart of the Gospel and Christian Hope* (Maryknoll, NY: Orbis, 1978); Denis Edwards, *Breath of Life: A Theology of the Creator Spirit* (Maryknoll, NY: Orbis, 2004); Celia Deane-Drummond, *Creation through Wisdom: Theology and the New Biology* (Edinburgh: T&T Clark, 2000); Stephen B. Bevans, "The Mission of the Spirit," *International Review of Mission* 103, no. 1 (April 2014): 30–33.

42. Peter de Mey, "Towards a Healthy Future of Catholicity in the Roman Catholic Church: Recommendations by Pope Francis," in *Catholicity Under Pressure: The Ambiguous Relationship between Diversity and Unity,* ed. Dagmar Heller and Peter Szentpétery (Leipzig: Evangelische Verlagsanstalt, 2016), 251–72.

43. E.g., Ivereigh, *The Great Reformer,* 290–94.

44. This is a growing field in mission studies. See, for example, Chandler H. Im and Amos Yong, eds., *Global Diasporas and Mission* (Oxford: Regnum, 2014); Martha Frederiks and Dorottya Nagy, eds., *Religion, Migration and Identity: Methodological and Theological Explorations* (Leiden: Brill, 2016).

45. Jacques Matthey, "Reconciliation, *Missio Dei* and the Church's Mission," in *Mission, Violence and Reconciliation,* ed. Howard Mellor and Timothy Yates (Sheffield: Cliff College Publishing, 2004), 116–17.

46. Kim, "Edinburgh 1910 to 2010."

47. Jacques Matthey, "Reconciliation, *Missio Dei* and the Church's Mission."

48. E.g., Gustavo Gutiérrez, *We Drink from Our Own Wells: The Spiritual Journey of a People* (Maryknoll, NY: Orbis Books, 1984 [1983]).

49. Conference website: www.overcomingviolence.org.

50. See chapter by Christopher Hrynkow in this volume.

51. By theologians such as Robert Schreiter, C.PP.S. See inter alia, Robert J. Schreiter, "The Theology of Reconciliation and Peacemaking for Mission," in Mellor and Yates, *Mission, Violence and Reconciliation,* 11–28.

52. CWME, "Mission as Ministry of Reconciliation" (2005), in Matthey, *You Are the Light of the World,* 90–126.

53. See, for example, Donal Dorr, *Mission in Today's World* (Blackrock, Co. Dublin: The Columba Press, 2000).

54. Pontifical Council for Interreligious Dialogue (PCID), World Council of Churches, and the World Evangelical Alliance, "Christian Witness in a Multi-Religious World: Recommendations for Conduct," 2011.

55. Brian Stanley, *The World Missionary Conference* (Grand Rapids, MI: Eerdmans, 2009), 88.

56. See Stephen B. Bevans and Roger P. Schroeder, *Constants in Context* (Maryknoll, NY: Orbis, 2004), 171–238.

57. Domenico Grasso, "Evangelizzazione. Senso di un termine," in Mariasusai Dhavamony, *Evangelisation,* Documenta Missionalia 9 (Rome: Gregorian University, 1975).

58. Ibid.

59. Karl Müller, "Missiology: An Introduction," in *Following Christ in Mission: A Foundational Course in Missiology,* ed. Sebastian Karotemprel (Mumbai: Paulines, 1995), 21–36, 29.

60. Roger P. Schroeder, "Catholic Teaching on Mission after Vatican II," in *A Century of Catholic Mission,* ed. Stephen B. Bevans (Oxford: Regnum Books, 2013), 113–14.

61. For an example of the breadth of evangelization, see Michael Hayes, ed., *Mission and Evangelization: The Vision of the Cardinals* (London: Burns and Oates, 2004).

62. In his encyclical *Redemptoris Missio* (*RM*; 1990), John Paul II returned to *mission* rather than *evangelization.* According to Frances Anekwe Oborji, this was to address a misunderstanding that the latter superseded the former and that in the stress on the multifaceted nature of evangelization, the traditional mission *ad gentes* had been undermined—*Concepts of Mission* (Maryknoll, NY: Orbis, 2006), 7–11. For Roger Schroeder, it was because the pope was wary that theology of inculturation had led to an overemphasis on the goodness of cultures and religion and that theology of liberation had lost the necessary focus on the importance of the church in mission—"Catholic Teaching after Vatican II," 115–16.

63. Priscilla Pope-Levison, "Evangelism in the WCC," in *New Directions in Mission and Evangelization 2: Theological Foundations,*

ed. James A. Scherer and Stephen B. Bevans (Maryknoll, NY: Orbis Books, 1994), 126–40.

64. WCC, "Christian Witness, Proselytism and Religious Liberty in the Setting of the World Council of Churches," *Ecumenical Review* 9, no. 1 (October 1956): 48–56. Note this is a somewhat different understanding of the word from that attributed to Pope Francis by Jacob Phillips is this volume.

65. Cf. J. Andrew Kirk, *What Is Mission? Theological Explorations* (London: Darton, Longman and Todd, 1999), 56–60.

66. Cf. Brian Stanley, *The Global Diffusion of Evangelicalism* (Downers Grove, IL: InterVarsity, 2013), 62–65, 151–55.

67. The classic treatment of *missio Dei* is Bosch, *Transforming Mission*. For its origins, see also John G. Flett, *The Witness of God: The Trinity, Missio Dei, Karl Barth, and the Nature of Christian Community* (Grand Rapids, MI: Eerdmans, 2010).

68. For a detailed analysis of these developments, see Bosch, *Transforming Mission*, 368–510.

69. *The Lausanne Covenant*, nos. 5, 6.

70. Jacques Matthey, Presentation of *Mission and Evangelism: An Ecumenical Affirmation*, in Matthey, *"You Are the Light of the World,"* 1–3.

71. For incisive criticism of the social Trinity, see Kathryn Tanner, "Trinity," in *The Blackwell Companion to Political Theology*, ed. Peter Scott and William T. Cavanaugh (Oxford: Blackwell, 2006), 319–32.

72. See, for example, R. Geoffrey Harris, *Mission in the Gospels* (Peterborough: Epworth, 2004).

9

Evangelii Gaudium

Good News for Ecumenism

JEREMY WORTHEN

Introduction

This chapter argues that *Evangelii Gaudium* (*EG*) has good news for ecumenism, but that this good news hinges on willingness to place the good news of the gospel at the heart of the ecumenical movement. It begins by recognizing the limits of *EG*'s overt treatment of ecumenism, which at first glance does not compare favorably with relevant earlier documents. Critical to Pope Francis's presentation in this text, however, is the twofold theme of evangelical ecclesiology and the ecclesial character of the gospel, a theme that binds ecclesial renewal to evangelization in a dynamic relationship. While the dual theme of evangelical ecclesiology and the ecclesial character of the gospel has the potential to draw together the diversity of contemporary Christianity, it also underlines the profoundly ecclesial character of Christian cooperation in sharing the gospel. Partnership in mission therefore could and should raise questions about visible unity and indeed incite our desire for it, just as growth in unity can only be fruitful where it is focused on receiving and proclaiming

Christ's message with new power. Such an approach holds out hope for a fresh integration of the ecumenical movement and also enables the connection between unity and renewal, a crucial strand in the ecumenical movement of the twentieth century, to be reaffirmed.

Where Is Ecumenism in *Evangelii Gaudium?*

On the face of it, *EG* is not an encouraging document for those who believe that the call to Christian unity remains an urgent one for today's churches. Its subject, evangelization, is undoubtedly of great interest and indeed an increasingly urgent concern to many, if not indeed all, Christian churches, and yet there is little explicit acknowledgment of readers outside the Catholic Church. The one place where *EG* explicitly addresses relations with other churches occurs in a section on "Social Dialogue as a Contribution to Peace," where a brief subsection on "Ecumenical Dialogue" appears sandwiched between subsections on "Dialogue between Faith, Reason and Science" and "Relations with Judaism" (*EG* 244–46). It is not the most promising of locations: Is dialogue, rather than cooperation or even partnership, the most that the Roman Catholic Church expects from other churches when it comes to evangelization? Is such dialogue not fundamentally different in kind from that with other religions and secular social actors?

In fact, the word *dialogue* only occurs once in these paragraphs, and that is in the specific context of a strongly affirmative reference to receptive ecumenism (without naming it as such) in the penultimate sentence of the subsection.[1] Earlier on, citing *Unitatis Redintegratio*, Vatican II's Decree on Ecumenism, Francis writes that "the credibility of the Christian message would be much greater if Christians could overcome their divisions and the church could realize 'the fullness of catholicity proper to her in those of her children who, though joined to her by baptism, are yet separated from full communion with her'" (*EG* 244).[2] The need to seek peace between Christians, to contribute to "the unity of the human family" (*EG* 245) and to minimize "the criticisms, complaints and ridicule to which the scandal of divided Christians gives rise" (*EG* 246) are all emphasized, but with no real exploration of what it might mean for Catholics to share the task of evangelization with Christians from other churches.[3]

This is all the more surprising given that the role of other churches as partners in evangelization was very clearly recognized in two of the most important background documents for *EG*, both from Pope Francis's recent predecessors: *Evangelii Nuntiandi*, Pope Paul VI's Apostolic Exhortation on evangelization from 1975;[4] and *Redemptoris Missio*, the 1990 encyclical of Pope John Paul II on the church's missionary mandate.[5] The former includes toward the end a remarkable passage about unity, where Paul VI says that his desire is

> for a collaboration marked by greater commitment with the Christian brethren with whom we are not yet united in perfect unity, taking as a basis the foundation of Baptism and the patrimony of faith which is common to us. By doing this we can already give a greater common witness to Christ before the world in the very work of evangelization. Christ's command urges us to do this; the duty of preaching and of giving witness to the Gospel requires this. (*Evangelii Nuntiandi* 77)

Not only, then, is collaboration with Christians beyond the Catholic Church in evangelization possible on the basis of common baptism and common faith; it is to be actively pursued, because it is demanded by faithfulness to what Christ asks of us. Fifteen years later, John Paul II could affirm, "Ecumenical activity and harmonious witness to Jesus Christ by Christians who belong to different churches and ecclesial communities has already borne abundant fruit" (*Redemptoris Missio* 50). Such partnership is not simply a pious aspiration but a reality, and if the fruit it bears is the fruit of John 15:16, then it comes from the presence and the activity of Christ in such endeavors. These are remarkable assertions from Pope Francis's predecessors, and ones that it might be said are no less deserving of re-reception and affirmation by all the churches today. Yet there is no overt parallel to be found in *EG*.

There is also at least one other context where positive reference to other churches and communions is a feature of Pope Francis's sources that does not appear to be sustained here. In the opening chapter of *EG*, he focuses on the importance of ecclesial renewal as integral to the call for the church to commit itself wholeheartedly to the task of evangelization; indeed, the relationship between renewal and evangelization is one of the pivotal themes for the text as a whole.[6] As he introduces it, he roots it in the heritage of Vatican II, citing Paul VI's *Ecclesiam Suam* and then, again, *Unitatis Redintegratio* from Vatican II: "Every renewal of the Church essentially consists in an increase of fidelity to her own calling.... Christ summons the Church as she goes her pilgrim way...to that continual reformation of which she always has need, in so far as she is a human institution here on earth" (*EG* 26). The sentence whose absence from the quotation is indicated by the first set of ellipses reads, "Undoubtedly this is the basis of the movement toward unity" (*Unitatis Redintegratio* 6). According to *Unitatis Redintegratio*, then, there is no doubt that the search for renewal and the search for unity are inseparable. Why would this claim not appear in the text of *EG*? Why is this sentence omitted?

Ecumenism, Evangelization, and the Renewal of the Church

It is often said that Vatican II represented the Roman Catholic Church's embrace of the twentieth-century ecumenical movement. One of the characteristic claims of that movement was that the renewal of the church perceived by so many Christians to be necessary, and indeed urged with growing intensity from the 1920s onward, was bound up with the growth of the churches toward visible unity. Church renewal would only come through growth in unity, while growth in unity was bound to foster renewal. As the then general secretary of the World Council of Churches claimed in 1956, "The basic theme of the ecumenical discussion has been and is the rediscovery of the Church as the new people of God. Now this conversation between the churches forces each church to ask in which ways it must be renewed in order to be the Church in the real sense of that word."[7] Much more recently, a leading figure in contemporary ecumenism asserted that "ecumenism has been a movement for unity through renewal and of renewal through unity."[8] It was not therefore just the ecumenical cause but that specific and highly charged claim that was adopted as its own by the Roman Catholic Church with Vatican II's Decree on Ecumenism.

Unitatis Redintegratio sets out a creative relationship between ecclesial renewal and ecumenical engagement that is very much in line with the self-understanding of the ecumenical movement at the time. For instance, the ecumenical movement leads all who participate in it "to examine their own faithfulness to Christ's will for the Church and accordingly to undertake with vigor the task of renewal and reform" (*Unitatis Redintegratio* 4). That is, ecumenism is a stimulus for renewal within each separate and separated church, and the text proceeds to spell out that this also applies to Roman Catholics: in their ecumenical work, "their primary duty is to make a careful and honest appraisal of whatever needs to be done or renewed in the Catholic household itself, in order that its life may bear witness more clearly and faithfully to the teachings and institutions which have come to it from Christ through the Apostles" (no. 4).

If ecumenical dialogue should lead to renewal, so also should renewal lead to deepening ecumenical relations; that is the point of the passage half-quoted in *EG* 26 from *Unitatis Redintegratio* 6. Ecclesial renewal draws us to seek the unity of the whole church. In words that followed the extract quoted by Pope Francis, the fathers of the Council proceed to identify this movement from renewal to unity in specific contemporary developments across the churches:

> Already in various spheres of the Church's life, this renewal is taking place. The Biblical and liturgical movements, the preaching of the word of God and catechetics, the apostolate of the laity, new forms of religious life and the spirituality of married life, and the Church's social teaching and activity—all these should

be considered as pledges and signs of the future progress of ecumenism. (no. 6)

Ecclesial renewal inspires and enables growth in unity, just
as growth toward unity releases new energy for renewal. If that is
so clear in the teaching of Vatican II, however, why does it not feature in the presentation of ecclesial renewal that is pivotal for *EG*?
To answer that question fully could involve more or less rehears-
ing the entire history of ecumenism over the past half-century,
but suffice it to say that Pope Francis's treatment here reflects the
widespread disconnection of renewal from ecumenism during the
period since Vatican II. Indeed, one might say that even as Vatican II was ending, the connection was weakening within the ecumenical movement itself, as a new sense of urgency gripped many
Christians who identified with it regarding the need to respond
as churches to moral issues raised by social and political developments: global economic inequality, apartheid in South Africa, the
struggle for civil rights, revolutionary movements against unjust
regimes, and after a slower start, the environmental crisis.[9]
   In this context, renewal could be associated with renewed
capacity for Christians to stand alongside one another for justice and peace and deal together with these pressing challenges,
whereas unity by contrast meant facing toward one another to
work out how church-to-church relations could be taken forward.
Indeed, by 1990, a study document from the World Council of
Church's Commission on Faith and Order was exploring the relationship between "the unity of the church" and "the renewal of
human community."[10] Once renewal was correlated with outward-
facing engagement with urgent contemporary issues, and unity
with an inward directed attention to institutional and theological
questions that began to look increasingly intractable in any case
from the 1970s onward, the claim that had given the ecumenical
movement much of its energy—that the cause of renewal and the
cause of unity are inseparable—inevitably began to be drained of
plausibility.
   As already noted, for Pope Francis, at the heart of the church's
renewal is participation in evangelization. Hence it is precisely
in its commitment to sharing the gospel with the world that the
church becomes open to the grace of God, who alone can renew

it. For what brings the church new life is nothing other than the newness of the gospel itself, and the gospel is only known as we share it: receiving it more deeply in order to preach it more powerfully, passing it on to others and thereby discovering more of its dazzling depths for ourselves—dynamics that will be analyzed further in the section that follows. There is no renewal for the church aside from the fuller reception of the gospel and its newness, and there is no reception of the gospel that can be separated from the work of drawing others to behold its beauty. Hence the deepest source for the church's renewal is not looking in at itself, even at itself in the multiplicity of churches, nor engaging with the questions asked of it by the society in which it is situated, but going out to the world with the good news of Christ, in faithful response to his word and in the power of the Spirit whom he sends.

Evangelical Ecclesiology and the Ecclesial Character of the Gospel

It is here that we might find, then, despite unpromising appearances, the good news for ecumenism in *EG*: in its insistent focus on the need to understand the good news of Christ and the church of Christ always in relation to one another. The vision that emerges is one that has the potential to bring back into alignment the historic priorities of the ecumenical movement. It could also become the opportunity for a renewed, kerygmatic affirmation and deeper discovery by the churches of their unity in the service of Christ.

The focus on relation between gospel and church in *EG* means that it proposes an ecclesiology that is profoundly evangelical, not in a sense that relates directly to evangelicalism as a distinctive movement within Protestant Christianity, but an ecclesiology that centers on the gospel and binds gospel and church together theologically in integral and dynamic relationship.[11] If one holds to such an evangelical ecclesiology, then it becomes plain that the renewal of the church can only happen on the journey of evangelization and not in any other way. Thus in an important passage from the

224

opening section of the first main chapter, having described the call of the people of God to "go forth" from Abraham onward, Pope Francis writes,

> The Church which "goes forth" is a community of missionary disciples who take the first step, who are involved and supportive, who bear fruit and rejoice. An evangelizing community knows that the Lord has taken the initiative, he has loved us first (cf. 1 Jn 4:19), and therefore we can move forward, boldly take the initiative, go out to others, seek those who have fallen away, stand at the crossroads and welcome the outcast. (*EG* 24)

The church is defined in this passage as "a community of missionary disciples" (a phrase also taken up elsewhere, e.g., *EG* 119–21), and as an "evangelizing community." It is not as if first there is the church, and then there is the activity of evangelization that the church may or may not decide to take up and to which it might accord a lower or higher priority. Rather, the dynamic of evangelization, of receiving and passing on the gospel, configures the life of the church at a fundamental level. The church exists from, in, and for evangelization as the integral process of receiving, proclaiming, and sharing the gospel.

Pope Francis is not sketching out a new doctrine of the church in these passages. Here too the roots of his approach reach back to Vatican II, which after all begins its Dogmatic Constitution on the Church with the assertion that "Christ is the Light of nations. Because this is so, this Sacred Synod gathered together in the Holy Spirit eagerly desires, by proclaiming the Gospel to every creature, to bring the light of Christ to all men, a light brightly visible on the countenance of the Church" (*Lumen Gentium* 1).[12] The ecclesiology of *Lumen Gentium* is thereby immediately put in relation to the gospel; the church is the body of the one who is the light of the world, and the Council's articulation of the doctrine of the church arises from a desire to proclaim "the Gospel to every creature." Conversely, the missiology of Vatican II is framed from the outset ecclesiologically in *Ad Gentes*, Vatican II's Decree on the Mission Activity of the Church: "The pilgrim Church is missionary by her very nature, since it is from the mission of the Son and the mission of the Holy Spirit that she draws her origin, in accordance with the decree of God the Father" (no. 2).[13]

The characteristic features of the evangelical ecclesiology found in *EG* then appear explicitly a decade later, in *Evangelii Nuntiandi*. The most directly relevant section of the text begins by stating, "Those who sincerely accept the Good News, through the power of this acceptance and of shared faith therefore gather together in Jesus' name in order to seek together the kingdom, build it up and live it. They make up a community which is in its turn evangelizing" (*Evangelii Nuntiandi* 13). Accepting the gospel means gathering together with others who accept it and belonging to a community committed to sharing it and passing it on: the church exists in the dynamic of evangelization. It is worth noting that the designation here of the church as an "evangelizing community" is taken up by Pope Francis in the passage quoted above (*EG* 24). In the paragraphs that follow, Pope Paul VI continues to stress the ecclesiological dynamic of evangelization very directly, writing that "evangelizing is in fact the grace and vocation proper to the Church, her deepest identity....The Church is an evangelizer, but she begins by being evangelized herself" (*Evangelii Nuntiandi* 14–15).

The other side of Pope Francis's evangelical ecclesiology is his presentation of an ecclesial gospel. The use of the term *evangelization*, which clearly indicates a process, rather than *evangelism*, which suggests an event, is not perhaps insignificant here. The gospel of Christ is offered by the church as the Body of Christ, and to hear and respond to the gospel is always already to be entering into the life of the church. Evangelization is not in the first place something done by and to individuals, who could and should subsequently come together in the church: sharing the gospel, offering it and receiving it, is an inherently ecclesial action. Thus at the beginning of chapter 3, on "The Proclamation of the Gospel," we read that "evangelization is the task of the Church": the church is "the agent of evangelization" (*EG* 111). Just as there is no church without evangelization, therefore, there is no evangelization without church. As Murray writes elsewhere in this volume, "The life, practices and structures of the church *are* the primary statement the church makes to the world, prior to any specific initiatives or actions *ad extra*."[14] The church that shares the gospel is not as it were a blank piece of paper on which anything might be drawn: it has a given reality, which includes the practice of the sacraments, the ordained ministry, and historic patterns of oversight. Pope Francis concludes the opening section of the first chapter by commenting on the liturgy: "The Church evangelizes and is herself evangelized through the beauty of the liturgy, which is both a celebration of the task of evangelization and the source of her renewed self-giving" (*EG* 24). While acknowledging the way that "God attracts us by taking into account the complex interweaving of human relationships entailed in the life of a human community" (*EG* 113), chapter 3 focuses on ecclesial practices such as liturgical preaching, catechesis, and *lectio divina* as critical sites for proclaiming and hearing the gospel.

At the same time, the ecclesial character of the gospel is about persons as well as practices. McCosker emphasizes that for Francis, "The gospel is not in fact primarily a message, an idea, or even a programme of action, but rather a person."[15] While his chapter in this book explores the roots of that claim in those who influenced the development of Francis's theology, it is also one with much wider currency. Thus the first world conference on Faith and Order in 1927 could affirm of Christ that "He Himself is the Gospel."[16] Moreover, in the mystery of salvation, Christ has united men and women with himself in the church, so that they become inseparable from him. We cannot therefore offer the gospel of Christ without also offering ourselves as the Body of Christ. Correspondingly, neither can we be united to Christ without being joined to his mission, his service, his reaching out to the whole world. As Rowan Williams once remarked, "The life of Christ ceases to be available when we want it merely for ourselves; it is active only when we are pushed beyond ourselves into mission."[17]

The Potential for Ecumenical Convergence

At this point, Anglicans at least may recall a book that has some claim to being their most significant contribution to twentieth-century ecclesiology, Michael Ramsey's *The Gospel and the Catholic Church*.[18] Ramsey wanted to argue that everything that was important in the life of the church was about the gospel and at the service of the gospel, and at the same time that receiving, expressing, and passing on the gospel were activities best held and sustained within the structures of "catholic" Christianity as Anglicans have tended to see it. Ramsey developed his thinking here partly in order to articulate a distinctive ecumenical vocation for Anglicanism, with its powerful Catholic and evangelical wings; toward the end of the book, he writes that "the further the question of reunion advances, the greater is the need for the Anglicans so to expound Church order and so to *live* it, that its relation to the Gospel is plain."[19] Although Pope Francis is by no means saying precisely the same thing, it would not be misleading either to suggest some significant parallels. For him too, an evangelical ecclesiology, where the call of the gospel is what creates, sustains, and renews the church, is inseparable from an ecclesial gospel, received in the texture of sacramental practices that shape and draw people into its unfathomable mystery. That combination may remain the best hope for a truly ecumenical theology of church and mission in the twenty-first century, affirming yet also challenging the theological instincts of both Catholics and Protestants, liberals and evangelicals, historic and newer churches.

Such an ecclesiology can take us beyond the sterile contrast between the church as *creatura verbi* in the theology of the Protestant Reformers and as *creatura sacramenti* in the theology of Catholics. Instead, it shows how Catholics can wholeheartedly affirm the church as created by the word of the gospel without thereby diminishing the significance of its sacramental life, including its sacramental order. The ecumenical potential of this line of thinking is affirmed by the attention given to it in the convergence text on ecclesiology published by the World Council of Churches' Commission on Faith and Order in 2013, *The Church: Towards a Common Vision*. It comes to the fore in an important section on "The Initiative of God, the Father, the Son and the Holy Spirit" in the second chapter of *The Church*, which builds on several decades of theological exploration around the relationship between mission and communion: "As a divinely established communion, the Church belongs to God and does not exist for itself. It is by its very nature

228

missionary, called and sent to witness in its own life to that communion which God intends for all humanity and for all creation in the kingdom."[20] The following paragraph then moves the focus from the category of mission to that of gospel, taking us closer to the characteristic style of *EG* and to its articulation of an evangelical ecclesiology, a theology of the church as configured by the twofold dynamic of evangelization in receiving and passing on the gospel: "The Church is centred and grounded in the Gospel, the proclamation of the Incarnate Word, Jesus Christ, Son of the Father....A defining aspect of the Church's life is to be a community that hears and proclaims the word of God. The Church draws life from the Gospel and discovers ever anew the direction for her journey."[21] Finally, there is a brief sketch of how this pattern can be found in Mary as "a symbol of and model for the Church and the individual Christian," receiving and sharing the word of God.[22] There is therefore a striking convergence between this short section of *The Church* and *Evangelii Gaudium* on the theme of evangelical ecclesiology.

We might also note that there is an important affirmation of missional ecclesiology in another recent document from the World Council of Churches, "Together towards Life: Mission and Evangelism in Changing Landscapes," in a brief section on "God's Mission and the Life of the Church."[23] Here too trinity, mission, communion, and gospel are drawn together in potentially rich ground for ecclesiology: "Living in that love of God, the church is called to become good news for all. The Triune God's overflowing sharing of love is the source of all mission and evangelism."[24] The text proceeds to assert that "it is not possible to separate church and mission in terms of their origin or purpose,"[25] taking up a theme that has become common across different theological traditions over the last thirty years and is indeed expressed very powerfully by Pope John Paul II in *Redemptoris Missio*. The difficulty here, however, is that this very ubiquity has been accompanied by a stretching of the range of meanings of *mission* that runs the risk of weakening its ability to unite those traditions. The foregrounding in *EG* of the specific theme of gospel and church, rather than mission and church more broadly, indicates one possible response to that situation.

The official Roman Catholic response to *The Church* is still awaited at the time of writing, but when it comes it will be a moment of potentially considerable ecumenical significance. There is clearly a contrast between the understanding of the church generated by churches that identify the Protestant Reformations of the sixteenth century positively as part of their heritage and those that do not, in particular the Roman Catholic Church but also the Orthodox churches. Such a dedicated Roman Catholic ecumenist as Walter Kasper has argued forcefully that the sacramental ecclesiology of Catholics and Orthodox, derived from the theology of the first millennium, is fundamentally different from that of Protestants, so different indeed that "when speaking of the Church, they do not mean quite the same thing."[26] For Kasper, this difference is one that inevitably affects and ultimately frustrates all moves toward greater unity between them, such that it becomes "the basic difficulty" raised by modern ecumenism.[27] *The Church* draws heavily on the theology of *missio Dei* and the concept of church as communion in order to try to address that, both much discussed over the last thirty years. Could an emerging convergence among the churches around an evangelical ecclesiology and an ecclesial gospel also, however, make a significant contribution to meeting this challenge, not least given the potential of this twofold theme for engaging evangelical and Pentecostal Christianity rather more directly than the dominant ideas of *The Church* may be able to do?[28]

Partnership in Evangelization and Mutual Recognition as Churches

Theological ideas only discussed among a small minority may not in and of themselves effect far-reaching changes in the churches, but part of the power of evangelical ecclesiology for ecumenism is its resonance with experience and practice. If the church lives in receiving and sharing the gospel, then where Christians from one church find themselves doing this alongside Christians from another church, then they simply have to ask ecclesiological questions. If people hear and receive the gospel together, then are they not thereby necessarily becoming the church together, whatever institutional labels may or may not apply? If people who love the gospel share the gospel together with others, are they not thereby necessarily acting as the church together, and thereby being the church together, across their ecclesial separations? Ecumenists talk about mutual recognition of churches. If we adhere to an evangelical ecclesiology, then it is impossible to recognize the gospel as received and proclaimed by a community of people without also recognizing that there is something of the reality of the church there. On the other hand, recognizing the reality of the church in other communities or indeed our own is not simply a matter of meeting some formal list of criteria, but rather of discerning the power of the gospel at work and therefore also discerning where human failings stand in the way of that power. Such mutual recognition cannot bypass the imperative of deepening conversion to the gospel on both sides, nor the invocation of God's grace for the church's renewal.

The fact that sacraments and church order continue to separate Christians cannot, however, be treated simply as an irritating irrelevance here; just as the church is evangelical, so the gospel is ecclesial. Here, too, there is scope for changing the character of the conversation about mutual recognition. How might churches that regard particular ecclesial practices around liturgy, sacraments, ministry, and *episcopē* as more than means to ends that could be achieved in other ways present them and enable others to see them as compelling forms of participation in the dynamic of evangelization? The same point also underlines the loss of effectiveness in shared reception and shared proclamation of the gospel that comes from continuing division between churches. Partnership in evangelization that is shorn of the fullness of sacramental communion cannot witness to the wholeness of the gospel; indeed, the danger is that without any consciousness of this diminishment, it actually communicates a nonecclesial and therefore distorted gospel to all involved. Ramsey urged in 1936 that "it is never true to say that separate persons are united to Christ, and then combine to form the Church."[29] The cleavage between gospel and church has become that much harder to resist in the hyperindividualistic cultures of the Western world, and both evangelizing separately and evangelizing in nonsacramental and uncommitted partnership can only widen it further. The reality in most parts of

231

the world today is that there are many churches seeking to share the good news, and the only choices are therefore whether to evangelize with one another, in competition against one another, or in indifference to one another. No church that is serious about responding to the commission of Christ can contemplate any of these except for the first. Yet a sharing in evangelization without ecclesial communion is at best wounded and weak. An evangelical ecclesiology therefore not only holds out the potential for theological agreement but also underlines the urgent practical imperative of Christian unity.

If ecumenism might find new resources in evangelical ecclesiology, what might this mean for the relation between unity and renewal that was at the heart of the twentieth-century ecumenical movement? *EG* indicates clearly enough that there is no convincing way of restating that claim in a direct way, although many within the ecumenical movement would still wish to do so. On the other hand, it also implies that it may be possible and indeed necessary to reformulate it with *evangelization* as the mediating term here. If Pope Francis is correct that the renewal of the church must come through deeper commitment to and participation in evangelization, and evangelization draws us inevitably into partnership with Christians from other churches and thereby into partial ecclesial relations with them that cause us to feel our ongoing divisions as serious wounds in the life of the church and obstacles to fruitful evangelization, then renewal through evangelization is inseparable from the search for Christian unity.

Recovering the Unity of the Ecumenical Movement

The story of the ecumenical movement over the last hundred years or so can be told in terms of three strands: "mission and evangelism," "faith and order" (addressing the challenges to visible unity at the level of doctrine and polity) and "life and work" (striving together for justice and peace). With connected but also distinct roots in the first half of the twentieth century, themselves reaching further back into the past, these strands were institutionally united when the World Missionary Council merged with the

World Council of Churches (born from the union of Faith and Order and Life and Work after World War II), the latter establishing its Division on World Mission and Evangelism in 1961. Yet by the end of that decade, they were already proving increasingly hard to hold together. The resurgent focus within mainstream ecumenism on life and work, in campaigns for civil rights, against apartheid, and against global economic inequality, led to concerns about marginalization by those focused on well-established faith and order questions. In a recent book, one of the leading ecumenists in America observed that "in the United States, we see such an extensive split between those whose priority is justice and those whose priority is church unity that it is often difficult to speak of one ecumenical movement."[30] Meanwhile, both those concerned with global mission and those confronting the challenges of evangelization in once Christian but now rapidly secularizing societies saw little or nothing in all of this that could be of relevance to them, with many turning away from formal ecumenism altogether.[31]

To return to the subject of the second section of this paper, the promise of renewal held out by the ecumenical movement in the mid-twentieth century gained its plausibility in large measure from the way these three strands were interwoven within it. Growth in relations between churches, fruitfulness in mission, and effective action for justice and peace would all flow from and into one another. The apparent unravelling of those strands explains not only the loss of influence among the churches of self-identified ecumenism but also why it no longer seems like a credible place to look for the sources of still-needed renewal. Is there any prospect of reconnecting them?

EG at least points to one way in which this might happen. As has just been argued, the twofold theme of evangelical ecclesiology and the ecclesial character of the gospel means that cooperation between churches in evangelization cannot be insulated from faith and order questions. As a profoundly ecclesial activity, evangelization cannot help but raise questions about ecclesial relations for churches sharing in it together. The price of holding theological questions about church unity at bay so that we can "just get on with sharing the gospel" is bound to be a de facto denial of the ecclesial character of the gospel, as if it were a disembodied message addressed to individuals who only come together in the church as a secondary consequence of their response. "Mission and evangelism" and "life and work" strands of ecumenism can only ignore "faith and order" via an instrumentalization of the church that makes it a means to ends that are ultimately perceived to be detachable from its life—the salvation of souls on the one hand, or social justice on the other.[32] These issues in fact take us back to the origins of the modern ecumenical movement, bound up with the ambivalence among Catholic Anglicans around involvement in the World Missionary Conference in Edinburgh in 1910. While the principal concern of English Anglo-Catholics was to prevent a Protestant-dominated body pronouncing on doctrinal matters, American Episcopalians grasped the point more quickly that commitment to an ecclesial gospel entailed that partnership in mission with other churches would have to involve seeking deeper theological agreement, including on ecclesiological matters relating to worship, ministry, and sacraments.[33]

At the same time, it should also be stressed that *EG* is by no means a vindication of the priority of faith and order ecumenism at the expense of its other two strands. Its overriding desire is for the whole gospel to be shared with the whole world, and it has no space for anything that does not evidently relate to that passion. This gospel cannot be detached from the church—but neither can the church of *EG* be detached from the work of evangelization. Faith and order that is not constantly listening to and addressing the concerns of mission and evangelism is therefore bound to be a sterile activity. Moreover, this whole gospel is also good news first and foremost for the poor, so that churches that come together to share the gospel will need to listen together to the cry of the poor and consider together what it means to seek the justice of God's kingdom, a concern that is also taken up in *LS* and considered in detail by a number of other contributors to the present volume.[34]

Conclusion

Evangelii Gaudium, therefore, is good news for ecumenism.

The primacy it gives to evangelical ecclesiology has significant potential for ecumenical theology and in particular for addressing the impasse around different understandings of the church that has been identified as a crucial issue for growth in unity. Such an evangelical ecclesiology implies that the kind of partnership in mission that is so clearly essential in the contemporary context of secularization, religious pluralism, and the proliferation of churches contains an ecclesial trajectory that cannot be ignored. If gospel and church are inseparable, then we cannot "do" the gospel together without "being" the church together. To imagine we can is to inhabit an ultimately anti-Christian individualism to whose dangers Catholic theology ought to be especially alert. Evangelization, therefore, must lead us to deal steadily and determinedly with obstacles to Christian unity. As Pope Francis teaches that the only way for the renewal of the church is through evangelization, then renewal is bound to the cause of unity. All this is only good news, however, for an ecumenism that is prepared to lose itself in the cause of the gospel, trusting that there alone will its true life and real meaning be found.

Select Bibliography

Avis, Paul. *Reshaping Ecumenical Theology: The Church Made Whole?* London: T & T Clark, 2010.

Clements, Keith. *Ecumenical Dynamic: Living in More Than One Place at Once.* Geneva: WCC, 2013.

Kinnamon, Michael. *Can a Renewal Movement Be Renewed? Questions for the Future of Ecumenism.* Grand Rapids, MI: Eerdmans, 2014.

Ramsey, Michael. *The Gospel and the Catholic Church.* 2nd ed. London: SPCK, 1990.

Stanley, Brian. *The World Missionary Conference, Edinburgh 1910.* Studies in the History of Christian Missions. Grand Rapids, MI: Eerdmans, 2009.

Vatican II. *Unitatis Redintegratio,* Decree on Ecumenism, 1964. http://www.vatican.va/archive/hist_councils/ii_vatican

_council/documents/vat-ii_decree_19641121_unitatis
-redintegratio_en.html.

World Council of Churches. *The Church: Towards a Common Vision,
Faith and Order Paper 214*. Geneva: WCC, 2013.

World Council of Churches. "Together towards Life: Mission and
Evangelism in Changing Landscapes." Edited by Jooseop
Keum. Geneva: WCC, 2013.

Notes

1. Paul D. Murray, ed., *Receptive Ecumenism and the Call to
Catholic Learning: Exploring a Way for Contemporary Ecumenism*
(Oxford: Oxford University Press, 2008).

2. The quotation is from Vatican II, *Unitatis Redintegratio*, Decree on Ecumenism, 1964, no. 4; see http://www.vatican
.va/archive/hist_councils/ii_vatican_council/documents/vat-ii
_decree_19641121_unitatis-redintegratio_en.html.

3. In the Aparecida document, in whose production in 2007
the then Cardinal Bergoglio had a major role, ecumenism is also
linked to evangelization via dialogue in a section on "Ecumenical
and Interreligious Dialogue," with the subsection heading, "Ecumenical Dialogue So That the World May Believe" (nos. 227–34).
Although not developed, it includes an assertion rather stronger
than anything in *Evangelii Gaudium*: "At this new stage of evangelization, we want dialogue and ecumenical cooperation to lead
to promoting new forms of discipleship and mission in communion." See the Fifth General Conference of the Bishops of Latin
America and the Caribbean, "Disciples and Missionaries of Jesus
Christ, So That Our Peoples May Have Life in Him: 'I Am the Way
and the Truth and the Life' (Jn 16:4)." Concluding Document,
2007, http://www.aecrc.org/documents/Aparecida-Concluding
%20Document.pdf.

4. Pope Paul VI, *Evangelii Nuntiandi*, Apostolic Exhortation of His Holiness Pope Paul VI, 1975, http://w2.vatican.va/
content/paul-vi/en/apost_exhortations/documents/hf_p-vi
_exh_19751208_evangelii-nuntiandi.html.

5. Pope John Paul II, *Redemptoris Missio*, On the Permanent

Validity of the Church's Missionary Mandate, 1990, http://w2
.vatican.va/content/john-paul-ii/en/encyclicals/documents/hf
_jp-ii_enc_07121990_redemptoris-missio.html.

6. I have developed this claim in more detail in "What's
New about Renewal in *Evangelii Gaudium?*" *Ecclesiology* 12 (2016):
73–90.

7. W. A. Visser 't Hooft, *The Renewal of the Church: The Dale
Lectures Delivered at Mansfield College*, Oxford, October, 1955 (London: SCM, 1956), 11; see esp. chap. 7, "Renewal and Unity."

8. Michael Kinnamon, *Can a Renewal Movement Be Renewed?
Questions for the Future of Ecumenism* (Grand Rapids, MI: Eerdmans,
2014), 2.

9. Jonas Jonson, *Wounded Visions: Unity, Justice, and Peace in
the World Church after 1968*, trans. Norman A. Hjelm (Grand Rapids, MI: Eerdmans, 2013).

10. World Council of Churches, *Church and World: The Unity of
the Church and the Renewal of Human Community*, Faith and Order
Paper 151 (Geneva: WCC, 1990).

11. Although written from a somewhat different theological perspective, the same overriding focus on the relationship
between gospel and church is evident in John Webster, "On Evangelical Ecclesiology," *Ecclesiology* 1, no. 1 (2004): 9–35.

12. Vatican II, *Lumen Gentium*, Dogmatic Constitution on
the Church, 1964, no. 1, http://www.vatican.va/archive/hist
_councils/ii_vatican_council/documents/vat-ii_const_19641121
_lumen-gentium_en.html.

13. Vatican II, *Ad Gentes*, On the Mission Activity of the Church,
1965, no. 2, http://www.vatican.va/archive/hist_councils/ii_vati
can_council/documents/vat-ii_decree_19651207_ad-gentes_en
.html.

14. See Paul Murray's chapter in this volume.

15. See Philip McCosker's chapter in this volume.

16. Text reproduced in Hans-Georg Link, ed., *Apostolic Faith
Today: Handbook for Study,* Faith and Order Paper 124 (Geneva:
World Council of Churches, 1985), 64.

17. Quoted in Philip Ind, "Rowan Williams and the Possibility of Dialogue: Part 2," *One in Christ* 49, no. 1 (2015): 91.

18. Michael Ramsey, *The Gospel and the Catholic Church*, 2nd
ed. (London: SPCK, 1990).

19. Ibid., 217.

20. World Council of Churches, *The Church: Towards a Common Vision*, Faith and Order Paper 214 (Geneva: WCC, 2013), no. 13.

21. Ibid., no. 14.

22. Ibid., no. 15.

23. World Council of Churches, "Together towards Life: Mission and Evangelism in Changing Landscapes," ed. Jooseop Keum (Geneva: WCC, 2013).

24. Ibid., no. 55. On the relationship between mission, evangelism, and evangelization in recent writing across different churches, see Kirsteen Kim's chapter in this volume.

25. Ibid., no. 57.

26. Walter Kasper, *The Catholic Church: Nature, Reality and Mission*, trans. Thomas Hoebel (London: Bloomsbury, 2015), 29.

27. Ibid., 158; cf. also 92–95, 151, 194–96, and 307–8.

28. See the comments of Catherine E. Clifford, "Catholic Perspectives on *The Church: Towards a Common Vision*," *One in Christ* 49, no. 2 (2015): 199–200.

29. Ramsey, *Gospel and the Catholic Church*, 36.

30. Kinnamon, *Renewal Movement*, 57. Cf. Konrad Raiser's comment in "Fifty Years after the Second Vatican Council: Assessing Ecumenical Relations from the Perspective of the World Council of Churches," *Ecumenical Review* 67, no. 2 (2015): 291: "After fifty years there are increasing doubts whether we are still dealing with one and the same ecumenical movement, or whether competitive understandings of ecumenism and its ultimate goal have emerged in the meantime."

31. Keith Clements, *Ecumenical Dynamic: Living in More Than One Place at Once* (Geneva: WCC, 2013), 197.

32. For a critical analysis of approaches that render the church a "means" only to the ends of mission, see Andrew Davison and Alison Milbank, *For the Parish: A Critique of Fresh Expressions* (London: SCM, 2010), 41–63.

33. Brian Stanley, *The World Missionary Conference, Edinburgh 1910*, Studies in the History of Christian Missions (Grand Rapids, MI: Eerdmans, 2009), esp. 38–41, 297–98.

34. E.g., Hrynkow, Lakeland.

Part 4

TRANSFORMING THE WORLD

CATHOLIC SOCIAL TEACHING

Is *Evangelii Gaudium* Disrupting or Enhancing Catholic Social Teaching?

AUGUSTO ZAMPINI DAVIES

Although Pope Francis asserts that his exhortation *Evangelii Gaudium* (*EG*)[1] "is not a social document" (*EG* 184), it provides the basis for a development of the social doctrine of the church, portrayed in his encyclical *Laudato Si'* (*LS*).[2] However, the *EG-LS* socioeconomic approach has raised some remarkably interesting, and unequivocally social questions for Catholic academics.

The North American political scientist Donald Devine claims that Pope Francis's notion of markets, human freedom, and science is questionable, because it is highly influenced by his experience of crony Latin American capitalism.[3] Consequently, Devine claims, Francis is slightly deviating from the social tradition of his predecessors St. John Paul II and Benedict XVI, something that sooner or later will be redressed by future popes. Similarly, P. A. McGavin, an Australian priest and economist, argues that Francis's vision of economic and environmental issues are too Latin American, meaning that they are influenced by a culture where economic backwardness and opportunistic behaviors prevail under weak governance regimes, and where an institutional approach to development is often overshadowed by a populistic personal way of governance.[4] Hence, McGavin argues, the pope

241

does not depict technology, finance, economics, production and consumption, pollution, climate change, and, most worryingly, the Catholic notion of integral human development, with the lens of traditional CST, but rather with this questionable populist Latin American vision.[5]

The Acton Institute, a Catholic North American think tank, has also expressed their concerns about *EG*'s economic remarks.[6] Its president, Fr. Sirico, wonders how Francis's criticism on the wealth mentality that drives economics could match with what arguably are demonstrable benefits to the poor due to the globalized markets. According to Sirico, it is precisely the economic mentality behind the markets that have permitted people to have more access to work, goods, and services than ever in history before. He also suggests that St. John Paul II has highlighted the benefits of free market and has warned against the socialist intervention, which contrasts with Francis's view of capitalism and social welfare. The latter's view, Sirico argues, is entirely due to Francis's experience of Latin American corrupt capitalism.[7] Finally, the Argentine moral theologian Gustavo Irrazábal explicitly argues that the pope disrupts Catholic social teaching (CST) because he respects neither its nuanced style nor its universal principles.[8] Instead, Irrazábal claims, the pope uses a prophetic but nonscientific tone based on his populist "Theology of the People,"[9] thus threatening the continuity of the social magisterium.

By analyzing some socioeconomic considerations of *EG*, further elaborated in *LS*, I argue that far from disrupting CST, Pope Francis has opened new avenues for the development of Christian social thought. We can identify at least three strands of development, which are analyzed in the corresponding three sections of this chapter. The first one is the confirmation of the inductive and ecumenical methodology of CST, first embraced by Pope John XXIII in 1959,[10] accepted by the Second Vatican Council in 1965,[11] and furthered by Paul VI in 1967[12] and John Paul II in 1987 and 1991.[13] It has also been developed by the Latin American bishops, who applied it in the last decades to analyze the context of their own countries and their continent.[14] This method, as Pope Francis clarifies, begins with the reality of the poor. Because, as the pope claims, reality is greater than ideas, it should always come first when analyzing social, economic, or ecological issues. And given that the standpoint to assessing reality is not neutral, the experiences and realities of people living in poverty or affected by social or ecological degradation should be prioritized. In this way, Pope Francis explicitly includes the CST principle of the preferential option for the poor—reaffirmed by John Paul II[15]—into CST methodology. Although some may argue that this method could hinder the work of those trying to connect CST with economics,[16] this chapter counters that it nevertheless helps others who try to promote a dialogue between CST and some economists with a humane vision that transcends the mere mathematical approach to economics, embodied in the work of the Nobel Economic laureate Amartya Sen—as also argued by Deneulin in chapter 12 of this collection. By facilitating this association, *EG* not only provides CST with a more solid socioeconomic basis, but also lays down the foundations for its actual transformation, because economists like Sen are "precious allies in the commitment to defending human dignity, in building peaceful coexistence between peoples, and in protecting creation" (*EG* 257).

The second strand of the development of CST found in *EG* is a refined elaboration of the CST notion of "integral human development," as explained by previous popes, especially by Paul VI,[17] John Paul II,[18] and Benedict XVI.[19] An integral model of development not only leaves no one behind, but it also integrates all dimensions of our existence, such as our faith and even the ecosystem that allows us to exist. Based on CST relational anthropology, which understands humans as persons in relation, *EG* builds up its critique on the prevailing economic model of progress, underpinned by the liberal myth of individual autonomy. Such an individualistic approach, the pope argues, not only elides the communitarian dimension of every person, pivotal for human flourishing, but it also foments the illusion of unlimited growth, which in turn fosters a consumerist and throwaway culture. Although some may consider this a rejection of the entire current economic system,[20] this chapter argues that *EG* is actually helping economics to recover its own ethos. A system where the "subject" of the economy is misconceived as a mere "object" of consumption, and whose freedom is distorted, cannot promote human development. Conversely, a system that has people at its center, rooted in deep anthropological ideas of relationships, freedom, and strong values such as those coming from faith, can widen the notion of economics while promoting integral human development. Moreover, *EG* expounds CST understandings of development by anticipating what *LS* will call "integral ecology," which links the socioeconomic growth with the personal-ecological one. The "cry of the poor" and the "cry of the earth" go *pari passu*, hence tackling poverty and promoting economic growth cannot be delinked from tackling ecological degradation and promoting holistic and sustainable well-being (*LS* 49).

The third strand of Catholic social development found in *EG* is the explicit affirmation that processes of inclusive public dialogue are key to social transformation. Based on the teachings of his predecessors, especially Benedict XVI,[21] who explains that international development necessitates economic, political, and religious dialogue, Pope Francis argues that faith in general cannot be omitted when considering development, and that religious narratives in particular can contribute to the dialogue on progress. While some may argue that the use of the Bible in the public arena is an imposition of a particular faith,[22] which cannot be accepted in a modern democratic secular society, Pope Francis, in line with authors such as Paul Ricœur,[23] conceives biblical narratives as religious classic art that help people to better understand humanity and the signs of the times. In other words, these religious narratives can enable us to discuss, publicly and inclusively, a wiser and creative way of designing models of growth that are truly human and sustainable. No wonder the economist Amartya Sen uses Sanskrit Hindu narratives to discuss arguments such as whether income is a good measure of quality of life,[24] the Christian narrative of the Good Samaritan (Luke 10:26–27) to introduce his argument about responsibility and universal concern for others,[25] and Buddhist narratives to argue that a consequential comparative assessment of states of affairs in development better serves the idea of justice. As Sen observes, some religious stories contribute to better public reasoning processes because they provide reasons for what matters to people's ordinary lives.[26]

In short, this chapter claims that these three new avenues of CST, expressed through the pope's prophetic style, reinvigorate rather than threaten the social magisterium of the church. The new vigor Francis brings, however, is only possible thanks to the foundational work of his predecessors, as also argued by Phillips, upon whose teaching the current pope builds.

EG: Realities Are Greater Than Ideas

EG sets the tone for a renewed methodology of CST that has a much stronger dialogical and ecumenical tone. The starting point of this methodology cannot be nuanced "general principles that challenge no one" (*EG* 182), but rather actual injustices and the view of those who suffer them. To hear the "cry of the poor" (*EG* 187–90) and redress their suffering, a profound dialogue with different sciences and creeds is needed (nos. 238–58). Similarly, as expounded in *LS,* to hear the "cry of the land," and to promote sustainable development, CST needs to start from the reality of the wounded mother earth, which is "among the most abandoned and maltreated of our poor" (*LS* 2). For that, it is necessary to listen to what is being witnessed by people working on the ground or in civic groups, and by the best scientific ecological research of today (*LS* 7, 10, 17–61). This "seeing" or "listening," Pope Francis argues, could "provide a concrete foundation for the ethical and spiritual" analysis, and, most importantly, should "touch us deeply" so as to move us to action (*LS* 15).

This analysis is particularly important for the church. As disciples of Christ, its members cannot be closed in, isolated from the actual world (*EG* 47, 87). On the contrary, they are called to be in the world and for the world, in a "permanent state of mission," not being afraid of transmitting the joy of the gospel to all, particularly to those in need (*EG* 22). This, of course, has serious consequences. One is that by being in the world, the church is questioned by the world, which helps in the church's constant renewal to increase its fidelity to its call, both individually and structurally (*EG* 26). The other is that Christ's disciples can become more aware of the actual social problems of the world. They can also contribute, through their faith—in dialogue with others—to propose creatively to "loosen the knots of human affairs, even the most complex and inscrutable" ones (*EG* 178). The evangelization mission of the church, hence, has less to do with protected isolated ideas or principles; it is more about how to discover and expound the kingdom of God "present in the world," and how this discovery can improve community building through healthy engagements with all peoples (*EG* 176).

This vision of the church's mission is applied in *LS* with the aim of helping to reduce the current socioecological degradation, and in *AL* in order to increase the joy of love. If the church's mission is *in* and *for* the world, and if such a mission is related to the overarching socioecological problem affecting the whole planet, then the church's principles need to interact *with* others' principles and the experiences of those who also live in the world. Put differently, in order to spread the joy of the gospel and discover creative paths for human advancement, Christians need to be engaged with the "seeing" and "analysis" of others. This comprises not only the experience of those who are being affected (the poor), or the vision of other faiths, but also those who contribute with their scientific ecological analysis (*EG* 182). Similarly, in order to transmit the "joy of love," Pope Francis proposes to start with the reality of the families as they are, rather than with principles which, occasionally, if they are "far removed from concrete situations and practical possibilities of real families," can fail to inspire God's grace and actual transformation (*AL* 1.36).

It is important to note how Francis's understanding of CST and its methodology is not presented through dry epistemological explanations, but through inspiring connections with the core of the gospel. It is this style that ignites the discussion on how CST should approach social problems. Not through an ideological approach, but through the seeing and listening to reality, which can only occur if we are immersed in the world of our time, in dialogue with other churches, faiths, and sciences, and closely related to those who suffer (*EG* 40, 142, 187). *EG*, therefore, confirms the traditional methodology of CST: *seeing-judging-acting*. When addressing social issues, the church proposes these three steps. We first need to see the reality, particularly through the eyes of the poor and disadvantaged. Once a concrete situation is addressed, we can move toward evaluating it in the light of the gospel and the tradition of the church (e.g., CST principles). Finally, we can promote decisions according to what we see and discern and consequently act. In *LS*, and following the Latin

American magisterium, Pope Francis adds a fourth stage of the method: "celebrating" God's love and goodness, which is crucial to bringing about hope and joy, and pivotal to seeing more clearly, judging more wisely, and acting more efficiently (*LS* 202–37).

This method, officially embraced by Pope John XXIII but with its roots in Catholic Action, breaks away completely from "the old dogmatic device" of prestating that if a situation is *hypothetically* intrinsically bad, the church is unavoidably obliged to reject it in *theory*, although it can occasionally tolerate it as a *modus vivendi*, as occurred with the notion of democracy until the mid-1950s.[27] Pope John therefore introduced a shift in the methodology of social analysis in the church. From the classical "deductive" method, which basically "understands reality in terms of the eternal, the immutable, and the unchanging," the Pope moves toward an "inductive" historical consciousness approach, which "gives more importance to the particular, the contingent, the historical and the individual."[28] *EG*'s and *LS*'s unique contributions, though, are found in the stress on the need to see reality through the experiences of the vulnerable, the weak, the marginalized, and not from general ideas (*EG* 182, 187, 190). For Pope Francis, scrutinizing the signs of the times through the reality of the poor is not only the "criterion of authenticity" of CST, but also enables us to "be deeply moved" and hence respond accordingly (*EG* 193–94). If Francis is confirming and enriching CST methodology, why do some academics such as those mentioned in the introduction argue that *EG* constitutes a deviation from the social doctrine of the church and her traditional principles, thus driving it toward self-destruction or extinction?

DOES *EG* BELITTLE OR REINFORCE CST PRINCIPLES?

As explained at the beginning of this chapter, criticisms of *EG* have been publicly expressed in the academic world. One of the sharpest critiques comes from the pope's home city, Buenos Aires. The Argentine theologian Irrazábal accuses Pope Francis of betraying CST methodology. He claims the pope is leaving aside a long tradition of addressing social problems through universal principles. By so doing, *EG* not only fails to follow a rich socio-theological tradition of the church, but also prevents eventual future dialogues with those who could redress the injustices, such as economic inequality. In particular, Irrazábal argues, the pope is putting at risk the enormous amount of work of theologians working on CST matters alongside other scientists, such as economists. Moreover, the pope seems to be unaware that, by trying to reinvent the wheel regarding CST methodology, he would need a strong theological background that could at least match CST universal principles, something that, according to Irrazábal, *EG* does not provide.[29]

However, criticisms such as Irrazábal's miss the point that *EG* is not reinventing the wheel in terms of CST methodology, but rather, as suggested before, delving deep into its very inductive and ecumenical roots.[30] The inductive and ecumenical method of seeing-judging-acting, which has a strong biblical background,[31] is implicitly incorporated in the patristic and the Scholastic tradition, and has been explicitly developed and explained in the twentieth century, is now taken up by *EG* and *LS*.[32] Therefore, accusing *EG* of betraying the Catholic tradition in general, or the social methodological tradition in particular, is not convincing.

One can understand Irrazábal's concern to maintain the current, fruitful dialogue between theology and economics. If *EG* were to prevent this dialogue from happening or developing, because its critique of economics alienates economists, then Pope Francis's pronouncements would be truly problematic for the social tradition of the church. However, by embracing and furthering traditional CST methodology, *EG* seems to open more possibilities for dialogue, especially with economists with a similar methodological approach and an idea of holistic human development.[33] A good example is the "capability approach" developed by Amartya Sen, which has enriched the understanding of development as a multidimensional process—hence not limited to material growth.[34] Such theoretical interventions have permitted the reopening of debate about economics and ethics, which were waning rapidly due to a deceptive technical interpretation of economic science,[35] which is precisely what Pope Francis advocates too. More importantly, Sen's approach has not just influenced the academic community. It has notably influenced many policies developed by international agencies such as the World Bank and United Nations (e.g., the creation of the United Nations Development Program and its Human Development Reports, published since 1990,[36] which measure development according to the capacity of people to convert wealth into well-being), and has garnered wide acceptance among policy makers.[37]

Still, however valuable Sen's approach could sound as a supplement to the social tradition of the church, Catholic theology needs to offer a solid methodology with which it can interact with the capability approach. It is precisely a bottom-up approach, reflected in the method adopted by *EG,* that enables such interaction. For Sen, in order to promote justice in economics, we cannot start by theoretically asking what a just society and perfect institutions are, and then design economic programs that would best suit our answers. By so doing, a theory of justice becomes not only unfeasible, but also redundant.[38] While the poor suffer grave injustices today, philosophers and policy makers are trapped in discussions about ideal scenarios, distracting them from the core issues of real unfair situations.[39] In Pope Francis's words, "realities are greater than ideas" (*EG* 231). Ideas and principles, hence, should rely on, develop upon, and respond to reality, as Sen also implies. Moreover, Sen proposes commencing by analyzing economic reality through a comparative approach toward policies that may actually reduce injustices and foster the advancement of justice.[40] This comparison is necessarily an interdisciplinary one. If economics is about free choices and the production of wealth, then its initial analysis cannot be disentangled from human values underpinning actual economic choices.[41] And given that there is no reason for excluding religious values in such an equation, Sen's approach and CST can jointly venture the readings of the signs of the times. Furthermore, the comparison of policies regarding the effect they have on real people requires, according to Sen, public debates, where representatives of all sectors involved in the problems weigh up reasonable value-laden propositions.[42] These debates need the voices of all, but in particular the voices of those who do not have access to official channels of public participation. In the words of Pope Francis, they need the participation of the marginalized.[43]

This example of coincidences and eventual collaboration between CST and Sen's approach to reading the signs of the time and their injustices shows how *EG,* aligned with the social tradition of the church of starting the socioethical reflection through the reality of those in need, helps rather than prevents the dialogue with social sciences, especially with economics. Thus, *EG* cannot be accused, as Irrazábal and the Acton Institute suggest, of risking the interdisciplinary work between theologians and other scientists who try to analyze together how to redress injustices. Furthermore, as the parable of *The Good Samaritan* (Luke 10:25–37) and *EG* and *LS* highlight, the seeing cannot be limited to our own religious (Catholic) eyes, but rather must be open to the eyes of social sciences, those of other faiths (and none), and social movements. Their sight is needed in present social theological ethics so as to judge ethically specific socioeconomic or political situations. This was the case with liberation movements in Latin America in the 1970s, or the Solidarity movement in Poland in the 1980–90s, or the interfaith movements in Asia in the 2000s, whose sight has enriched Catholic theology and its analysis of the social realm. This is also the case with civic and ecological movements regarding the "seeing" of environmental degradation and its roots, whose work is praised and taken by the new social document of church (*LS* 14).

The importance *EG* and *LS* give to CST method does not come out of the blue. To be fair to criticisms such as Irrazábal's, the "seeing" of the method has not always been understood as starting from the reality of the most vulnerable. In fact, *The Compendium of the Social Doctrine of the Church* (*Compendium*),[44] which intended a complete overview of the pontifical teachings from Leo XIII onward and champions the triple movement of seeing-judging-acting (no. 7), conceives the starting point—the seeing—as "principles" for reflection rather than empirical reality.[45] So one could argue, alongside Irrazábal, that not starting from these principles is weakening rather than strengthening the opportunities for CST to interact with other faiths and sciences so as to tackle social injustices. Yet, what this position depicts is the methodological tensions within Catholic social tradition.

POLITICAL FEARS AND CST INDUCTIVE METHODOLOGY

Although officially launched by Pope John XXIII and confirmed by the Pastoral Constitution *GS*, and despite being further advanced by all subsequent popes, the inductive and inclusive

CST method has been used ambiguously during recent decades.[46] The reason involved liberation theology and the Latin American social magisterium. The social teachings of the Latin American bishops more clearly and concretely explained and applied the inductive method than the popes in their universal magisterium. In particular, the bishops highlighted the need to start any social analysis from the basis of the community, that is, from the poorest.[47] When this happens, the bishops argued, the discernment of the signs of the time cannot but include those social structures, whether economic, cultural, or political, that prevent people from flourishing.

However, fear of a merely political reading of biblical and Christian justice, especially due to the influence of liberation theology in the region during times of political upheaval, moved John Paul II[48] and Joseph Ratzinger, as prefect of the Congregation of the Doctrine of the Faith,[49] to warn the bishops about the risks of a "too political" approach to the social teaching of the church that could confuse God's plan for salvation with a specific sociopolitical order, socialism. These warnings, plus the bishops' growing anxiety regarding the perils of supporting—even indirectly—responses to social injustices with violent or antireligious approaches,[50] put the bishops gathered in Santo Domingo in 1992 under immense pressure. Consequently, they decided to set aside the method of seeing-judging-acting, and took refuge in the safe fortress of deductive theology.

Nonetheless, given that the option for the poor and the need for a prophetic attitude were ratified at that same conference, the "safe" enclosed theological methodology was not able to keep its citizens (theologians, pastors, community agents, and so on) inside their "safe" walls. Moreover, the method had already been accepted by the Latin American theological and pastoral ethos and was being implemented across the whole continent. Thus, a document contradicting the ethos of previous Conferences of Bishops and of the Second Vatican Council did not carry enough weight to bury the incipient hermeneutic method. For this reason, this Latin American legacy regarding methodology has not been negated and in the new millennium, the bishops of that continent, led by Cardinal Bergoglio, officially reappropriated the methodology, which they recognized was already being applied by a great number of theologians, pastors, and communities.[51]

EG: ENHANCING THE METHOD

Before *EG*, Pope Francis gave strong and clear signs of approval for the inductive/bottom-up/interdisciplinary method in CST. While addressing the Latin American bishops on his trip to Brazil, Francis explicitly mentioned the CST method of seeing-judging-acting. Not only did he praise the bishops for continuing to apply that method in their later document of Aparecida,[52] but also critically pointed out the risk comprised in the method, that is, to have an "aseptic" view of reality, as if the seeing could ever be neutral and impartial. The new pope has openly admitted that the seeing of reality is always affected by our view, our sight. A great temptation, he argues, is to pretend to have *aseptic-impartial-objective* views of socioeconomic problems and therefore attempt to impose it on others who have *contaminated-partial-subjective* views.[53] For Christians, a possible way to avoid this temptation is to take "the path of discipleship." The views of the disciples of Christ, while chiefly influenced by the values of the kingdom of God, were also affected by the historic and cultural milieu.[54] Thus, the current disciples of Christ need to address the new social realities with the eyes of the kingdom connected to the eyes of the world. When the views of the kingdom and of the world (e.g., other sciences) go *pari passu*, the creativity to find effective actions that can redress injustices is possible.

The incorporation of this thought in *EG* comes as no surprise. It is clearly not intending to close the doors to dialogue with economics, as some critics argue. On the contrary, by setting the tone of the biblical roots of the CST method, it offers social theologians better guidance to delve deeper into an interdisciplinary approach. The exhortation explains why, in order to spread the joy of the gospel and discover creative paths for human advancement, Christians cannot be detached from community life, their local contexts, and the engagement with others in their particular social, geographical, and historic realities (*EG* 11, 177, 178, 234). Francis therefore not only accords great importance to the inductive-historical approach of social theological methodology, but also highlights the correlation between such methodology and the anthropological stress on freedom, inclusion, and participation. An inclusive seeing of the signs of the time necessitates an inclusive dialogue, from which creative programs fostering an inclusive society can ensue. For that, the dialogue must aim at generating an inclusive model of development able to buttress the well-being of all people. On this point, I argue, we find the second contribution from *EG* to CST.

EG: "Integral" Development, Faith, and Ecology

Critics of *EG* protest that the pope denounces what he believes is wrong without referring to research on the causes of the supposedly socioeconomic evil, but simply based on his personal perception,[55] which many understand as antibusiness or anticapitalist.[56] However, regardless of the assumptions of Francis's personal views, his economic statements in *EG* are based on CST classic understanding of "integral and authentic development," rooted in a relational anthropology.

RELATIONAL ANTHROPOLOGY

For CST, human beings are conceived as "persons" rather than as "individuals" (*GS* 12–22). A person has an individual uniqueness, but cannot be developed outside or above society, because she exists exclusively in society and for other people. Likewise, a society cannot truly develop outside or above persons, because social life is always "an expression of its unmistakable protagonist: the human person," who is the "subject, foundation and goal" of any community (*Compendium* 34, 106).[57]

A balance between individual freedom and its social context, or in other words, between the person, his or her interpersonal relations, and his or her wider social relations, is pivotal for human flourishing. As Paul Ricœur argues,[58] without "institutional mediations," "individuals are only the initial drafts of human persons." The reason is that, unless humans belong to a political body—where institutions are crucial—they cannot flourish as such.

Therefore, institutional-political-communitarian mediation cannot be revoked when aiming at human development. However, Ricœur clarifies, this belonging has been explained differently by one version of liberalism, the one embedded in the social contract tradition. For this approach, the individual is already a complete person (and a subject with rights) before entering into the contractual relation. "He gives up real rights...natural rights in exchange for security, as with Hobbes, or for civil status or citizenship, as with Rousseau and Kant."[59] But given that this understanding of association is "insecure and revocable," Ricœur prefers the previously explained one, which is anthropologically irrevocable, because it sees social relationality as an essential requirement for human advancement. Yet, as Hannah Arendt[60] claims and Ricœur concurs, the risk of admitting this fundamental social dimension in order to progress as human beings, is to belittle the personal and interpersonal identity, stressing too much on the collective one: a perfect scenario for authoritarianism.

INTEGRAL HUMAN DEVELOPMENT

The social tradition of the church has never accepted the absolute sovereignty of either the individual or the collective dimension of our existence—*EG* is no exception. Based on a relational anthropology, CST conceives human flourishing as holistic—this means, as "integral and authentic development" for the *whole person* and for *all peoples*. Consequently, when growth is boosting only one dimension of humanity (e.g., material), or is benefiting merely one sector of the population (e.g., the affluent), then development is not entirely human and lacks authenticity. The main reason is that humans cannot flourish and reach their full potential if they develop only partially, whether this partiality is individual (just one dimension of the person's existence) or social (just for one or for a group of individuals).

It is on this basis that *EG* builds up its critical analysis on economics. The prevailing economic model of progress is not integral because it foments exclusion and inequality (*EG* 53), being underpinned by the myth of individual autonomy, which belittles interpersonal bonds and the necessary communitarian dimension of humans to flourish (no. 67). The model is also inauthentic because it does not acknowledge the reality of the limits to prosperity (*EG* 54). Following uncritically the idols of Mammon (i.e., money) and the market, which, as false gods rule rather than serve humanity (*EG* 57), the current economic model is complicit in distorting the idea of the person created in the image and likeness of God. For these idols and their models, individuals are defined more according to their consumptive power (consumers) and to what they "have," rather than according to what they really "are." Worse, often "human beings are themselves considered consumer goods to be used and then discarded," being the "left-overs" or victims of a "throw-away culture" where "the priority is given to the outward, the immediate, the visible, the quick, the superficial and the provisional" (*EG* 53–62).

This criticism is not against the economy in itself, but against a particularized application of an economic model. Francis's contribution to the debate is more on the ethical side of economics, rather than on the engineering-mathematical side.[61] Put differently, Francis is trying to bring economics to the place where it once belonged, that is to the terrain of ethics, "to the art of achieving a fitting management of our common home, which is the world as a whole" (*EG* 206). The fact that this contribution entails only general anthropological comments does not mean they are superficial or poorly grounded. On the contrary, they go deep into the meaning of human beings and progress. However, these anthropological contributions might not be enough for critics of *EG*, who argue that Francis is excoriating the entire political-economic system without proposing an alternative, or even offering some core universal values in order to find it. This resembles more, they argue, the old authoritarian clerical style rather than the humble scientific approach that the twenty-first century needs from the Catholic Church.[62]

The lack of economic details in *EG*, far from being a disadvantage to CST in its attempt to promote a better development model, is actually an advantage. First, because the pope is talking about the church's anthropological and ethical expertise, he invites other experts "to complete and enrich" his "diagnosis" (*EG* 108). Had he proposed a concrete economic alternative, as critics demand, he would have gone beyond a pope's "ambition" and "mission" (*Octogesima Adveniens* 4). What Francis is arguing, based on the CST notion of integral development, is that "the dignity of each human person and the pursuit of the common good... ought to shape all economic policies" (*EG* 203). He is also claiming that economic growth needs to be accompanied by a "growth in justice" (*EG* 204), something that is difficult to achieve through either "irresponsible populism" or a "naïve trust in the goodness of those wielding economic power" or "the free market" (no. 54). This does not sound like a personal, isolated, and populist idea of a Latin American bishop who ignores the social and institutional role of economic markets.[63] Second, the pope is overtly expressing that CST is "open to discussion," hoping that in such a discussion CST principles can be augmented so as to eventually become more concrete in the promotion of human flourishing and the common good (*EG* 182). This openness and humbleness does not sound patronizing at all, and it is even boosting—rather than hindering—the scientific work of CST tradition.

INTEGRAL CHRISTIAN FAITH

Aside from ethical principles and the invitation to dialogue, *EG* also offers a nuanced, novel contribution to the debate on integral development, which is now linked with integral faith and, as further developed in *LS*, with integral ecology.

An "integral and authentic faith," as presented in the exhortation, is part of the "missionary option" of the church (*EG* 27). Driven by the "liberating work of the Spirit," the church struggles to move from an "ostentatious preoccupation for the liturgy, for doctrine, and for [its own] prestige," toward forging communion in "all social bonds" (*EG* 95, 178). Indeed, Francis argues, "to evangelize is to make the kingdom of God present in our world," which "has a clear social content" (*EG* 176–77). At the heart of Christian faith lies "the profound connection between evangelization and human advancement" (*EG* 178), the inseparable bond of communion and justice (no. 179). This implies, for example, that when we ask for forgiveness of our trespasses (The Lord's Prayer), we cannot but link the "personal and social" discernment (*EG* 181), meditating on the habits and personal attitudes that prevent our fulfillment, as well as on the structures that hinder social development (no. 189). "The Church cannot and must not remain on the sidelines in the fight for justice," because it is called to help to build a "better world" (*EG* 183), to "heal wounds, to build bridges, to strengthen relationships, and to bear one another's burdens" (no. 67). "An authentic faith—which is never comfortable or completely personal—always involves the deep desire to change the world...to leave the world somehow better than we found it" (*EG* 183).

Yet, consistent with the CST methodology, *EG* proposes a change of perspective, commencing by the inclusion of those excluded from the benefits of the system, because—precisely— "there is an inseparable bond between our faith and the poor" (*EG* 49). In this work of socioeconomic inclusion, however, the poor are not to be considered merely passive beneficiaries. Once freely able to take part in their society (*EG* 187), they can contribute with their creativity (*EG* 192), especially with the wisdom of their popular culture, "which contains values of faith and solidarity capable of encouraging the development of a more just and believing society" (*EG* 68).

We can see how *EG* is linking the very basis of Christian faith with economics and integral human development, a link that is further explored in *LS* (nos. 62–100, 202–46). For Pope Francis, Christian spirituality can contribute to sustainable development because it "proposes an alternative understanding of the quality of life...one capable of deep enjoyment free of the obsession with consumption," and hence it "encourages a prophetic and contemplative lifestyle" (*LS* 222). In this way, Christian spirituality ignites personal and social love (*LS* 231), because it favors "sobriety and humility" at a personal level (*LS* 224), while increasing "the capacity for living together in communion" (no. 228). Moreover, Christian spirituality, rooted in the encounter with Jesus Christ, becomes evident in the relationship between Christians and the world around them (*LS* 217). Now the world (the land and the poor) is crying out for help (*LS* 49). In response, "the rich heritage of Christian spirituality" encourages personal and community conversion so as to be reconciled with others, with creation, and with the Creator (*LS* 216, 218–19). This comprises a change of attitude, from indifference to loving awareness, from utilitarianism to gratuitousness, from selfishness to generosity, from self-advantage to solidarity (*LS* 220). In short, integral faith not only permits believers to have a deep understanding of the quality of life that can counter the current consumeristic society. It also motivates a deep individual and social conversion, so as to transform our society into a better place for all.

INTEGRAL ECOLOGY

EG contains the germ of a further elaboration of integral development and integral faith: integral ecology (*LS* 138–62). This is a *logos* that acknowledges the inextricable connection between all webs of life, capable of caring for the entire *oikos* (home). The interdependency of human beings in their search for development, therefore, should include not only all human beings on the earth, but also, as demanded by our faith, future generations, other creatures, and the rest of creation too.

According to *EG*, therefore, integral development (for the entire person and for all people), is intimately linked with an integral understanding of our faith. Christians not only believe in God the almighty, but also in the goodness of his creation (and creatures). As good stewards of such a beautiful creation, and as disciples who have been redeemed by Christ, we believe we are entrusted with care for the gift of creation, and with the joyful mission of expounding the kingdom of God on earth, our common home. This socioecological mission of love and justice is integral to Christian faith. Yet, the mission transcends the environmental problem; it is about the ecological one, the webs of life on earth, both social and natural. Therefore, integral development and integral faith are inextricably related with an integral vision of the ecology. This is not limited to the earth, its natural elements, the climate, and wildlife. It is also about human life, which is part of the ecology, and which plays a fundamental role in the ecological crisis.

We can see how, by connecting integral development with integral faith and integral ecology, Pope Francis is being faithful to CST's deepest anthropological and biblical roots. Still, one could argue that the Bishop of Rome is trying to impose Christian faith on the public processes of human development. This would be, as Irrazábal points out, highly problematic.[64] In the following and final section, I will briefly explore how *EG* and *LS* are proposing the link between faith and development beyond the church and into the public arena.

EG: Public Reasoning Processes

Far from being patronizing, unscientific, or imperative, as some critics argue, *EG*, and its subsequent social document *LS*, are dialogical propositions bringing different voices and values into public debates about integral and sustainable development. Regarding Christian faith, the pope is well aware that we can neither deduce absolute interpretations of social realities, nor propose *the* solution to concrete contemporary problems from it (*EG* 184). In order to help find these concrete and practical solutions seeking for integral development, we need the contribution and participation of different faiths, sciences, and cultures (*EG* 31, 182). Although the church cannot but present the truth of the gospel when participating in any debate, her approach cannot be a "doctrinal or moral...or ideological" one, because it would lose the actual "fragrance of the Gospel" (*EG* 31). The church, in fact, is always growing in her interpretation and understanding of the revealed truth, not just by its theological research or sacramental life, but also through public "dialogue" (*EG* 40). Dialogue, as described in *EG*, is "much more than the communication of a truth" (*EG* 142). It is a path, a process of listening and responding that not only helps the discovery of new dimensions of the truth, but also heals the deepest roots of evils disrupting relationships (see *EG* 4, 238, 205).

DIALOGICAL CREATURES

Based on the personal-relational anthropology of CST, the church is convinced that human beings, who are created in the image and likeness of the triune God, are able to pay disinterested attention to others, to hear what the other says without simultaneously thinking how we can respond. Indeed, the only way of comprehending what the other appreciates is to somehow empty oneself and embrace the other, going beyond the limits of language and trying to reach the unique and loving being behind the words.[65] This way of listening opens a path for freedom and human flourishing. As the persons of the Trinity can empty themselves so as to listen fully in order to allow new things to happen (crucifixion-resurrection), so can humans created in her likeness. When dialogue is based on a healthy and respectful pluralism, as the pope argues, it generates processes that yield new ideas (*EG* 255, 232). This helps to create a new culture of "encounter" that fosters respect and inclusion, which seems to be the right path to defend human dignity, to promote full human development, and to pursue the common good (*EG* 220, 257, 238–39).

We can find some examples of this way of dialoguing in the ecumenical and interreligious dialogue, as highlighted by Jeremy Worthen in the previous chapter of this volume. Despite the tensions (and even wars) in the name of faith in our modern era, healthy and trinitarian models of dialogue are aiding the advancement of the conversation.[66] A revealing case is the forum organized a decade ago by Hans Küng, where representatives of different religions deployed the virtue of listening by emptying themselves of a priori arguments. This does not mean that they set aside their own beliefs, but that in the interchange of convictions, by enabling the core ethos of the others to flourish, they were also able to rediscover and reaffirm their own central values, generating a fruitful outcome.[67]

DIALOGUE AND STRUCTURAL IMPEDIMENTS

Still, the grounds for this dialogue, with this particular way of listening, as Küng's case shows, need not be just the participants' virtue of listening and debating, but also a structure that permits those virtues to flourish. When structures for the debate are set in such a way that the strongest voices do not impose themselves over the weakest ones, where the unique being of each participant is respected, regardless of majorities or minorities of followers, then the ground for people to deploy their potential conversational virtues is cleared and thus the chances for the dialogue to succeed increase. What the example of world religious dialogue depicts is that a public dialogue, in order to enable human flourishing, requires a proper structural environment or organization.

It cannot depend exclusively on the individual capacities of the people involved, as seems to be the narrative of prevailing economic programs.

Structures impeding a culture of encounter and dialogue are, for CST, structural sins (*Sollicitudo Rei Socialis* 36). To change these structures, both a conversion in personal attitudes and in social relationships is required (*EG* 188–89). The pope trusts "in the openness and readiness of all Christians" to work together for this change (*EG* 201) so as to generate a different global public mindset that "could help bring down the wall of separation between the economy and the common good of society" (no. 205), between "individualistic, indifferent and self-centered" approaches and actual integral human fulfillment (no. 208).

But what can we do against such structural evils? One means of fighting structural sin is to enhance our relational dimension and to strengthen our capacity to cooperate with others. This is not limited to intimate or friendly relationships only, but also comprises societal or communal association, generally channeled through churches, NGOs, political groups, families, social movements, and so on. For CST, when our capacity to cooperate is transformative, and when it generates cultures of encounter in which people can flourish, it proves the existence of the human capacity for "public-love."[68] While *EG* highlights the social dimension of our faith and mission, *LS* further explains how our love is also civic and political, not limited to the relationships between individuals, but applied in the "macro-relationships" of politics and economics as well (*LS* 231). Although not everybody has a specific political or economic vocation, as inhabitants of the earth or citizens of our societies, we all have something to contribute. Engaging in healthy processes of dialogue, therefore, helps persons and groups to "bear fruit in significant historical events" (*EG* 223). This, as *EG* explains, is a crucial dimension of our faith.

PUBLIC DIALOGUE AND BIBLICAL NARRATIVES

In order to motivate this participation and dialogue of Christians in the new Areopagi (*EG* 257), and in order to present our faith as a factor of inspiration for social change, Pope Francis proposes going beyond CST traditional principles. He suggests a

Christian contribution to the public dialogue for integral development should stress the importance of the great biblical narratives, which say a lot "about the relationship of human beings with the world" and with each other (*LS* 65). "Religious classics can prove meaningful in every age; they have an enduring power to open new horizons, to stimulate thought, to expand the mind and heart" (*EG* 256). I argue this is a definitive development of CST. The pope seems not only to follow the Vatican II proposal "to draw more fully on the teaching of Holy Scripture" (*Optatum Totius* 16)[69] but also to echo the biblical scholar Sandra Shneiders who, following Gadamer, Ricœur, and Tracy, offers a compelling explanation for treating some biblical texts as "great art."[70] As such, biblical texts, when being interpreted by modern people, come alive; they are actualized, renewed, and furthered, opening for the reader new ways of understanding their own reality.

Note that the analogy is with *great* art only. Not every piece of writing is a work of art, and even some of those that are considered art have had little influence on people. Following Ricœur and Schneiders,[71] we can define great written art (or a "classic text"), as those texts having aesthetic beauty in their style and composition, steady relevance throughout the centuries (not merely for a few years or decades), and lively permanent effective interaction with a large group of readers. Although all classic texts are influenced by their cultural tradition, it is precisely through the sensibility of a particular culture that this great piece of art is able to bring universal truths to human existence. The classic,[72] unlike other texts, is not imprisoned in its culture nor in its generation, but rather is alive among different cultures and times through the effort of readers who, apart from criticizing and translating it, appropriate it and recontextualize it in their current situations. Indeed, "the classic text is classic…because it does not merely convey information but affects existentially the life of its readers."[73]

In this regard, just as we speak of Latin, Greek, or Chinese classics, we can also speak of Christian classics, among which "the New-Testament is *the* religious classic of Christianity."[74] Its aesthetic style, its constant relevance for millions of people throughout twenty centuries, and its capacity to impact on the lives of its readers, especially by offering them a new set of possibilities for their well-being, makes this religious book a true classic. Its stories are "more than a reservoir of citations used to illustrate moral insights" or merely something about the past. They rather open a new world of meaning, offering "generative metaphors" that contribute to a novel vision of the present (*Sollicitudo Rei Socialis* 54).[75]

It is not a coincidence that, as mentioned earlier, Amartya Sen draws upon religious narratives to discuss arguments around quality of life, economics, justice, assessment of development, and so forth. Many religious narratives can be seen as part of a literature genre that can facilitate public dialogue, precisely because they start with ordinary situations of life that people can easily identify with. In addition, they reveal the ambiguity of those situations where suffering and injustice seem to prevail, although they are not the final destiny of human existence. Religious stories, hence, can trigger people's imagination to respond to particular injustices in a creative way. For example, they can invite listeners to position themselves in relation to the story's protagonists in order to work through their own social commitments, as Sen points out when discussing the parable of the Good Samaritan.[76]

In times when economics cannot give creative answers to financial and environmental crises on its own, Bible stories can provoke readers not only to rethink the text in itself, but also to rethink the world, as suggested in *EG*. They can break the present narrow hermeneutic horizon or biased interpretation of wealth creation by opening new alternatives,[77] and they can challenge root metaphors, those basic modern assumptions, such as the exclusive utilitarian-ridden intention for decision-making, or that unregulated markets will forge justice and spread wealth (*EG* 204), that are used to depict (and distort) the nature of society and our experience.[78]

EG and *LS* confirm the CST position about the need for processes of public dialogue where faith values are taken seriously into account. Yet, Catholic social values can be introduced in complementary ways to that of the universal CST principles. According to Pope Francis, biblical narratives, with their universal truth, which transcends local cultures, may also be considered in public debates on integral human development. Not with the idea of forcing people to believe in a particular creed or religious story, but as a contribution to the dialogue that can help people interpret their own existential stories, question the prevailing economic narrative of the time, and trigger their imagination to seek for novel solutions regarding economic-socioecological problems (*LS* 62).

Conclusion

This chapter has analyzed why *EG* (and its subsequent social document, *LS*) neither disrupts nor distorts the social teaching of the church, as some critics imply. On the contrary, by reaffirming CST's inductive and inclusive methodology, that is, its starting from the reality of the marginalized and vulnerable of society, *EG* buttresses a principle that is the nucleus of the gospel: the preferential option for the poor. Similarly, *EG* has clearly owned another core principle of the Catholic social tradition: the need to develop as humans in an integral and authentic way. Still, in a subtle way, *EG* provides such a principle with a deeper meaning, not only because it connects it with the natural environment but also because it explains why it is so crucial to our faith (integral faith). By so doing, *EG* has emphasized, more than any previous papal documents, the need to participate in processes of dialogue seeking for social transformation. Nonetheless, *EG* is not merely a description of good principles. It is rather an exhortation for action. Hence, in order to encourage Christians to deploy the beautiful mission of announcing the joy of the gospel, an announcement that can change and improve the way we live as persons and as social beings, *EG* suggests we should unashamedly bring into the public arena those inspiring biblical stories that, like classic art, can help us bring about a world of possibilities.

In short, *EG*, with its inclusive and ecumenical vision of scrutinizing the signs of the times, with its integral understanding of growth, and with its broad conception of evangelization—which is enriched through processes of public discussions—stands as a noble and refined pastoral and theological document. Those who accuse *EG* of emanating from an unsubstantial and populist liberation theology are adopting a fundamental misreading of this text. Ultimately, *EG* attempts to discover the gospel in all our relationships: to discover a joy that can set us free from the inhuman culture of unfettered prosperity in which we are trapped.

Select Bibliography

Boileau, David A. *Principles of Catholic Social Teaching*. Milwaukee: Marquette University Press, 1994.

De Schrijver, Georges. "Paradigm Shift in the Third-World Theologies of Liberation: From Socio-Economic Analysis to Cultural Analysis?" In *Liberation Theology on Shifting Grounds*, 3–84. Leuven: Leuven University Press, 1998.

Devine, Donald. "A libertarian view of Francis' *Laudato Si*." *Library of Law and Liberty* (2015).

Himes, Kenneth et al, eds. *Modern Catholic Social Teaching. Commentaries & Interpretations*. Washington, DC: Georgetown University Press, 2005, 41–71.

Irrazábal, Gustavo. "*Evangelii Gaudium* y la Doctrina Social de la Iglesia." *Teología* 114 (2014): 131–43.

McGavin, Paul A. "What Is Wrong with *Laudato Si'*?" http://chiesa.espresso.repubblica.it/articolo/1351226.

Scannone, Juan C. "Papa Francesco e la teología del popolo." *La Civiltà Cattolica* 165 (2014): 571–90.

Sen, Amartya. *Development as Freedom*. New York: Anchor Books, 1999.

———. *The Idea of Justice*. London: Allen Lane, 2009.

Verstraeten, Johan. "Catholic Social Thought as Discernment," *Logos* 8, no. 3 (2005): 94–111.

Notes

1. Pope Francis, Apostolic Exhortation *Evangelii Gaudium*, 2013. Note: All documents of popes are available from http://www.vatican.va/holy_father/index.htm.

2. Pope Francis, Encyclical Letter *Laudato Si'*, On Care for Our Common Home, 2015.

3. Donald Devine, "A Libertarian View of Francis' *Laudato Si'*," *Library of Law and Liberty* (2015). Available from http://www.libertylawsite.org/2015/07/30/a-libertarian-view-of-francis-laudato-si/.

4. Paul A. McGavin, "What Is Wrong with *Laudato Si'*?"

L'espresso (2015). Available from http://chiesa.espresso.repubblica
.it/articolo/1351224.

5. For McGavin, this approach does not help to forge the relationship between wealth creation and poverty reduction, a critical point in CST.

6. See Robert Sirico, "Initial Comments on *Evangelii Gaudium*," Acton Institute radio podcast (2013). Available from http://
blog.acton.org/archives/63200-audio-sirico-comments-evangelii
-gaudium-blaze-radio-larry-kudlow-show.html.

7. Acton's economic researcher, Samuel Gregg, has gone further, arguing that while *EG* is a great spiritual document, it has many economic assumptions, something that is worse in *LS*. For example, the pope's condemnation of the "absolute autonomy of the markets" (*EG* 202) missed the fact that the current world's economy is highly regulated. In fact, the argument continues, *EG* and *LS* fail to critique the left-populist regimes that, due to excessive state intervention, have brought economic destruction and increased poverty to countries such as Argentina and Venezuela. For Gregg, Pope Francis's economic views seem to resonate with the dependency theory formulated by Latin American economists in the 1950s, which have never worked in practice. Thus, Francis's concern about people not succumbing to self-enclosed individualism that produces injustice, needs to be connected with the reality of economics, not just with flawed ideas about market economics, especially if we need to follow Francis's advice that "ideas disconnected from realities give rise to ineffectual forms of idealism" (*EG* 232). In the end, what Gregg argues is that *EG* and *LS* are distancing themselves from a more subtle Catholic social tradition, which has been more aware of economic realities. See also S. Gregg, "Pope Francis and Poverty," *National Review*, November 26, 2013, http://www.nationalreview.com/corner/365004/pope
-francis-and-poverty-samuel-gregg; and "*Laudato Si*: Well Intentioned, Economically Flawed," *The American Spectator*, June 19, 2015, https://spectator.org/63160_laudato-si-well-intentioned-econo
mically-flawed/.

8. Gustavo Irrazábal, "*Evangelii Gaudium* y la Doctrina Social de la Iglesia." *Teología* 114 (2014): 131–43, http://bibliotecadigital
.uca.edu.ar/repositorio/revistas/evangelii-gaudium-doctrina
-social.pdf. Given that his critique has a strong theological input,

is clearly explained, and he comes from a similar background than Pope Francis, I am focusing more on this critique than the rest.

9. Cf. ibid., 133–35. For an explanation of the theology of the People, see Juan C. Scannone, "Papa Francesco e la teología del popolo," *La Civiltà Cattolica* 165 (2014): 571–90. Available in Spanish from http://www.seleccionesdeteologia.net/selecciones/llib/vol54/213/213_Scannone.pdf.7/.

10. Pope John XXIII, Encyclical *Mater et Magistra* (1961).

11. Pope Paul VI (Second Vatican Council), Pastoral Constitution on the Church in the Modern World, *Gaudium et Spes* (1965); and Dogmatic Constitution on Divine Revelation, *Dei Verbum* (1965).

12. Pope Paul VI, Encyclical *Populorum Progressio* (1967) and Apostolic Letter *Octogesima Adveniens* (1971).

13. Pope John Paul II, Encyclical *Sollicitudo Rei Socialis* (1987) and Encyclical *Centesimus Annus* (1991).

14. CELAM (Consejo Episcopal Latinoamericano). 2da Conferencia General: Medellín, Colombia, (1968); 3era Conferencia General: Puebla, México (1979); 4ta Conferencia General; 5ta Conferencia General: Aparecida, Brasil (2007). (CELAM's documents are available from http://www.celam.org/ [accessed on August 13, 2016].)

15. Sollicitudo *Rei Socialis* (1987).

16. See, e.g., Irrazábal, *"Evangelii Gaudium* y la Doctrina Social de la Iglesia."

17. *Populorum Progressio.*

18. *Sollicitudo Rei Socialis.*

19. Pope Benedict XVI, Encyclical *Caritas in Veritate* (2009).

20. See, e.g., Devine, "A Libertarian View of Francis's *Laudato Si'*," and McGavin, "What Is Wrong with *Laudato Si'?*" For a good journalist article that questions the understanding of capitalism of *EG*, see David Harsanyi, "What the Pope Gets Wrong about Capitalism," *The Federalist*, December 2013, http://thefederalist.com/2013/12/03/pope-wrong/. For a brief explanation on the different ways the economic teachings of *EG* have been received by Catholic businesspeople, see UNIAPAC, "Socio-economic Aspects of the Exhortation *Evangelii Gaudium*," 2014, http://www.uniapac.org/filesPDF/StateG.pdf.

21. Pope Benedict XVI, *Caritas in Veritate*.

22. For arguments against including religion in the public arena, see Richard Dawkins, *The God Delusion* (Boston: Houghton Mifflin, 2006).

23. Paul Ricœur, *Hermeneutics and the Human Sciences: Essays on Language, Action and Interpretation*, ed., trans., and with an introduction by J. B. Thompson (Cambridge: Cambridge University Press, 1981).

24. Amartya Sen, *Development as Freedom* (New York: Anchor Books, 1999), 13–14.

25. Amartya Sen, *The Idea of Justice* (London: Allen Lane, 2009), 171–72.

26. Amartya Sen, "The Contemporary Relevance of Buddha," *Ethics and International Affairs* 28, no. 1 (2014): 15–27.

27. Marvin L. Mich, "Commentary on *Mater et Magistra* (Christianity and Social Progress)," in *Modern Catholic Social Teaching: Commentaries & Interpretations*, ed. K. Himes et al (Washington, DC: Georgetown University Press, 2005), 191–216.

28. Charles E. Curran, "Catholic Social and Sexual Teaching: A Methodological Comparison," *Theology Today* 44 (1988): 427.

29. Cf. Irrazábal, "*Evangelii Gaudium* y la Doctrina Social de la Iglesia," 133–35.

30. CST inductive method, alongside the universal principles based on natural law, has permitted the Catholic to dialogue with politicians, economists, and sociologists of different backgrounds and faiths. For the link between CST and natural law, see S. Pope, "Natural Law in Catholic Social Teaching," in Himes, *Modern Catholic Social Teaching*, 41–71. For a study of CST principles, see D. A. Bolieau, *Principles of Catholic Social Teaching* (Milwaukee: Marquette University Press, 1994). For a thorough analysis of the biblical and theological roots of the CST method, see Augusto Zampini Davies, "Amartya Sen's Capability Approach and Catholic Social Teaching in Dialogue: An Alliance for Freedom and Justice?" (PhD thesis, Roehampton University, 2014), https://roehampton.openrepository.com/roehampton/bitstream/10142/604356/1/PhD_Thesis_A_Zampini_electronic_version.pdf.

31. The Good Samaritan (Luke 10:25–37) is considered the paradigmatic one. See Rudolf Schnackenburg, *El Mensaje Moral*

del Nuevo Testamento. II: Los primeros predicadores cristianos (Barcelona: Herder, 1991). The parable depicts how the sight of a Levite, a priest, and a Samaritan affected their judgment and actions. Unlike the liturgical officers, the Samaritan, when "seeing" the same unjust situation of a wounded man lying half dead along the road on their way to Jericho, was moved by compassion. The unknown Samaritan, a socioreligious rival for those who were listening to the story, becomes paradoxically the one who better reflects the image and likeness of God. He then behaves as a neighbor (πλησίον: friend, close relative), seeing with compassion the wounded and defenseless man, judging with solidarity the situation, and acting with justice. Indeed, by behaving as a neighbor, he has done "what is right and good," which is the response to the question that triggered the parable. For a good and concise analysis of the parable, see Luis A. Schökel, *Biblia del Pelegrino. Nuevo Testamento* (T.3) (Estella, Navarra: Mensajero-Verbo Divino, 1998).

32. Implicit precedents can be found in Augustine of Hippo, Thomas Aquinas, and Francisco de Vittoria. See C. E. Curran, *Catholic Social Teaching: 1981–present. A Historical, Theological, and Ethical Analysis* (Washington, DC: Georgetown University Press, 2002).

33. While interacting with political economics, CST has always intended to redress some imbalances of the anthropologies underpinning economic systems. Thus, while advocating individual freedom, CST has also insisted on the relational aspect of human beings and on the "common" good. This has allowed CST to highlight the elements of economics that hinder integral human development, whether from a liberal or from a socialist point of view. This is reflected in the first official document of CST, *Rerum Novarum* (*RN*), where Pope Leo XIII denounces "the misery and wretchedness pressing so unjustly on the majority of the working class," who are "surrendered, isolated and helpless, to the hardheartedness of employers and the greed of unchecked competition" (*RN* 3). At the same time, the pope warns about the misconceptions of socialism, particularly on issues of private property and the role of the state (cf. *RN* 4). See Pope Leo XIII, Encyclical *Rerum Novarum*, On Capital and Labor, 1891. For more on this topic, see Michael Walsh, and Brian Davies, eds., *Proclaim-*

ing Justice & Peace: Papal Documents from Rerum Novarum through Centesimus Annus (Mystic, CT: Twenty-Third Publications, 1991).

34. Séverine Deneulin and Lila Shahani, eds., *An Introduction to the Human Development and the Capability Approach: Freedom and Agency* (London: Earthscan and International Development Research Centre, 2009).

35. Hilary Putnam, *The Collapse of the Fact/Value Dichotomy, and Other Essays, Including the Rosenthal Lectures* (Cambridge, MA: Harvard University Press, 2002); and Vivian Walsh, "Sen after Putnam," *Review of Political Economy* 15, no. 3 (2003): 315–91.

36. UNDP (United Nation Development Programme), Human Development Reports (1996–present), http://www.undp.org/content/undp/en/home/librarypage.html.

37. Harry Brighouse and Ingrid Robeyns, eds., *Measuring Justice: Primary Goods and Capabilities* (Cambridge: Cambridge University Press, 2010). Pedro Flores-Crespo and Rodolfo de la Torre, "Adopting the Human Development Idea: Lessons Drawn from Some Initiatives to Reduce Poverty in Mexico," Human Development and Capability Association Annual Conference, New York, September 16–25, 2004, https://www.researchgate.net/publication/242418429_Adopting_the_Human_Development_Idea_Lessons_drawn_from_some_initiatives_to_reduce_poverty_in_Mexico.

38. Sen, *The Idea of Justice*, 192; Sen, *On Ethics and Economics* (Oxford: Basil Blackwell, 1988); Sen, "The Contemporary Relevance of Buddha," 15–27.

39. Sen, *The Idea of Justice*, 390.

40. Ibid., 9.

41. Sen, *On Ethics and Economics*.

42. Sen, *The Idea of Justice*, 234.

43. For a careful consideration of the potential alliance between CST and Amartya Sen's approach, see Zampini Davies, "Amartya Sen's Capability Approach and Catholic Social Teaching in Dialogue."

44. Pontifical Council of Justice and Peace, *Compendium of the Social Doctrine of the Church*, 2004, accessed on October 13, 2011, http://www.vatican.va/roman_curia/pontifical_councils/justpeace/documents/rc_pc_justpeace_doc_20060526_compendio-dott-soc_en.html.

45. The principles for reflection are grouped in the *Compendium* as follows: solidarity and subsidiarity, human dignity, human rights, and common good; participation and social-relational life; private property and universal destiny of goods; the fundamental underpinning values of truth, freedom, justice, and charity (*Compendium* 105–208).

46. Lisa Sowle-Cahill, "Caritas in Veritate: Benedict's Global Reorientation," *Theological Studies* 71 (2010): 291–99.

47. CELAM, Medellín (1969) and Puebla (1979).

48. Pope John Paul II, "Discurso Inaugural de la IV Conferencia General del Episcopado Latinoamericano (CELAM)," Santo Domingo, 1992, http://w2.vatican.va/content/john-paul-ii/es/speeches/1992/october/documents/hf_jp-ii_spe_19921012_iv-conferencia-latinoamerica.html.

49. CDF (Congregation for the Doctrine of the Faith), *Instruction on Certain Aspects of the "Theology of Liberation,"* 1984, http://www.vatican.va/roman_curia/congregations/cfaith/documents/rc_con_cfaith_doc_19840806_theology-liberation_en.html. CDF, *Instruction on Christian Freedom and Liberation*, 1986, http://www.vatican.va/roman_curia/congregations/cfaith/documents/rc_con_cfaith_doc_19860322_freedom-liberation_en.html.

50. G. De Schrijver, "Paradigm Shift in the Third-World Theologies of Liberation: From Socio-Economic Analysis to Cultural Analysis?" in *Liberation Theology on Shifting Grounds* (Leuven: Leuven University Press, 1998), 3–84.

51. Cf. Aparecida (no. 19).

52. Ibid.

53. This seems to be the case of Devine, McGavin, and Gregg, who accuse Francis of being too Latin American, by which they mean that the pope has a contaminated view of economics due to his experience of crony capitalism, as opposed to their supposedly purist economic view coming from North America or Australia. Apart from wondering if crony capitalism is exclusive to the "Latinos," it is worth noting that a key element explained in *LS* is the "interconnection" between people, nations, and regions (*LS* 70, 138, 240). This applies to economics as well, especially in the current globalized economic system. Therefore, what happens economically in Latin American countries is closely connected

with global economic policies, often determined by powerful countries or by global institutions where such countries have a great influence. Consequently, as Pope Benedict XVI has argued before Francis, "In the face of the unrelenting growth of global interdependence, there is a strongly felt need for a reform" of those institutions (*Caritas in Veritate* 67).

54. Aparecida (nos. 20–32).

55. For Devine, McGavin, and Gregg, the flawed economic approach of *EG* and *LS* is due to Francis's experience of crony capitalism in Latin America, linked with a weak institutional practice and an easily manipulated rule of law. They also argue, alongside Irrazábal, that a social populist background and a personal tendency of populist leadership do not help Francis to grasp the subtleties of institutional economics and the critical role it plays in promoting integral development.

56. See, for instance, the BBC Analysis program debate, conducted by Edward Stourton: "Is the Pope a Communist?" (BBC News, 2014). Written summary and audio available from http://www.bbc.co.uk/news/magazine-33024951. Accessed on June 25, 2015.

57. On a personal note, in January 2014, I introduced this idea of "persons" (instead of individuals) to development agencies in Sri Lanka. The reception of the idea was quite positive, particularly because, they argued, it has helped them to further expound to Buddhist believers the principle of subsidiarity of CST (Meeting, National Council for Reconciliation and Peace, Colombo January 1, 2014).

58. Paul Ricœur, *The Just* (Chicago: The University of Chicago Press, 2000), 10.

59. Ibid., 9–10.

60. Hannah Arendt, *Eichmann in Jerusalem: A Report on the Banality of Evil* (New York: Penguin, 2005; 1st ed. 1944).

61. Sen explains how these two dimensions of economics need to come together when designing economic policies that can promote actual well-being. See Sen, *On Ethics and Economics*.

62. E.g., Irrazábal, "*Evangelii Gaudium* y la Doctrina Social de la Iglesia."

63. See Irrazábal, "*Evangelii Gaudium* y la Doctrina Social de la Iglesia" and McGavin, "What Is Wrong with *Laudato Si'*?"

64. Irrazábal, *"Evangelii Gaudium* y la Doctrina Social de la Iglesia."

65. Enrique Cambón, *La Trinidad: Modelo Social* (Madrid: Ciudad Nueva, 2000).

66. LWF (The Lutheran World Federation) and PCPCU (The Pontifical Council for Promoting Christian Unity, *From Conflict to Communion* (Lepipzi: Evangelische Verlagsanstalt and Bonifatius, 2013), http://www.lutheranworld.org/sites/default/files/From% 20Conflict%20to%20Communion.pdf.

67. Hans Küng and Karl-Josef Kuschel, *Hacia una ética mundial. Declaración del parlamento de las religiones del mundo* (Madrid: Trotta, 1994).

68. Pope Benedict XVI, Encyclical *Deus Caritas Est* (2005).

69. Pope Paul VI (Second Vatican Council), Decree on Priestly Training, *Optatum Totius*, 1965.

70. Sandra M. Schneiders, *The Revelatory Text: Interpreting the New Testament as Sacred Scripture* (San Francisco: Harper-San Francisco, 1991); Hans-Georg Gadamer, *Truth and Method* (New York: Crossroad, 1989); and Paul Ricœur, *Hermeneutics and the Human Sciences.* David Tracy, *The Analogical Imagination: Christian Theology and the Culture of Pluralism* (New York: Crossroad, 1981).

71. Ricœur, *Hermeneutics and the Human Sciences*; Schneiders, *The Revelatory Text.*

72. For a thorough analysis of the category of "classical" as key to hermeneutics, see Tracy, *The Analogical Imagination*, 99–229.

73. Schneiders, *The Revelatory Text*, 151.

74. Ibid., 151.

75. See also Johan Verstraeten, "Catholic Social Thought as Discernment," *Logos* 8, no. 3 (2005): 94–111.

76. Sen, *The Idea of Justice*, 170–73.

77. Schneiders, *The Revelatory Text*, 148.

78. Verstraeten, "Catholic Social Thought as Discernment," 106.

11

"Let Us Not Leave in Our Wake a Swath of Destruction and Death"

Evangelii Gaudium and Socioecological Flourishing

CHRISTOPHER HRYNKOW

Introduction

Evangelii Gaudium was Pope Francis's first substantively multidimensional exercise of his magisterial office. This Apostolic Exhortation deals with many issues relevant to social, political, cultural, and ecological worlds. Though it conforms to his early reign's feature of not changing any dogma or principal doctrine of the Catholic Church (*EG* 104), it is nonetheless also characteristic of a noteworthy shift in his approach to the papacy (no. 41). This chapter will bring some of the content of that shift into focus by employing a green theo-ecoethical lens as its interpretive and mapping framework. As explored more fully below, this nomenclature points to three characteristics of the lens: in reverse order these are its ecoethical, theological, and green features. The latter is grounded with the help of six green principles: ecological wisdom, social justice, nonviolence, participatory democracy, sustainability, and respect for diversity.

274

In this chapter, these principles organize a mapping of the green theo-ecoethical content of *EG*. In a point that will be addressed in a section dealing with the relationship between what have been Francis's most prominent magisterial documents, his first Apostolic Exhortation and his first social Encyclical, this mapping of *EG* will help illustrate that despite the publicity surrounding its release, *Laudato Si'* (*LS*) was not Francis's first sustained foray into social ecology.

In this case of *EG*, the above-mentioned shift in approaching the papacy extends to Francis's method of exercising his magisterial office. For example, the pope's first Apostolic Exhortation is written in a comparably more pastoral style than can be found in much papal teaching. Given its subject, the joy of the gospel, and despite it being addressed "to the bishops, clergy, consecrated persons and the lay faithful" (*EG* cover page; cf. no. 200), it is important to consider not only how *EG* relates to the Roman Catholic tradition but also its significance to the wider church, whose non-Catholic members are also concerned with "the proclamation of the Gospel in today's world" (*EG* cover page). Indeed, the main text of *EG* recognizes this point (no. 3). Further, Francis explicitly names an ecumenical call to justice, which invites a socioecological reading: "All Christians, their pastors included, are called to show concern for the building of a better world" (*EG* 183). This normative ecumenical remit is also active in Francis's reiteration of the value of exegetes, theologians, and social scientists in helping the church's doctrine mature and in aiding in the discernment of its mission (*EG* 40).[1]

In light of that foundation, the present chapter assesses select contributions of *EG* to socioecological flourishing by employing a green theo-ecoethical lens, which is ecumenical in the sense of being informed by both Roman Catholic and other-than-Catholic Christian sources. It begins by delineating the importance of socioecological flourishing from an ecumenical perspective. Next, it turns to situating the lens, before applying its constitutive elements and the above-mentioned six principles to a mapping of the green theo-ecoethical content of *EG*. A penultimate section comments on some of the relationships between Francis's encyclical, *LS*, and *EG*. It concludes by linking the renewal called for in

EG to socioecological flourishing as previewed in the image of abundant life presented in the Gospel of John.

An Ecumenical Perspective on the Importance of Socioecological Flourishing in the Present Context

Lynn White Jr., the medieval historian and son of a Calvinist minister who also held a graduate degree in theology from Union Theological Seminary, wrote arguably the most significant article on Christianity and ecology in the 1960s. A reductionist, but frequent, citation of his article, "The Historical Roots of Our Ecological Crisis," emphasized that Christianity is the most anthropocentric of religions and almost irredeemably responsible for the ecological crisis.[2] This reading has been so popular that it has served in several instances as a barrier to mainstream Anglophone environmentalists forming partnerships with Christian actors in the service of a green common good. For example, Martin Palmer, an Anglican and secretary general of the Alliance of Religions and Conservation, recounts that during the late twentieth century, many environmental groups assumed Christians would be hostile to their activist projects and, thus, should be avoided: "What Lynn White did is that he overstated and he gave ammunition to those who wanted to keep religion firmly out of the [environmental] debate."[3]

Notwithstanding Palmer's analysis, it should be emphasized that while White does argue that "Christianity made it possible to exploit nature," he nevertheless encourages us to "ponder the greatest radical in Christian history since Christ: Saint Francis of Assisi," because Francis "tried to depose man from his monarchy over creation and set up a democracy of all God's creatures." White closed his article by suggesting Francis be named the patron saint of ecology.[4]

In making this argument, White ignored the contributions of Eastern Christians who retained integral concepts, fusing the material and the spiritual, throughout much of their theological development.[5] The above-described, common reading of White also ignores the case of socioecological concern from within Western Christian traditions in the contemporary period. For example, the work of the American Lutheran thinker Joseph Sittler on Christianity and ecology preceded White's contribution by more than a decade and was more firmly focused on solving the problem of Christians valuing the earth, with reference, for example, to the continuing relevance of the doctrine of the incarnation.[6] In 1979, Pope John Paul II took up White's recommendation and declared Francis of Assisi to be the patron saint of ecologists,[7] later noting, "As a friend of the poor who was loved by God's creatures, Saint Francis...gives us striking witness that when we are at peace with God we are better able to devote ourselves to building up that peace with all creation which is inseparable from peace among all peoples."[8]

Perhaps more substantively, contemporary Christians working on ecological issues in both the academic and activist realms have often taken their cues from a variety of sources within the Christian intellectual and practical experience. These certainly include the Franciscan example upheld by White,[9] but also range from close readings of the Bible that emphasize the goodness of creation,[10] to the church fathers and mothers,[11] to drawing upon a wide range of contemporary ascetic practices.[12] Those engaged in constructing Christian foundations for a strong ecological ethic draw upon diverse perspectives and resituate them within the faith tradition. Namely, among others, these sources include contemporary ecology sciences,[13] movements for inclusion,[14] and secular philosophers.[15] Such contributions can be taken as evidence that, despite Christianity's uneven environmental record, it is nevertheless possible to construct an integrated worldview critically sourced from Christian theologians and green initiatives, in order to offer positive responses to the challenges facing the Earth community due to anthropogenic ecological degradation.

Citing the challenges that accompany such degradation, the Canadian ecofeminist theologian Heather Eaton shades her reflections on human-earth and intrahuman relationships within a framework of "socio-ecological crisis."[16] This notion of interrelated crises, with crises considered in the present chapter primarily in the plural for their multiple manifestations, demands an ecojustice response, which couples social justice and a concern for ecological health often understood in light of the integrity of creation; this coupling is a central feature of many Christian initiatives to address anthropogenic ecological degradation. Eaton's work can be situated within a certain approach to ecofeminist liberation theologies, which casts the religious project "in light of making justice, of right relationships with women, men, and all living beings."[17] At the heart of such efforts lies a basic orientation centered on the belief that a Christian faith that takes the Jesus story seriously, when combined with a concern for social and ecological sustainability, will bear moral witness to "the intrinsic connection between all forms of oppression, and especially between that of poor people and degraded nature."[18]

The planet's over two billion Christians can help in this regard when they act as if the dignity of the human person and the integrity of the natural world are inextricably linked. Further, this notion has a long ecumenical pedigree. For instance, the above-cited consensus may be a way to understand one of the goals of the WCC and several Roman Catholic orders who seek to have "Justice, Peace, and the Integrity of Creation" as a mutual set of commitments or a covenant underlying all their programming.[19] These groups often use JPIC as an acronym, which has the advantage of invoking these three concepts together[20] to symbolize how these foundational principles are essentially joined.[21]

For people with privilege, applying these principles means that we must also humbly accept socioecological limits. This acceptance need not result in an overly austere asceticism, but there remains an imperative to limit consumption through a type of green asceticism that frequently activates the potential for joy among "deep greens" of both the secular and religious variety.[22] This ultimately represents a more emancipatory dream for all members of the Earth community than does the (inaccessible for far too many) "American dream" expressed through a big detached house, multiple carbon-burning vehicles, or processed food at every meal as part of a ubiquitous "addiction to commercial-industrial progress."[23] As Pope Francis notes, under present conditions, people can be pulled in multiple, decontextualizing directions:

> People get caught up in an abstract, globalized universe,
> falling into step behind everyone else, admiring the glit-
> ter of other people's world, gaping and applauding at
> all the right times. At the other extreme, they turn into
> a museum of local folklore, a world apart, doomed to
> doing the same things over and over, and incapable of
> being challenged by novelty or appreciating the beauty
> which God bestows beyond their borders. (*EG* 234)

Hence, a cogent mantra for our millennium, brought into focus
by a green theo-ecoethical perspective as developed below, may
be "limitation for ecological, social, and self-growth." This mantra
represents a paradox, but perhaps a "true paradox," which could
become a campaign slogan for a healthy future when we learn to
"live simply so that others can simply live"[24] and, ultimately, have
a chance to flourish.

A Green Theo-ecoethical Lens: An Interpretive and Mapping Framework

The preceding discussion raises two issues for the moral
project of "not leav[ing] in our wake a swath of destruction and
death" (*EG* 215). First, it encourages us to consider how the papal
magisterial office, as a branch of the educational project with
transformative goals,[25] serves to lend rhetorical support for (or
detracts from) the promotion of socioecological flourishing. That
subject will be addressed below. However, it also raises another
important point: papal teaching is not the last word on the promotion of ecojustice by Christians, or even for Catholics. Several
grassroots initiatives undertaken by Christians, sometimes within
the context of broad coalitions of action, do contribute to the
fostering and realization of relationships that support the incarnation of ecojustice principles in this world. To provide a map
linking this concern to the intimately related area of socioecological flourishing, this chapter employs a green theo-ecoethical
lens. The aforementioned six green principles serve as a key to
organize this map.

Making a point relevant to constructing such a hermetical lens, Usher, Bryant, and Johnston note that it is "precisely through the interplay between one's interpretative framework...and that which one seeks to understand that knowledge is developed."[26] In *EG*, Pope Francis adds, "Conceptual tools exist to heighten contact with the realities they seek to explain, not to distance us from them" (*EG* 194). It is with such epistemological dynamics in mind that this chapter employs a green theo-ecoethical lens as its interpretive and mapping framework. The lens's nomenclature points to each of its constitutive parts—green, theological, ecoethical dimensions. Each of these constitutive parts was initially selected primarily for its potential to contribute contextual cogency to a hermeneutical lens (cf. *LS* 17). Yet, particularly when acting in combination, the three constitutive parts also add other significant characteristics that serve to give a green theo-ecoethical lens a robust set of abilities that extend beyond the hermeneutical to the synthetic and the possible. In addition, the lens fosters a methodology that is at once critical and normative, holding that a necessary response during the "terminal phase of the Cenozoic era"[27] is to turn the human project toward incarnating substantive visions of socioecological flourishing.

The lens is green because it employs as its organizational framework the green principles of ecological wisdom, social justice, participatory democracy, nonviolence, sustainability, and respect for diversity. A number of persons concerned with planetary health have used the term *greenwashing* to describe, in rough parallel with the more common use of *whitewashing*, a certain phenomenon of misdirection becoming increasingly evident in consumerist societies. The collaboratively edited activist website Sourcewatch defines greenwashing as "the unjustified appropriation of environmental virtue by a company, an industry, a government, a politician or even a non-government organization to create a pro-environmental image, sell a product or a policy, or to try and rehabilitate their standing with the public and decision-makers after being embroiled in controversy."[28] Notably, this definition highlights how greenwashing extends beyond corporate marketing to encompass sociopolitical realities. This phenomenon is so complete that the term *green* has often been misappropriated to serve segmented interests and to justify ecologically destructive products, policies, and consumptive practices. As a result, unfolding what *green* is meant to signify can be considered important to Christians concerned with ecojustice.

In employing *green*, this chapter seeks to invoke the type of distinctions that can be raised by contrasting environmental and green politics in a certain light. While environmental politics can be constructed in a manner that serves segmented interests, green politics are meant to be more holistic, notably including a social justice component as part of an integral goal of fostering truly sustainable societies. In filling in the deep sustainability-nourishing content of *green*, it is helpful to reference the events in April 2001, when green party members, activists and academics among them, from around the world came together in Canberra, Australia, for the first Global Greens Congress. One of the key outcomes of the Canberra conference was the approval of the *Global Greens Charter*, which stipulated that greener politics ought to be based on the principles of ecological wisdom, social justice, participatory democracy, nonviolence, sustainability, and respect for diversity. These principles were selected as they are based on a contextualization of academic research, a desired transformation of the negative impacts on marginalized people and the planet of current political practices, and insights emerging from the work of those committed to such transformation. They draw on the constitutions and charters of green parties from around the world as well as the *Earth Charter*, the *Millennium Declaration* made at Oaxaca in 1999, the *Accord between the Green Parties of the Americas and the Ecologist Parties of Africa*, along with statements and insights growing from the First Planetary Gathering of Greens held in advance of the Rio Earth Summit in 1992. After a two-year, cross-cultural consultative process (much of which took place via e-mail, lowering the document's carbon footprint), a draft was compiled by Dr. Louise Crossley (1942–2015), a distinguished Australian Antarctic research scientist who also holds a PhD in the history and philosophy of science. That draft was then debated and modified until consensus was reached among representatives from green parties all over the world in Canberra in 2001. This consensus is all the more remarkable given that there were over eight hundred participants from seventy-two countries, including youth representatives, at that Global Greens Congress.[29]

As the author experienced himself while campaigning during the 2008 Canadian general election, the green principles also provide a valuable communicative framework for unfolding green transformative politics and programming to people with varying levels of knowledge on socioecological issues, undoubtedly owing to their cross-cultural and dialogical origins.[30] These principles were also reaffirmed at the 2012 Global Greens Congress in Dakar, Senegal. Significantly, the *Global Greens Charter*, like many documentary contributions to Christian peace witness (e.g., *GS* 77–97),[31] then states that peace is more than the mere absence of war.[32] An underlying premise of this chapter is that remaining cognizant of these six principles helps to prevent an all too common slippage in use and misappropriation of the term *green*. More significantly, they simultaneously give a fuller meaning to the term, serving to elaborate on some of the nourishing content of *green*.[33]

In this regard, the lens is theological since Christian ethical traditions, inclusive of but not limited to ecotheological ethical perspectives, are employed in this chapter to help ground these green theo-ecoethical principles. In dialogue with *EG*, the main objective here is to engage in the act of harvesting, in parallel with what Peter Phan characterizes as the liberationist project of employing other disciplines' "third generalities," in order to provide a basis for naming important contextual realities from a Christian perspective.[34] The lens is ecoethical in that it takes inspiration from Christian ecological ethicists but also draws upon other religious, spiritual, and secular traditions. These ethicists hold worldviews that locate humans in essential relationships with each other and the natural world.[35] We are now in a period of planetary history when the globe's Christians are, out of necessity, involved in interrelated social and ecological crises. Moreover, in part because of the reality of a shared fate with all humanity and the rest of the created world, all persons may be shown to have a responsibility to support visions for a sustainable future. As such, it is expected that a green theo-ecoethical lens will have a certain resonance in our times when visions of socioecological flourishing are desperately needed to assist in driving the holistic healing of an Earth community in peril. Additionally, the lens is "colligational," serving to link its constitutive elements that may otherwise appear disparate.

Furthermore, through synthesizing its three constitutive parts, this hermeneutical lens is notably (1) religiously and spiritually literate; (2) critically normative,[36] able to effectively consider matters of contextual pertinence; and (3) teleological with a goal of adding a measure of momentum to both visions and practices supportive of socioecological flourishing. These features combine to give the lens a certain epistemological wholeness (cf. *LS* 138, 141), which is marked by an organically self-justifying character as both revealing and healing in multiple senses. As a result, ecological wisdom, social justice, participatory democracy, nonviolence, sustainability, and respect for diversity are understood to have relevance within Christian moral thought. These principles are conceived as dialogical and interrelated, with each informing the others in significant ways, offering a vision of other possible worlds characterized by socioecological flourishing. It is this green theo-ecoethical light that the six principles are now employed to map *EG* in the remainder of this chapter.

EG Mapped through a Green Theo-ecoethical Lens

ECOLOGICAL WISDOM

Francis gives several nods to ecological wisdom in *EG*. The theological anthropology he presents notes humanity's embodied nature and how that connects us to the rest of the natural world on an immediate and sensory level: "Thanks to our bodies, God has joined us so closely to the world around us that we can feel the desertification of the soil almost as a physical ailment, and the extinction of a species as a painful disfigurement" (*EG* 215, cf. *LS* 19). As a primary basis for the initial and essential proclamation of the gospel, he notes its wisdom-filled nature before asserting, "All Christian formation consists of entering more deeply into the kerygma" (*EG* 165, cf. *LS* 214). Further, since ecological wisdom is premised on connectivity and valuing what is substantive,[37] it is significant that while decrying a reductionist anthropology that views humans as mere consumers (*EG* 54), Francis teaches about the fragility of the natural world: "The thirst for power and possessions knows no limits. In this system, which tends to devour everything which stands in the way of increased profits, whatever is fragile, like the environment, is defenceless before the interests of a deified market, which become the only rule" (*EG* 56). The socioecological link implied in that passage is laid bare later in the document when, after discussing the plight of marginalized people, Francis proclaims, "There are other weak and defenceless beings who are frequently at the mercy of economic interests or indiscriminate exploitation" (*EG* 215).

Francis bookends this statement as antithetical to ecological wisdom and removes a major rhetorical basis for presently existing unsustainability, stating succinctly and emphatically that "money must serve, not rule!" (*EG* 58). Indeed, it is evident that he is pointing to a materiality that is of a more ecospiritual type than one that makes money the normative measure of all things.[38] In this regard, it is informative to note the link Francis makes between the embodied nature of the incarnation and the actual quenching of contemporary spiritual hunger:

> Today, our challenge is not so much atheism as the need to respond adequately to many people's thirst for God, lest they try to satisfy it with alienating solutions or with a disembodied Jesus who demands nothing of us with regard to others. Unless these people find in the Church a spirituality which can offer healing and liberation, and fill them with life and peace, while at the same time summoning them to fraternal communion and missionary fruitfulness, they will end up by being taken in by solutions which neither make life truly human nor give glory to God. (*EG* 89)

Here, very much in the spirit of a green theo-ecoethical lens, and through its application to the question of humanity's truest nature, healing and liberation come into focus as intimately coupled with ecological wisdom.

SOCIAL JUSTICE

In *EG*, Francis is clear that "none of us can think we are exempt from concern for the poor and for social justice" (*EG* 201). He continues that in order to avoid "a constant risk of distorting the authentic and integral meaning of the mission of evangelization," the social dimension of the kerygma must be "properly brought out" (*EG* 176, cf. no. 258).[39] Further, Francis asserts the gospel "is not merely about our personal relationship with God" (*EG* 180).[40] In connecting personal liberation with sensitivity to the needs of others (*EG* 9), Francis names an important solidarist dimension to social justice: "Whenever our interior life becomes caught up in its own interests and concerns, there is no longer room for others, no place for the poor" (*EG* 2). Indeed, he emphasizes a clear imperative to seek the common good as a primary invitation flowing from Christian truth: "Before all else, the Gospel invites us to respond to the God of love who saves us, to see God in others and to go forth from ourselves to seek the good of others" (*EG* 39). Francis is specific, yet pastoral, in his exhortation to "a generous solidarity" that generates moral imperatives for the economically wealthy: "The Pope loves everyone, rich and poor alike, but he is obliged in the name of Christ to remind all that the rich must help, respect and promote the poor. I exhort you to generous solidarity and to the return of economics and finance to an ethical approach which favours human beings" (*EG* 58). Moreover, he explicitly names solidarist praxis as a path toward positive social change: "Convictions and habits of solidarity, when they are put into practice, open the way to other structural transformations and make them possible" (*EG* 189). In Francis's rendering, moving out from narrow self-interest further provides a communitarian framework for incarnating the joy of the gospel (*EG* 188), giving us the context of one of the more famous quotes from *EG*:

> An evangelizing community gets involved by word and deed in people's daily lives; it bridges distances, it is willing to abase itself if necessary, and it embraces human life, touching the suffering flesh of Christ in others. Evangelizers thus take on the "smell of the sheep" and the sheep are willing to hear their voice. (*EG* 24)

As would surprise few commentators, a central focus of the social justice content of *EG* is the Catholic social teaching principle of a preferential option for those living in poverty.[41] Indeed, within the Apostolic Exhortation, Francis names basic features of the imperative for social justice in an unequivocal and ecumenical manner: "In all places and circumstances, Christians, with the help of their pastors, are called to hear the cry of the poor" (*EG* 191, cf. *LS* 49).[42] Francis further bonds this fundamental option with the primary mission of the "whole Church," through the assertion that the gospel itself supports "above all the poor and the sick, those who are usually despised and overlooked" (*EG* 48). Thus, Francis asserts, "There is an inseparable bond between our faith and the poor" (*EG* 48). As such, one of the goals of the proclamation of the Word, even in homiletics, ought to be to strengthen "commitment to fraternity and service" (*EG* 155).

Supporting a faith-inspired understanding of justice as the community of equals, where brotherhood and sisterhood in Christ "must surely apply to everybody,"[43] Francis also invokes the notion that social justice outreach work correlates with the continuing relevance of a religious tradition when he asserts that one of the reasons a couple might not seek baptism for their child is "lack of pastoral care among the poor" (*EG* 70). Here, we come to another of the famous phrases from *EG*, charmingly linked to Francis's former magisterial office in Buenos Aires[44] but repeated here for the benefit of the "entire Church" (*EG* 49). The pope writes, "I prefer a Church which is bruised, hurting and dirty because it has been out on the streets, rather than a Church which is unhealthy from being confined and from clinging to its own security" (*EG* 49). Indeed, recalling the concept of flourishing discussed above, he stipulates that the church is called to be "at the service of a difficult dialogue," which overcomes segregation and violence through bridging the gap between (1) "people who have the means needed to develop their personal and family lives," and (2) those who are denied access to sociopolitical opportunity structures to the point they become '"non-citizens," "half-citizens," and "urban remnants"' (*EG* 74, cf. *LS* 22). Francis's vision can thus be seen as fostering space for the substantive peace, marked by social justice, which is so crucial to a green theo-ecoethical lens.

PARTICIPATORY DEMOCRACY

During the author's formative primary and secondary education in parochial schools, it was an often-repeated mantra that the Catholic Church is not a democracy. Inasmuch as this is true, even fewer people would tend to think of the Catholic Church as a participatory democracy. Yet, there are several rhetorical exhortations of participation and participatory structures in *EG*. In general terms, Francis defines a regrettably recurring feature of "sociopolitical activity is that spaces and power are preferred to time and processes" (*EG* 223). A particularly interesting example, challenging the notion that the Bishop of Rome is the universal ordinary, with primacy over all local churches,[45] Francis writes, "It is not advisable for the Pope to take the place of local Bishops in the discernment of every issue which arises in their territory. In this sense, I am conscious of the need to promote a sound 'decentralization'" (*EG* 16). This orientation dovetails well with Francis's words on the continuing relevance of the "placed" nature of the parish:

> While certainly not the only institution which evangelizes, if the parish proves capable of self-renewal and constant adaptivity, it...really is in contact with the homes and the lives of its people, and does not become a useless structure out of touch with people or a self-absorbed group made up of a chosen few. The parish is the presence of the Church in a given territory, an environment for hearing God's word, for growth in the Christian life, for dialogue, proclamation, charitable outreach, worship and celebration. (*EG* 28)

This praise of the "grounded" parish dovetails well with Francis's exhortation of the need for integration in order to avoid "becoming nomads without roots" (*EG* 29). It follows that place and particular churches are important in evangelization processes (*EG* 30). This place-based approach is certainly something that resonates with Christian visions of participation,[46] as evidenced in Francis's exhortation that "we need to sink our roots deeper into the fertile soil and history of our native place, which is a gift of God. We can work on a small scale, in our own neighbourhood, but with a larger perspective" (*EG* 235). Francis gives another nod in the direction of subsidiarity-based participation at the end of his discussion on the importance of a role for national bishops' conferences: "Excessive centralization, rather than proving helpful, complicates the Church's life and her missionary outreach" (*EG* 32). Also, citing the problem of "excessive clericalism," he urges that spaces be made for lay participation in "decision-making" (*EG* 102). Francis further extols the need for youth movements to "actively participate in the Church's overall pastoral efforts" (*EG* 105). He adds that, in particular, spaces must be fostered for the participation of women "both in the Church and in social structures" (*EG* 103). Significantly in this regard, Francis promotes a gender inclusive (but anthropocentric) exegesis marking both men and women as created in the image of God (*EG* 274). In support of participatory ethics, Francis further extols the need "to give priority to actions which generate new processes in society and engage other persons and groups who can develop them to the point where they bear fruit in significant historical events" (*EG* 223). In accord with notions of deep participation,[47] Francis also embraces the normative value of consensus among the faithful, regardless of their rhetorical abilities:

> As part of his mysterious love for humanity, God furnishes the totality of the faithful with an instinct of faith—*sensus fidei*—which helps them to discern what is truly of God. The presence of the Spirit gives Christians a certain connaturality with divine realities, and a wisdom which enables them to grasp those realities intuitively, even when they lack the wherewithal to give them precise expression. (*EG* 119)

These dynamics are further fostered through a certain humbleness on the part of all members of the church, inclusive of priests. In particular, Francis emphasizes that all Christians must realize that they too are in need of evangelization (*EG* 164). It is in this light of such humbleness that another of Francis's well-known phrases from *EG* is perhaps best read, a passage that we might also note reverses the assumed direction of evangelization, invoking a participatory image of community:

> I want a Church which is poor and for the poor. They have much to teach us. Not only do they share in the *sensus fidei*, but in their difficulties they know the suffering Christ. We need to let ourselves be evangelized by them. The new evangelization is an invitation to acknowledge the saving power at work in their lives and to put them at the centre of the Church's pilgrim way. We are called to find Christ in them, to lend our voice to their causes, but also to be their friends, to listen to them, to speak for them and to embrace the mysterious wisdom which God wishes to share with us through them. (*EG* 198)

Through acts of deep listening, this essential Christian orientation can then be incarnated into a participatory praxis.[48] Such an approach to wrestling with diverse perspectives is supported by Francis's assertion that "we need to practice the art of listening, which is more than simply hearing. Listening, in communication, is an openness of heart which makes possible that closeness without which genuine spiritual encounter cannot occur" (*EG* 171). This orientation is at the heart of a green theo-ecoethical perspective on participation, wherein important insights expressed by Francis not only inform this chapter's interpretive and mapping lens but come into focus through its application as supporting transformative projects so sorely needed in a time of intertwined social and ecological crises.

NONVIOLENCE

There are many resonances within *EG* with perspectives on principled nonviolence.[49] For example, Methodist biblical theologian and peace activist Walter Wink described Jesus's "third way" as leaving behind passivity and violence in favor of transformative active nonviolence.[50] Similarly, Francis proposes that a transformative "third way...is the best way to deal with conflict. It is the willingness to face conflict head on, to resolve it and to make it a link in the chain of a new process" (*EG* 227). Reflecting on such processes, John Dear argues that the twentieth-century papal affirmations of scholarly approaches to biblical interpretation that are supported by the documents of the Second Vatican Council[51] can serve to downplay the natural law and just war traditions, helping move Catholics toward an active (re)embrace of the "Gospel of Peace." For Dear, the sometimes amorphous "spirit of Vatican II"[52] recovers Jesus's much needed nonviolent peace witness.[53] In accord with Dear's characterization of the peace witness of the Second Vatican Council, Francis connects peace building and the new evangelization:

> The Church proclaims "the Gospel of peace" (*Eph* 6:15) and she wishes to cooperate with all national and international authorities in safeguarding this immense universal good. By preaching Jesus Christ, who is himself peace (cf. *Eph* 2:14), the new evangelization calls on every baptized person to be a peacemaker and a credible witness to a reconciled life. (*EG* 239)

Also recalling Wink's concern for naming and countering systems of domination,[54] Francis presents a vision of positive peace (*EG* 219). Filling in his view of substantive peace as consisting of much more than the mere absence of war, Francis writes,

> Peace in society cannot be understood as pacification or the mere absence of violence resulting from the domination of one part of society over others. Nor does true peace act as a pretext for justifying a social structure which silences or appeases the poor, so that the more affluent can placidly support their lifestyle while others have to make do as they can. Demands involving the distribution of wealth, concern for the poor and human rights cannot be suppressed under the guise of creating a consensus on paper or a transient peace for a contented minority. The dignity of the human person and the common good rank higher than the comfort of those who refuse to renounce their privileges. When

these values are threatened, a prophetic voice must be raised. (*EG* 218)

Employing language that also has resonances with Wink's project,[55] Francis connects to a responsible citizenship that does not conform to "the powers that be" (*EG* 220). Thus, "progress in building a people in peace" (*EG* 221) is fostered through "an ongoing process in which every new generation must take part: a slow and arduous effort calling for a desire for integration and a willingness to achieve this through the growth of a peaceful and multifaceted culture of encounter" (*EG* 220). That process, in turn, is connected to an inclusive and justice-oriented participation as described previously. Francis continues, "In a culture which privileges dialogue as a form of encounter, it is time to devise a means for building consensus and agreement while seeking the goal of a just, responsive and inclusive society" (*EG* 239). Mitigating against the manifestations of conflict that serve to fracture relationships, Francis's "culture of encounter" actively seeks to foster unity (*EG* 220). This ethical orientation informs his image of worldly existence as akin to a pilgrimage, presumably of craftspeople, wherein "trusting others is an art and peace is an art" (*EG* 244) and "ecumenism can be seen as a contribution to the unity of the human family" (*EG* 245). It is this type of approach to nonviolent earthly sojourning that augments the prospects of Christian orthopraxis, contributing to the incarnation of the green theo-ecoethical principles.[56]

SUSTAINABILITY

Turning his attention to the common home of all families, the harms perpetrated by people against "our Sister, Mother Earth, who sustains and governs us" (*LS* 1) are exposed by the pope in the opening of *Laudato Si'* as not only relational on an intersubjective level but also as deeply personal.[57] Providing part of his theological basis for a solution to the resultant relational malaise, Francis's remark from *EG*, "all creation shares in the joy of salvation" (*EG* 4; cf. no. 181), addresses the issue of the natural world's eschatological status in a manner that can strengthen an ethic for sustainability in a green sense.[58] From a green theo-ecoethical perspective, it is

291

worth emphasizing this point because the moral community in Christian terms is frequently placed within the bounds of those who are understood to be saved. Creation, redemption, and the scope of the moral community are herein linked. Therefore, one key implication for sustainability in Francis's statement may be that other-than-human elements of the ecological world are accorded a measure of moral respect. This ethical extension can only help in processes of "reenchantment of the world,"[59] and lends support to a biospiritual worldview that mitigates against the wanton destruction of the natural world.[60] Indeed, in the field of religion and ecology, a biospiritual worldview is firmly associated with an ethical orientation that assigns intrinsic value to both human and other-than-human members of the Earth community, thus preventing processes of commoditization[61] that Francis associates with an unsustainable "'throw away' culture" that wastes life and food, wherein excluded people are the "leftovers" (*EG* 53). To further ground this point, Francis asserts, "We may not always be able to reflect adequately the beauty of the Gospel, but there is one sign which we should never lack: the option for those who are least, those whom society discards" (*EG* 195). This imperative transfers into a realm of socioecological duty that Francis frames in ecumenical terms with reference to his medieval namesake (see *LS* 10): "Small yet strong in the love of God, like Saint Francis of Assisi, all of us, as Christians, are called to watch over and protect the fragile world in which we live, and all its peoples" (*EG* 216). Such faithful vigilance, practiced widely, would help ensure the deep sustainability so central to a green theo-ecoethical lens.

RESPECT FOR DIVERSITY

Before upholding the Trinity as a location of diversity "where all things find their unity," Francis states clearly that "when properly understood, cultural diversity is not a threat to Church unity" (*EG* 117). It follows that the subject matter of the Apostolic Exhortation, the joy of the gospel, cannot be confined to a single culture (*EG* 118) or even a small group of cultures (*EG* 117). Moreover, in accord with a green theo-ecoethical perspective, diversity is associated with overcoming entropy and stagnation through resilience, strength, health, dynamism, creativity, and participation (cf. *EG* 129). Indeed, Francis supports this position with reference to the very heart of the Christian faith tradition: "We would not do justice to the logic of the incarnation if we thought of Christianity as monocultural and monotonous" (*EG* 117). Francis further connects solidarity with a peace-building concord: "Solidarity, in its deepest and most challenging sense, thus becomes a way of making history in a life setting where conflicts, tensions and oppositions can achieve a diversified and life-giving unity" (*EG* 228).

Returning to this overarching, central theme of joyful proclamation, Francis asserts that one reason cultural diversity deserves respect is because it ensures the vitality of the gospel. This is a cyclical process so that when the gospel and particular cultures meet in the context of faith communities, evangelization is so closely coupled to diverse cultures that they become integral to each other's processes of meaning making:

> Once the Gospel has been inculturated in a people, in their process of transmitting their culture they also transmit the faith in ever new forms; hence the importance of understanding evangelization as inculturation. Each portion of the people of God, by translating the gift of God into its own life and in accordance with its own genius, bears witness to the faith it has received and enriches it with new and eloquent expressions. (*EG* 122)

Tying this process back to social justice's featured role in the proclamation of the gospel, Francis defines one of the challenges of "inculturated preaching" as strengthening the "bond of charity," understood to be infused with the covenantal love between "God and his people" (*EG* 143).

In accord with a common feature in the field of theo-ecoethical ethics,[62] *EG* invokes an image of diversity from the natural sciences. In proposing an appropriate integral model, he writes,

It is the polyhedron, which reflects the convergence of all its parts, each of which preserves its distinctiveness. Pastoral and political activity alike seek to gather in this polyhedron the best of each. There is a place for the poor and their culture, their aspirations and their potential. Even people who can be considered dubious on account of their errors have something to offer which must not be overlooked. It is the convergence of peoples who, within the universal order, maintain their own individuality; it is the sum total of persons within a society which pursues the common good, which truly has a place for everyone. (*EG* 236)

In rough parallel with the evolutionary consciousness that is connected to a green theo-ecoethical lens (cf. *LS* 83),[63] Francis also extends the imperative associated with respecting cultural diversity to the respecting of multiple charisms, emphasizing the importance of holding those that renew and build up the church through a creative tension, "in communion, even when this proves painful" (*EG* 130). In harmony with the concept of panentheism,[64] for Francis, within this endeavor, the third person of the Trinity is properly held up as the binding force: "Diversity must always be reconciled by the help of the Holy Spirit; he alone can raise up diversity, plurality and multiplicity while at the same time bringing about unity" (*EG* 131). If the Christian community can incarnate what Francis exhorts as a proper life-giving and nonviolent response to this challenge of diversity, then "the Church can be a model of peace in our world" (*EG* 130). This imperative for social justice and peace extends to work with people of all faiths (*EG* 259) and none. In the latter case, an imperative for a state of being-in-the-world akin to what is described above as socioecological flourishing is upheld in *EG*'s endorsement of "the commitment to defending human dignity, in building peaceful coexistence between peoples and in protecting creation" (*EG* 257). With that point, this chapter has come full circle in its mapping of the green theo-ecoethical content of Francis's first substantively multidimensional exercise of his magisterial office.

Evangelii Gaudium as Previewing *Laudato Si'*

Many of the themes mentioned above are taken up in Francis's social encyclical dealing extensively with ecological issues, *LS*. Despite Francis's note of caution that the Apostolic Exhortation is not a social document (*EG* 184), an ecumenically informed lens helps to map a good deal of green theo-ecoethical content in *EG*. Much of this content relates to the promise of the papal magisterial office, as identified above, to help foster socioecological flourishing in a time of socioecological crises. Indeed, a good summary of this potential is expressed by Francis himself:

> An authentic faith—which is never comfortable or completely personal—always involves a deep desire to change the world, to transmit values, to leave this earth somehow better than we found it. We love this magnificent planet on which God has put us, and we love the human family which dwells here, with all its tragedies and struggles, its hopes and aspirations, its strengths and weaknesses. The earth is our common home and all of us are brothers and sisters. (*EG* 183)[65]

In terms of threats to our common home, a theme so central to *LS* that its working title (now preserved in the subtitle) was *Domus Communis*,[66] one meta-issue in play at the moment is the prospect of irreversible, anthropogenic global climate change, which can be taken to ignite the Christian "apocalyptic imagination."[67] Throughout much of *EG*'s drafting process, it was certain that Pope Francis was preparing an encyclical on social ecology, which we now know as *LS*, with an expressed goal of moving forward the political process for an effective and binding global agreement to mitigate the negative effects of climate change.[68] A certain preview of the political content of the present pope's first social encyclical can be found in *EG*, where Francis also fills in some of the content of what constitutes human flourishing:

> I ask God to give us more politicians capable of sincere and effective dialogue aimed at healing the deepest

roots—and not simply the appearances—of the evils in our world!…I beg the Lord to grant us more politicians who are genuinely disturbed by the state of society, the people, the lives of the poor! It is vital that government leaders and financial leaders take heed and broaden their horizons, working to ensure that all citizens have dignified work, education and healthcare. (*EG* 205)[69]

Additionally, this passage points to how any focused papal treatment of social ecology will necessarily be unable to limit itself to a single issue, even if that issue is as momentous as how anthropogenic global climate change negatively affects the prospects for the continuance of human life on the planet. Rather, it will likely take an integral approach to socioecological crises. In 1989, John Paul II named the ecological crisis as a moral crisis,[70] and Pope Francis provides a more detailed description of this ethical problem and necessary responses in *LS*. Now, we wait to see if the human project can effectively respond to the ethical challenges faced today. The green theo-ecoethical lens presented above shows that such a response cannot be limited to damage control, nor can it consist simply of a crisis response or a passive waiting. Indeed, "Truly, much can be done!" (*LS* 180).

In contrast to Francis's aforementioned and questionable assertion that *EG* is not a social document, the pope is clear in his ambition for *LS*: "It is my hope that this Encyclical Letter, which is now added to the body of the Church's social teaching, can help us to acknowledge the appeal, immensity and urgency of the challenge we face" (*LS* 15). This is a helpful distinction considering the spaces that are opened up within Catholic, ecumenical, inter-religious, and secular contexts by this pope broadly endorsing integral responses to present socioecological crises. Indeed, such is the gravity of these crises, combined with (1) the basic fact that continuing ecological degradation is reducing our capacity to respond as a species to this malaise, and (2) the concomitant importance of tenable solutions aimed at socioecological flourishing as supported within *LS* at this juncture in planetary history, that Francis, invoking the example of *Pacem in Terris*, moves beyond even the example of John XXIII in addressing his first social encyclical to "every person living on this planet" (*LS* 3).

This choice of address is based upon a personal desire to "enter into dialogue with all people about our common home" (*LS* 3).[71] This pastoral twist on talking to the world, which phrased differently or coming from another pope may have been taken as imperialist or condescending, also has substantive green theo-ecoethical content that can unite people in the service of a "dialogue and action, which would involve each of us as individuals, and also affect international policy" (*LS* 15) that, in turn, fosters a socioecological common good.

It is within this multifaceted, ethical paradigm that Francis seeks to address the democratic deficit and ecological debt that is accruing because, to put it rather charitably, "politics and business have been slow to react in a way commensurate with the urgency of the challenges facing our world [and]...recent World Summits on the environment have not lived up to expectations because, due to lack of political will, they were unable to reach truly meaningful and effective global agreements on the environment" (*LS* 165–66). Turning its attention specifically to the area of climate change, *LS* characterizes the lack of effective global governance regimes to protect the poor and planetary systems as a failure of "honesty, courage and responsibility, above all on the part of those countries which are more powerful and pollute the most" (*EG* 169). Of course, as Francis notes (*LS* 168), some authentic progress has been made in regard to ecologically beneficial agreements, such as through international treaties that result in a certain measure of consensus and cooperation in the form of global agreements largely respected by nation-states and business corporations. Such agreements, like the *Montreal Protocol* concerning ozone layer depletion,[72] help to show that Francis is not working within a framework of negative utopia when he names a faith-based imperative to take socioecological action and not to delay in activating conscience and exercising responsibility in a manner that does not burden people living in poverty. Indeed, the pope's grounded vision in this regard can be characterized as an important prophetic faith witness, despite the presence of debates that obscure socioecological duties.

Carrying on another trajectory that can be sourced in *EG*, this prophetic quality of naming important truths in the face of rhetorical interference is explicitly referenced in *LS*. "Even as this

Encyclical was being prepared, the debate was intensifying. We believers cannot fail to ask God for a positive outcome to the present discussions, so that future generations will not have to suffer the effects of our ill-advised delays" (*LS* 169). As such, from a green theo-ecoethical perspective, the prospect of Francis helping to transform this pathological situation also coalesces with the possibility of the realization of an adequately greener world characterized by socioecological flourishing (cf. *LS* 105).[73] As mapped in this chapter, *EG* emerges as a clear, accessible document that can contribute to such green theo-ecoethical transformation.

Conclusion: A Renewal for Abundant Life

In *EG*, Francis emphasizes, "Jesus' whole life, his way of dealing with the poor, his actions, his integrity, his simple daily acts of generosity, and finally his complete self-giving, is precious and reveals the mystery of his divine life" (*EG* 265). It follows that *imitatio Christi* in our present context calls for more than merely ensuring we do "not leave in our wake a swath of destruction and death which will affect our own lives and those of future generations" (*EG* 215). The contemporary imitation of Christ most certainly must guard against such a negative outcome. However, beyond the minimum of not promoting a culture of death and destruction, *imitatio Christi* today must also reflect the mission of Jesus in the world as presented in the Gospel of John[74] and rendered poignantly into English in the King James Bible: "I am come that they might have life, and that they might have it more abundantly" (John 10:10). This chapter suggests that such abundant life is cogently represented through the concept of socioecological flourishing. In this regard, Francis's magisterial contributions highlight an imperative to support actively abundant life for all members of the Earth community. Though certainly not perfect in this regard,[75] *EG* does offer sound resources for constructing an integrated ethic supportive of socioecological flourishing, which can be brought into focus through a green theo-ecoethical lens. It remains to be seen whether *LS* and Pope Francis's concomitant efforts for transformation of political and economic processes can bear substantive green fruit.[76] If they do, not only the world's Christian population but also the entire Earth community will be able to be counted as beneficiaries of the transformative power of the gospel as extolled in *EG*. Indeed, in light of the material presented previously, a further significant point can be asserted: faithful living intentionally aimed toward increasing socioecological flourishing in this world though the transformative power of the gospel can be counted as a moral project of making "all things new" (*EG* 288) or, rather, renewed (cf. *EG* 24, 132; *LS* 63, 106), in a deeply ecumenical sense.

Select Bibliography

Berry, Thomas. *The Christian Future and the Fate of the Earth*. Edited by Mary Evelyn Tucker and John Grim. Maryknoll, NY: Orbis, 2009.

Boff, Leonardo. *Cry of the Earth, Cry of the Poor*. Translated by Phillip Berryman. Maryknoll, NY: Orbis, 1997.

———. *Virtues for Another Possible World*. Translated by Alexander Guilherme. Eugene, OR: Cascade Books, 2011.

McFague, Sallie. *A New Climate for Theology: God, the World and Global Warming*. Minneapolis: Fortress Press, 2008.

McKay, Stan. "An Aboriginal Perspective on the Integrity of Creation." In *Liberating Faith: Religious Voices for Justice, Peace and Ecological Wisdom*, ed. Roger S. Gottlieb, 519–52. Lanham, MD: Rowan & Littlefield, 2003.

Pope Francis. *Laudato Si'*, Encyclical Letter of the Holy Father Francis on Care for our Common Home. Vatican City: Libreria Editrice Vaticana. http://w2.vatican.va/content/dam/francesco/pdf/encyclicals/documents/papa-francesco_20150524_enciclica-laudato-si_en.pdf.

Schaefer, James. *Theological Foundations for Environmental Ethics: Reconstructing Patristic and Medieval Concepts*. Washington, DC: Georgetown University Press, 2009.

Wink, Walter. *The Powers That Be: A Theology for the New Millennium*. New York, NY: Galilee Doubleday, 1999.

Notes

1. Cf. Stephen Bevans, *Models of Contextual Theology* (Maryknoll, NY: Orbis Books, 2002), 4.

2. Lynn White Jr., "The Historical Roots of Our Ecological Crisis," *Science* 155, no. 3767 (1967): 1203–7.

3. Martin Palmer, interview during "Beyond Belief: The Environment," March 24, 2014, http://www.bbc.co.uk/programmes/b03yn6xt.

4. White, "Historical Roots," 1205–6.

5. See, e.g., Anestis G. Keselopoulos, *Man and the Environment: A Study of St. Symeon the New Theologian* (Crestwood, NY: St. Vladimir's Seminary Press, 2001).

6. See Joseph Sittler Jr., "A Theology for Earth," *The Christian Scholar* 37, no. 3 (September 1954): 367–74.

7. John Paul II, *Inter Sanctos* (Vatican City: Libreria Editrice Vaticana, November 29, 1979), http://w2.vatican.va/content/john-paul-ii/la/apost_letters/1979/documents/hf_jp-ii_apl_19791129_inter-sanctos.html.

8. John Paul II, "Message of His Holiness Pope John Paul II for the Celebration of the World Day of Peace 1 January 1990: Peace with God the Creator, Peace with All of Creation," (Vatican City: Libreria Editrice Vaticana, December 8, 1989), no. 16, http://www.vatican.va/holy_father/john_paul_ii/messages/peace/documents/hf_jp-ii_mes_19891208_xxiii-world-day-for-peace_en.html.

9. Cf. Dawn M. Nothwehr, *Ecological Footprints: An Essential Franciscan Guide for Faith and Sustainable Living* (Collegeville, MN: Liturgical Press, 2012).

10. See, e.g., Jonathan R. Wilson, *God's Good World: Reclaiming the Doctrine of Creation* (Grand Rapids, MI: Baker Academic, 2013).

11. See, e.g., Jame Schaefer, *Theological Foundations for Environmental Ethics: Reconstructing Patristic and Medieval Concepts* (Washington, DC: Georgetown University Press, 2009).

12. See, e.g., Dennis Patrick O'Hara, "Thomas Merton and Thomas Berry: Reflections from a Parallel Universe," *The Merton Annual* 13 (2000): 222–34.

13. See, e.g., Gretel Van Wieren, *Restored to the Earth: Christianity, Environmental Ethics and Ecological Restoration* (Washington, DC: Georgetown University Press, 2013).

14. See, e.g., Daniel T. Spencer, *Gay and Gaia: Ethics, Ecology, and the Erotic* (Cleveland: Pilgrim Press, 1996).

15. See, e.g., Michael S. Hogue, *The Tangled Bank: Toward an Ecotheological Ethics of Responsible Participation* (Cambridge: James Clarke and Co, 2010).

16. Heather Eaton, "Forces of Nature: Aesthetics and Ethics," in *Aesth/Ethics in Environmental Change: Hiking through the Arts, Ecology, Religion and Ethics of the Environment*, ed. Sigurd Bergmann, Irmgard Blindow, and Konrad Ott (Berlin: LIT Verlag, 2013), 105.

17. Ivone Gebara, "Ecofeminism: A Latin American perspective," *Cross Currents* 53, no. 1 (Spring 2003): 103.

18. Sallie McFague, "An Ecological Christology: Does Christianity Have It?" in *Christianity and Ecology*, ed. Dieter T. Hessel and Rosemary Radford Ruether (Cambridge, MA: Harvard University Press, 2000), 33.

19. World Council of Churches Staff, "Justice, Peace, Creation: History," 1998, http://www.wcc-coe.org/wcc/what/jpc/hist-e.html; Missionary Oblates of Mary Immaculate Staff, "Justice, Peace and the Integrity of Creation," 2015, http://omiusajpic.org/.

20. Cf. Freda Rajotte, "Justice, Peace, and the Integrity of Creation," *Religious Education* 85, no.1 (Winter 1990): 5–14.

21. Cf. Martin Robra, "Theology of Life—Justice, Peace, Creation: An Ecumenical Study," *The Ecumenical Review* 48, no. 1 (1996): 28–37.

22. Cf. Bron Taylor, "Earth and Nature-based Spirituality (Part 1): From Deep Ecology to Radical Environmentalism," *Religion* 31, no. 2 (2001): 175–93.

23. Brian Swimme and Thomas Berry, *The Universe Story: From the Primordial Flaring Fourth to the Ecozoic Era; A Celebration of the Unfolding Cosmos* (New York: HarperCollins, 1992), 254.

24. Here, this chapter is borrowing from a phrase that is often erroneously credited to Gandhi but certainly reflects Gandhian insight and has resonance for those concerned with issues of peace, justice, and the integrity of creation.

25. Cf. Edmund O'Sullivan, "Emancipatory Hope: Trans-

formative Learning and the Strange Attractors," in *Holistic Learn-ing and Spirituality in Education: Breaking New Ground*, ed. John P. Miller, Selia Karsten, Diana Denton, Deborah Orr, and Isabella Colalillo Kates (Albany, NY: University of New York, NY Press, 2005), 69–78.

26. Robin Usher, Ian Bryant, and Rennie Johnston, *Adult Education and the Postmodern Challenge: Learning beyond the Limits* (New York, NY: Routledge, 1997), 184.

27. Thomas Berry, *The Great Work: Our Way into the Future* (New York, NY: Bell Tower, 1999), 79.

28. The Center for Media and Democracy, "Greenwash-ing," April 7, 2013, http://www.sourcewatch.org/index.php/Greenwashing.

29. See Global Greens, "Global Greens Congress 2001," April 2001, https://www.globalgreens.org/canberra2001. Particularly helpful for sourcing the above was the *Spinifex* newsletters com-piled at this link (though these now have to be searched inde-pendently due to a website update). A literature search reveals citations of the *Global Greens Charter* in diverse academic fields from the study of politics to health research. E.g., Michael Bent-ley, "An Ecological Public Health Approach to Understanding the Relationships between Sustainable Urban Environments, Public Health and Social Equity," *Health Promotion International* 29, no. 3 (2014): 528–37.

30. This experience of the green principles' communicative qualities was a prime stimulus for the development of this colliga-tion framework on this point and the earlier described drafting process.

31. Second Vatican Council, Pastoral Constitution on the Church in the Modern World, *Gaudium et Spes*, (Vatican City: Libreria Editrice Vaticana, December 7, 1965), http://www.vatican.va/archive/hist_councils/ii_vatican_council/documents/vat-ii_cons_19651207_gaudium-et-spes_en.html.

32. Global Greens, *Global Greens Charter*, (2001, 2012), no. 9, http://www.global greens.org/globalcharter-english.

33. In his 2014 Boyle Lecture, Alister McGrath, building on the work of William Whewell and Margaret Morrison and employ-ing these terms, upholds the value of colligation to provide better refutations of the new atheism. Beyond this apologetic applica-

tion, in the green theo-ecoethical case, the aspiration here is to better foster socioecological flourishing. Cf. Alister McGrath, "New Atheism—New Apologetics: The Use of Science in Recent Christian Apologetic Writing," Boyle Lecture, January 22, 2014, 6–7, https://s3-eu-west-1.amazonaws.com/content.gresham.ac.uk/data/binary/585/22jan14alistermcgrath_newatheism.doc.

34. Expanding upon Clodovis Boff's reflections in this regard, during his discussion of hermeneutical mediation, Phan includes the possibilities of theology, social sciences, and humanities acting as "first generalities" in the articulation of liberation theologies' "third generalities." Indeed, Phan views this employing of third generalities as a key feature of the methods that serve to unite diverse Christian liberation theologies. See Peter C. Phan, "Method in Liberation Theologies," *Theological Studies* 61, no. 1 (2000): 52–55.

35. E.g., Sallie McFague, *Life Abundant: Rethinking Theology and Economy for a Planet in Peril* (Minneapolis: Augsburg Fortress, 2001).

36. Ken Booth describes peace studies as possessing a quality of "critical normativity" in his discussion of the normative elements that inform critical security studies. This quality identifies the presence of normative commitments within a critically constructed discourse. Critical normativity in this sense is present in Christian ethics, in general, and theo-ecoethical praxis, in particular, both of which inform the methodology for this research. On the initial point, see Ken Booth, "Critical Explorations," in *Critical Security Studies and World Politics*, ed. Ken Booth (London: Lynne Rienner Publishers, 2005), 1–20; cf. *EG* 50.

37. E.g., Sallie McFague, *A New Climate for Theology: God, the World and Global Warming* (Minneapolis: Fortress Press, 2008).

38. Leonardo Boff, *Virtues for Another Possible World*, trans. Alexander Guilherm (Eugene, OR: Cascade Books, 2011). Interestingly, recalling his actions during what was also the drafting period of *Evangelii Gaudium*, Leonardo Boff has cited a Spanish version of the *Earth Charter* (indicating as common source with the *Global Greens Charter*) as one of the documents, along with a selection of his books and a draft UN document on the common good of Mother Earth and humanity, that he passed to Pope Francis through trusted intermediaries to provide "bricks" that

would help the pope build the foundations for *Laudato Si'*. Boff, "An Unworthy Servant in the Service of Francis," 7, 9; cf., Harvey Cox, *The Silencing of Leonardo Boff: The Vatican and the Future of World Christianity* (Oak Park, IL: Meyer Stone Books, 1988).

39. Cf. Synod of Bishops, *Justice in the World*, 1971, 6, http://www.shc.edu/theolibrary/resources/synodjw.htm.

40. Cf. John Howard Yoder, *Christian Attitudes to War, Peace, and Revolution* (Grand Rapids, MI: Brazos Press, 2009).

41. See Donald Dorr, *Option for the Poor and for the Earth: Catholic Social Teaching* (Maryknoll, NY: Orbis Books, 2012).

42. Cf. Social Affairs Committee of the Assemblée des évêques catholiques du Québec, "Cry of the Earth; Cry of the Poor," May 1, 2001, http://www.eveques.qc.ca/documents/2001/20010501e.html.

43. Walter J. Houston, *Justice: The Biblical Challenge*, Biblical Challenges in the Contemporary World Series (London, UK: Equinox, 2010), 91.

44. Cf. Deneulin's chapter in this volume.

45. See Richard R. Gaillardetz, *Teaching with Authority: A Theology of the Magisterium in the Church* (Collegeville, MN: Liturgical Press, 1997), 50–56.

46. Cf. Glasgow Quaker Meeting Staff, "Quaker Business Meetings: How Friends Make Decisions," August 2002, http://www.qis.net/~daruma/business.html.

47. Cf. Synod of Bishops, no. 6.

48. Cf. Glasgow Quaker Meeting Staff, "Quaker Business Meetings."

49. On the distinction between principled and pragmatic nonviolence from a Gandhian perspective, cf. L.K. Bharadwaj, "Principled versus Pragmatic Nonviolence," *Peace Review: A Journal of Social Justice* 10, no. 1 (1998): 79–81.

50. Walter Wink, *The Powers That Be: A Theology for The New Millennium* (New York: Galilee Doubleday, 1999), 97.

51. See, in particular, Second Vatican Council, Dogmatic Constitution on Divine Revelation, *Dei Verbum* (Vatican City: Libreria Editrice Vaticana, November 18, 1965), http://www.vatican.va/archive/hist_councils/ii_vatican_council/docments/vat-ii_const_19651118_dei-verbum_en.html.

52. Cf. John W. O'Malley, *What Happened at Vatican II?* (Cam-

bridge, MA: Belknap Press of Harvard University Press, 2008), 310–11.

53. John Dear argues that Vatican II's orientation toward *ressourcement* and Scripture allows for an important recovery of the gospel of peace. See John Dear, *The God of Peace: Toward a Theology of Nonviolence* (Eugene, OR: Wipf and Stock, 2005), 115–25.

54. Walter Wink, *Engaging the Powers: Discernment and Resistance in a World of Domination* (Minneapolis: Fortress Press, 1992), 314.

55. Cf. Wink, *The Powers That Be*, 184–85.

56. On nonviolence in this, cf. Jim Wallis, "The Power of Protest at Mizzou," November 12, 2015, https://sojo.net/articles/power-protest-mizzou.

57. Cf. Stan McKay, "An Aboriginal Perspective on the Integrity of Creation," in *Liberating Faith: Religious Voices for Justice, Peace and Ecological Wisdom*, ed. Roger S. Gottlieb (Lanham, MA: Rowan & Littlefield, 2003), 521; Oren Lyons, "The Politics of Human Beings against Mother Earth: The Nature of Global Warming," Sol Kanee Lecture on Peace and Justice, University of Manitoba, Winnipeg, MB, November 8, 2007, https://www.youtube.com/watch?v=HiA4_e4YwZE; Larry L. Rasmussen, *Earth Community, Earth Ethics* (Maryknoll, NY: Orbis Books, 1996).

58. See, e.g., Rita Nakashima Brock and Rebecca Ann Parker, *Saving Paradise: How Christianity Traded Love of this World for Crucifixion and Empire* (Boston, MA: Beacon Press, 2008), 388.

59. Cf. Morris Berman, *The Reenchantment of the World* (Ithica, NY: Cornell University Press, 1981); Avihu Zakai, "Jonathan Edwards and the Language of Nature: The Re-enchantment of the World in the Age of Scientific Reasoning," *Journal of Religious History* 26, no. 1 (2002): 15–41.

60. Cf. Thomas Berry, *The Dream of the Earth* (San Francisco: Sierra Club Books, 1988), 11.

61. Cf. Berry, *The Great Work*, 59.

62. See, e.g., Rosemary Radford Ruether, *Gaia & God: An Ecofeminist Theology of Earth Healing* (San Francisco: HarperCollins, 1992).

63. See, e.g., Bruce Sanguin, *Darwin, Divinity and the Dance of the Cosmos: An Ecological Christianity* (Kelowna: Copper House, 2007), 27.

64. See, e.g., Keselopoulos. For a liberationist application of "panentheism" in light of ecojustice concerns, see Leonardo Boff, *Cry of the Earth, Cry of the Poor*, trans. Philip Berryman (Maryknoll, NY: Orbis Books, 1997), 152–54.

65. This theme of common home is also brought forward in Pope Francis's first social encyclical (e.g., *LS* 13).

66. Pope Francis asked several people, including James Martin, SJ, to draft their versions of a short encyclical under the title *Domus Communis* (our common home), which indicates the centrality of the common home (a solidarist image) to the project that became the present pope's first social encyclical. Viewed through a green theo-ecoethical lens, the fact that the main title of the encyclical became *Laudato Si'* (praise be), with "on care for our common home" now the subtitle, can still be taken as a solidarist image, emphasizing how duties to God permeate our duties to our fellow human beings (with special duties to people living in poverty) and to the rest of the created world. On his contribution, see James Martin, "The Theologians Respond: *Laudato Si*," June 18, 2015, https:// www.youtube.com/watch?v=EdAJO-anDmY.

67. Cf. Stefan Skrimshire, ed., *Future Ethics: Climate Change and Apocalyptic Imagination* (London: Continuum, 2010).

68. Cf. Elise Harris, "Pope's Environmental Encyclical to Be Titled 'Laudato Si' (Praised Be You)," May 31, 2015, http://www.catholicnewsagency.com/news/popes-environmental-encyclical-to-be-titled-laudato-sii-praised-be-72899/. The *Paris Agreement* drafted late in 2015 did not achieve a truly effective and binding agreement of the type invoked by Francis. See Conference of the Parties, "Adoption of Paris Agreement," December 12, 2015, http://unfccc.int/resource/docs/2015/cop21/eng/l09r01.pdf.

69. On the topic of human flourishing, cf. *LS* 192.

70. John Paul II, "Peace with God the Creator, Peace with all Creation," no. 5.

71. Although Francis, in what is perhaps an unfortunate inconsistency, also states at the beginning of chap. 2 that the encyclical is "addressed to all people of good will" (*LS* 62).

72. For information on this and other UN instruments to mitigate against ozone layer depletion, see United Nations Environment Protection Agency, "Ozone Secretariat: Treaties and Decisions," 2014, http://ozone.unep.org/en/treaties.php.

73. Cf. Christopher Hrynkow, "The Pope, The Planet, and Politics: A Mapping of How Francis Is Calling for More Than the Paris Agreement," *The Journal of Church and State* (July 07/2016), https://doi.org/10.1093/jcs/csw030.

74. Cf. Nakashima Brock and Parker, *Saving Paradise*, 40.

75. In terms of gender justice, e.g., cf. *EG* 104. See also Beattie in this volume.

76. Cf. Hrynkow, "The Pope, The Planet, and Politics."

12

Evangelii Gaudium and Amartya Sen's *Idea of Justice*

Informal Economy Workers in Argentina

SÉVERINE DENEULIN[1]

Situating the Context

In the conceptual chapter introducing the fourth part of this volume, Zampini Davies argues that far from disrupting Catholic social teaching, *EG* strengthens and expands its central principles. Many arguments of the papal exhortation are found in the encyclical *LS* and are now part of Catholic social teaching. Among them, he emphasizes an inductive methodology that starts with the reality of the cry of the poor and the earth, an inclusive public dialogue as key to social transformation, an invitation for theology to engage with the social sciences for this task, and a recognition of those who live in conditions of poverty as active shapers of their lives rather than passive victims of economic and social policy. Zampini Davies proposes Amartya Sen's capability approach as a dialogue partner with *EG*, and Catholic social teaching more broadly, given their common ground. Both are normative frameworks that aim at evaluating situations from the perspective of human flourishing, at identifying the conditions that constrain the full development of persons, and at transforming them. This chapter discusses in greater depth how *EG*, and other theological resources such as the Catholic social teachings on work, the economy, and solidarity, and the Second Vatican Council documents on ecclesiology and liturgy, can enter in fruitful dialogue with Amartya Sen's capability approach, and more specifically his conceptualization of social justice.[2]

In its discussion of whether Pope Francis was indebted to liberation theology or not, the chapter by Lakeland in this volume argues that what characterizes the current incumbent of the papacy is a very strong inductive methodology and a distance from ideologies. *EG* introduces "reality" as a "principle":

> Realities are greater than ideas. This principle has to do with incarnation of the word and its being put into practice....The principle of reality, of a word already made flesh and constantly striving to take flesh anew, is essential to evangelization. It helps us to see that the Church's history is a history of salvation, to be mindful of those saints who inculturated the gospel in the life of our peoples and to reap the fruits of the Church's rich bimillennial tradition, without pretending to come up with a system of thought detached from this treasury, as if we wanted to reinvent the gospel. At the same time, this principle impels us to put the word into practice, to perform works of justice and charity that make that word fruitful. Not to put the word into practice, not to make it reality, is to build on sand, to remain in the realm of pure ideas and to end up in a lifeless and unfruitful self-centredness and gnosticism. (*EG* 233)

LS provides an extensive analysis of the reality that "the earth, our home, is beginning to look more and more like an immense pile of filth" (*LS* 21). It links the situation in which the world finds itself today to the "modern myth of unlimited material progress" (*LS* 78), and to a technological advancement that has lost sight of its ends, namely the promotion of human dignity through work (*LS* 128). *LS* takes the reality of work or labor as integral to its ecology: "Any approach to an integral ecology, which by definition does not exclude human beings, needs to take account of the value of labor" (*LS* 124). It observes that the deterioration of the environment and the violation of the dignity of human life often go together and that this joint deterioration is connected to an economic system that prioritizes financial gains over human dignity (*LS* 56). This chapter takes the reality of informal economy work in Argentina as the background to the dialogue between *EG* and Amartya Sen's *Idea of Justice.*

Any passenger on the Argentine capital city's metro, or other public transport, as the then Jorge Bergoglio was, would have encountered the reality of the informal economy—vendors trying to sell goods of all kinds in train carriages, ranging from chewing gums, socks, books, tissues, to even kitchen knives.[3] Anyone walking the streets of Buenos Aires would also have noticed men pushing carts full of rubbish in the midst of car traffic. They are known locally as *cartoneros*, named after the cardboard (*cartón* in Spanish) they collect from the city's bins and then recycle to make a living. The creativity of people to produce work in order to survive is limitless: recycling rubbish, cleaning car windscreens or juggling to entertain drivers waiting at traffic lights, selling goods on pavements or in the public transportation system, or using motorbikes to make deliveries. What is known in Latin America as "popular economy" is thriving.

According to the Confederation of Popular Economy Workers of Argentina (CTEP in its Spanish acronym),[4] the popular economy refers to the production of goods and services by people who, unable to secure waged employment or regularized self-employment, nevertheless work in a myriad of ways in order to provide for themselves and their families. It is characterized by the means of production in the hands of the workers themselves and not investors external to the economic activity, by meeting people's needs and not maximizing profit, by low capital investment and inadequate technology, by geographical concentration of its workers at the periphery of urban centers, by a lack of legal recognition, and by an absence of social protection and services that are readily available to other workers.[5]

The popular economy includes what is commonly referred to as the informal economy, but can also include formal economy elements such as cooperatives that are legally recognized. The dependence of popular economy workers on the formal economy is another reason why the CTEP finds the formal/informal economy distinction inadequate to capture the essence of the economic activities that a large number of people invent to survive. Popular economy workers often require the formal economy for some necessary components of their work. For instance, the *cartoneros* depend on companies buying their goods, such as the multinational dairy company Danone buying their plastic to recycle it into yogurt pots. However, despite their self-ascription as "popular economy workers," this chapter will continue to use the traditional designation of "informal economy workers."[6] The reason for this is that workers still call themselves "popular economy workers" when the work they do has passed from insecure and informal to secure and formal. This is an important distinction to keep, and the "popular economy" designation blurs it.

About 1.5 billion people worldwide are estimated to work in informal employment; that this, about half of the global labor force is working outside the jurisdiction of labor legislation and social protection.[7] According to estimates from the International Labor Organization (ILO), about 46.9 percent of the working population in Argentina did so in the informal sector in 2011, of which 11.7 percent were informal workers in the formal sector and 5.1 percent were domestic workers.[8] These figures reflect the Latin American reality, with an estimated 47.7 percent of the Latin American working population employed in the informal sector in 2012.[9] The ILO counts as informal economy workers people who work in productive units that do not constitute a legal entity, have no formal accounting system, or have no registration of their production activities, and people who work in formal companies but are employed without a legal contract.

Because their work is neither connected to a stable income, nor coming with protection against labor accidents, pension, or access to health insurance, informal economy workers are among the country's most marginalized groups, with many living in the mushrooming shantytowns of Argentinian cities. According to official data for 2010,[10] the federal capital city of Buenos Aires, which numbers 3 million people, had 41 informal settlements in which more than 200,000 people live.[11] More than 75 percent of the population who live in Buenos Aires's shantytowns work in the informal economy in order to survive.[12]

Informal economy workers are what Pope Francis calls in *EG* the "excluded," who are not only "exploited" but also "leftovers" of an economic system that does not need them, and that sees them as "consumer goods to be used and then discarded" (*EG* 53). As the chapter by Mangiarotti in this volume notes, the foundations of *EG* are found in the Latin American bishops' conferences. The words of *EG* 53 are a direct echo of paragraph 65 of the document of the 2007 Latin American bishops' conference in the Brazilian city of Aparecida, which Bergoglio led and wrote.[13] It invites the reader to contemplate the faces of those who suffer: indigenous and Afro-American communities, women, young people who have no opportunities to work or study, unemployed workers, informal economy workers, children who are victims of sexual trafficking, unborn children aborted, families who face hunger, those suffering from drug addictions, elderly people, those who suffer from loneliness, prisoners. The Aparecida document refers to them as the "excluded who are not only exploited but also leftovers and disposable." This language is also found in *LS*, which talks of the "more hidden areas [of cities] where the disposable of society live" (*LS* 45).

EG is an exhortatory document that does not pretend to give a full analysis of social realities. It aims at giving a normative compass about the direction of human actions in the light of the gospel. Or to put it in bare terms: it signals areas where human suffering is greater, and it gives pointers for transforming this suffering into joy and establishing the necessary conditions for each and every person to live fully human lives. As such, however, it does not give an academic conceptual framework with which to analyze social realities from the perspective of human dignity or flourishing. This is why social scientific analysis, and especially the normative social analytical framework proposed by Amartya Sen, can be a powerful ally to *EG* in its exhortation to bring the joy of the gospel to the concrete realities of people's lives—"to go forth from our own comfort zone in order to reach all the 'peripheries' in need of the light of the Gospel" (*EG* 20).

The next section discusses some of the analytical tools offered by Amartya Sen's conceptualization of injustice, and why it can be an enriching complement to *EG*. The remainder of the chapter will then narrate the journey of informal economy workers in Buenos Aires, with whom Bergoglio was and remains closely associated, to transform work from undignified to dignified, and examine how theological resources, such as social teachings, ecclesiology, and liturgy, can help mediate the actions of marginalized groups to become protagonists of their own lives and create better opportunities for human flourishing.

Amartya Sen's Idea of Justice

Social sciences, and in particular the discipline of economics, have had a tendency to eschew explicit discussion of values.[14] With its utilitarian foundations, economics has aspired to be a value-free science where the assumptions that people act to maximize their utility and firms to maximize their profits are rarely questioned. One of Amartya Sen's major contributions to the social sciences has been to bring ethics back into economics.

In his book on *Ethics and Economics*, Sen contrasts "the engineering approach" to the "ethical approach" in economics. He argues that the former "is characterized by being concerned with primarily logistic issues rather than with ultimate ends and such questions as what may foster 'the good of man' or 'how should one live?' The ends are taken as fairly straightforwardly given, and the object of the exercise is to find the appropriate means to serve them."[15] He compares the failure to deliberate about ends to "a decision expert whose response to seeing a man engaged in slicing his toes with a blunt knife is to rush to advise him that he should use a sharper knife to better serve his evident objective."[16] Sen urges economics to recover its ethical foundations, in the sense that discussion about ends should become once again central to the discipline.

Behind what Sen has called the "engineering approach" lie hidden normative assumptions about the end of human actions in the maximization of utility. Sen's works have questioned these assumptions. The standard of living, he argues, does not lie in the possession of commodities or satisfaction or happiness levels but in the actual living.[17] The starting question to assess states of affairs is not how much people have or how they feel, but what kinds of lives they are able to live. Following Aristotelian ethics, he argues that the pursuit of a good life is not about mental states or feelings of happiness, but about "beings and doings," which he calls "functionings."[18] These can be, among others, appearing in public without shame or pursuing knowledge, being healthy or being with family and friends, being well nourished, adequately sheltered, participating in the life of the community, or having a say in decisions that affect one's life.

Because Sen considers human freedom as intrinsic to a good human life,[19] he adds to the concept of functionings the one of "capabilities," which he defines as "the set of functioning vectors within his or her reach,"[20] or "a person's ability to do valuable acts or reach valuable states of being."[21] There is a difference between someone suffering from hunger because she or he has chosen to be on hunger strike for the sake of an objective she or he values, and someone suffering from hunger because she or he has no access to food. While Sen considers choice as the main distinction between functionings and capabilities, others have interpreted the distinction more in terms of the ability to sustain a certain level of functionings than choice per se.[22] There is a difference between someone performing a job on a one-year temporary contract and another person performing exactly the same job on a permanent contract. Both have the same level of "functionings" (working) but one has less opportunity to sustain that functioning in the future than the other. They have, in other words, different "capability sets."

One of the reasons for Sen's distinction between functioning and capability in the evaluation of states of affairs is the concern for human agency, which Sen defines as the "pursuit of whatever goals or values he or she regards as important."[23] The centrality of agency is a key feature of what has come to be known as the "capability approach" in the social sciences.

There are many similarities between the capability approach and *EG* and *LS*. Both Sen and Pope Francis strongly advocate for the need to redefine the notion of progress and development, to make it people centered and not wealth or income centered (*EG* 55, 203; *LS* 194). Both have an inductive methodology, using the kinds of lives that people live as the starting point of their reflection. In that respect, the capability approach could give a fuller account of the sufferings of the faces that paragraph 64 of the Aparecida document referred to,[24] and a more in-depth analysis of the constraining factors, which prevent people from having access to valuable beings and doings (functionings), such as living in a nonovercrowded dwelling with access to safe water and sanitation, being adequately nourished, working, being healthy, and making plans for oneself and one's family. Finally, both stress the importance of agency and the responsibility of people to shape their environment in a way that is conducive to the human flourishing of each and all on a shared planet (*EG* 122, 199; *LS* 144).[25]

The capability approach is what underpins the conceptualization of social justice proposed by Sen, and that brings further areas of similarities with Pope Francis. Two of the main features of Sen's *Idea of Justice*, namely his nonideal and comparative view of justice and the centrality of public reasoning to make situations less unjust, are also found in *EG* and *LS*. They are particularly relevant for analyzing the actions of informal economy workers to create better conditions for them and their family members so as to develop fully as persons.

For Sen, to ask what constitutes a just society is not a good starting point for thinking about justice or injustice. He advances the argument that "questions of justice" are best based "first, on assessments of social realizations, that is, on what actually happens (rather than merely on the appraisal of institutions and arrangements); and second, on comparative issues of enhancement of justice (rather than trying to identify perfectly just arrangements)."[26] Or as he has recently put it, reminiscent of Pope Francis's reality principle, "The basic argument for a realization-focused understanding, for which I would argue, is that justice cannot be divorced from the actual world that emerges."[27] In discussing the demands of justice, "Should we not," Sen asks, "also have to examine what does emerge in the society, including the kind of lives that people can actually lead, given the institutions and rules and also other influences?"[28]

The evaluation space he proposes for this comparative assessment of the kinds of lives that people live is the capability space. One situation is better, or more just, than another if people have more opportunities to enjoy valuable beings and doings. Thus, a situation where informal economy workers enjoy health insurance and protection against labor accidents would be comparatively better than the current one, and therefore more just. This does not entail that all capability deprivations have to be eliminated, for the reality of a fully just society is always beyond human reach. What matters is that a situation can be made less unjust by creating better conditions for people to enjoy some valuable sets of functionings, even if other valuable functionings remain absent.[29] Waste pickers may continue to live in a shantytown with little access to public services and next to a polluted river, but having minimal social protection such as access to preventive health care, insurance against labor accidents, and a small pension, would already make their situation more just.

It is this comparative element that sets justice in motion in Sen's account of justice. It is "the contrast between what is happening and what could have happened that is central to the advancement of justice."[30] It is also a contrast that sets justice in motion in Pope Francis's documents: "Cities create a sort of permanent ambivalence because, while they offer their residents countless possibilities, they also present many people with any number of obstacles to the full development of their lives. This contrast causes painful suffering" (*EG* 74); "at the same time, we have a sort of 'superdevelopment' of a wasteful and consumerist kind which forms an unacceptable contrast with the ongoing situations of dehumanizing deprivation, while we are all too slow in developing economic institutions and social initiatives which can give the poor regular access to basic resources" (*LS* 109).

Sen's capability account of social justice, however, goes further than simply assessing situations and laying down the contrast between those who enjoy valuable sets of beings and doings and those who do not. He argues that this contrast, when submitted to public discussion, is precisely the starting point for remedying action. Public reasoning is the central mechanism in Sen's account of justice to reduce the contrast between what the current situation is and what it could be, should other policy decisions be made.

Sen does not give a single definition of his account of public reasoning. From his writings,[31] one can infer three main features:

voice, dialogue, and empathy. In a short article on what it is like to be a human being and how to avoid social arrangements that are painful, Sen writes, "Only the wearer may know where the shoe pinches, but pinch-avoiding arrangements cannot be effectively undertaken without giving voice to the people and giving them extensive opportunities for discussion."[32] In Sen's idea of justice, injustice reductions—or actions aimed at "pinch-avoiding arrangements"—start with expressing what ails one in one's life, crying out the sufferings and deprivations experienced (voice), making one's voice heard and seeking interlocutors who will listen, and discussing ways of reforming existing or creating new institutional arrangements that would eliminate the "pinch" (dialogue).

A critical feature of such dialogue that Sen highlights is seeing other people's perspectives, the ability to put oneself in the position of another person and being able to revise one's own position if need be (empathy): "When we try to assess...which kind of societies should be understood to be patently unjust, we have reason to listen and pay some attention to the views and suggestions of others, which might or might not lead us to revise some of our own conclusions."[33] Sen sees "the ability to sympathize and to reason" as core human faculties.[34] He speaks of the importance for the "non-victims" of capability deprivation to "take on" the eradication of their deprivation as "their *own* commitment."[35]

In other words, reasoning is connected to the existence of certain virtues, understood in the classical sense of acquired moral dispositions or character traits: disposition to listen to another person even if her views are different from one's own, to learn from her and possibly change one's view, and to see the world from another person's perspective. The case for the importance of voice, dialogue, and empathy is also made extensively by Pope Francis, such as in *EG* 238–54 on "social dialogue as a contribution to peace," and *LS* 3, which describes the encyclical as an invitation "to enter into dialogue with all people about our common home." The next section discusses how this "public reasoning" takes place in the reality of the lives of informal economy workers in Buenos Aires.

Making the Lives of Informal Economy Workers Better

Sergio Sánchez is a waste picker in the city of Buenos Aires who was thrust into the international spotlight when sitting on the front row in his waste picker uniform in the Basilica of St. Peter in Rome at the installation of Jorge Bergoglio as Pope Francis in March 2013. He also later made headlines by having his newborn son baptized by the pope in the Vatican in October 2015.[36] Sergio started to search for waste to recycle in the 1990s after losing his factory job. In 2002, he met a group of students who had set up a street soup kitchen in response to the December 2001 economic crisis.[37] Little by little, they got to know each other and the problems waste pickers faced—the exploitation of intermediaries, the bribes, the dangerous work conditions, child labor, economic insecurity, inability to plan their lives, and so forth. The student initiative was a response to engage in politics in a new way: seeing people as persons and not clients for political gains, hence the emphasis on listening to their stories and entering into their lives.[38] The students taught them about their rights, and helped them value more the work they were doing. They also made them realize that it was wrong to have to pay bribes in order to work—because waste picking was illegal, *cartoneros* had to make "agreements" with the police to work. With time, an organization was formed, the Movement of Excluded Workers, as a more institutionalized platform to speak in the public domain. As Sergio puts it, "Before, every *cartonero* looked after him/herself only, but we had to speak with one voice. I was lucky to have had good teachers who taught me I had rights and had to fight for them."[39]

The waste pickers of Buenos Aires acquired greater confidence to speak up in the public sphere, and voice "what ailed in their lives," when they encountered the then Cardinal Bergoglio in 2007. The archdiocese had initiated, as an annual event, an initiative to put tents in a public square for one day where the city's marginalized residents tend to conglomerate and to make pastoral agents available for passersby to talk. It became known as *carpa misionera* (or missionary tent)[40] and one can see this pastoral initiative as a direct consequence of the Aparecida document's call to make missionary disciples that is also reflected in

EG's call for a missionary church that goes to the margins of society. Bergoglio was celebrating the closing liturgy, and this is where he came to meet the waste pickers.[41] Their relationship with the cardinal strengthened the public legitimacy of their claims. On May 1, 2014, on the eve of a march to demand the right of informal economy workers to form a union, the now Pope Francis sent a video message in which he insisted on the importance of their work and affirmed their social action.[42]

Today, Sergio works as an urban recycler in a cooperative directly contracted by the city government. The waste is sorted in a recycling center with proper technology and hygiene conditions. He earns a modest but stable income and benefits from a pension, health security scheme, and insurance against accidents. He is one of the lucky twenty thousand informal economy workers to enjoy such opportunities to work in safe conditions, earn a stable income, and have health insurance.[43] What led to this improvement has not been the result of state beneficence but a result of the agency of the informal economy workers themselves and of "public reasoning" in which voice, empathy, and dialogue were key mechanisms for making their situation less unjust, that is, decreasing the number and intensity of their capability deprivations.

A first improvement in their lives was the legalization of their work. Collecting waste had been, since 1976, an illegal activity in Buenos Aires. Those who did so had to bribe the police in order to work. Given the significant increase of waste pickers in the aftermath of the December 2001 economic crisis, the decriminalization of waste picking became a political issue. The voice of waste pickers was channeled to the city government assembly through their newly formed collective organization. The argument that scavenging was a form of work and that its prohibition violated the constitutional right to work, won.[44] The repeal of the law considerably changed the public perception of waste pickers and contributed to the transformation of their identity from scavengers to urban recyclers. It also led to the elimination of an exploitative situation with intermediaries. Until then, waste pickers worked separately and depended on middlemen for selling their goods. Intermediaries bought their products at the lowest possible price. Through cooperatives, workers were able to pool their resources

319

together to contract trucks themselves, to send their products directly to companies, and to negotiate a fair price.

A second improvement came in 2008. The waste pickers who lived in Greater Buenos Aires and had their work in the city center had achieved an agreement with train companies to reserve one carriage empty of seats so they could commute with their carts. Given public hygiene preoccupations and complaints from passengers, this facility was abruptly ended. In reaction to this decision, waste pickers occupied public squares and generated a social conflict with the public authorities who tried to remove them by force. The conflict was overcome when information came to light that the city government was paying large sums of money to a private contractor to recycle much less waste than them. After dialogue, an agreement was concluded and the social conflict ended—we can note here echoes in *EG* about social dialogue being a way to peace. The contract with the private contractor was terminated and the money redirected to subsidize their work. The local government provided uniforms to make the work safer, made designated recycling centers available, and supplied appropriate technology. Another result of the dialogue was the granting of labor accident insurance and the provision of child nurseries.

The three features of Sen's account of "public reasoning"—voice, empathy, and dialogue—were critical for improving the lives of some informal economy workers in the city of Buenos Aires. The changed legal status of waste picking was the result of a dialogue, where the voice of waste pickers had become such that they could no longer be ignored, and where different positions were discussed in the city's assembly and an agreement found. The cooperative movement provided a space for their voice to be strengthened and for waste pickers to eliminate the need for middlemen, and therefore their exploitation. This collective voice was facilitated by many *cartoneros* living in the same neighborhoods and having to commute together. Other workers, such as vendors on public transport, have less opportunity to organize collectively given the individual nature of their work.[45] Empathy was also at play when members of the city assembly changed their perspective on waste-picking work, seeing it as an environmental service to the city and no longer as something negative.

The waste pickers of the city of Buenos Aires were not the only informal economy workers to engage in public reasoning to improve their situation. Joining with other sectors, the Confederation of the Popular Economy Workers (CTEP) was formed in December 2011. It is organized under a National Secretariat with different representative branches, such as garment workers, motorcyclists, street vendors, stallholders, small farmers, and vegetable producers. It has created an integral health and education program, which includes a mutual insurance scheme, medical and dental consultations, and health prevention. In December 2015, the CTEP was granted union status, which has been one of its biggest objectives since its creation.[46] This gives informal economy workers a platform for their voices to be heard and for dialogue to take place. As an urban recycler who went to Geneva for a conference on the transformation of the informal economy at the International Labor Organization expressed it, "Nobody can represent a worker like me, no union, no business, no government. I do not want to be a second or third class worker, but a worker like any other worker."[47]

Public reasoning—or voice, dialogue, and listening—can be at the same time facilitated by theological resources. As noted above, the Aparecida document led to the creation of a missionary tent that brought Bergoglio into contact with the waste pickers, which gave them moral support for their collective organizing.[48] The next section explores how theological resources can play a mediating role in public reasoning and the reduction of injustice. It focuses on Catholic social teaching regarding work and the economy, and the Second Vatican Council with regard to liturgy and ecclesiology.

The Mediation of Theological Resources

The encyclical *Rerum Novarum* (Of new things, 1891) by Pope Leo XIII has traditionally been seen as the foundational document of Catholic social teaching.[49] It was a response to the problems of industrialization and the exploitation of workers. It urged governments to legislate for minimum wages, to guarantee labor rights such as protection against illness and accidents, and affirmed the right of workers to form unions.

The encyclical *Laborem Exercens* (Through work) by Pope John Paul II, promulgated in 1981, reinforced the teachings of *Rerum Novarum*. It emphasized that working was part of one's humanity: "Work is a good thing for man [*sic*]—a good thing for his humanity—because through work man [*sic*] *not only transforms nature*, adapting it to his own needs, but he also *achieves fulfilment* as a human being and indeed, in a sense, becomes 'more a human being'"(*LE* 9; emphases in original). The teachings that work is part of one's humanity, that the work of someone who collects urban rubbish on his or her cart has value and transforms nature and makes a contribution to society, have played a mediating role in the public reasoning in which informal economy workers of Buenos Aires have been engaged. The direct intervention of Pope Francis to support the CTEP's demand to be recognized as a union at their May 1, 2014, march could be seen as a direct expression of these teachings. When asked who the teachers were who taught him he had rights as an informal economy worker, Sergio Sánchez responded that Bergoglio had been one of them.[50]

Another teaching from *LE*, which transpires in the activities of the CTEP, is the importance of the family from whom the worker cannot be isolated: "It must be remembered and affirmed that the family constitutes one of the most important terms of reference for shaping the social and ethical order of human work.... In fact, the family is simultaneously *a community made possible by work* and the first *school of work*, within the home, for every person" (*LE* 10; emphases in original). This is why the CTEP has recreation facilities for workers' children, and healthcare provision for their entire families. One can note here that close links between work and family have also been made in the most recent exhortation of Pope Francis, *Amoris Laetitia*, following the two synods of bishops on the family (see *AL* 25).

A second set of teachings that informal economy workers have used in their public reasoning are those about the economy. That the economy should serve the person, and not vice versa, has been the main message of the encyclical *Centesimus Annus* (The one hundredth year) by John Paul II in 1991, and the major aim of the CTEP. It is a major theme of *EG* (nos. 53–58) and also the main goal of Amartya Sen's capability approach. There are echoes between *EG* and what can be read in the formative booklets of the CTEP regarding an economy that excludes:

> When they deny us work, they deny us the very belong-
> ing to society. They exclude us. We are neither bosses
> nor employees: we are surplus. And as we are surplus,
> they treat us like waste: they put us in sanitary belts so
> that there is no bad smell in the city. For us not to get
> out of our waste tip, they use two tools: police and assis-
> tance. They give us a bit of bread and a bit of stick.[51]

In addition to the teachings on the economy, one can also mention those on solidarity, which the encyclical *Sollicitudo Rei Socialis* (On social concern) by John Paul II in 1987, defined as "a firm and persevering determination to commit oneself to the common good; that is to say to the good of all and of each indi-vidual, because we are all really responsible for all" (*SRS* 38). The Latin American bishops reaffirmed in 2007 the role of the church in accompanying permanently the efforts of the most vulnerable and excluded to be subjects of change and transformation of their situation, as an expression of that solidarity:

> Solidarity likewise springs from our faith in Christ as
> a permanent attitude of encounter, brotherly and sis-
> terly spirit, and service, which is to be manifested in
> visible options and gestures, primarily in defense of life
> and of the rights of the most vulnerable and excluded,
> and in continual accompaniment in their efforts to be
> agents for changing and transforming their situation.
> The Church's service of charity among the poor "is an
> aspect which must clearly mark the Christian life, the
> Church's whole activity and her pastoral planning."[52]

This understanding of the mission of the church as stand-ing in solidarity with those who suffer, who are oppressed and excluded, and accompanying them in their efforts to change the structures that oppress, exclude, and harm them, was central to the documents of the Second Vatican Council. As Mangiarotti notes in his chapter, one of the main remits of the Latin American bishops' conference, CELAM, after it was formed in 1955, was the implementation of the Council in the Latin American context. The Pastoral Constitution of the Church, *Gaudium et Spes* (Joy and hope, 1965) invited "every person of goodwill" to respond to the "signs of the times" and make the "joys and the hopes, the griefs and the anxieties of the men [and women] of this age, especially those who are poor or in any way afflicted" their own.[53] This is where ecclesiology (how the church understands itself and what it is about) meets liturgy in the transformation of people's lives.[54]

Liturgy, ideally understood, should operate as resource for social transformation at two levels: building community and generating hope. Liturgy opens up a space where people who would otherwise not meet can come together. The "missionary tent," and its closing Mass, celebrated annually since 2007, provided a common space for workers to voice their difficulties and find common ways to overcome them.[55] In his video interview, Sergio Sánchez mentions the difficulty informal economy workers had baptizing their children because many were undocumented migrants.[56] The eucharistic liturgies brought them together and were a means of finding ways to overcome bureaucratic hurdles. From this practical problem of baptism, they went on to tackle other common problems they faced, like work exploitation and insecurity.

Participating in liturgy is not about merely a collective meeting attendance. As eucharistic liturgy is celebrated to commemorate the life, death, and resurrection of Christ and the inauguration of the kingdom of God that Jesus came to announce, it is also about making present the reality of redemption here and now and of the world to come, a world where evil and suffering is undone, a world in which the whole creation is reconciled with its Creator. As highlighted earlier, it is precisely in that comparative gap, in the contrast between a reality that is and one that could be—a situation with suffering or capability deprivation and a situation with fewer deprivations—that other institutional arrangements can be found to improve people's lives. In other words, liturgy can also generate an important social function in creating hope that the situation currently lived does not have to be what it is, it can be changed.[57] This was particularly salient in the liturgy celebrated by Pope Francis in October 2014 at a gathering of social movements of excluded people—waste pickers, landless peasants, unemployed, slum dwellers, and homeless—around the themes of work, land, and housing (or *labor, terra, domus* as its logo puts it).[58] Symbols of the struggles of the excluded were brought as offerings at the altar of St. Peter's Basilica: a makeshift house to symbolize their hope to live in adequate housing, a cart of a rubbish picker to symbolize their hope to work in conditions that enable them and their families to develop fully as persons, and a basket of fruit and vegetables to symbolize their hope to protect the environment and farm sustainably so that all can have enough to eat.

Conclusion

This chapter has discussed some of the similarities between *EG* and *LS* and Sen's *Idea of Justice,* and how theological resources can contribute to "public reasoning" in reducing injustice and improving people's lives. Among other effects, they offer resources to construct a space where relationships can be built with those who suffer from capability deprivation that facilitates listening to their voices; they can provide sets of normative guidelines about social analysis; and they can help organize people collectively and generate hope. Such contribution is, however, not without its risks.

One of the biggest risks is the use of theological resources for partisan political ends. It is one thing to create a space of dialogue for different views to be heard and another to transform that space into a political platform for the given agendas of a certain political group. The merging of theological resources to create a more just society with a specific political party is a risk to which the Argentine Catholic Church is particularly prone. In the 1960s and 1970s, it was not unusual for some Catholic priests to identify the church with the Peronist political party.[59] This risk of political partisanship has become obvious in the pope's initiative in convening a meeting of movements of excluded people. The first meeting of the World Meeting of Popular Movements was held in the Vatican in October 2014 and offered a global platform for dialogue and encounter. However, the second meeting in July 2015 in Santa Cruz in Bolivia had more partisan political undertones, with organizations brandishing banners supporting specific political parties during the pope's speech.[60] A national gathering of the Meeting of Popular Movements in Argentina organized on church land in December 2015 had similar political partisanship.

The Latin American bishops urged in their meeting in Aparecida in 2007 to make the church's service among the poor a mark of the church's whole activity and pastoral planning, and to accompany them in their efforts to be agents for changing and transforming their situation (no. 394). The bishops have not, however, spelled out on how to go about making this a reality. Amartya Sen's idea of justice could help in that regard. It emphasizes that the reduction of injustice involves listening to other people's perspectives—even the ones with whom one may profoundly disagree, and trying to see the world from other people's eyes—whether one is a landless farmer or a Monsanto engineer, whether one is a waste picker or a Coca-Cola manager, whether one is a supporter of communism or a Cuban political dissident. Going beyond our "comfort zone in order to reach all the 'peripheries' in need of the light of the Gospel" (*EG* 20) is not without risk. Pope Francis prefers a "Church which is bruised, hurting and dirty because it has been out on the streets, rather than a Church which is unhealthy from being confined and from clinging to its own security" (*EG* 49). Perhaps Sen's works could help set up some bruise-mitigating arrangements, even if not all bruises can be avoided.

Select Bibliography

Calderisi, Robert. *Earthly Mission: The Catholic Church and World Development.* New Haven, CT: Yale University Press, 2013.

Clarke, Gerard, Michael Jennings, and Timothy Shaw, eds. *Development, Civil Society and Faith-Based Organisations.* Basingstoke: Palgrave, 2008.

Clarke, Matthew, ed. *Handbook of Research on Development and Religion.* Cheltenham: Edward Elgar, 2013.

Deneulin, Séverine, and Masooda Bano. *Religion in Development: Rewriting the Secular Script.* London: Zed Books, 2009.

Marshall, Katherine. *Global Institutions of Religion: Ancient Movers, Modern Shakers.* Hoboken: Taylor and Francis, 2013.

Rubin, Jeffrey, David Smilde, and Benjamin Junge. "Lived Religion and Lived Citizenship in Latin America's Zones of Crisis: Introduction to Special Issue." *Latin American Research Review* 49 (2014): 7–26.

Tomalin, Emma. *Religions and Development.* London: Routledge, 2013.

Notes

1. With thanks to Maria del Mar Murga, Carolina Palacio, and Juan Grabois for facilitating the empirical material on the Confederation of Popular Economy Workers.

2. Amartya Sen, *The Idea of Justice* (London: Allen Lane, 2009).

3. The empirical material for this chapter has been collected by the author during three fieldwork trips in July–December 2014, December 2015, and May 2016.

4. Confederación de los Trabajadores de la Economía Popular, see http://ctepargentina.org (accessed June 13, 2016).

5. For a discussion of popular economy in Latin America, see Thomas Bauwens and Andreia Lemaitre, "Popular Economy in Santiago de Chile: State of Affairs and Challenges," *World Development* 64 (2014): 65–78; Angelique van Zeeland, "The Interaction between Popular Economy, Social Movements and Public Policies: A Case Study of the Waste Pickers' Movement," *United Nations Research Institute for Social Development Occasional Paper,* September 11, 2014.

6. For a discussion on what counts as informal economy, see Martha A. Chen, "The Informal Economy: Definitions, Theories and Policies," *WIEGO (Women in Informal Employment: Globalizing and Organizing) Working Paper No. 1,* August 2012, http://wiego .org/informal-economy/history-debates; and Martha A. Chen, "Informal Employment and Development: Patterns of Inclusion and Exclusion," *The European Journal of Development Research* 26, no. 4 (2014): 397–418.

7. United Nations Development Programme, *Human Development Report: Work for Human Development* (New York: UNDP, 2015).

8. ILO, *Panorama Laboral 2012: América Latina y el Caribe* (Geneva: ILO, 2012), 44.

9. ILO, *Panorama Laboral 2013: América Latina y el Caribe* (Geneva: ILO, 2013), 65.

10. Ann Mitchell Suárez and Eduardo Lépore, eds. *Las Villas de la Ciudad de Buenos Aires: Territorios Frágiles de Inclusión Social* (Buenos Aires: Universidad Católica Argentina, 2014), http://www.uca.edu.ar/index.php/site/index/es/uca/programa-interdisciplinario-sobre-desarrollo-humano-e-inclusion-social/publicaciones.

11. According to a survey of seven urban agglomerations that contain 60 percent of the total Argentinian population, there were 1,834 informal settlements in Argentina in 2013, totalling about 532,800 families. The survey considered as informal settlement a set of dwellings with a minimum of eight families, of which more than half lack land titles and access to at least two basic services like water, electricity, or sewage. See TECHO Argentina, *Relevamiento de asentamientos informales 2013* (Buenos Aires: TECHO), http://www.techo.org/informate/techo-argentina-relevamiento-asentamientosinformales.

12. See Suárez et al., *Las Villas de la Ciudad de Buenos Aires*.

13. See http://www.aecrc.org/documents/Aparecida-Concluding%20Document.pdf (accessed June 10, 2016).

14. For a discussion on the importance of values in the social sciences and the ethical evaluation of social norms and institutions, and the contribution of Sen's works in that regard, see Andrew Sayer, *Why Things Matter to People: Social Sciences, Values and Ethical Life* (Cambridge: Cambridge University Press, 2011).

15. Amartya Sen, *Ethics and Economics* (Oxford: Oxford University Press, 1987), 3–4.

16. Amartya Sen, "Rationality and Social Choice," *American Economic Review* 85, no. 1 (1995): 1–24, at 16.

17. Amartya Sen, *Commodities and Capabilities* (Amsterdam: North-Holland, 1985). See also Amartya Sen, "Equality of What?" in *Tanner Lectures on Human Values*, ed. Sterling McMurrin (Cambridge: Cambridge University Press, 1980), 197–220.

18. Amartya Sen, "Capability and Well-Being," in *The Quality of Life*, ed. Martha Nussbaum and Amartya Sen (Oxford: Clarendon Press, 1993), 30–53.

19. Amartya Sen, "Well-Being, Agency and Freedom: The Dewey Lectures 1984," *Journal of Philosophy* 82, no. 4 (1985): 169–221; Amartya Sen, *Inequality Re-examined* (Oxford: Oxford University Press, 1992).

20. Sen, "Well-being, Agency and Freedom," 201.

21. Sen, "Capabilities and Well-being," 30.

22. Jonathan Wolff and Avner De-Shalit, *Disadvantage* (Oxford: Oxford University Press, 2007).

23. Sen, "Well-being, Agency and Freedom," 203.

24. For a discussion of what counts as valuable functionings/capabilities whose absence deserves policy attention, see Martha Nussbaum, *Creating Capabilities* (Cambridge, MA: Harvard University Press, 2011).

25. For Sen, "The importance of the agency aspect, in general, relates to the view of persons as responsible agents" ("Well-being, Agency and Freedom," 204). The 2010 *Human Development Report*, based on the capability approach, defines development as "the expansion of people's freedoms to live long, healthy and creative lives; to advance other goals they have reason to value; and to engage actively in shaping development equitably and sustainably on a shared planet" (United Nations Development Programme, *Human Development Report 2010: The Real Wealth of Nations*, 2, accessed June 8, 2016, http://hdr.undp.org/en/content/human-development-report-2010).

26. Sen, *Idea of Justice*, 410.

27. Amartya Sen, *The Country of First Boys and Other Essays* (New Delhi: Oxford University Press, 2015), 182.

28. Ibid., 182.

29. Amartya Sen, "What Do We Want from a Theory of Justice," *Journal of Philosophy*, 103, no. 5 (2006): 215–38.

30. Sen, *Idea of Justice*, 389.

31. See, among others, Sen, *Idea of Justice* and *Country of First Boys*, and Jean Drèze and Amartya Sen, *An Uncertain Glory: India and Its Contradictions* (London: Allen Lane, 2013).

32. Amartya Sen, "What Is It Like to Be Like a Human Being?" in United Nations Development Programme, *Human Development*

Report 2013 (New York: UNDP, 2013), 24, http://hdr.undp.org/en/2013-report.

33. Sen, *Idea of Justice*, 88.

34. Ibid., 414–15.

35. Sen, *Country of First Boys*, xxxvii. Original full quote reads, "The political compulsion in a democracy to eliminate famines depends critically on the power of public reasoning in making non-victims take on the need to eradicate famines their *own* commitment. Democratic institutions can be effective only if different sections of the population appreciate what is happening to others, and if the political process reflects a broader social understanding of deprivation."

36. See "Pope Baptizes the Son of His Friend, the 'Waste-Pickers' Leader from Buenos Aires," *America Magazine*, November 1, 2015, http://americamagazine.org/content/dispatches/pope-baptizes-son-his-friend-waste-pickers-leader-buenos-aires.

37. Personal communication, December 2014. For a short video of the story of Sergio's life told by him, accessed June 10, 2016, see http://hosting.soundslides.com/tcfcz.

38. Personal communication, Rafael Chamky, CTEP coordinator, December 2014.

39. Personal communication, December 2014.

40. Virginia Azcuy and José Juan Cervantes, "Plaza Pública," *Ciudad vivida. Prácticas de Espiritualidad en Buenos Aires*, ed. Virginia Azcuy (Buenos Aires: Editorial Guadalupe, 2014), 35–71.

41. Personal communication, Sergio Sánchez, December 2014.

42. See "Mensaje del Papa Francisco para todos los trabajadores de la economía popular en el 1 de Mayo 2014," available at http://www.youtube.com/watch?v=w74dI3nyq9w (accessed June 10, 2016).

43. There are no official government figures. This is an estimation from the Confederation of the Popular Economy Workers. Personal communication, Carolina Palacio, September 2014.

44. Mariano Perelman, "El Cirujeo en la Ciudad de Buenos Aires: Vizibilización, Estigma y Confianza," *Revista de Antropologia Iberoamericana* 5, no. 1 (210): 94–125.

45. Personal communication, Julio, street vendor organization leader, November 2014.

46. See http://ctepargentina.org/la-ctep-escribe-un-nuevo-capitulo-en-la-historia-del-movimiento-obrero (accessed June 10, 2016).

47. Personal communication, Clara, December 2014.

48. Personal communication, Sergio Sánchez, December 2014.

49. All documents of Catholic social teaching can be found at http://www.catholicsocialteaching.org.uk/principles/documents (accessed June 10, 2016).

50. Personal communication, December 2014.

51. Document 3, p. 11, http://ctepargentina.org/documentos (accessed June 10, 2016).

52. Para. 394, http://www.aecrc.org/documents/Aparecida-Concluding%20Document.pdf.

53. Para. 1 and 4, http://www.vatican.va/archive/hist_councils/ii_vatican_council/documents/vat-ii_const_19651207_gaudium-et-spes_en.html.

54. For a discussion on how liturgy and ecclesiology are intrinsically connected, see Massimo Faggioli, *True Reform: Liturgy and Ecclesiology in Sacrosanctum Concilium* (Collegeville, MN: Liturgical Press, 2012).

55. Personal communication, Sergio Sánchez, December 2014.

56. See http://hosting.soundslides.com/tcfcz (accessed June 10, 2016).

57. Ana C. Dinerstein, and Séverine Deneulin, "Hope Movements: Naming Mobilization in a Post-development World," *Development and Change* 43, no. 2 (2012): 585–602.

58. Michael Czerny and Paolo Foglizzo, "The Strength of the Excluded: World Meeting of Popular Movements at the Vatican," *Thinking Faith: Online Journal of the Jesuits in Britain,* January 2015, https://www.thinkingfaith.org/articles/strength-excluded-world-meeting-popular-movements-vatican. For the meeting's website (in Spanish), see http://movimientospopulares.org (accessed June 13, 2016).

59. José Pablo Martín, *El Movimiento de Sacerdotes para el Tercer*

Mundo: Un Debate Argentino (Buenos Aires: Editorial Universidad Nacional del General Sarmiento, 2010).

60. According to a person closely involved in the meeting, organizations that were critical of Evo Morales's government were not given permission by the Bolivian government to attend. Personal communication, December 2015.

Transforming Words, Transforming Relationships

An Afterword

ROWAN WILLIAMS

One central strand of argument in Pope Francis's Apostolic Exhortation is the reference to a "crisis of communal commitment" in the contemporary environment (*EG* 50). The pope offers an analysis of various "dehumanizing" trends (*EG* 51) that include social exclusion, waste, competition, and everything that colludes with the treating of persons as disposable (*EG* 53); and this opens out into a catalogue of those underlying aspects of global culture that the church has to reject—the idolatry of money, the sovereignty of the market, the unthinking acceptance of radical inequality, all that nurtures short-term attitudes and a focus on immediate gratification (*EG* 61–62). But he is also careful to note that there can be religious responses to all this that simply mirror the sickness they try to cure (*EG* 63). What authentic evangelization must address is the failure or deficit of corporate fidelity; and Christians must do so by a discipleship that accords proper value not only to the person but to every material other in the universe (not the only way in which this document anticipates the more recent encyclical on the environment).[1] Patterns of religious privilege and exclusion are inimical to the gospel, because they do not embody God's own commitment to the neighbor of any and every background or conviction.

Proclaiming the gospel is thus a "word" that *denies the denial of commitment.* It is an act that begins simply in *witnessing* to commitment, to God's embodied promise, and moves from this to become a *summons* to commitment. It declares that God has, eternally and in time, committed himself to the world and in that gift of divine fidelity has made it possible for us to be faithfully committed to one another in the same way. So the challenge to any strategy of evangelization is very much what Bonhoeffer in his prison letters famously announced—the challenge to find words that will transform reality, that will both represent and create the bonds of faithfulness.[2]

This entails not only listening to the ambient culture but listening to what I hear in myself—that is, in myself as always already addressed and engaged by God. I must listen for my own apprehending and absorbing of God's word. It is in that listening that I understand what it means that—to use one of the most resonant phrases in the document—"I am a mission" (*EG* 273). My transformed existence in Christ constitutes my personal being as a word of good news. Christ's existence and identity are entirely defined as mission: both his eternal life and his incarnate existence are nothing but the living out of divine promise and faithfulness—in eternity as the unfailing expression of the Father's will and self-gift, in time as the fulfillment of prophecy and the sustained will to be with his people whatever violence or rejection is set in opposition. We are called to live in such a way: not searching for dominance nor seeking the submission or absorption of the other, but, in and with Christ, embodying God's commitment to be there in and for every person and situation.

This is why evangelization is a nonnegotiable aspect of the church's life, not a second thought or an extra. If we are in Christ, the sacrament of divine fidelity, we cannot but live faithfully; and we cannot live faithfully if we either seek to dominate our world or retreat in embarrassment, failing to witness to what God has declared in Jesus. Pope Francis has a telling aside on the uniqueness of Christ and the inadequacy of syncretism: we certainly do not despise or seek to overturn all non-Christian visions of the good and the holy, but the idea that all visions are essentially the same amounts (paradoxically) to a "totalitarian gesture" (*EG* 251). It forecloses the possibility that in Jesus there is truly a universal possibility of change of a distinctive kind, change into the liberty of God's children.

The pope is clear that when words do effect change, they do so initially by *attracting*: beauty is emphatically a dimension of what is offered in proclamation, and the attraction conveyed is one of the ways in which we experience the presence and action of Christ. So what evangelization seeks to do is to be transparent to Christ. This search for transparency to Christ is the heart of all our prayer, personal and liturgical. Pope Francis is very critical of a focus on liturgy that is narrow and precious, but he recognizes that evangelization has a "mystagogic" aspect, that it has to do with the prayerful appropriation of the events of salvation in the ritual act of the community, which becomes Christ's act through his promised gift of the Spirit. If anything, this dimension of the sharing of the gospel is understated in the document, quite clearly because of the anxiety that concentrating on the liturgy can easily distract us from actual social transformation (and there is also perhaps a characteristically Jesuit caution about too strong an emphasis on the externals of worship). But there are materials here for a further development of this theme.

We might take up some of these ideas and push the argument further in respect of liturgy and sacrament. Thus it is clear that the church has to live out its calling through *practices of commitment,* and its liturgical and sacramental life exists so that we are regularly confronted with the enacting of God's commitment. Our words and acts as church are oriented to the renewal of relation with Jesus Christ, who is, as we have seen, the embodiment of God's self-commitment to creation. Sacramental life in turn embodies Christ's fidelity to us and enables us to embody him in our practice. St. Teresa of Avila, in her *Way of Perfection,*[3] eloquently characterizes the Eucharist as enacting Christ's will to be with us always, whatever we do to him, to abide in the heart of a world that is perennially rebellious and violent. But it is possible to see all the sacraments of the church as signs of divine faithfulness—reconciliation, marriage, orders, and so on. The words and acts of the sacramental life change relations; they introduce the presence of the Spirit of the age to come into our world. So they realize the copresence of Christ in and with our actions, as the decisive agency without which nothing changes. We alone cannot resolve the "crisis of commitment," because we are ourselves caught up in the various forms of infidelity that characterize fallen humanity: we do not sustain our love or attention, we are seduced by the same short-term perspective that our world (more and more) encourages. So the sacramental encounter is good news for *us*: human action can be "adopted" into the faithful pattern of God's agency in the corporate acts of the church as church, and so we may discover that "adoption" in the rest of our work and service, as we try to embody God's promise in our love and service for the neighbor. We are reminded that commitment is possible because God has lived it out in our midst; and so we look on our service, on our patterns of relating, on our personal prayer, in a new light, as potentially carriers of God.

This is not to criticize the document, simply to suggest how its vision may be elaborated in a way that further dissolves the false opposition between worship and service that Pope Francis is evidently seeking to repudiate. While the theology of *Evangelii Gaudium* is often latent rather than fully expressed, it should be plain that the whole logic of the document is consistently christological and trinitarian. The theology of mission here is a theology resting on the conviction that the second person of the Trinity *is* the mission of the Father, the eternal purposeful act of the Father in sharing divine life. And our incorporation into that life is the ground of our becoming mission—becoming the means by which created words and action can transfigure the diseased and frustrated human relations in the midst of which we live into the channels of true life. The joy of the gospel is thus not a sense of satisfaction in a job well done, or a euphoric emotion, but a share in the trinitarian bliss, God's joyful welcoming of his life returning to him in the other. And this joy is what we seek to open for others: the hidden beauty into which the world may fully grow.